Barcelona

INSIGHT GUIDES

BARCELONA

APA PUBLICATIONS L

Part of the Langenscheidt Publishing Group

☆ INSIGHT GUIDES
BARCELONA

ABOUT THIS BOOK

Editor
Catherine Dreghorn
Picture Editor
Tom Smyth
Cartography Manager
Zoë Goodwin
Series Editor
Rachel Lawrence
Publishing Manager
Rachel Fox

Distribution

UK & Ireland
Dorling Kindersley Ltd, a Penguin Group company
80 Strand, London, WC2R 0RL
customer.service@dk.com

United States
Ingram Publisher Services
One Ingram Blvd, PO Box 3006
La Vergne, TN 37086-1986
customer.service@ingrampublisher services.com

Australia
Universal Publishers
PO Box 307
St Leonards, NSW 1590
sales@universalpublishers.com.au

Worldwide
Apa Publications GmbH & Co. Verlag KG (Singapore branch)
7030 Ang Mo Kio Ave 5
08-65 Northstar @ AMK
Singapore 569880
apasin@signet.com.sg

Printing

CTPS - China

What makes an Insight Guide different? Since our first book pioneered the use of creative full-colour photography in travel guides in 1970, we have aimed to provide not only reliable information but also the key to a real understanding of a destination and its people.

Now, when the internet can supply inexhaustible (but not always reliable) facts, our books marry text and pictures to provide that more elusive quality: knowledge. To achieve this, they rely on the authority of locally based writers and photographers.

This book turns the spotlight on a city that is forever reinventing itself. The heart and legs of Catalonia, Spain's leading economic region, it is one of Europe's most vibrant cities with a huge amount to offer visitors. As Miguel de Cervantes wrote in *Don Quixote*: "Barcelona: innately courteous, offering shelter to the travel-weary, hospitals for the poor, home for the brave, revenge for the offended, reciprocating friendship and unique in situation and beauty."

CONTACTING THE EDITORS

We would appreciate it if readers would alert us to errors or outdated information by writing to:

Insight Guides, P.O. Box 7910, London SE1 1WE, England. insight@apaguide.co.uk

THE CONTRIBUTORS

This seventh edition of *City Guide: Barcelona* was commissioned and edited by **Catherine Dreghorn**, Assistant Editor at Insight Guides.

This new edition has been thoroughly updated by **Judy Thomson**, a writer and translator living just off La Rambla, Barcelona's most famous thoroughfare. A long-time contributor to Insight Guides, Thomson built on work she did on previous editions of the book, including writing the photo features on festivals, shopping and the city's best beaches, as well as the features on Catalan food and wine, and the city's design aesthetic. Thomson also penned the new chapter 21st Century Barcelona, looking at Poble Nou, Diagonal Mar and 22@.

Other photo features – on markets, Montserrat and Park Güell – were written by long-term devotee of the city **Roger Williams**, the author of Insight's *Step by Step Barcelona*.

The design was created by **Klaus Geisler** and the principal photographer was **Gregory Wrona**, a regular contributor to Insight Guides, who made two trips to the city to capture its ever-changing architecture, restaurants, shops and bars.

This edition of *City Guide: Barcelona* draws on earlier versions edited by **Dorothy Stannard**, **Pam Barrett** and **Andrew Eames**. Contributors to those editions whose work is still evident in this book include **Marcelo Aparicio**, **Xavier Martí**, **George Semler**, the historian **Dr Felipe Fernández-Armesto**, **Valerie Collins**, **Anne Michie** and architect **Jane Opher**.

The book was proof-read by **Catherine Jackson** and indexed by **Liz Cook**.

THE GUIDE AT A GLANCE

The book is carefully structured both to convey an understanding of the city and its culture and to guide readers through its attractions and activities:

◆ The Best Of section at the front of the book helps you to prioritise. The first spread contains all the Top Sights, while Editor's Choice details unique experiences, the best buys or other recommendations.

◆ To understand Barcelona, you need to know something of its past. The city's history and culture are described in authoritative essays written by

specialists in their fields who have lived in and documented the city for many years.

◆ The Places section details all the attractions worth seeing. The main places of interest are coordinated by number with the maps.

◆ A list of recommended restaurants, bars and cafés is printed at the end of each chapter.

◆ Photographs throughout the book are chosen not only to illustrate geography and buildings, but also to convey the moods of the city and the life of its people.

◆ The Travel Tips section includes all the practical information you will need, divided into five key sections: transport, accommodation, shopping, activities (including festivals, nightlife and sports), and an A–Z of practical tips. Information may be located quickly by using the index on the back cover flap of the book.

◆ Two detailed street atlases are included at the back of the book, complete with a full index. On the second one, you will find all the restaurants and hotels plotted for your convenience.

PLACES & SIGHTS

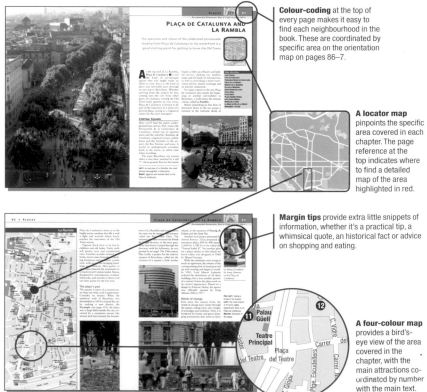

Colour-coding at the top of every page makes it easy to find each neighbourhood in the book. These are coordinated by specific area on the orientation map on pages 86–7.

A locator map pinpoints the specific area covered in each chapter. The page reference at the top indicates where to find a detailed map of the area highlighted in red.

Margin tips provide extra little snippets of information, whether it's a practical tip, a whimsical quote, an historical fact or advice on shopping and eating.

A four-colour map provides a bird's-eye view of the area covered in the chapter, with the main attractions coordinated by number with the main text.

PHOTO FEATURES

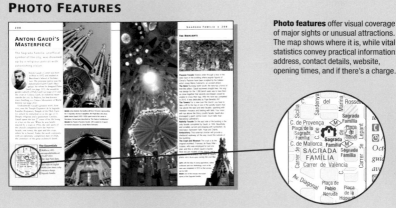

Photo features offer visual coverage of major sights or unusual attractions. The map shows where it is, while vital statistics convey practical information: address, contact details, website, opening times, and if there's a charge.

RESTAURANT LISTINGS

Restaurant listings feature the best establishments within each area, giving the address, phone number, opening times and price category followed by a useful review. The grid reference refers to the atlas at the back of the book.

Txapela

Passeig de Gràcia, 8–10
☎ 93-412 0289 ☞ *Tapes*
daily. € [p306, B4]
This place seems to be
from a do-it-yourself kit for
Basque restaurants, but
nevertheless it has a surprising range of tasty hot
and cold *pinchos* (snacks

TRAVEL TIPS

GETTING AROUND

From the Airport

Barcelona is only 12km (7 miles) from El Prat airport and is easily reached by train, bus or taxi. Trains to Sants and Passeig de Gràcia depart every 30 min-utes from 6am–11.38pm and about 25 minutes.

Advice-packed Travel Tips provide all the practical knowledge you'll need before and during your trip: how to get there, getting around, where to stay and what to do. The A–Z section is a handy summary of practical information, arranged alphabetically.

Contents

THE BEST OF BARCELONA: TOP SIGHTS

At a glance, everything you can't afford to miss in Barcelona, from Gaudí's Sagrada Família and Casa Milà to the Miró Foundation and the beaches

△ The **Park Güell** Colourful ceramics in the park Gaudí designed for his patron, Eusebi Güell. *See pages 224–5*

◁ **La Boqueria** This covered market on La Rambla selling wonderful fresh produce is one of Europe's most attractive markets. *See page 100*

△ The **Palau de la Música Catalana** Recently extended, the Palau is a *modernista* dream. *See page 127*

◁ The **Sagrada Família** Gaudí's glorious, unfinished cathedral. *See pages 208–9*

◁ The **beaches** Barcelona's waterfront has become the city's playground. *See pages 172–3*

△ The **Museu Picasso** One of the most popular attractions in Barcelona, the city where the artist grew up. *See page 130*

◁ **Santa Maria del Mar** The city's most beautiful church. *See page 132*

▷ **Fundació Joan Miró** An open airy space that displays Miró's works to their best advantage. *See page 186*

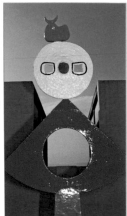

◁ **La Rambla** Barcelona's famous tree-lined avenue is a good starting point for any visit. *See pages 95–107*

▽ **La Pedrera** The "witch-scarer" chimneys of Casa Milà, known as La Pedrera. *See page 202*

THE BEST OF BARCELONA: EDITOR'S CHOICE

Unique attractions and festivals, top museums and shops, family outings and money-saving tips personally selected by our editor

BEST VIEWS

● **Barcelona Bus Turístic** Worth every cent to see the city from the open top deck of the Tourist Bus. *See page 250.*

● **Torre de Collserola** The lookout platform on the 10th floor of this communications tower gives you a 360° view of Catalonia, including, on a good day, the Pyrenees. *See page 217.*

● **Transbordador Aeri** Get the city into perspective by gliding over the port in the cable car from Montjuïc, the Torre de Jaume I or the Torre Sant Sebastià. *See pages 161, 189.*

● **Waterfront** From the beach end of Passeig Joan de Borbó at sunset, look back at the silhouette of the Old Town's skyline, especially La Mercè, the Virgin holding her child. *See page 162.*

● **La Pedrera** Thumbnails of the Sagrada Família and other Eixample monuments from the roof. *See page 202.*

ABOVE: among the spooky chimneys on the roof of La Pedrera. **LEFT:** view of the Torre Agbar.

BEST BUILDINGS

● **CaixaForum** An award-winning *modernista* textile factory converted into cultural centre. *See page 179.*

● **Palau Baró de Quadras** This Puig i Cadafalch house is the headquarters of the Casa Asia and is open to the public. *See page 203.*

● **La Pedrera** If you see no other Gaudí building, don't miss this 1910 apartment block. It gives an insight into the brilliance of the city's most famous architect. *See page 202.*

● **Torre de Martí I** A Renaissance tower in the Plaça del Rei, in the Barri Gòtic. *See page 121.*

● **Pavelló Mies van der Rohe** Less is more in this seminal building of the Modern Movement, designed as the German Pavilion for the 1929 International Exposition. *See page 179.*

● **Torre Agbar** The headquarters of a water company at Plaça de les Glòries, this sleek tower is a 21st-century addition to the Barcelona skyline. *See page 195.*

● **Santa Maria del Mar** A beautiful Catalan-Gothic church, with stunning stained-glass windows, that will make your spirit soar. *See page 132.*

BARCELONA FOR FAMILIES

● Barcelona is child-friendly in true Latin tradition: locals, shops and restaurants welcome children, street performers abound and the many traffic-free areas in the old town are good for bikes and skateboards.

● **Aquàrium** One of the largest aquariums in Europe. *See page 158.*

● **Beaches** Barceloneta and Nova Icària beaches are sheltered by the Port Olímpic and have climbing frames. *See pages 172–3.*

● **Ciutadella** Park with rowing boats, ducks, picnic areas, play areas and a great zoo. *See page 135.*

● **Club Nataciò Atlètic Barceloneta** Swimming club with an outdoor pool shal-low enough for children. Plaça del Mar, 1. *See page 161.*

● **Jardins de la Torre de les Aigües** is unique: a small outdoor pool (late June–early Sept) set within an Eixample block. Best for the very young. Roger de Llúria, 56.

● **Granja Viader** A magnificent milk bar. Good for thick hot chocolate and the nutty drink *orxata*. Xuclà, 4.

● **Tibidabo** A 100-year-old funfair overlooking the city. *See page 218.*

● **Concerts and theatre** The Auditori concert hall, the CaixaForum, Fundació Miró and even the Liceu run regular family programmes.

BEST MUSEUMS

● **CCCB** Technically a cultural centre, this wonderful space stages intriguing exhibitions as well as diverse festivals – film, music and performance. *See page 146.*

● **CosmoCaixa** The born-again science museum has hands-on exhibits for all ages, plus a recreation of the Amazon. *See page 220.*

● **Fundació Miró** Flooded with Mediterranean light, this purpose-built museum has one of the largest collections of Miró's work. *See page 186.*

● **MNAC** The Museu Nacional d'Art de Catalunya houses a millennium of Catalan art from its famed Romanesque collection to 20th century photography. *See page 181.*

● **Museu Picasso** Comprehensive display of Picasso's startling early work and some later pieces in five medieval palaces. *See page 130.*

TOP SQUARES

● **Plaça del Rei** The essence of medieval Barcelona. Best early in the morning or on summer nights, when it is sometimes a concert venue. *See page 120.*

● **Plaça Reial** Daytime bustle, petty crime and night-time partying don't detract from this handsome 19th-century square. *See page 103.*

● **Plaça Sant Felip Neri** The very heart of the Gothic Quarter. To feel its peace, wait for the children in the adjacent school to return to class. *See page 116.*

● **Plaça del Sol** One of several fine squares in the district of Gràcia, it is a meeting place for young and old. *See page 213.*

● **Plaça Vicenç Martorell** Just off La Rambla in El Raval and popular for its terrace cafés and playground. *See page 143.*

ABOVE: children love Tibidabo, and the views are stunning, too. **BELOW:** a bicycle tour taking a break in Plaça del Rei in the heart of medieval Barcelona.

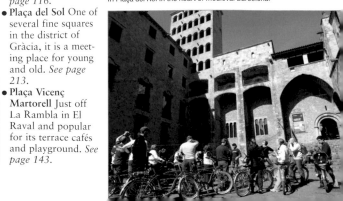

FLAVOURS OF BARCELONA

● **La Boqueria** All the food markets are a trip for the senses, but this one takes first prize for its colours, tropical flavours, Mediterranean aromas and overwhelming vitality. Also includes several good restaurant-bars. *See page 100.*

● **La Seu** An indulgent range of farmhouse cheeses from all over Spain, kept to perfection. Tastings take place on Saturday mornings. Also offers excellent olive oils. Dagueria, 16.

● **Herbolari** One of many herbalists who can advise on and mix your particular potion from drawers full of aromatic herbs. Also sells honey and natural cosmetics. Xuclà, 23.

● **J. Múrria** A traditional small grocer's shop in the Eixample with its original painted glass facade and a mouth-watering array of goods from the finest hams and cheeses to the most expensive wines. Roger de Llúria, 85. *See page 204.*

●*Pa amb tomàquet* When the bread is fresh, the tomatoes hand-picked and the olive oil cold-pressed, this traditional accompaniment is a meal in itself and cannot be bettered.

ABOVE TOP LEFT: fresh, hand-picked tomatoes. **ABOVE TOP RIGHT:** the *sardana* is danced every Sunday, as well as at festivals. **ABOVE:** cured ham.

BEST BARCELONAN TRADITIONS

● **Correfoc** Part of the La Mercè festivities, this is the wildest of celebrations, when fire-spitting dragons and their accompanying devils threaten to engulf in flames anyone fool enough to taunt them.

● **Dancing** Barcelonans of all ages love to dance the *sardana,* the Catalan national dance.

● **Fiestas** Whether it's buying red roses on the day of Sant Jordi, the patron saint, or roasting chestnuts in the autumn, the people of Barcelona continue their traditions with enthusiasm.

● **Going out for break-fast** Sitting up at a classic steel bar with your favourite daily newspaper, fresh crusty sandwich and piping hot coffee is a cherished part of life.

● **Paella** Meeting up with friends or family for a paella on the beach or in the woods is possible even on sunny winter days, and always a treat. This is a dish often cooked by the man of the house.

● **Sunday lunches** Not a Sunday goes by without Catalan families reuniting for a big family meal, usually in the grandparents' house. Someone will bring a dessert, fresh from the pastry shop and wrapped up with paper and ribbon.

● **Weekend escapes** Catalans work hard all week, but weekends are sacrosanct. They escape to the ski slopes in winter and the beaches in summer.

BEST BUYS

- **Leatherwear** Spain is still a good place to buy shoes and bags. The best areas are Portal de l'Angel, Rambla de Catalunya, Passeig de Gràcia and Diagonal. *See page 264.*
- **Fashion** Apart from the ubiquitous Zara and Desigual, more upmarket Spanish designers include Adolfo Domínguez and Antonio Miró. Independent boutiques are mostly in the Old Town. *See page 265.*
- **Bric-à-brac and antiques** Visit Els Encants flea market in Glòries, the antiques market in the Cathedral Square and the art market in Plaça Sant Josep Oriol. *See page 117.*
- **Interior design** From Vinçon in Passeig de

Gracia to Cosas de Casa in Plaça Sant Josep Oriol, the city is full of design ideas. *See page 265.*
- **Wine and edibles** From cava to handmade chocolates. *See page 266.*

BELOW: the sound and light show at La Font Màgica on Montjuïc is hugely popular.

FREE BARCELONA

- **La Font Màgica** Designed for the 1929 exhibition, the Magic Fountain offers free *son et lumière* displays most of the year. *See page 178.*
- **Open-air museum** The side streets off Passeig de Gràcia and Rambla Catalunya are like a museum of *modernisme*: buildings, balconies, stained-glass windows and carved doors can all be appreciated as

you wander around the neighbourhood. *See page 200.*
- **Neighbourhood fiestas** Hardly a month goes by without a fiesta with giants, parades and *castells* (human pyramids).
- **Street performers** Human statues, musicians, opera singers – the streets of the Old Town are full of free entertainment – although they all appreciate a donation in the hat.

MONEY-SAVING TIPS

Articket The ticket that gets you into seven art centres for €25 (which when you think La Pedrera alone charges €14 is excellent value). Also includes CCCB, MACBA, Museu Picasso, Fundació Joan Miró, Fundació Tàpies and MNAC. Purchase online (www.barcelonaturisme.com) or at a tourist office.

Menú del dia Most restaurants offer a set menu at lunchtime, with three courses and a drink at a price well below the sum of its parts. It's a good idea to eat your main meal at

lunchtime and snack in the evening, although the cost of *tapes* can add up.

Museum entrance Some museums (Picasso, History of Catalonia, Museu d'Història de la Ciutat, CosmoCaixa, DHUB, Ceramic, MNAC) can be visited free on the first Sunday of the month, and all municipal museums (Disseny Hub, Picasso, MUHBA) are free on Sunday afternoons. Others have a reduced rate on certain days, e.g. the MACBA on a Wednesday. The CaixaForum and the Catalunya Caixa exhibition space in La Pedrera are free.

T10 card A card of 10 journeys for use on metro, bus, train or tram for around €8. If you transfer from metro to bus, tram, funicular or inner-city stations of the FGC (the Generalitat-run suburban train) within an hour and a quarter of leaving the metro (or vice versa) it is considered part of the same journey, and the ticket is not re-punched when it is passed through the machine.

You can also travel from one bus line to another, and to train lines as far as stations within Zone 1, like the airport, and Castelldefels beach in the south. Excellent value.

THE BARCELONANS

Life in Barcelona is characterised by dynamic commercial activity and a vibrant social scene – seasoned with a dash of cosmopolitanism thanks to the many outsiders who come here to work and play

Catalans in general, and Barcelonans in particular, are famed for their business acumen, passion for work and economic ability. The laid-back *mañana* attitude of the old Spanish stereotype scarcely exists in Barcelona. But then, as Catalans never tire of telling you, Catalonia and its capital are *not* Spain. In Barcelona, 10 o'clock means 10 o'clock, not 11.30. "*Anem per feina*" is a common expression, once pressed into service as a Catalan nationalist election slogan: "Let's go to work."

Market trading

Like England, Catalonia has been dubbed a nation of shopkeepers, and indeed, Barcelona has a staggering number of shops. This is not so surprising when you consider its mercantile background, going back to the Phoenicians. This bourgeois city was built up through family enterprise, and has now become one of *the* places to shop. The slogan once sported by carrier bags of the famous Vinçon design store puts it in a nutshell: "I shop, therefore I am."

Barcelona exudes an air of prosperity, and is no longer a particularly cheap city. The standard of living is high, but it has to be paid for, and the work ethic is especially noticeable if you come here from elsewhere in Spain. You can see it in the comparatively early closing (by Spanish standards) of bars and restaurants. Efficiency, punctuality and reliability are of the essence. Barcelona works *very* hard.

PRECEDING PAGES: dancing devils at the Gràcia festival; looking out from Park Güell. **LEFT:** crowds and stalls on La Rambla. **RIGHT:** musicians in Parc Güell.

In Andalucía they have a saying: "The Andalucian works to live, the Catalan lives to work." But it is not as straightforward as this. For how do we square this view of Catalans with the wild celebrations of La Mercè, the

> Barcelona bustles with immaculately groomed urban professionals, striding in and out of offices with briefcases and laptops, mobile phones clamped to their ears.

week of festivities around 24 September, the day of Barcelona's patroness, when giants and fantastical creatures parade around on stilts, free concerts are put on with no regard for cost, and fiery dragons career through the crowds in the hair-raising *correfoc* or "fire-running"?

THE CATALAN LANGUAGE

First lesson to visitors: Catalan is not a historical relic, surviving only in the countryside. It is spoken by some 6 million people in Catalonia, Valencia, the Balearics, Andorra, the Roussillon region of France and the town of Alghero in Sardinia, and Catalan-speakers form far the largest linguistic community in Europe without their own state.

Catalan is a Romance language, like Castilian Spanish, French and Italian, but with a sharp, staccato quality that gives it a very distinctive sound. It was used in public life very early on, and Catalan literature enjoyed a Golden Age from the 13th to the 15th century, producing the chronicles of Catalan count-kings, the philosophy of Ramon Llull, a huge range of poetry and in 1490 Joanot Martorell's *Tirant lo Blanc*, considered the first European novel.

Absorption into the Spanish monarchy, however, led to a downgrading of the language, and after the abolition of Catalan institutions by Felipe V in 1716 Castilian was imposed as the sole language of government, law and education. Nevertheless, a century later industrialisation and the rise of a native middle class provided a backdrop for Catalonia's cultural *Renaixença* or "rebirth". Literature, music and the Catalan press all flourished. With the restoration of the Generalitat in 1931, Catalan was again the primary language of Barcelona, in public life, the arts and on the street.

This made the total shutdown after Franco's victory in 1939 all the harder to bear. Catalan was banned from public use, with penalties even for speaking it on the street. A generation grew up unable to read or write in the language they spoke at home.

Catalans are intensely attached to their language, and whenever the pressure upon it has relaxed, Catalan has revived. So it was after Franco's death in 1975. Catalan and Castilian are now both official languages, but in practice Catalan is the primary language in education, media, documents, signs and so on. The "linguistic normalisation" undertaken by the Catalan government since 1980 has been a remarkable success, but also controversial, and the many ramifications of linguistic politics remain a constant local topic.

Barcelona itself remains a linguistic soup, since half or more of its population are Castilian-speakers. There are determined Catalan-only speakers, as well as their opposites; most people, though, want to get along, and readily hop back and forth. Catalan is a richly expressive language, with a blend of abruptness and Latin sinuosity that seems rooted in the Catalan character. And who could reject a tongue that has such vocal satisfactions as *xiuxiuejar* (to whisper) and *pastanagues* (carrots)?

Prudence versus impulse

The Catalans call these apparently contradictory facets of their character *el seny* and *la rauxa*. The former is a combination of prudence, profound common sense and good judgement, the latter a fit, impulse or emotional outburst: a kind of attack of wildness.

You can see both sides of the Catalan character in the way they drive. Unlike in other flamboyant cities, the traffic in Barcelona is orderly. Drivers stop on red, and go on green. But if you hesitate a split second, or worse still, stall, you'll be deafened by furious honking. When traffic gets really snarled up, *rauxa* takes over. Patience is no longer a virtue: you must get going, be on the mark, have your wits about you.

Barcelonans may work until they're blue in the face, but they're still a Mediterranean people: creative, fun-loving, noisy and gregarious. As Barcelona's celebrated Olympic Games of 1992 set out to show the world, Mediterranean high spirits and street life do not have to be synonymous with sloth and inefficiency, and Barcelonans are capable of first-class technology and efficiency without relinquishing any of their vibrancy and zest.

A clash of cultures

Barcelonans work hard all week, then sit in traffic jams every Friday afternoon so they can enjoy weekends by the sea or in the mountains. They have little time for the wishy-washy: theirs are the strong, bright primary colours of Miró. They are adventurous travellers, visiting the most remote corners of the world. They value initiative and pioneering enterprise. Barcelona is intensely involved internationally in science, education, ecology and other fields.

But they do come over as reserved and serious beside the many citizens originally from other parts of Spain, the migrants who flooded in during the 1950s and 1960s in search of work. Coexistence has sometimes been a thorny matter, with ethnic, class and cultural differences all intertwined: the Catalan middle classes often take a dim view of the ebullient non-Catalan working class, and vice versa. Sometimes still referred to by the derogatory label *xarnegos* (the original meaning of which

> *The key to the Barcelonans' unique exuberance is the "passionate energy" noted by George Orwell in 1936 as he watched Barcelonan men, women and children build barricades in the war-torn city.*

LEFT: young Barcelonans in Pile 43, a cosy bar in the Barri Gòtic. **ABOVE:** concoting cocktails at Dry Martini. **ABOVE RIGHT:** comedian at Teatre Llantiol.

is a child of a Catalan and a non-Catalan), some of these "other Barcelonans" form distinct communities, mostly in the outer neighbourhoods. Barcelona's *Feria de Abril* (April Fair), held in Parc del Fòrum near the beach, is no longer a pale, homesick imitation of the Andalucian original, but a big event in its own right that attracts nearly a million visitors. And, of course, the second and third generations of so-called *xarnegos* are Barcelona born and bred.

> Barcelonans love dashing around, being busy and generally having lots of irons in the fire. Ask them how they are and they'll say "vaig de bòlit!" – "I'm speeding!"

Barcelona Football Club is more than the city's main football team, it is one of Catalonia's flagship institutions *(see box, right)*. It is also a force for local unity. Barcelonans and Catalans of all ages, classes, genders, shapes, sizes and even ethnic origins now happily unite to dance in the streets when Barça beats Madrid or wins any kind of trophy. The red and gold of the Catalan flag combine with

Barça's *blaugrana* in a swirling mass down La Rambla. Corks pop and cava sprays far into the night.

Peaceful coexistence, solidarity, citizen participation – these are just a few of the buzzwords bandied about by Barcelona's policymakers, and personified by the volunteers who give free Catalan classes to the ever-increasing immigrant community, determined to integrate them as new Catalans.

Barcelonans' identity

Like all good Mediterraneans, Barcelonans are a street people. All it takes is a few tables squeezed onto a postage stamp of pavement, and they'll sit for hours over their drinks and olives, apparently oblivious to the fumes and traffic noise. When it rains, the milling throngs leap into cars and taxis, causing the traffic to "collapse", as they put it, in a cacophony of blasting horns.

One of the highest accolades a Barcelonan can receive is that he or she is *espavilat* or

ABOVE LEFT: café life in Poble Nou. **ABOVE TOP:** a handy kiosk on La Rambla. **ABOVE:** La Boqueria market stall. **RIGHT:** funfair at Tibidabo. **FAR RIGHT:** sweet shop in La Boqueria.

espavilada, which can be translated as awake or alert. This proactive zooming around encompasses not only work, but a host of other activities – from culture, shopping and social life to voluntary work, chauffering children, sports... you name it, Barcelonans do it with gusto.

Barcelonans are devoted to their traditions, as anyone witnessing them dancing the *sardana*, Catalonia's intricate dance, can testify *(see box, page 24)*. Yet at the same time they are open to innovation. Creativity is part of the Catalan identity. Its traditions are bound up with Catalonia's defence of its identity as a nation – a cultured and tolerant nation that is open to new ideas and influences.

trade fairs and meetings makes for an exciting cosmopolitan buzz. As technology makes physical location less relevant, more foreigners are choosing Barcelona as a place in which to live, attracted by its climate and lifestyle.

Seductive city

Barcelona has worked magic on foreigners as well. In his *Homage to Catalonia*, George Orwell chronicled the Barcelona of 1936, filled with young foreigners who had come to defend democracy. In the 1960s, as the Spanish-language publishing capital, the city was home to intellectuals such as Gabriel García Márquez and Mario Vargas Llosa.

This foreign presence has grown massively since the 1990s. Irish pubs, Japanese restaurants and Pakistani groceries abound. Barcelona's popularity as a venue for international

FOOTBALL CRAZY

Barcelona Football Club – Barça – was founded in 1899 by Hans Gamper, a Swiss living in Barcelona. One of its slogans is that it is *més que un club* – more than a club – but one of its special features is that it really is a club: its 105,000+ paid-up fans are members who vote for the board, not "season-ticket holders". This huge fan base comes from the whole of Catalonia, not just the city. Barça is a symbol of Catalonia, even when its stars are from Brazil, Argentina or Mali.

The club gained its curious political role as a champion of Catalan freedom during times when Catalan identity was blocked everywhere else, under Primo de Rivera in the 1920s and, far more intensely, under Franco. Stadium crowds are hard to censor, and the blue-and-maroon *(blaugrana)* flag of Barça became a substitute for the Catalan colours.

Catalan emotions came to a head in meetings with Real Madrid, a symbol of the regime and right-wing Spain.

After the return of democracy this kind of football politics did seem to fade for a while, and it even seemed possible that football could just be a game, but it has revived with vigour. Currently Barcelona has one of the best teams in the world, universally admired and flying higher than ever *(see page 276)*.

Infanta Cristina of Spain (daughter of the King of Spain) lived in the Sarrià district for years, with no intrusive interest from locals.

Barcelona is also one of the most tolerant places in Spain. Gay and feminist movements were largely pioneered here, and alternative medicine, self-help and New Age culture thrive. The respect for creativity extends to eccentrics. Look at Gaudí: far from being the archetypal misunderstood artist, he was positively sought out and encouraged in his creative flights.

Above all, good humour rules. Walk through any Barcelona market. The stallholders have been up since dawn, buying stock, loading and unloading, cooking lentils, chickpeas and the like. Yet they're filled with good cheer, cracking jokes and gossiping, their talk peppered with endearments like *rei*, *reina*, *maco*, *maca*. They're shopkeepers to the core, but enjoy themselves.

Independence and tolerance

Catalan tradition places a high value on independence, both collective and personal. Their climate allows Barcelonans to live life outside. They are masters of sociability when out in the streets and squares, bars and restaurants; they engage fully in the community life of offices and shops, parks and sports fields. However, they are fiercely protective of their homes, their safe haven. This translates into a great respect for individual privacy – the

Putting on a show

This good humour and flair for combining work, fun and creative imagination is the essence of life in Barcelona. On Carnival

IN THE RING: DANCING THE *SARDANA*

The *sardana* is Catalonia's national dance, one of the region's most recognisable symbols. In its present form it grew out of the 19th-century *Renaixença*, when Catalans rediscovered their cultural identity. No festival is complete without it.

In Barcelona *sardanes* are danced in the cathedral square each Sunday at noon, Saturday at 6.30pm and Wednesdays at 7pm, and at weekends there is a *sardana* school for children in Plaça de Catalunya. The band, the *cobla*, is unique to the dance: the leader plays a *flabiol*, a three-holed pipe, and a *tabal*, a small drum strapped to his elbow. Woodwind instruments are also traditional –

especially the *tenora*, the special Catalan clarinet, while the brass section is more conventional. Each tune lasts about 10 minutes, and, just as you think it is dying away, it starts up anew.

As the music gets going, a few people in the crowd start to dance, linking hands to form a small circle. Soon others join in, making their own circles or joining existing ones, until the whole square is filled with dancers, solemnly counting the short sedate steps, which suddenly change to longer, bouncy ones. True aficionados wear espadrilles with coloured ribbons, but most people dance in their ordinary shoes, be they Sunday best or trainers.

Thursday, for example, it's business as usual at the Boqueria market on La Rambla – but in fancy dress. A cardinal in full regalia blesses shoppers trundling their carts in and

> Barcelona is a meritocracy, with little regard for petty titles and nobility, but a huge respect for creativity.

out. Ballet dancers, chest hair bristling from pink tutus, cart crates of potatoes. Plumed cavaliers slice chorizo, while Moorish princesses gut fish.

In the old districts of Gràcia and Sants locals work all year to prepare for their *festa major* (annual fête) in mid-August. Entire streets are turned into decorative fantasies, with prizes for the best. Each street or square organises its own programme. Kids get puppet shows and hot chocolate parties; live salsa and rock bands play through the night. By

day it's still business as usual, except you'll go shopping in *Jurassic Park*, or something out of the *Arabian Nights*.

A day of roses, books and dragons

The epitome of the Barcelona personality is the feast of Sant Jordi (St George), patron saint of Catalonia, on 23 April. This is also the anniversary of the deaths of Shakespeare and Cervantes, and is celebrated by giving gifts of books and roses. Sant Jordi is an inspired blend of culture, moneymaking and fun: it's not actually a public holiday, so everyone is sucked into the *festa* as they go about their business.

Bookshops set up stalls on La Rambla and in streets and squares, and give discounts. TV shows interview authors on La Rambla. It's a field day too for florists and hawkers, who sell roses in metro stations. Children in Catalan national dress greet their parents at school gates with paper roses and paintings of expiring dragons. Later, as men hurry home, each one bears a red rose beautifully wrapped and tied with red-and-yellow ribbon, and record book sales figures appear on the late-night news. ❑

FAR LEFT: lacemakers gather on La Rambla. ABOVE LEFT: father and daughter during festivities on the Plaça Sant Jaume. ABOVE: shining shoes on La Rambla.

FURIOUS FIESTAS

The Barcelonans' reputation as sober workaholics is seriously undermined when one of the city's many annual festivals erupts onto the streets

Hardly a month passes in Barcelona without at least one excuse to party, like a *festa major* (celebration of local patron saint), which calls for a public holiday, enormous family meals, flowing cava and noisy antics in the streets.

Depending on the *festa*'s status, it will probably entail dancing *gegants* (giants), *dracs* (dragons), *dimonis* (devils) and legendary beasts, plus processions of dignitaries and mounted guards *(guardia urbana)*, *castells* (human towers), and *sardanes* (the traditional Catalan dance) in public squares which are taken over by rock or jazz bands at night. There is nearly always an air-raid of fireworks.

There are also more demure festivals, such as the Fira de Sant Ponç (11 May), when medicinal herbs, honey and crystallised fruits are sold. At the other extreme are the wild festivals like La Mercè, the *festa major* in September, which consists of a whole week of uproarious fun culminating in the *correfoc*, a pyromaniac's dream. It is also worth looking out for the numerous cultural festivals, including the Grec, a five-week-long summer festival of music and the arts.

LEFT: the five-year-old *anxeneta* crowning a five-storey or more *castell* is the most breathtaking and unmissable moment of a *festa*.

ABOVE: each neighbourhood has its own *festa major*. One of the most popular is in Gràcia in mid-August, when neighbours get together to decorate their streets elaborately and bands play late into the night.

ABOVE: La Mercè is the festival to beat all festivals when the city celebrates its patroness, Mercè, for a whole week around 24 September. With fireworks, devils and concerts by night, *castells* (human pyramids, *see left*), *gegants* (giants) and *dracs* (dragons) by day, there's something for everyone.

OTHER FESTIVAL HIGHLIGHTS

BAM Barcelona Acció Musical is now an established part of the Mercè fiesta in September, providing free music concerts in locations around the city, from the cathedral esplanade to the Rambla del Raval.

Castanyada An autumnal festival held around All Saints' Day (1 November) in homes, schools and public squares. Roast chestnuts and sweet potatoes are eaten, followed by *panellets* (small almond-based cakes) with muscatel sweet wine.

Grec For over 35 years the city has held this festival of music and the arts, using locations all over the city. Runs for several weeks (June to July).

L'Ou com Balla Often missed, this low-key celebration of Corpus Christi is one of the most delightful: an egg dances in the beautifully decorated fountains of the medieval courtyards of the Gothic Quarter.

Sant Jordi celebrates St George, the patron saint of Catalonia on 23 April. According to legend, the blood of the slain dragon transmutes into a rose. Men and women exchange gifts of books and roses, as this is also the date of Cervantes's anniversary.

BELOW: brilliant firework displays accompany many festivals, including La Mercè in September and Sant Joan in June. Bonfires, fireworks and flowing cava last all night long on the eve of Sant Joan (23 June). The festival is an explosive start to summer when young and old alike take to the streets with firecrackers. Luckily the 24th is a public holiday and the streets are quiet as everyone recovers.

ELS FUTBOLISTES RECLAMEN
L'AJUT ALS REFUGIATS

ORGANITZAT PER COMISSIÓ
PRO REFUGIATS U.G.T. S.R.I. i
SINDICAT PROFESSIONALS FUTBOL
DIUMENGE 27 A LES CORTS

THE MAKING OF MODERN BARCELONA

The city rose to power under Catalonia's medieval count-kings, then fell into decline only to wake up to find itself under the control of Madrid. The urge to break out of this inertia, and a deep Catalan identity, are at the core of Barcelona's inventive energy

Barcelona has all the attributes of a great metropolis and the self-consciousness of a capital city, but much of its dynamism has come from its always having had something to prove. In the Middle Ages it was the centre of the greatest Mediterranean empire since Roman times, but never became a sovereign city in its own right, like Venice or Genoa. Until 1716 it was the capital of a Catalan state, but as Catalonia was absorbed into the Spanish monarchy Barcelona fell into the status of disregarded subordinate to its upstart rival Madrid, the source of endless frustrations.

In the 19th century, a once-more economically vibrant Barcelona became the centre of a resurgent Catalan culture and the groundbreaker for everything modern in Spain. And recently Barcelona has leapt out of its seclusion again to win an image as one of Europe's most fashionable, most inventive, liveliest cities.

Roman beginnings

The Roman colony that grew into Barcelona was founded around 15 BC. It fed well off its "sea of oysters", and had such amenities as porticoed baths and a forum, but was a small town, covering about 12 hectares (30 acres). Its city walls were dwarfed by those at nearby Tarragona. Roman Barcino was built on top of a small hill, roughly where the cathedral is today.

For half a millennium after the end of Roman rule, Barcelona's history is sparsely

documented. Thanks to its walls it remained a coveted stronghold, but most of the surrounding region was a no-man's-land. Of the occupiers of those years – the Visigoths, the Moors, the Franks – only the first seem to have esteemed the city much. In 415 the Visigoth king Ataülf seized Barcino from its last Roman governor, and briefly made it his capital.

> Barcelona's Roman walls, built around AD 300, made it a valued stronghold for 1,000 years.

The ramshackle Visigothic kingdom fell apart, though, when Muslim armies swept over the Iberian peninsula in 711. For 80 years Barcelona was ruled by a Moorish governor under the caliphs of Córdoba, rulers of Al-Andalús. Its

---

LEFT: the footballers' union organises aid for Republican refugees during the Civil War. **RIGHT:** part of the Roman wall and reconstructed aqueduct at the Portal del Bisbe.

He was a man of the mountains, who from his stronghold in Ripoll managed in the 880s to unite most of the patchwork of Catalan counties under his authority, including Barcelona.

Once incorporated into Wilfred's inheritance, though, the old Roman citadel rapidly gained importance. Around 911, Wilfred II founded the monastery of Sant Pau del Camp outside the city, and chose to be buried there. It was this sort of princely patronage that began to turn the former backwater into a medieval metropolis.

Moorish threat

In 985 Barcelona was a rich enough target to be sacked by Al-Mansur, the great vizier of Córdoba. Frankish authority over the counts of Barcelona had been ephemeral for a century, but in theory they were still feudal vassals of the Frankish king. Count Borrell II accordingly sent off a request for aid to his lord in this crisis.

next change of ownership came in 801, when Louis the Pious, son of the Frankish Emperor Charlemagne, seized control of the territory as far south as Barcelona, making it the Marca Hispànica or "Spanish March" of his father's empire, to protect it from Moorish invasions.

The birth of Catalonia

To guard this new frontier, Frankish aristocrats were left as counts to rule the Pyrenean valleys. Catalonia grew out of these counties, and this is one of the differentiating facts of Catalan history. The Christian kingdoms in western Spain descended from communities who had retreated north before the Muslim advance; Catalonia had its roots north of the Pyrenees. Hence the Catalan language, for example, is closer to French and above all Provençal than it is to Castilian.

Barcelona itself long remained a remote frontier fortress. Its potential only began to be realised with the emergence of a nascent Catalan state. Wilfred the Hairy – the precise translation of *Guifré el Pilós* – the man acclaimed as the founder of the House of the Counts of Barcelona, actually had little to do with the city.

From the 10th to the 12th century Catalonia was an important centre of Romanesque art and architecture, producing jewels such as the church of Sant Pau del Camp (see page 149).

Nothing came back, so Borrell renounced all obligations to the kings of France, effectively declaring his independence.

Barcelona recovered from its sacking, and the Moorish threat did not survive Al-Mansur's death in 1002. The caliphate was enfeebled by internal intrigue, and in the 1030s dissolved into competing emirates called *taifas*. This allowed the Christian states to make big advances, and the Catalan counts expanded their lands to the south and west. Barcelona enjoyed a bonanza on the proceeds of booty, ransom and trade.

Wealth and empire

By 1075, 95 percent of transactions in Barcelona were in gold. For the next 500 years, maritime enterprise supplied the city's wealth and formed its character. In 1060, the Barcelonans were still hiring galleys from Moorish ports. By 1080 the counts had a fleet of their own.

For years, the counts of Barcelona still divided their attention between both sides of the Pyrenees, acquiring lands in the Languedoc as well as towards the Ebro. In 1150, however, Ramón Berenguer IV married Petronella, daughter of the King of Aragón. Their successors would be "count-kings", rulers of a complex inheritance known as the Crown of Aragón. Since a king was inherently more important than a count, this entity was often known just as Aragón, but its political and economic hub was Barcelona,

INTERNATIONAL TRADE

Barcelona's count-kings were often at war with Muslim rulers, but its merchants traded with the entire Mediterranean, in grain, wines, silks and spices. Charters from the counts make clear the scope of this trade: in 1105 Ramón Berenguer III gave a profitable monopoly to four Jews of Barcelona on shipping home ransomed Muslim prisoners. In 1160 the Jewish chronicler and traveller Benjamin of Tudela reported seeing ships from "Pisa, Genoa, Sicily, Greece, Alexandria and Asia" all lying off the beach at Barcelona waiting to unload.

FAR LEFT: a lord and his vassal, from an early Catalan manuscript. **ABOVE LEFT:** the marriage of Ramón Berenguer IV and Petronella of Aragón, 1150. **LEFT:** Sant Pau del Camp. **ABOVE:** Barcelona's merchants traded throughout the Mediterranean.

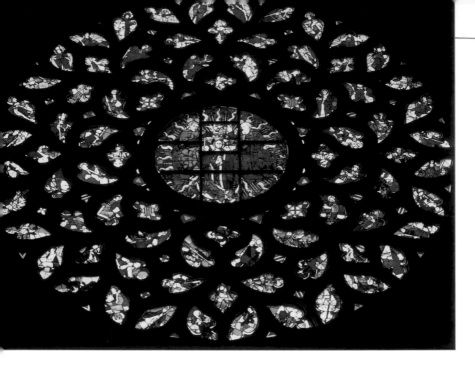

and for centuries its main language would be Catalan. The title King of Aragón initially served the House of Barcelona mainly to ensure them due respect from other monarchs.

Island invasions

In 1213 the count-kings lost their main lands north of the Pyrenees to France, after Pere I of Aragón died at the battle of Muret. This, however, was only a prelude to the Catalan monarchy's greatest expansion, as it directed all its energies towards an onslaught against the Muslim kingdoms to the south.

Barcelona had to gain access to the Balearic Islands, then under Moorish rule, to become a trade centre rivalling Genoa or Pisa. The seizure of Mallorca in 1229 was celebrated as a great triumph. Conquests of Ibiza (1235), Valencia (1238), Sicily (1282), Menorca (1287) and Sardinia (1324) gave the count-kings control of a network of Mediterranean ports, landmarks of an empire of grain and gold, silver and salt. In governing his new lands, however, Jaume I kept the complicated legal structures the Catalans had inherited from the Franks. Already sovereign of two entities, Aragón and Catalonia, he did not absorb the new territories into either, but made Valencia and Mal-

GOLDEN AGE

The Middle Ages were the first great period of Catalan literature. Like its neighbour Provençal, Catalan was already used to write poetry and documents in the 12th century, when most of Europe wrote only in Latin, and the Catalan law code or *Usatges* was written down in Catalan in about 1190. The court was unusually literate, and Jaume I (1213–76) and Pere III (1336–87) both wrote memoirs in their own language. In the 1280s, the great scholar Ramón Llull *(left)* became the first European for centuries to write philosophy in anything other than Latin or Greek. A huge amount of medieval Catalan writing survives, including *Tirant lo Blanc*, written by Joanot Martorell in 1490 – the first true European novel.

lorca two more kingdoms under the crown – a system that would never coalesce into a cohesive state.

Medieval metropolis

Imperial exploits were matched by Barcelona's desire for adornment at home. The Gothic cathedral is the prime monument of the late 13th century, and the decades after its construction began in 1298 were a time of frenzied building. The chapel of Santa Agata, in the count-kings' Palau Reial in Plaça del Rei, was built by Jaume II (1291–1327). The first stone of Santa Maria del Pi was laid in 1322, and that of the exquisite Santa Maria del Mar in 1329.

Not even the Black Death – which killed half the city council – crushed the city's confidence. Never was Barcelona so spectacularly embellished as in the reign of Pere III (1336–87); he built the vaulted halls of the Saló de Cent in the Ajuntament (town hall) and the Saló del Tinell in Plaça del Rei, and rebuilt on a vast scale the royal shipyards, the eight great bays of the Drassanes at the foot of the Ramblas (now the Maritime Museum). Private builders filled the Carrer Montcada with ornate town mansions.

LEFT: one of the glories of Catalan Gothic, the rose window of Santa Maria del Mar. **ABOVE:** Jaume I presides over the Catalan *Corts* or Parliament. **RIGHT:** a Catalan merchant ship, from a woodcut of 1502.

The passing of glory

However, as the empire grew, its costs came to exceed its benefits. The ambition to control the western Mediterranean led to wasteful wars with Genoa, and Sardinian resistance to Catalan rule exhausted the conquerors.

The empire that made a metropolis of Barcelona also sucked the rural life-blood out of Catalonia, as the population balance shifted. The countryside could no longer keep armies supplied with men or the city with food. In 1330 Barcelona had its first serious famine.

> Barcelona's medieval elite were a merchant aristocracy, and their ideal residences were the Gothic palaces of Carrer Montcada (see page 129).

In 1410 the line of count-kings descended from Wilfred the Hairy came to an end with Martí I, and the Crown of Aragón passed to a Castilian noble dynasty, the Trastámaras. Over the next century, the influence of Barcelona within the monarchy diminished. Alfons V "the Magnanimous" (1416–58) mainly governed the

Crown of Aragón from as far away as Naples.

In the century after 1360, not a decade went by without a plague or famine in Barcelona. Insecurity led to violent unrest. In 1462, Catalonia exploded in civil war, combining urban discontent with a peasants' revolt. Barcelona rose against Joan II, but the siege that ended the war in 1473 was devastating.

THE MISSING RENAISSANCE

No visitor to Barcelona can fail to be struck by the relative dearth of great Renaissance and Baroque buildings. Examples of grandeur are few and far between: the Ajuntament (Town Hall, *below*) hides its medieval core behind a Renaissance facade. The Carrer Ample was opened as a gesture to Renaissance town planning, but most of what survives from this time reflects private effort, not public wealth or patronage.

This is largely due to the fact that the Habsburg monarchs and ministers were mainly concerned with their empire, its wars and their great seat of power in Castile, Madrid.

Marriage of power

Barcelona was thus at a low ebb when the political framework around it was transformed. In 1469 Fernando (Ferran, in Catalan) of Aragón married Isabel of Castile, a union that for the first time would bring all the main Christian kingdoms of Spain under the same rulers. Legally, each part kept its institutions for another 200 years – as the different elements already did in the Crown of Aragón – but nevertheless, as the joint monarchy developed, Catalonia became increasingly regarded as an annexe of Castile.

Multinational takeover

In contrast to Catalonia, Castile was on a rising curve of expansion. In 1492 Granada, last Muslim state in the Iberian peninsula, was conquered, and Fernando and Isabel sponsored Columbus's first voyage to America. American conquests would bring unheard-of power and booty, but Barcelona got little share of this or the new Atlantic trade, as Catalans were not allowed to trade directly with the colonies for over 270 years. On Fernando's death in 1516 his Spanish kingdoms went to his grandson Charles V of Habsburg (Carlos I of Spain), who was also ruler of Burgundy, the Netherlands and Austria, and Holy Roman Emperor. Catalonia became a minor part of a global empire. The Habsburg rulers mainly visited Barcelona on their way to somewhere else, and so it progressively lost the courtly status that had been one of the foundations of its fortune.

Differences in Castilian thinking were a worsening source of conflict. In Castile, civic liberties normally rested in a charter from the king, and royal authority could rarely be resisted long – especially after Charles V crushed the revolt of the Castilian *comuneros* in 1521. The identity of Barcelona, however,

> The Habsburg monarchs often saw Catalonia's representatives as a gaggle of disloyal, troublemaking lawyers.

was bound up with its status in law, and that of Catalonia and its *Corts* (Parliament) as a partner in the Spanish monarchy. In Catalonia, the Habsburgs had to negotiate a patchwork of traditional assemblies, each determinedly aware of its historic rights. To an aristocracy accustomed to absolute power, this attitude looked like simple disloyalty.

FAR LEFT: 16th-century Catalan tiles showing typical crafts and occupations. **ABOVE LEFT:** gold coin of the joint monarchs Fernando and Isabel. **ABOVE:** Barcelona falls to the armies of Felipe V, 11 September 1714.

Rebellion and defeat

In the early 17th century the Spanish monarchy began to totter under the effects of over-ambition and endless wars. In their attempts to stop the rot the ministers of Felipe IV (1621–65) made insistent demands for money and man-power from non-Castilian territories of the crown. Catalans feared for their rights.

The cost of the Thirty Years War and war with France brought the monarchy's demands to a peak. Catalonia rose in revolt in 1640, after an attempt to conscript Catalans into the royal armies, and the rebels tried to transfer their allegiance to Louis XIII of France. However, a controlled rising by Barcelona lawyers exploded into a ferocious peasants' revolt. The war dragged on for years, and the siege of Barcelona in 1652 ended only when the citizens were "reduced to eating grass". The victorious Habsburgs were unusually generous, and allowed the Catalan institutions to remain in place.

The end of the Habsburgs

In 1700 the chronically infirm Carlos II, last Spanish Habsburg, died without an heir. Two candidates disputed the throne in the War of the Spanish Succession: one French, Felipe V, grand-

Expansion

The city was prostrate and revival slow, but the 18th century was also an era when sustained economic growth began in Barcelona, thanks to new activities such as direct trade with the Americas – finally open to Catalans in the 1770s – and the beginnings of industrialisation based on American cotton. In the 1780s, the Catalan economy accelerated fast.

War and revival

In 1808, Napoleon seized King Carlos IV and the Spanish royal family and put his brother Joseph on the Spanish throne. He tried to win over Catalonia by offering a separate government, but perhaps surprisingly the Catalans had none of it, and supported the Spanish monarchy throughout the war (1808–14).

This war and its aftermath reduced the Spanish state to chaos. Barcelona's manufacturers, though, were not deflected from their plans, and Catalonia became one of very few areas in southern Europe to join the Industrial Revolution before 1860.

The walls come down

Barcelona was the most insanitary and congested city in Europe. Observers blamed the cholera epidemic of 1854, which took 6,000 lives, on overcrowding. It was still a militarised city, contained by walls and watched over by two hated fortresses, Montjuïc and the Ciutadella. Strict ordinances banned building outside the walls. Inside, every metre was occupied. Barcelona was bursting at the seams.

Permission to tear down the walls and the Ciutadella came in 1854, and ordinary people, eager for fresh air, joined in the demolition.

son of Louis XIV, and one Austrian, the Archduke Charles. After a slow start, the Barcelonans became the most committed opponents of Felipe V, and clung on even after their British and Dutch allies withdrew in 1713. The final siege lasted from August 1713 to 11 September 1714, when the city fell, a date commemorated as the *Diada de Catalunya* – Catalonia's national day.

In 1716 Felipe V finalised his decrees of *Nova Planta*, which, following lines set down by his grandfather in France, finally made Spain a single, centralised state. All the assemblies and rights of Catalonia and other Aragonese territories were abolished, and Castilian was made sole language of law and government. Barcelona was reduced to a provincial city, and suffered the indignity of an occupying army billeted in a glowering new fortress, the Ciutadella.

Barceloneta was designed by a French army engineer, Prosper Verboom, to house thousands of people expelled from the Old City to make way for the Ciutadella, the huge fortress built to keep Barcelona in check.

An idealistic engineer, Ildefons Cerdà, drew up a plan for the "Extension and Reform" of Barcelona.

Cerdà's design for the Eixample (Extension) joined Barcelona to Sants, Gràcia and other hinterland towns by means of a giant grid of crisscrossing streets, broken by two great diagonal avenues. It was a utopian dream, but with

> In 1836, the first steamship rolled off a slipway in Barceloneta, gaslight was introduced in 1842, and in 1848 Spain's first railway linked Barcelona to Mataró, 30km (19 miles) north.

a scientific basis. Most criticisms of today's Eixample – such as the lack of open space – result from the debasement of Cerdà's plan that has been allowed by successive city councils.

Catalan rebirth

The September Revolution of 1868, which swept Queen Isabel II from the Spanish throne, brought another promise of democratic reform, and another brief time – six years – when repression was cast aside and ideas and movements proliferated in Barcelona. Workers' unions blossomed, and the first anarchist groups were formed. Barcelona had a flourishing café society, and new ideas – the Catalan *Renaixença* or rebirth, socialism, anarchism –

were avidly debated. Radical forces, however – in Catalonia and Spain as a whole – were chronically weak and divided. Spain briefly became a federal republic in 1873, but this was soon toppled by a military coup, followed by the restoration of the Bourbons under King Alfonso XII.

EXHIBITION FEVER

As Barcelona's prosperity grew in the 19th century, the city's movers and shakers, ignored by the government in Madrid, felt they needed to do something to bring their city to the world's attention. Their exuberance was ideally expressed by the 1888 Universal Exposition. With less than a year to prepare, Barcelona threw itself into a frenzy of construction: most of the Parc de la Ciutadella (the main exhibition site), the Arc de Triomf *(below)*, the Columbus Column and more, all date from 1888. The exhibition knocked up huge debts, but Barcelona felt it had been worth it – so much so that it staged another expo' in 1929, which led to the redesign of Montjüic and Plaça d'Espanya, and these collective memories clearly fed into the huge enthusiasm for the Olympic project in the 1980s.

FAR LEFT: Barcelona in 1706. **LEFT:** engraving showing workers at a Barcelona metalworks, 1877. **ABOVE:** citizens in their finery on La Rambla in the 19th century. **ABOVE RIGHT:** the Guardia Civil retake control of Barcelona's streets, 1909.

A new era

The restoration of the monarchy, and the renewed suppression of radical movements, did not halt the expansion of Barcelona. Rather, it allowed it to take off, as the middle classes felt

> *The* modernista *style combined a strong sense of Catalan tradition with a powerful enthusiasm for the new: intricate, elaborate, but set against the rationality of the machine age.*

a new burst of confidence. The building of the Eixample went on apace, as the fashionable quarter for the wealthy and professional classes. Its owners competed with each other to commission the most opulent buildings, so it became the great showcase for Gaudí and other Catalan *modernista* architects *(see pages 54–7)*.

By 1900 two forces were most prominent: the new Catalan bourgeoisie, who sought modernisation and economic and political autonomy within the established social order, and the new working class, among whom revolution was the stuff of everyday conversation. Dissent grew with the loss of Spain's last

colonies and their markets in 1898. Anarchism gained strength. There were general strikes in 1901 and 1902, and in 1909 the city suffered the *Setmana Tràgica*, a week of rioting when 70 religious buildings were burnt down.

The 20th-century crisis

The early 1900s were the peak years of the Lliga Regionalista, a conservative Catalan nationalist party that sought to give respectable expression to the sentiments of the *Renaixença*. In 1914 they won from the Madrid government the *Mancomunitat* or confederation of the four Catalan provinces, the first pan-Catalan institution since 1714. Their confident plans, though, would be knocked aside by bitter conflicts within Catalan society.

With World War I Barcelona saw a whole new opulence, generated by supplying the Allies. This also brought massive inflation, which postwar triggered a social and economic crisis. Workers flocked to the anarchist union, the CNT.

ABOVE: Montjuïc all lit up for the 1929 Exposition.
TOP RIGHT: *miliciana* on guard above the Plaça de Catalunya, July 1936. **ABOVE RIGHT:** queuing for food after Barcelona fell to Franco, February 1939.

In 1923 the army commander in Barcelona, Miguel Primo de Rivera, used this chaos as justification for a military coup, taking over the Spanish government as first minister under King Alfonso XIII. The Catalanist elite, terrified by unrest, gave him their support, only to be rewarded with the renewed banning of the Catalan flag and public use of the language.

The Second Republic

Primo de Rivera retired to his Andalucian estate in 1930. Alfonso XIII sought to stabilise the situation with local elections in April 1931, but when these were overwhelmingly won by anti-monarchist candidates the king went into exile. Spain's Second Republic was proclaimed. Left-wing nationalists had won the elections in Catalonia, and their popular leader Francesc Macià became provisional president of a restored Catalan Generalitat, or autonomous government. What cellist Pau Casals called a "veritable cultural renaissance" began. The five years between 1931 and the Civil War are seen by Catalans as another very brief golden age, when Barcelona, in euphoric mood, threw itself into another of its bursts of enthusiasm for new projects and creative ideas.

The Spanish Civil War *(see box, below)* ushered in one of Spain's darkest periods, and

BARCELONA IN THE CIVIL WAR

The Spanish Civil War began on 18 July 1936, when the army launched a coup against the left-wing Popular Front government in Madrid and its allies, such as the Catalan Generalitat. In Barcelona, leftist parties and unions fought back, and were victorious by 19 July.

Barcelona then underwent a revolution: normal authorities were suspended, and trams, factories and stores became workers' collectives – a time captured by Orwell in *Homage to Catalonia*. This euphoria, though, had shaky foundations. The Nationalists led by General Franco had been successful in many parts of Spain, and were advancing on Madrid.

They were armed by Germany and Italy, while the Republicans, cold-shouldered by Britain and France, had no other source of arms than the Soviet Union, which gave the Communists disproportionate influence. In Barcelona tension mounted between Communists and Anarchists, coming to a head in street battles in May 1937.

The Republican army, meanwhile, made little headway against Franco's troops, and behind the lines there were acute shortages and hunger. In 1938, Barcelona was heavily bombed by the Italian air force. For months, the Republic struggled to turn the tide at the battle of the Ebro, in southern Catalonia. When this failed it had no strength left, and Franco's army took Barcelona in January 1939. Nearly half a million refugees crossed into France, and 35,000 Republicans were executed by the new regime.

under Franco's iron hand Catalan identity, language and culture were subjected to brutal repression for nearly 40 years.

Getting by in the grey years

During the Franco regime, the middle classes worked hard, looked after their businesses and made money, reinforcing Barcelona's status as the manufacturing capital of Spain. Madrid, which held the purse strings, neglected and underfunded "Spain's factory". Waves of immigrants from Spain's impoverished south poured in looking for work in the 1950s and 1960s, and cheap, drab housing blocks were thrown up in a ring of badly serviced satellite suburbs.

By the late 1960s, the iron grip Franco had held over Spain was becoming enfeebled. Tourism, the basis for an economic boom, also opened the country to the world. In Barcelona, opposition movements were ever more active.

Autonomy and a new beginning

Legend has it that on 20 November 1975, when Franco died, Barcelona partied so hard the city ran out of cava. A few months later, King Juan Carlos appointed an obscure Francoist official, Adolfo Suárez, as prime minister

with the task of returning Spain to democracy.

Spain's first democratic elections since 1936 came in June 1977. In Catalonia the main winners were the Socialists and the conservative nationalist Convergència party of Jordi Pujol. Suárez saw that a democratic Spain had to admit Catalan aspirations, and an autonomy statute gave Catalonia substantial potential self-government. In every local election since 1978 the Socialists have held control of Barcelona council until 2011 when the Convergència i Unió candiate, Trias, became mayor.

Radical change

Politics were only one aspect of a drastic change in the whole of Barcelona as the city shook off the repressive years *(see box, below)*. A key element in this was the hosting of the 1992 Olympic Games – as a pretext for attracting international attention and investment to help carry out the

---

CREATIVE REGENERATION

In the post-Franco years, long-frustrated creativity was released and Barcelona rediscovered its artistic traditions. The pinch-spirited drabness of Francoism was left behind by a stylish, inventive, clearly Catalan style. Barcelona's Socialist council, under charismatic mayor Pasqual Maragall from 1982, sought to harness this new mood; it enlisted Barcelona's creative community, typified by architect Oriol Bohigas, the city's chief planner, who set in motion a renovation of the whole city. Nor was this just a matter of image and quality of life: by attracting service industries they could compensate for the decline of the city's traditional economic core – textiles, chemicals and engineering.

plans for a new city. What could beat the Olympics to put the city back on the global map?

Post-Olympic city

Apart from major new infrastructures, the most stunning transformation has been on the waterfront. In the 1980s, Barcelona had a grimy industrial harbour, and a grubby, unloved beach. A key part of the Olympic plan was to open Barcelona to the sea, with the creation of the Olympic Village and port and the opening up of kilometres of clean beach.

It's often unnoticed that many of Barcelona's projects were carried out *after* 1992, like the transformation of the Port Vell into a spectacular leisure area. Barcelona's Ajuntament has been an international benchmark for dynamic city administration, and its love affair with the world's architects is unending. However, with the retirement of both Pujol and Maragall by

2006 – key leaders in shaping post-Franco Catalonia – the political scene entered a grey period. It was difficult to emulate the large strides that had been made in the '80s and '90s and the advent of recession slowed down some grand designs. By 2011 young people all over Spain, including Barcelona, were protesting peacefully about soaring unemployment and

> With its return to the sea, Barcelona seems to have distilled the essence of a Mediterranean city.

corrupt politicians and there was a sense that the "new democratic" Spain was losing its way.

General elections are due in 2012. In Catalonia, Artur Mas of the Convergència i Unió party has taken over the Generalitat and Barcelona City Council, seemingly reflecting a national move towards the right.

Meanwhile Barcelona's latest brainchild, the 22@ business district, is progressing. History has proven that it is hard to crush the Catalans' rebellious and inventive spirit. It is to be hoped that the 21st century is no exception. ❑

FAR LEFT: the opening ceremony of the 1992 Olympics. **ABOVE LEFT:** Jordi Pujol *(left)* and Pasqual Maragall, the foremost political figures of modern Catalonia. **LEFT:** Vila Olímpica under construction. **ABOVE:** the transformed Port Vell lit up for the Festes de la Mercè.

DECISIVE DATES

Early History:
c.700 BC–AD 415

c.700 BC
The Iberians settle in the fertile area between the Rivers Llobregat and Besòs.

c.600 BC
Greek ships appear off the Catalan coast, and found the city of Empòrion on the Costa Brava.

c.300 BC
The Carthaginians occupy parts of Catalonia.

264–200 BC
In the Punic Wars between Rome and Carthage, the Romans capture the area around the future Barcelona in about 200 BC.

c.15 BC
Roman soldiers found Barcelona as a small town on the road between Rome and Tarraco (Tarragona), during the reign of the Emperor Augustus. The colony's full name is Julia Augusta Faventia Paterna Barcino.

c. AD 350
Roman city walls (left) built.

415
The Visigoths enter Spain and capture Barcelona. Their leader Ataülf makes it his capital, but this later moves to Toledo.

Moors, Franks and the Catalan-Aragonese Monarchy: 711–1469

711
The Moors invade Spain and capture Barcelona in 713.

801
The Franks under Louis the Pious take Barcelona and found the Marca Hispànica (Spanish March) in what would become Catalonia.

c.880
Wilfred the Hairy (Guifré el Pilós), Count of Ripoll, unifies the Catalan counties and establishes the House of Barcelona, a dynasty that lasts 500 years.

985
Al-Mansur, Grand Vizier of the Caliph of Córdoba, sacks Barcelona.

988
Count Borrell II (above) renounces all obligations to the kings of France after receiving no help against Al-Mansur, making Catalonia effectively independent.

1137
Count Berenguer IV of Barcelona marries Petronella, heiress to the throne of Aragón, forming the joint Catalan-Aragonese monarchy.

c.1190
The Usatges, the Catalan legal code (below), is compiled and written in Catalan.

1213
Count-King Pere I is killed at the battle of Muret in Languedoc, and loses lands in southern France.

1229
Jaume I takes Mallorca, first of a series of major conquests that led to dominance in the Mediterranean.

1274
Barcelona's city government, the Consell de Cent, is established.

13th–14th century
The Catalan-Aragonese monarchy extends its power to Sardinia and Sicily. Barcelona's maritime law, the *Llibre del Consolat del Mar*, governs sea trade. Splendid buildings go up in Barcelona's Barri Gòtic.

1347–50
Black Death kills half Barcelona's population.

1359
Corts Catalanes or Catalan Parliament established, with a council, the Generalitat de Catalunya, to administer finances.

1391
Anti-Jewish pogroms in Barcelona and throughout Aragón and Castile.

1462–73
Catalan civil war.

Imperial Spain: 1469–1808

1469
Fernando II of Aragón marries Queen Isabel I of Castile, uniting all the Spanish Christian kingdoms in one inheritance.

1492
Granada falls, Columbus discovers America, and all Jews are expelled from all the Spanish kingdoms.

1522
Charles V denies Catalans permission to trade directly with the American colonies, insisting they can only do so via Seville.

1640
After the governments of King Felipe IV demand Catalonia contribute more to the Thirty Years War, Catalans rise in revolt in the War of the Reapers *(Guerra dels Segadors)*, and the Generalitat tries to place the country under the authority of French king Louis XIII. Spanish troops are unable to recapture Barcelona until 1652.

1659
In the Treaty of the Pyrenees, all of Catalonia north of the Pyrenees – Roussillon and Perpignan – is ceded to France.

1702–14
Barcelona sides with the Habsburg Archduke Charles in the War of the Spanish Succession, against the French Bourbon Felipe V. French and Spanish troops take the city after a year-long siege on 11 September 1714.

1715–16
The victorious Felipe V issues his decrees of *Nova Planta*, abolishing the remaining Catalan institutions and establishing Spain as a single, centralised state. In Barcelona half of La Ribera district is destroyed to make space for a fortress, the Ciutadella.

1808–14
Napoleon's troops occupy most of Spain, including Barcelona. Catalans rise up against the French. Experiments are made in democratic government, but when King Fernando VII is restored in 1814 he only seeks to reinstate the absolute monarchy.

The Modern Era
1814 onwards
Barcelona's trade and industry steadily expands, and from the 1830s it has the first steam-driven factories in Spain.

1836–8
Dissolution of most of Barcelona's monasteries, opening up large areas for new building.

1842
Barcelona is bombarded from Montjuïc to suppress a radical revolt.

1848
Spain's first rail line is built from Barcelona to Mataró.

1854–6
The Ciutadella and the medieval city walls are demolished.

1860
The building of the city's grid (Eixample), designed by Ildefons Cerdà, begins.

1868–73
September Revolution, against Queen Isabel II, begins six years of agitation. The first anarchist groups are formed, and in 1873 Spain briefly becomes a republic.

1888
Barcelona hosts its first Universal Exposition.

1901–9
Radicalisation and anarchist influence in the workers' movement are reflected in general strikes, and the *Setmana Tràgica* (Tragic Week) in 1909, when churches are destroyed in riots after the government tries to conscript extra troops for its colonial war in Morocco.

1914
The *Mancomunitat*, a joint administration of the Catalan provinces, is set up. Industry flourishes during World War I.

1919
General strike begun at La Canadiense electricity company initiates period of intense social conflict.

1923–30
Military dictatorship of Primo de Rivera suppresses unions and Catalan freedoms.

1929
A second Universal Exposition is held on Montjuïc. The Plaça d'Espanya, Palau Nacional and Poble Espanyol are all built.

1931
Second Spanish Republic
proclaimed: Catalonia is
given autonomy, with a
restored Generalitat under
Francesc Macià *(above)*.

1936–9
Spanish Civil War: right-
wing generals revolt
against the Republic, but in
Barcelona are initially
defeated by the people in
the streets. But, after three
years of war, bitter fighting
and destruction, Barcelona
falls to Franco's troops on
26 January 1939.

1959–60
After years of scarcity, local
economy begins to revive
as tourism and foreign
investment enter Spain.

1975
Franco dies on 20 Novem-
ber. King Juan Carlos oversees moves towards a
restoration of democracy.

1977–8
First democratic general
elections since 1936, and
first local elections, won in
Barcelona by Socialists.
Catalan autonomy statute
granted and Catalan recognised as official language.

1980
Jordi Pujol is elected first
president of restored
Catalan Generalitat.

1982
Pasqual Maragall becomes
Mayor of Barcelona.

Barcelona'92

1992
Barcelona Olympic Games.

1997
Maragall resigns and is
succeeded by Joan Clos.

2003
Jordi Pujol retires; Pasqual
Maragall heads left-wing
coalition. Barcelona holds
one of the largest demon-
strations in Europe against
the Iraq War *(above right)*.

2004
Socialists led by José Luis
Rodríguez Zapatero take
over Spanish central
government after Partido
Popular is discredited by its
response to 11 March Al-
Qaeda bombings in Madrid.

2006
Maragall coalition in
Generalitat replaced by
one under fellow Socialist
Josep Montilla. New
Statute for Catalonia
passed in Congress.

2008
AVE rail link finally connects
Barcelona and Madrid.

2009
Despite world recession,
the 22@ business district
forges ahead.

2010–11
Beleaguered by the eco-
nomic situation, Socialists
suffer defeats in municipali-
ties and regionally. This is
reflected in Catalonia where
centrist Convergència i Unió
take over Generalitat and
city council.

ARCHITECTURE

Barcelona has a rich architectural heritage, from soaring Gothic arches to flamboyant *modernista* mansions. And a spate of exciting new building projects has rejuvenated the city's image over the past two decades

I n 1999, the Royal Institute of British Architects awarded their annual gold medal, the most prestigious award for architecture in the world, not to an individual but, for the first time, to a city: Barcelona. The award stated: "Inspired city leadership, pursuing an ambitious yet pragmatic urban strategy and the highest design standards, has transformed the city's public realm, immensely expanded its amenities and regenerated its economy, providing pride in its inhabitants and delight in its visitors."

Since the 1980s Barcelona has attracted the attention of architects from all over the world for its bold contemporary architecture, urban design and successful programme of renewal. The effect has been to catapult the city from a dusty European backwater to a shining example of how cities should be managed.

Architecture has always been on any visitor's agenda due to the works of Antoni Gaudí and his *modernista* contemporaries, but their work, extraordinary though it is, comprises only a part of the city's rich architectural heritage.

Understanding the city

Set between the sea and the Collserola mountains, and contained by Montjuïc to the south and the River Besòs to the north, Barcelona is one of the most densely populated cities in Europe. At its heart lies the Casc Antic, the medieval area which, until the middle of the 19th

century, contained the entire city within its walls – the oldest of which date back to the Romans.

Catalan Gothic has a distinctive character: dignified but somewhat dour. The interiors are often strikingly large. Some are very fine, embodying the secular and religious splendour of the time. Not to be missed are the Saló del Tinell, with its enormous arches, in the Palau Reial Major, the Museu Marítim/Drassanes, where the galleons of the Armada were made, and the Església de Santa Maria del Mar, for its elegance and serenity. The area's dwellings are mixed: dingy flats rub shoulders with splendid merchants' palaces in Montcada, which house the Museu Picasso and other institutions.

LEFT: the ceiling of the nave of Santa Maria del Mar, a prime example of Catalan Gothic. **RIGHT:** 15th-century architecture in the Barri Gòtic.

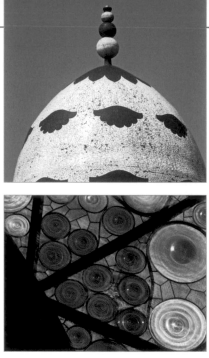

Inventive restoration

Restoration of such palaces has been carried out as part of the city's regeneration programme. Contemporary insertions and details sit proudly beside medieval structures in a style that does not seek to create exact replicas. The purpose has been to complement the existing buildings rather than to imitate past architectural styles.

This attitude is prevalent in all restoration work carried out in the city. A notable example is the 18th-century Casa de la Caritat, in El Raval, which has been transformed into the stunning Centre de Cultura Contemporània (CCCB, *see page 146*) by architects Vilaplana and Piñón.

A radical solution

By the 1850s, it was necessary to build an expansion, or "Eixample", to relieve over-crowding. Engineer Ildefons Cerdà proposed an enormous grid that would spread out over the surrounding plain, intersected by avenues lined with trees. The project was radical, proposing a vision of the city that would be full of sunlight, air and open spaces, and well ordered, with integrated public facilities and transport networks.

> Modernisme *was considered the epitome of bad taste in the years following its heyday, but the pendulum has swung back again, and* modernista *buildings are now symbols of the city.*

The existing Eixample, however, is very different. Almost as soon as the grid was laid out, the council allowed plots of land to be bought up, and families made their fortunes building speculative housing. The quality of housing was graded depending on location; the fashionable streets became the sites for some extremely grand *modernista* blocks, with glazed balconies and tiled and carved facades. In the

more obscure locations are poorer imitations – badly built, narrow, dark flats, with similar but smaller layouts, sometimes with a touch of *modernista* detailing on the entrance and facade. The internal spaces of each block, originally intended as communal parks, became factories, workshops and, later on, car parks.

Development has been a continuous process from the early *modernista* housing, through 1960s architecture, to contemporary apartments. Height restrictions and building lines of the strict grid layout have generally been maintained, resulting in a lively but homogeneous design. The population of the Eixample is great enough to sustain the small shops and bars that give it its pulse, and the area has adapted well to changes in transport and lifestyle.

Urban villages

The city has a number of outlying "villages", such as Gràcia, Sants and Sarrià. Although encroached on by the Eixample, these areas retain a strong and vibrant identity, with their own local history, fiestas and culture. The

buildings are generally smaller, with narrower streets, small squares and parks, four- to five-storey blocks of flats and a limited amount of single-occupancy housing. The whole city is ringed by blocks of flats built in the 1960s to house the thousands of immigrant workers from the rest of Spain. These blocks are variable in quality, and some estates have severe social problems.

RADICAL ARCHITECT

Built by Ludwig Mies van der Rohe (1886–1969), the German Pavilion for the 1929 International Exposition on Montjuïc challenged contemporary notions of space, with no windows, doors or walls in the conventional sense; steel columns support the roof, and the space flows seamlessly from interior to exterior rooms. Frameless glass blurs the concept of thresholds, with panels and screens used to create particular spatial effects.

One of the most influential buildings of the 20th century, it still appears extremely modern. Controversially, a replica of the original was built in 1986 to mark the centenary of the architect's birth.

FAR LEFT: Gaudí's Casa Viçens. **LEFT:** details on the Plaza de Toros, and on Mercat de la Boqueria. **ABOVE:** the Mies van der Rohe Pavilion, Montjuïc.

Architectural regeneration

After the stagnation of Franco's rule (ending with his death in 1975), the new Barcelona City Council was quick to implement plans for regeneration. By the time the Olympic bid was won in 1986, the city was already receiving international attention for its architecture programme. Design was the highest consideration. Each area was subject to a plan based on a study of all aspects of the urban fabric, from the provision of schools and parks to traffic organisation and major infrastructure projects.

International profile

For the high-profile public buildings, and to lend international status to the programme, "star" architects were invited to contribute: Japanese architect Arata Isozaki built the Palau Sant Jordi *(see page 185)*, a huge steel-and-glass indoor arena with a levitating roof, on Montjuïc hill; English architect Norman Foster built the Torre de Collserola *(see page 217)*, now an icon of the skyline and sometimes known as the Torre Foster; US architect Frank Gehry constructed the huge copper fish glittering on the seafront *(see*

ARCHITECTURE OF THE VALL D'HEBRON

The Vall d'Hebron Olympic site, located on metro line 3 at Mundet, is home to some of the most interesting, if lesser known, Olympic buildings.

The most impressive is the Velodrome, built by Esteve Bonnell. It is a beautifully simple, modern interpretation of an ancient, essentially Mediterranean, building type, set in a landscape surrounded by cypress trees. It was built in 1984, at a time when postmodernism was prevalent, incorporating a characteristically classical pastiche and superficial decoration, using high-quality materials such as stone, marble, steel and glass. The site also contains the now dilapidated archery range by Enric Miralles

and Carme Piñón. Nearby is a replica of the pavilion of the Spanish Republic, designed by Josep Lluís Sert for the 1937 Paris Exhibition, and used to exhibit Picasso's *Guernica*. Sert established modern architecture in Barcelona in the 1920s and 1930s after coming into contact with other European modernists, most notably Le Corbusier, but was later exiled to the United States.

The pavilion was rebuilt in 1992 using the original cheap materials of thin steel sections and asbestos panels, but it is nevertheless very sophisticated. It currently houses a university and research centre (Av. Cardenal Vidal i Barraquer).

page 163), while another American, Richard Meier, designed and built the contemporary art museum (MACBA, see page 144).

The extensive Posa't Guapa (Get Beautiful) campaign in the Casc Antic placed an emphasis on restoring facades and houses; EU grants were obtained for the purpose.

Home-grown talent

The planning authorities also invested trust in many virtually unknown Catalan architects, and the support of the city's inhabitants, plus an appreciation of their cultural and architectural heritage, have enabled them to flourish.

The many buildings constructed or renovated for the Olympic Games in 1992 continue to be fully functional, like the Institut Nacional

d'Educació Fisica de Catalunya, a sports university, and the Palau Sant Jordi, which is used for concerts.

Catalan architects have always designed more than just buildings. Street furniture, kiosks, paving slabs, tree grilles and shopfronts are all architect-designed. Such work tends to be craft-based, and the continued existence of small metalworking shops, marble masons and stained-glass ateliers allows buildings to be creatively detailed.

Although in the post-Olympic period building work slowed, the regeneration programme continued. This resulted in more public housing and facilities such as university buildings and projects like Rafael Moneo's Auditori concert hall and Ricardo Bofill's Teatre Nacional, as well as commercial ventures like French architect Jean Nouvel's Torre Agbar, an office block.

LEFT: Centre de Cultura Contemporània. **ABOVE TOP:** the 2004 Fòrum building designed by Herzog and de Meuron. **ABOVE:** Gehry's copper fish in the Port Olimpic. **RIGHT:** Jean Nouvel's stunning Torre Agbar at night.

Some excellent architectural guidebooks, many in English, can be obtained from the shop in the Col·legi d'Arquitectes in Plaça Nova (see page 112).

The port area of Barcelona was opened up with Maremàgnum, a major shopping and leisure district, and the World Trade Centre. Several large new shopping centres have been built, such as L'Illa and Diagonal Mar. Leading national and international architects such as Herzog and de Meuron were brought in for some of the Fòrum 2004 building work *(see page 170)*.

Ongoing projects

The new business district known as 22@ *(see page 168)*, a showground for national and international architects, is work in progress. It should eventually tie in with a major new station for the AVE high-speed train. On a more domestic level renovation of the city's food markets continues, like the wonderfully colourful Mercat de Santa Caterina, part of an impressive urban regeneration scheme. Despite recession there are still plenty of grandiose projects on the drawing board, such as further development of the port and smaller social and cultural ones, but the question now hovers "Will they ever get off it?".

Barcelona has an ideal climate for fine architecture, the strong light allowing sculptural forms to be read more clearly. The lack of weathering also makes flat facades and the use of rendering and tiling appropriate.

The city has always nurtured its architects, indulged their idiosyncracies and encouraged them to be forward-thinking and individualistic. Though they understand the history of Barcelona's architecture, and love Gaudí and Domènech i Montaner, they are not intimidated by them, building alongside this legacy in a confident and contemporary style. Their achievements are as good as their predecessors', and have their roots in the same traditions of attention to detail and local craftsmanship. ❑

Urban Regeneration

Plans begun in the post-Franco era to bring light and space into this notoriously dense city continue today, with new public spaces appearing in neglected areas. It all began in 1981, when architect Oriol Bohigas was asked to establish a

new department of urban design for Barcelona City Council. Previously, he had been the head of the city's School of Architecture, so he took with him his most able students, who became known as the Golden Pencils. Each architect was allocated an area of Barcelona and asked to develop a plan for its regeneration. There was a desperate shortage of public space and, since buildings were expensive, parks and squares became the main focus. The proposals ranged from small areas of paving to large parks on derelict land, from the opening up of the Eixample blocks to the renovation of traffic interchanges.

A symbolic development for Catalans was the creation of the Plaça Fossar de les Moreres, next to Santa Maria del Mar, to commemorate the Catalan Martyrs of 1714.

Parc Creueta del Coll by architect firm Martorell-Bohigas-Mackay lies in the site of an old quarry in an outlying area (metro L5 El Coll/Teixonera). An enormous sculpture by Eduardo Chillida is suspended above a public swimming pool. The Parc de l'Escorxador on the site of the old abattoir near Plaça d'Espanya, once a dry and dusty

space, has been transformed into a series of rectilinear terraces and walkways, highlighted by an enormous Miró sculpture. Difficult to categorise, the park has been described as a cross between a formal garden and a wild Mediterranean landscape.

In Gràcia, architects Bach and Mora redesigned eight existing but neglected squares. Plaça del Sol now has lampshades resembling the setting sun, while the design of Plaça del Diamante contains references to the book of the same name by Catalan writer Mercè Rodoreda (1908–83).

In 2007 the International Urban Landscape Award went to a regeneration project by architects Arriola and Fiol, in an outlying district – the Parc Central de Nou Barris. This sustainable urban space, the second-largest in the city, was praised for its function as a recreational area and its role in integrating the district.

A more recent example is the new Rambla del Raval which entailed controversial demolition of old housing and relocation of residents. Originally envisaged by 19th-

century town planner Cerdà to breathe life into a conflictive neighbourhood, it was finally achieved in the 21st century. This broad walkway between jacaranda and palm trees is used for community events and as a meeting place in this multicultural district. ❑

LEFT: ME hotel, designed by Dominique Perrault, in 22@ district. **ABOVE:** Parc de l'Espanya Industrial. **RIGHT:** Parc Central de Nou Barris.

MODERNISME

The city's defining architectural style looked to the past for its principal influences

Modernisme is Barcelona's great contribution to architecture. Colourful and flamboyant, it was a mix of then-current technology and former styles. It began at the time of the Universal Exposition in 1888, continued until around 1930, and corresponded to the Arts and Crafts and Art Nouveau movements in the rest of Europe, with which it shared a pre-occupation with sinuous line, organic form and ornament.

Its greatest practitioners were Lluís Domènech i Montaner (1850–1923), a professor at Barcelona University's School of Architecture, and one of his pupils, Josep Puig i Cadafalch (1867–1957). For the Universal Exposition, Domènech designed El Castell dels Tres Dragons, now part of the Museu de Ciències Naturals, based on Valencia's red-brick Gothic Stock Exchange. It afterwards became a workshop for ceramics, wrought iron and glass-making. Furnishings and details were an essential ingredient in *modernista* buildings.

Modernisme was a part of the Catalan *Renaixença* (renaissance), and it looked to the past, taking on Catalan Gothic with its tradition of ironwork, while acknowledging the styles of Islamic Spain. The 19th-century expansion of the city (the Eixample) gave architects the freedom and space to experiment, and this is where most *modernista* buildings are to be found.

LEFT: a griffin acts as a bannister stop on the courtyard staircase in Casa Amatller. In seeking references from the past, artists and architects returned to the Catalan *Renaixença*, when Gothic flourished. Gargoyles, dragons and other mythical beasts animated many buildings.

TOP: Puig i Cadafalch's Dutch-gabled Casa Amatller and Gaudí's scaly-tiled Casa Batlló jostle for attention on the "Block of Discord".
ABOVE: knuckled columns on the undulating windows of Casa Batlló represent the dragon's victims in the legend of St George.
RIGHT: the Hospital Sant Pau, designed by Domènech i Montaner.

THE HIGHLIGHTS

Illa de la Discòrdia The best starting point to understand *modernisme* is the "Block of Discord", three neighbouring buildings in Passeig de Gràcia. Within a few metres of each other are Domènech i Montaner's Casa Lleó Morera, Puig i Cadafalch's Casa Amatller and Gaudí's Casa Batlló *(see pages 198–9)*. Gaudí did not regard himself as a *modernista*, but it is impossible not to compare his work with theirs, and though there are some differences in style, the discord is not obvious.

Palau de la Música Catalana A Unesco World Heritage Site, this is a sumptuous building, though its main facade, crowded with sculptures and dazzling mosaics, is rather cramped. There are tours of the building, but it is best if you can attend a concert beneath the stained-glass dome that suffuses the auditorium with a mellow light *(see page 127)*.

Hospital de la Santa Creu i de Sant Pau Domènech i Montaner's extraordinary hospital was the most advanced in Europe when it was completed in 1901. It is essentially a series of pavilions connected by underground tunnels *(see page 205)*.

CaixaForum The Casaramona textile factory built by Puig i Cadafalch at the foot of Montjuïc is now the CaixaForum cultural centre *(see page 179)*.

Palau Güell One of Gaudí's first major commissions, this extravagant town house (1885–90) reopened after nine years of refurbishment, and is crammed with detail, from the stables in the basement to the highest chimney pot *(see page 224)*.

TOP: ornate cupola on the top of Casa Lleó Morera, on the corner of Illa de la Discòrdia in Passeig de Gràcia.

ABOVE: knights and damsels are a recurring theme: like the Arts and Crafts movement, *modernisme* harked back to a romantic Golden Age. This ensemble symbolising music is by Miguel Blay and dominates a corner of the Palau de la Música Catalana.
RIGHT: coloured mosaics and fancy ironwork pervaded commercial premises as well as private houses. This Rambla chocolate shop has been run since 1820 by the Escribà family.

Modernista architects paid great attention to the detail of buildings both inside and out. Stained-glass, wood, stone, marble, iron, brass, ceramics – every available material was considered for embellishment. Doorknobs, hinges and light switches all had to be in keeping. Furniture was important, too, and the decorative arts were often included in an architect's overall scheme. In their time, some of these interiors might have been almost overwhelmed with decoration, as they were in Victorian England. But today, stripped of their furnishings, the lines and intent of the interiors can be fully grasped.

Modernista furniture and decorative art can be seen in the MNAC on Montjuïc *(see page 181)*, and in the Museu de les Arts Decoratives at the Palau Reial in Pedralbes, soon to move to the new Design Museum *(see page 214)*.

ABOVE LEFT: the lustrous floor-to-ceiling and wall-to-wall oak infuses this first-floor room of Gaudí's Casa Batlló with a rich warmth, aided by careful positioning and colouring of windows. Most riveting, perhaps, is the fireplace, a sensual inglenook backed by earthy coloured tiles. **LEFT:** the stained glass of a country scene brightened mealtimes in the dining room of Domènech i Montaner's Casa Lleó Morera.

WHERE TO EAT AND SLEEP MODERNISME

Casa Calvet, Casp 48. Classy restaurant in the converted offices of a building designed by Gaudí in 1899 for a textile magnate. *(See page 206.)*

Casa Fuster, Gran de Gràcia 132. Domènech i Montaner's last work was the city's most expensive private building, becoming a popular café and dance hall. Now a 5-star hotel, you can try jazz sessions in the ground-floor Café Vienés. *(See page 259.)*

Els Quatre Gats, Montsió 3. Seminal café by Domènech i Montaner, where Picasso first showed. *(See page 125.)*

La Font del Gat, Passeig Santa Madrona 28. Outdoor restaurant-café near the Miró Foundation on Montjuïc, designed by Puig i Cadafalch. *(See page 182.)*

Hotel España, Sant Pau 9–11. Now a superior-grade hotel, the recent revamp highlights the Domènech i Montaner architectural details and the murals by Ramón Casas in the dining room. *(See page 257.)*

London Bar, Nou de la Rambla 34. One of the oldest bars in the city; has a good atmosphere that will take you back in time, with live music. *(See page 273.)*

Escribà, La Rambla 83. A coffee and pastry on the terrace of this famous chocolate shop gives you time to study its ornamental exterior. *(See page 109.)*

ABOVE: the main feature of the auditorium in the Palau de la Música Catalana is the ceiling's kaleidoscopic inverted stained-glass dome. Few other music halls benefit from natural light. The bust beneath the exuberant Tree of Life on the proscenium arch is of Anselm Clavé, founder of the Orfeó choral society, sculpted in white pumice by Pau Gargallo.
LEFT: a coffee pot from Casa Batlló; no item was left undesigned.

TOP: Café Vienés in luxury hotel Casa Fuster, where once all of Barcelona society dropped by. **LEFT:** a *modernista* café sign.

ART AND INSPIRATION

With a legacy left by Picasso and Miró, Tàpies still making his mark, and a lively contemporary aesthetic, art in the city has never been more alive and exciting

To visit Barcelona is to breathe in a complex and exciting visual art history. The streets map the impressions that have inspired three of Spain's prime movers in the story of modern art: Pablo Picasso, Joan Miró and Antoni Tàpies. Ironically, Picasso only spent a few years here before moving on to Paris; Miró also came and went. Only the still-living Tàpies made his permanent base here, but the legacy left by these three great artists is clearly appreciable through the work of young contemporary Catalan artists.

Pablo Picasso

Pablo Ruiz Picasso (1881–1973) was born in Málaga, in southern Spain. His family soon moved on to La Coruña in Galicia before arriving in Barcelona in 1895, where his father took up the post of Painting Professor at the city's La Llotja School of Art *(see page 130)*. As a young man, before leaving the city, first for Madrid then for Paris, he was to encounter Barcelona's artistic circle that met at the now famous Els Quatre Gats (The Four Cats) café. It was here, on 1 February 1900, that Picasso exhibited for the first time.

The 150 drawings of friends included portraits of Jaume Sabartés, Picasso's lifelong friend and secretary. The Museu Picasso in Barcelona was initially founded largely thanks to Sabartés, who donated his personal collection of the artist's work. Picasso also designed

the menu cover for Els Quatre Gats, which was influenced by Henri de Toulouse-Lautrec (1864–1901). This influence was just one stage of many during Picasso's phenomenal development. Picasso entered his melancholy Blue Period (1901–4) after the death of his Catalan friend Casagemas, before emerging into the warmth of the Rose Period (1904–6).

Then came the pioneering breakthrough into Cubism, which he was to develop over the next 20 years. He returned to Catalonia on several occasions, and donated a considerable number of paintings (almost all his youthful works and the *Las Meninas* series from the 1950s) to the Museu Picasso in Barcelona *(see page 130)*.

LEFT: *Feníxia* by Silvia Gubern, on Montjuïc, is one of many public works of art. **RIGHT:** the young Picasso, drawn by Ramón Casas.

The Picasso Museum occupies a series of 15th-century palaces. In the same medieval street, Montcada, several more palaces serve as art venues, including the new Disseny Hub.

City of art

Barcelona is exceptional for the quantity and quality of exhibition venues and is a sheer delight for any visitor interested in art. You will find well-produced catalogues, usually with texts in English, and shows on a par with those in most capital cities. Start at the Palau de la Virreina in La Rambla for information about current shows throughout the city, including its own, or the revamped Arts Santa Mònica at the end of La Rambla, an exciting space with avant-garde and experimental work.

Joan Miró

Outside Terminal 2 at Barcelona airport you will find one of Miró's ceramic murals, a collaboration with his friend Llorens Artigas. Barcelona born and bred, Miró (1893–1983) returned here throughout his life, between periods spent in Paris and Mallorca. While studying at La Llotja School in Barcelona, he joined the arts society Cercle Artístic de Sant Lluc, which still exists.

Miró was already aware of Dada at this time, though Fauvism, Cubism and Paul Cézanne (1839–1906), in particular, were the major influences on his work. Catalan landscapes featured strongly. *The Farm* (bought by

Ernest Hemingway and now in Washington), a major painting of his *detalliste* period, portrays the family farm, Mont-Roig, near Tarragona. It features many of his subsequent motifs: stars, insects and animals, as well as showing a characteristic respect for manual labour. Gradually, realism gave way to suggestion and poetry, a progression aided by his contact with French Surrealism.

Like his friend Picasso, Miró suffered greatly during the Civil War, and he produced (among other things) the *"Aidez L'Espagne"* poster to raise funds for the Republic. Miró's works, showing limited use of certain colours, were precisely composed. He also had wideranging skills, turning his hand to theatre design, printmaking, tapestry, ceramics and bronze sculptures as well as painting and drawing. The permanent collection at the Fundació Miró *(see page 186)* on Montjuïc covers all of these areas. This building is testimony to the understanding Miró had with his friend, architect Josep Lluís Sert, who designed both this and Miró's studio in Mallorca. It is a celebration of Miró's work, and showcases a varied programme of exhibitions, as well as other important works such as Alexander Calder's *Mercury Fountain*.

You will find evidence of Miró all over the city, whether walking over his ceramic pavement in La Rambla, admiring the monumental *Woman and Bird* sculpture in the Parc Joan Miró *(see page 205)*, or simply noticing the La Caixa bank logo he designed.

Antoni Tàpies

Antoni Tàpies (born 1923) is probably Spain's best-known living artist. His work forms an artistic link between Miró's generation and the new work being produced in the Catalan contemporary art world. Tàpies knew Miró and revered his work; the latter's influence is seen in Tàpies's early work, on view at the Fundació Tàpies *(see page 199)*. The museum,

which redeploys an important Domènech i Montaner building, has a permanent collection of work by Tàpies as well as high-quality contemporary exhibitions. Tàpies is "deeply committed to pluralism and diversity" in art. The first thing you see when you arrive at the building is the mass of metal wires on the roof. Entitled *Cloud and Chair*, this is Tàpies's emblem for the building.

MIRÓ AND THE SURREALISTS

An apocryphal story about Miró tells of how, in his desire to be considered a member of the Surrealist group, he went about trying to get himself arrested – the surest way to attain credibility among his peers. Although he was peaceful by nature, Miró summoned up the courage to walk around the streets of Paris shouting: "Down with the Mediterranean!"

Miró was invoking the Mediterranean in its symbolic role as the cradle of Western civilisation, but his choice of words was ironic given the importance of Mediterranean light and colour in his work. Of course, no one arrested him and the rest of the group scorned his efforts.

FAR LEFT: detail of a Nativity frieze designed by Picasso, on the exterior of the Col·legi d'Arquitectes.
LEFT: *Donna amb mantellina* from Picasso's pointillist period, in the Picasso Museum.
ABOVE AND RIGHT: various works in the Fundació Miró, Montjuïc.

A dirty aesthetic

During the repression under Franco, when all Catalan culture was effectively illegal, methods of expression became highly creative. In 1948 the *Dau al Set* (Dice on Seven) group was set up, with members Tàpies, Tharrats, Cuixart, Ponç, Puig and Brossa. The "visual poems" of Joan Brossa (1919–98), a long-neglected Catalan artist-poet, have been at the forefront of recent Catalan art *(see box, below)*.

Catalan artists also employed street graffiti to voice dissent. The use of signs and symbols, already seen in Miró's painting, appeared to different effect in Tàpies's work. In keeping with the international Arte Povera and Art Autre movements, Catalan Informalism combines existentialist ideas with simple materials to produce the so-called "dirty aesthetic" that still reigns in Barcelona. The Joan Prats Gallery in Rambla de Catalunya displays representative work from contemporary and earlier artists. Or try Consell de Cent, the commercial gallery street one block down from the Fundació Tàpies.

The art scene today

The Informalist legacy is tempered by Catalan Conceptualism nowadays, as represented in the Museu d'Art Contemporani's (MACBA) permanent collection. There is also work from the Dau al Set group, and the bed-piece hanging at the entrance is by Tàpies.

THE PHENOMENON OF STREET ART

Street art is prevalent in all areas of the city, thanks to the initiatives in the 1990s to create new urban spaces. Eduardo Chillida's heavyweight sculpture *Elogi de l'Aigua*, in the Parc Creueta de Coll, is a fine example. Artist-poet Joan Brossa is ever-present in the city: his giant-sized letters are scattered about the Passeig Vall d'Hebron, and his bronze tribute to "Barcino" is set in front of the cathedral.

In the Passeig Picasso, Tàpies pays homage to his idol with a large glass cube containing planks, a piano and painted blankets. The cube itself was designed by the great-grandson of Lluís Domènech i Montaner.

On the beach at Barceloneta is Rebecca Horn's reminder of the original beach huts and restaurants which were torn down to make way for the new waterfront development. Models of the huts, cast in bronze and lit like beacons from within, lie piled one on top of the other. Nearby is Juan Munoz's typically enigmatic and melancholic piece *A room where it always rains* which is a caged "room" filled with his figures that could perhaps roll on their round bases, but for their weight of cast bronze. Also down by the port is Lichtenstein's *Barcelona Head*, in front of the main post office. It uses Gaudí's technique of setting broken pieces of ceramic into cement.

Visit the theatre at the Mercat de les Flors (see page 271) and look up at the ceiling to get some idea of Miguel Barceló's vision.

Miguel Barceló is another contemporary Catalan artist with work in the MACBA's collection. This Mallorcan painter now carries the torch for art in Barcelona. His stays in Mali, West Africa, have produced some epic "relief" paintings.

Pere Jaume's work is great fun, neatly fusing questions of representational art and how to frame it. This theme is on permanent display in his ceiling of the Gran Teatre del Liceu, rebuilt and reopened in October 1999.

Susana Solano, another internationally known Catalan artist, finally gained an ample retrospective of her enigmatic metal constructions here in the late 1990s. Other artists representative of established trends include painters Xavier Grau, Ràfols-Casamada, Hernàndez-Pijuan and Grau Garriga. Artists producing work in multidisciplinary techniques include Carlos Pazos, José Manuel Broto, José María Sevilla and Sergi Aguilar.

The Museu d'Art Contemporani is situated right next door to the Centre de Cultura Contemporània de Barcelona (CCCB). This labyrinthine building was set up as a force for social, urban and cultural development, and has a full programme of striking, thought-provoking exhibitions, talks, music, dance and videos.

Preserving the past

On Montjuïc hill, the Museu Nacional d'Art de Catalunya (MNAC, *see page 181*) is unmissable. It offers a fabulous opportunity to marvel at Catalonia's wealth of Gothic and Romanesque painting and sculpture, including medieval wall paintings. In a bid to collect 1,000 years of Catalan art under one roof, the pieces from the former Museu d'Art Modern were transferred here in 2004, including important works by Ramón Casas, Santiago Rusiñol and other major *modernista* artists from the late 19th and early 20th centuries. ❑

FAR LEFT: interior of the CaixaForum. LEFT: *Núvol i Cadira* (Cloud and Chair) by Tàpies. LEFT: Roy Lichtenstein's *Barcelona Head*. ABOVE: MNAC is a splendid showcase for Catalan art.

DESIGNER CITY

In Barcelona your whole day can be a designer experience, from breakfast in your boutique hotel to dinner in a stylish restaurant, via shops and museums that have all been given the designer treatment

Buying the greens in your local market in Barcelona can be a designer experience, as can going to pay your dues in the Town Hall, and, if you have the misfortune to need attention in the Hospital del Mar, console yourself with the fact you are walking into a carefully planned space where sleek seats in the waiting room offer views over a sculpted promenade and landscaped beaches where even the showers have the stamp of a well-known design name. Exaggeration? Well, no, because this is the city where design forms part of daily life.

Liberation of ideas
The great boom in design that swept through Barcelona in the 1980s following Franco's death is legendary. Fuelled by the challenge of preparing for the Olympics, it forms the basis of contemporary Barcelona. But awareness of design – above all architecture – and an individual approach to it is nothing new here.

Style consciousness
Catalan Gothic already stood out from other European Gothic architecture in the 14th century. As Robert Hughes comments: "Catalan architects did not want to imitate the organic profusion of detail in northern Gothic. They liked a wall." Similarly, with *modernisme*, Catalonia had its own take on Art Nouveau. The extraordinary creativity of Gaudí was an extreme case for any society to accept, yet bourgeois industrialists were his patrons and had homes built by him. They had a designer hospital too, Domènech i Montaner's radical Hospital de la Santa Creu i Sant Pau, in use until 2009 when it expanded into a new building.

> Innovative design has never been an alien concept in Catalonia, a society that has always striven to represent its individuality to the world.

The first "design bars", among them Nick Havanna and Torres de Avila, dazzled in the 1980s, and architecture magazines began to applaud Barcelona's urban spaces. From there, the design movement gained momentum, eagerly supported by city authorities keen to enhance Barcelona's image and promote local

talent. Street furniture is designed by the likes of Oscar Tusquets, and drinking fountains by Santa & Cole. City markets have had multi-million-euro facelifts *(see page 68)*.

The same is true of the public Hospital del Mar, which has a catchment area that is one of the city's most needy. Visiting the hospital, one is struck by the Mediterranean light filtering through skylights, the space, the sea outlook, and the healthy breezes sweeping through patios where patients stroll.

Altered images

There was a time when visitors were drawn to Barcelona for its heady mix of Mediterranean culture and the kind of decadence associated with a dirty old port. Bars selling absinthe and seedy Barri Xino cabarets were sought out by night, while restaurants with starched tablecloths and grumpy waiters were patronised by day. Nowadays visitors swarm in for a sophisticated blend of culture and

> *In Barcelona, impersonal chain hotels are snubbed for new boutique hotels, such as Neri, Casa Camper and Omm (see pages 256, 257 and 260).*

commerce. Hand luggage on return flights is a walking advertisement for brands such as Zara, Custo and Camper.

Following the trend of the Born with its boutique prettification, the once notorious El Raval neighbourhood has been the most recent subject of the designer makeover. Already home to the MACBA, the CCCB (Centre for Contemporary Culture) and FAD (Foment de les Arts Decoratives, promoting new design and located in a Gothic convent), it is sprouting galleries, shops, restaurants and hotels. It's still to be seen whether the balance will be kept between all these newcomers and old local groceries and cobblers.

The designer city has its attractions, and its pursuit is in the Catalan genes, but the other traits of Barcelona that give it its colour and charm will never be totally eclipsed. ❏

LEFT: Vinçon, high temple of interior design.
ABOVE: a suite at Hotel Omm.

RETAIL THERAPY

Barcelona's myriad shops range from traditional grocery store to cutting-edge fashion boutique

Whether you are after a sharp Toni Miró suit or a unique outfit by a young Catalan designer hot from the catwalk, handmade rope-soled shoes or Camper sandals, rustic ceramics or oven-roasted nuts, antiques or handicrafts, it's all here. And finding it can be the ultimate pleasure as you stroll along the elegant avenues of the Eixample, where you'll find top national and international names, or through the medieval lanes of the Born in the Old Town, best for one-off independent boutiques. There's even a shopping centre lapped by the Mediterranean in the harbour, Maremàgnum, and another, Diagonal Mar, right by the beach. The shopping can be accompanied by coffee breaks at terrace cafés or lunchtime *menús* in a local bar, or even a dip into a gallery or museum en route. The streets off Plaça Catalunya, like Portal de l'Angel and Pelai are best for young fashion. *See listings under Shopping on pages 263–7 of Travel Tips, and under the relevant chapter.*

ABOVE: located in a handsome *modernista* house right next to Gaudí's La Pedrera on Passeig de Gràcia, Vinçon has the ultimate in interior design, from chef's choice kitchen knives to state-of-the-art sofas by local and international designers. Visiting it is a quintessential Barcelona experience: see what anyone who's anyone furnishes their homes with, while you admire the 19th-century setting, once the home of painter Ramón Casas.

LEFT: one of Spain's most successful commercial stores, the Zara empire has now spread across the world, selling good-value fashion for all tastes at such a rate there's little fear of meeting someone in the same outfit. Sister shops Bershka, Pull & Bear, Massimo Dutti, Oysho, Zara Home, Uterqüe and Stradivarius follow suit.

RIGHT: born in Barcelona of Swiss parents, Desigual has grown fast into a brand with a totally Barcelonan identity. True to its name its clothes are just not the same – wacky designs, bright colours, with a spirit of fun and top quality. Stores are located all over the city, in shopping centres, on La Rambla and in Passeig de Gràcia, and are starting to spread around the globe.

ONLY IN BARCELONA

One of the joys of shopping here is that traditional shops still run by the third or fourth generation of the family hold out among the hip and cool.

Get off the beaten track and you'll find curious little shops selling everything from earthenware pots to perfumes in styles which are hard to resist.

The heady scent of fresh flowers in the sunshine is intoxicating as you wander down La Rambla de les Flors, lined with flower stalls.

Even chocolates have been given the designer treatment in Xocoa (Vidriera, 4) and other outlets. Expect exotic fillings like green tea.

Be guided by experts when choosing from the range of Spanish wines from lesser known regions on offer at Vila Viniteca (Agullers, 7).

Take a look inside one of the many old chemists' shops, with fixtures and fittings from the height of the *modernista* period.

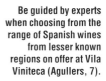

An essential for football fans: Barça T-shirts and other gifts from one of the official stores, such as Jaume I, 18, or in Maremàgnum.

ABOVE: Sombreria Obach (Call, 2) is a treasure just off Plaça Sant Jaume, run by the two grandsons of its founder. Gaze at the array of hats in the polished window, from traditional berets to suave panamas, but don't miss its impeccable interior.

LEFT: latest on the fashion scene are small boutiques where young designers sell their ultra-creative collections. On Land (Princesa, 25) stocks several Catalan designers, like Miriam Ponsa, Josep Abril, Name and their own label. *(See also Shopping, page 265.)*

MARKETS

Discover enticing markets
bursting with produce from
farms, mountains and the sea

There are more than 40
municipal markets in
Barcelona. The largest of
them – La Boqueria,
Sant Antoni and El Born
(now closed) – are
impressive late 19th-
century iron-and-glass
structures built on the
site of former monaster-
ies. These cathedrals to
food are ideal places to display Catalonia's wide variety
of produce from the mountains,
rich farmlands and the sea, often sold by third-
and fourth-generation vendors. In recent years,
however, tradition has been giving way to trend,
with juice bars and fusion food, and prices,
particularly in touristy La Boqueria, have been
rising. Santa Caterina and Barceloneta have been
dramatically overhauled, and Sant Antoni is next.

Elsewhere, squares and open spaces are put to
use with regular stamp, book, craft, antiques and
bric-à-brac markets. The latest is the lively multicultural weekend market in Rambla del Raval.
The main flea market is El Encants in Glòries. Get
there early to dig out a bargain.

ABOVE: in every market you'll find stalls with a tantalising array of
local and regional specialities, such as hams and spicy sausages.
BELOW: fresh produce, such as the fish and seafood on sale in
La Boqueria, is carefully selected and prepared according to the
customer's demands.

BELOW: Santa Llúcia Christmas market in front of the cathedral.
The rest of the year there is an antiques market on Thursdays.

WHERE TO EAT MARKET PRODUCE

For a visitor, much of the food on offer at the city's markets is merely for looking at. Fresh bread, olives, cheese and charcuterie make for a delicious impromptu picnic, but to really savour the range of produce, visit the market cafés and restaurants. Many of the established ones are institutions. In La Boqueria, **Pinotxo**, run by the Bayen family, opens at 6am and specialises in oysters and cava. Foodies gather for breakfast from 8am at **Quim de la Boqueria** towards the back of the market, where Quim Márquez produces innovative dishes. In Mercat Santa Caterina, **Cuines Santa Caterina**, from the Tragaluz group, serves fusion food in a cool, modern space while **Bar Joan** offers excellent traditional dishes at an economic price. The revamped Mercat de Barceloneta offers the gourmet experience at **Els Fogons de la Barceloneta** and Michelin-starred **Lluçanès** by chefs Francesc Miralles and Àngel Pascual, serving seafood such as tartar of escalopes with white truffles.

ABOVE: glitzy bric-à-brac at El Encants flea market in Glòries. Arrive early in the morning for the best buys.
BELOW: Mercat Santa Caterina was recently rebuilt by architects Enric Miralles and Benedetta Tagliabue with a distinctive multi-coloured roof. Building work revealed the ruins of the monastery on which it stands.

TOP: explore food markets off the beaten track for the most genuine experience.
BELOW: architectural detail, La Boqueria.

A PASSION FOR FOOD

In Barcelona you will find some of the best food in Spain.
An abundance of fresh fish, superb meat and cheese, a
cornucopia of great vegetables, plus Catalan inventiveness,
have produced a distinctive and delicious cuisine

N o one should visit Barcelona without making some attempt to get to know Catalan food. The experience would be incomplete otherwise, and any assessment of its people merely superficial. Eating is an important part of Catalan culture, something to be valued, taken seriously and enjoyed to the full, in true Catalan style.

The acerbic political commentator and eminent writer Manuel Vázquez Montalbán was passionate about food; he bestowed a certain grace on any restaurant where he chose to eat. In his opinion, "Catalan cooking is one of the most distinguishing signs of the national identity." It is also a composite of the nation's past, embodying the many influences of the different peoples and cultures that have swept through, settled in or bordered Catalonia, to say nothing of the lands dominated by Catalonia over its millennial history. The original fusion food, perhaps.

Nature's bounty

Catalan cooking is also a reflection of the geographical and physical characteristics of the country. Many dishes are based on the nuts, garlic, olive oil, tomatoes, herbs and dried fruits that are indigenous to these lands. Catalans are justifiably proud that their region can offer miles of rugged coastline and sheltered beaches, as well as awesome mountain ranges and rich valleys, and all within easy reach of each other.

Similarly, the cooking combines the natural products of the sea, the fertile plains and the mountains in a style known as *mar i muntanya* (sea and mountain). It makes for strange-sounding, though delicious, marriages on the menu, such as *mandonguilles amb sèpia* (meatballs with cuttlefish), or *gambes amb pollastre* (prawns with chicken).

Simple pleasures

The health-giving properties of a Mediterranean diet are almost a cliché these days, and a selling point in many an advertising campaign, but here such a diet still exists in a pure, unadulterated form. One of the most famous

LEFT: eating in the Plaça Reial. **RIGHT:** the oyster bar at Tragafishhh, in the restaurant Tragaluz.

Catalan dishes is perhaps the most simple, yet one of the best: the ubiquitous *pa amb tomà-quet*. This fresh "peasant" bread rubbed with tomato, a trickle of virgin olive oil and a pinch of salt is the Mediterranean answer to northern Europe's thinly sliced bread and butter, and not surprisingly provokes a certain amount of south-ern pride. It's a delicious accompaniment to

OCTOBER HARVEST

October is a great time to be in Barcelona, because it's mushroom season, when fans of wild fungi will be in their element. The market stalls are rich in autumnal colours, and the smell of damp woods is intoxicating. The generic name for the various wild mushrooms is *bolets*. *Rovelló* is one of the best, especially just grilled with garlic and parsley, but also delicious in stewed meat dishes at this time of the year. For the best range of fresh, dried (or, if need be, frozen) mushrooms, and un-usual fresh herbs, go to Petras, Fruits del Bosc, at the very back of La Boqueria market. Ignore the arrogant service and enjoy the super-ior products.

meals, and can also be eaten as a snack served with anchovies, cured meats or cheese.

Breakfast time

Breakfast veers wildly from being a dull, cursory affair of milky coffee and biscuits, to a full-blooded *esmorzar de forquilla* (fork breakfast), which is a mid-morning meal of hearty dishes like pigs' trotters and bean stews. This is more of a rural market-town tradition, not meant for an efficient morning in the office. It is common, though, to have a large ham sandwich or wedge of traditional Spanish omelette (*truita* in Catalan, *tortilla* in Spanish) with a glass of wine around 10am, and to chase the morning coffee with a *conyac*. For the faint-hearted, bars and cafés serve good *cafè amb llet* (large coffee with milk), *tallat* (a shorter version) or *cafè sol* (small, black and intense) with a range of pastries or croissants.

Lunchtime treats

Visitors can indulge in what is more of a week-end treat for residents: an aperitif around 1pm. This consists of a drink such as red vermouth, often with soda, served with olives and other

tapes (snacks) like *boquerons* (pickled anchovies) or tinned *escopinyes* (cockles). The temptation to turn this into a light lunch is where visitors often lose the local rhythm.

> *Try to adapt to local timing: have breakfast when Barcelonans do, lunch with them, even have "tea" with the old ladies and children, and then you'll be able to wait until after 9pm for dinner.*

The advantages of having lunch *(dinar)* are manifold: the food has just arrived from the market and is at its best; it can be slept or walked off; the whole city is tuned in to lunch – a sacred quiet descends, especially on Sunday, and many offices and small shops are closed until 4 or 5pm.

Peak lunchtime is 2pm, lingering on to 4pm or even later at weekends – although there is a danger of not being served after 3.30pm. Lunch is also the most economical meal, when nearly every restaurant has a *menú del dia* (set menu). Even the most basic of these offers a choice of starters (soup, salad or vegetables), a main course of meat or fish, a dessert, and wine, beer or a soft drink. Obviously the standard and the price vary from one restaurant to another, but for €10–14 you can expect an excellent, balanced meal.

Sauces may be rich but can be outweighed by a crisp fresh salad and fruit to follow. The option of simple grilled fish or meat, garnished with a *picada* of garlic and parsley, is hard to equal, especially when accompanied by *allioli* (a strong garlic mayonnaise that is also served with rice dishes).

Local specialities

Look out for *menús* that include any of the following: as starters, *arròs negre*, black rice, a more interesting version of paella made with squid and its ink; *escalivada*, grilled peppers and aubergines dressed with oil; *esqueixada*, salad of raw salt cod, onions and peppers; *xató*, a salad from Sitges of frisée lettuce with tuna, salt cod, anchovies and a *romesco* sauce;

ABOVE LEFT: meat and cheese stalls in the market.
LEFT: wild mushrooms fill market stalls in autumn.
ABOVE: El Raval's Rita Rouge, where a Venezuelan chef adds a twist to local produce.

espinacs a la Catalana, spinach sautéed with raisins and pine nuts; *faves a la Catalana,* small broad beans stewed with herbs, pork and sausages (best in spring); *canalons,* a Catalan

SPOILT FOR CHOICE

Getting to know Catalan food is hardly a chore. Along with Basque cooking, its reputation ranks highest in Spain. And with nearly 3,000 restaurants in Barcelona, the only problem is which one to choose. Sightseeing and museum-visiting can and should be interrupted to recharge the batteries and experience the culinary offerings of the city. Some recommended restaurants are listed at the end of each chapter in the Places section of this guide.

Restaurants serving dinner before 9pm are probably oriented towards tourists but can still be good. However the more traditional places may not open their doors before 9pm.

tradition brought from Italy, always eaten on 26 December; *fideuà,* an excellent and lesser-known variation on paella, comprising noodles cooked in a fish stock, and *escudella,* the most traditional Catalan soup, a strictly winter dish. *Escudella* is usually followed by *carn d'olla,* that is, the meat and vegetables that have been cooked to make the soup. Now a traditional Christmas dish, this used to be part of the staple diet of every Catalan household.

The main event

Among the main courses, be sure to try the very Catalan *botifarra amb mongetes,* a tasty sausage served with haricot beans; *fricandó,* braised veal with *moixernons,* a small, delicate wild mushroom; *bacallà,* salt cod served in many ways such as *a la llauna* (garlic, parsley and tomato) or *amb xamfaina* (tomato, pepper and aubergine sauce, also served with meat); *suquet,* a seafood stew; *calamars farcits,* stuffed squid; *oca amb naps,* goose with turnip; *conill,* rabbit, either grilled and served with *allioli,* or stewed; *xai,* lamb – the cutlets *(costelletes)* are especially good.

Fish *(peix)* and shellfish *(marisc)* should not be missed in Barcelona: the simplest and per-

haps the best way is grilled (a mixed grill, *graellada*, is a good option for two) or done in the oven, *al forn*. It is worth going to a good restaurant for a paella; cheap imitations are usually disappointing.

If you have any room for dessert, don't miss the famous *crema catalana*, a cinnamon-flavoured custard with a burnt caramel top. Other traditional *postres* include *mel i mató*, a curd cheese with honey, *postre de músic*, a mixture of roast nuts and dried fruits, usually served with a glass of sweet *moscatel*, and *macedonia* (fruit salad).

Berenar and later

The advantage of the light-lunch option is being able to face a *berenar* (afternoon snack). From around 5 to 7.30pm *granjes* (milk bars) overflow as people manage to drink extremely thick chocolate (the authentic version is made with water and needs to be "drunk" with a

spoon – sometimes the spoon will almost stand up in the thick liquid) and very creamy cakes. For a classic *berenar* try the cafés around the Plaça del Pi, especially in Petritxol, or sit at a marble table in the Granja M. Viader in Xuclà, the oldest *granja* in Barcelona, where *cacaolat* (a children's favourite) was invented.

PASTRY HEAVEN

In Barcelona the number of pastry shops per square metre must rank among the world's highest. For each feast day and festival there is a corresponding traditional sweetmeat: *bunyols* (a small doughnut) during Lent, *la mona* (a sort of brioche, often with fancy decorations) for Easter, *panellets* (little marzipan cakes decorated with pine nuts) for All Saints Day and for

castanyades (autumnal parties centred on roasting chestnuts). Throughout the summer months the different neighbourhood and village feast days are celebrated with fireworks, cava and *cocas* (pastries covered in sugar, crystallised fruits and pine nuts).

FAR LEFT: Oriol Ivern, chef at Hisop restaurant.
LEFT: prawns and squid feature on many menus.
ABOVE: *berenar* is served. **ABOVE RIGHT:** tempting choices in Mauri, a famous pastry shop. **RIGHT:** *churros* (fried pastries) – not for calorie counters.

EAT YOUR WAY ROUND THE CITY – A GUIDE TO SNACKS

TAPAS

Not originally a Catalan tradition but available in most bars in Barcelona, tapas (in Spanish, *tapes* in Catalan, both pronounced the same) are snacks to accompany a drink, so can range from a few olives to a small portion of a main dish.

PINCHOS

The Basques specialise in *pinchos*, which come on a toothpick, usually on a slice of bread. There are now chains of Basque bars across the city with names like Euskal Etxea, Irati, Sagardi and Taktika Berri, where platters of hot *pinchos* emerge from the kitchen at regular intervals or are laid out on the bar. Trust prevails, and the sum of your toothpicks is the bill. Beware how they add up.

MENU DECODER

(a mixture of Catalan and Spanish)
albóndigas meatballs
bunyols de bacallà salt cod fritters
cabrales a potent blue cheese from Asturias wrapped in vine leaves
calamares a la plancha/a la romana grilled squid/fried squid rings

croquetas croquets
ensaladilla rusa Russian salad – diced vegetables in mayonnaise
formatge cheese
fuet spicy dried sausage
llonganissa another kind of spicy dried sausage
manchego seco strong Spanish cheese
pa amb tomàquet bread rubbed with tomato and oil
patates allioli fried potatoes with garlic mayonnaise
patates braves fried potatoes with a hot spicy sauce
pebrots de Padró green peppers, sometimes spicy hot
pernil salat cured ham cut from the bone (*jamón serrano* in Spanish)
pescaditos small fried fish
pulpo octopus, a speciality from Galicia
queso de cabra goat's cheese
torrades slices of toast with which you can make your own *pa amb tomàquet* and request different toppings
tortilla Spanish omelette
truita Spanish omelette, which may be *espanyola* (potatoes and onions),

espinacs (spinach), *pagès* (mixed vegetables), *alls tendres* (young tender garlic) or *francesa* (the classic French omelette without a filling). *Truita* also means trout in Catalan.

DRINKS

un blanco glass of white wine
una caña small glass of draught beer
una cerveza beer
una jarra glass of draught beer
una mediana bottle of beer
una sidra light cider
un tinto glass of red wine
txakolí Basque white wine

Shops and offices are open until 8 or 9pm, so family dinner is around 10pm, and is usually quite light: soup and an omelette, for example. Restaurants don't normally start serving until around 9pm.

Creative cooks

Apart from these traditional dishes, the creative spectrum is broadening into many variations on the basic Catalan theme, in both *tapes* and main dishes. There is a new generation of chefs, many inspired or even trained by world-famous Ferran Adrià, whose El Bullí restaurant is closed until 2013. Their rebellious spirit, combined with the essential Catalan love of food and passion for the Mediterranean, is a formula that makes for exciting results. You can get a taste of this in restaurants like Alkimia, Commerç 24 or Hisop, to name but a few.

International influences

As an increasingly cosmopolitan capital, Barcelona has a broad range of restaurants that reflect the tastes and demands of its inhabitants. There are restaurants from other

> Restaurants don't usually have a set menu at night, so eating out can cost more than at midday. If you've had a good lunch, this is the time to "do tapes" – visit several bars for a glass of wine and a snack in each.

regions of Spain, particularly Galicia, from top-notch, top-price Botafumeiro with fine oysters and fish, to the average corner bar. And then there are French, Italian, Greek, Lebanese, Moroccan, Mexican, South American, Indian, Pakistani, Chinese and Japanese, plus a growing number of vastly improved vegetarian restaurants – vegetarians used to have a hard time in Spain, but this, too, is changing. There really is no excuse to resort to one of the fast-food outlets insidiously taking root in some of the most historic streets and squares – the latest, inevitable, sign of cultural colonisation.

So get out there, make new discoveries, and immerse yourself in local culture in one of the most enjoyable ways possible. ❑

FAR LEFT: you can eat at one of several stalls in La Boqueria market. **LEFT:** grilled squid is a popular *tapes* choice. **ABOVE:** the *tapes* tradition has caught on in Barcelona and is a great way of experimenting with lots of different dishes.

WINE

The reputation of Spanish wine has changed enormously in recent years, and Catalonia is one of the regions that is now attracting attention from international connoisseurs as well as visitors with a taste for the good things in life

its white wines, on the outskirts of Barcelona; the well-known **Penedès**, to the southwest of Barcelona; the most recent, **Pla de Bages**, near Manresa; **Conca de Barberà**, with its *modernista* wine cellars, in Tarragona; **Costers del Segre**, home of Raimat wines, to the west in Lleida; and **Tarragona, Terra Alta, Montsant** and the **Priorat** with terraced vineyards on steep, slatey hillsides in the south.

In a bid for stronger identity in the international market, a recent controversial move by the large companies backed by the Generalitat (Catalan autonomous government) to introduce a denomination for the region as a whole, **D.O. Catalunya**, has been successful. The smaller denominations will continue to exist within this framework.

> In restaurants the house wine (vi de la casa) *is often a young wine or, in rural areas, a dark red wine. Don't be surprised if red wines are served chilled in summer.*

There was a time when Spanish wine meant plonk, and the only Spanish vintage to have any international acclaim was Rioja. Today, these misconceptions are in the past, and anyone who appreciates a decent glass of wine will be aware that Spain has many different wine-growing regions, producing a range of interesting and increasingly high-quality wines.

Catalonia's wine regions

Catalonia itself has 10 wine regions officially classified as D.O. (*Denominació d'Origen*, similar to the French *appellation contrôlée*): **Empordà-Costa Brava**, near the French border; **Alella**, in the Maresme, a tiny area known for

The Catalan region with the highest profile abroad is the Penedès, mostly due to the giant Torres, a family firm in Vilafranca del Penedès that exports wine to more than 90 countries, has vineyards in Chile and California and is held in high esteem in the wine world. With the sixth generation of the family now in the business, they continue to produce award-winning wines such as Gran Coronas Black Label, Fransola, Gran Viña Sol and Viña Esmeralda.

Over the past few years there has been a lot of activity among the smaller bodegas across Catalonia, involving experimentation, new techniques, different grape varieties and maximising of the indigenous grapes such as *xarel·lo* and *macabeo* (white), and *carinyena*, *garnatxa* and *monastrell* reds. It is reflected in improved quality, and some notable wines are emerging.

Up-and-coming labels

One of the most fascinating areas is the Priorat, traditionally known for cheap, strong wines bought from barrels, but now producing some of the best-quality wine in the country. Large companies from La Rioja and the Penedès have started working there, and some highly prized wines are emerging from its low-yield, high-alcohol-content grapes.

La Ermita, from Riojan winemaker Alvaro Palacios, can sell for over €600 a bottle, depending on the vintage. Other wines to look out for, not necessarily so highly priced, are Cervoles, a red from Costers del Segre, Can Rafols dels Caus, Can Feixes and the ecological Albet i Noia wines from the Penedès, and Oliver Conti, from another up-and-coming area, the Empordà. An increasing number of organic wines from small bodegas are available.

• *For suggestions on where to buy wine in Barcelona, see page 266.* ❑

THE HOME OF CAVA

Ninety-five percent of Spain's cava is produced in Catalonia and the greater part from the Penedès, where it was created by Josep Raventós in 1872. From that celebrated first bottle grew the Codorníu empire, which along with Freixenet leads the cava industry. This sparkling wine, made by the *méthode champenoise*, is oblig-atory at fiestas and a ubiquitous compan-ion to Sunday lunch (when it is served with dessert). One of the world's great sparkling wines, cava is warmer, earthier and less acidic than champagne *(see page 233).*

LEFT: there's an extensive range of wines to choose from. **ABOVE:** busy wine bar in the Barri Gòtic.

ORIENTATION

The Places section details all the attractions worth seeing, arranged by area. The areas are shown on a colour-coordinated map on pages 86–7. Main sights are cross-referenced by number to individual maps

The Places section of this guide is divided geographically, beginning with La Rambla, the city's famous spine, and then exploring the distinctive areas spreading either side, and the waterfront stretching east from the foot of La Rambla.

If you can get to one of the city's high points early in your visit – Montjuïc, Tibidabo, the Park Güell, or even Columbus's column – it will put the city into focus. It is not surprising that this is one of the world's densest cities (15,977 inhabitants per sq km): packed in between the Collserola range of hills and the Mediterranean, and bordered by Montjuïc and the River Besòs, all the available space has been consumed. Parks tend to be in rocky knolls where no building could have been erected, or created latterly in disused industrial spaces.

The latest developments are centred on the sea, with planned extensions to the port and the reclaiming of land by the Diagonal Mar.

The city's layout

Plaça de Catalunya is a good place to get one's bearings. From this crossroads between the Old Town (the Ciutat Vella) and the New Town (the 19th-century Eixample), it is easy to get a sense of place and history. The Old Town, containing most of the city's historical landmarks, is divided into the Barri Gòtic, La Ribera and El Raval. The Barri Gòtic (Gothic Quarter) is in the middle, bordered by La Rambla and Via Laietana. La Ribera is the district on the other side of Via Laietana, including some medieval streets, and El Raval lies on the other side of La Rambla, where convents-turned-cultural centres rub shoulders with the last remnants of the notorious Barri Xino.

Plaça de Catalunya, like an all-encompassing terminal, is also a good departure point for most excursions. Airport buses arrive there, buses to most parts of town and beyond can be caught there, two metro lines run through it and the FGC trains uptown to the Parc de Collserola leave from there. Even trains to the coast and the mountains depart from beneath this central square.   ❏

PRECEDING PAGES: night view of La Pedrera; the roof of the Mercat de Santa Caterina.
LEFT: view from the spires of Sagrada Família.

La Boquería
page 100

La Pedrera
page 202

La Rambla
pages 95–107

Fundació Joan Miró
page 186

Beaches
pages 172–3

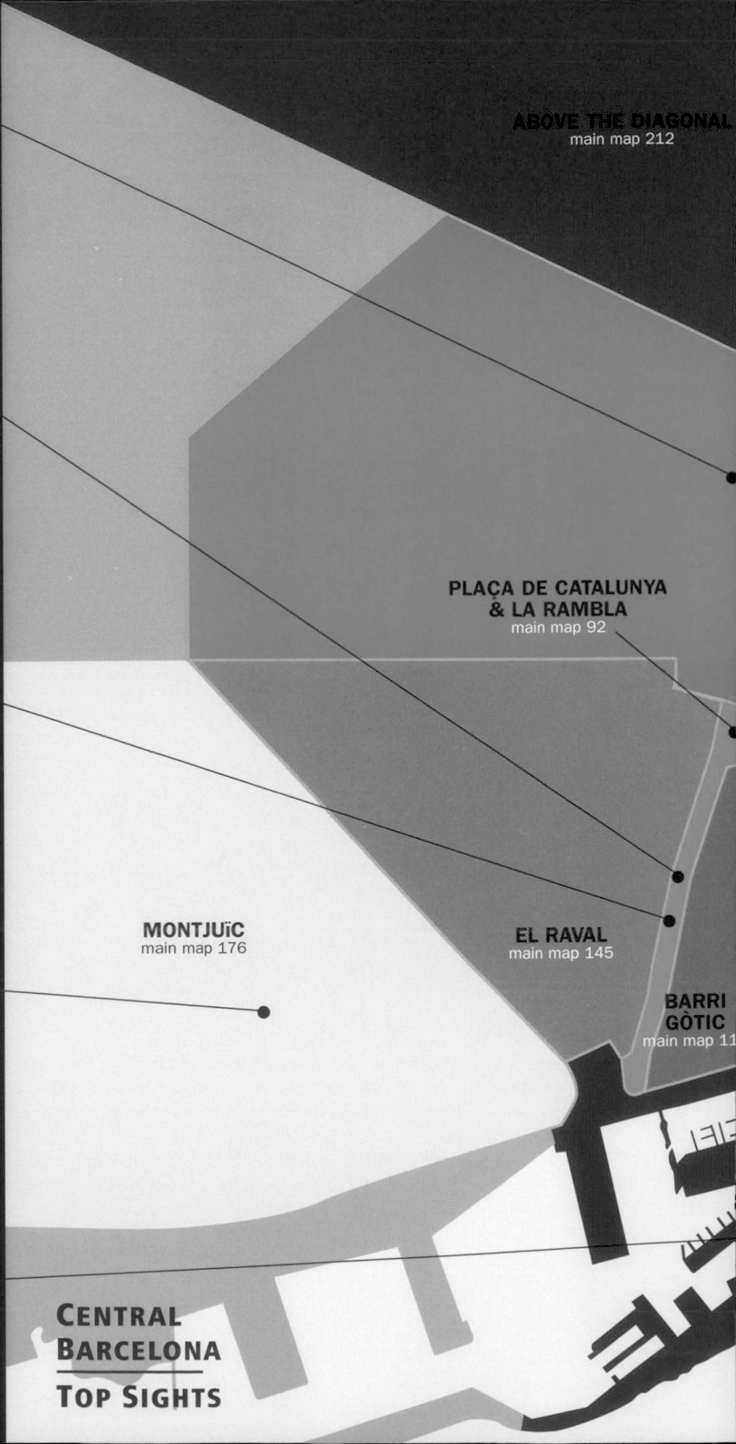

ABOVE THE DIAGONAL
main map 212

**PLAÇA DE CATALUNYA
& LA RAMBLA**
main map 92

MONTJUÏC
main map 176

EL RAVAL
main map 145

**BARRI
GÒTIC**
main map 11

**CENTRAL
BARCELONA**
——
TOP SIGHTS

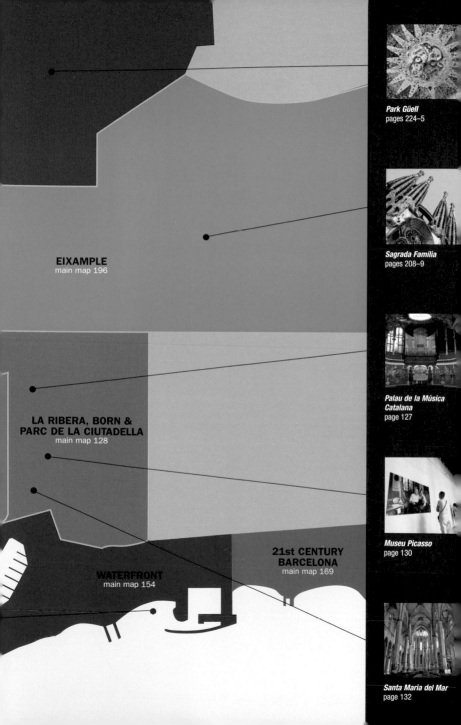

EIXAMPLE
main map 196

LA RIBERA, BORN &
PARC DE LA CIUTADELLA
main map 128

21st CENTURY
BARCELONA
main map 169

WATERFRONT
main map 154

Park Güell
pages 224–5

Sagrada Família
pages 208–9

*Palau de la Música
Catalana*
page 127

Museu Picasso
page 130

Santa Maria del Mar
page 132

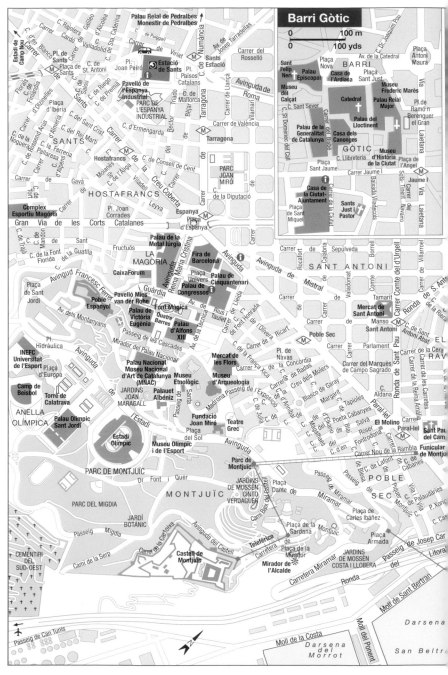

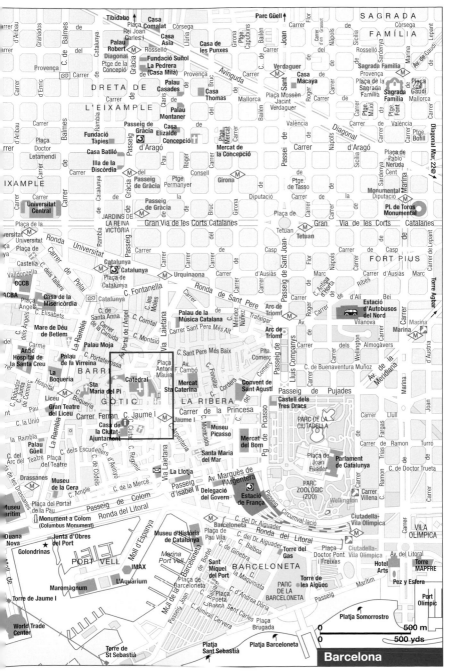

Barcelona

Recommended Restaurants, Bars & Cafés on pages 108–9

PLAÇA DE CATALUNYA AND LA RAMBLA

The spectacle and colour of the celebrated promenade leading from Plaça de Catalunya to the waterfront is a good starting point for getting to know the Old Town

At the top end of La Rambla, Plaça de Catalunya ❶ is not the kind of picturesque square that you might make an effort to visit, but it *is* the kind of place you inevitably pass through on any trip to Barcelona. Whether arriving from the airport by bus, coming into the city from other parts of Catalonia, visiting the Old Town from uptown or vice versa, Plaça de Catalunya is bound to be part of the trajectory. It is more of a pivotal *plaça*, acting as a logistical centre for the city's transport.

CENTRAL SQUARE

Here you'll find the metro underground train service, FGC trains (the Ferrocarrils de la Generalitat de Catalunya, which run to uptown areas and the suburbs), Rodalies de Catalunya (regional trains), public buses and the Aerobús to the airport, the Bus Turístic and taxis. A world of underground corridors leads to the trains, so allow time when travelling.

The main Barcelona city tourist office is also here, marked by a tall "i" above ground. Run by the tourist board, it offers an efficient and helpful service, dishing out leaflets, maps and all kinds of information, as well as providing a hotel reservation service, money exchange and an internet connection.

For many visitors to the city, Plaça de Catalunya also marks the beginning of another inevitability in Barcelona: a walk down the famous avenue called **La Rambla**.

Before embarking on that flow of humanity down to the sea, pause a moment in the welcome shade of

Main attractions

CAFÉ ZURICH
FONT DE CANALETES
PARRÒQUIA MAJOR DE SANTA ANNA
PALAU DE LA VIRREINA
MERCAT DE LA BOQUERIA
PLA DE LA BOQUERIA
GRAN TEATRE DEL LICEU
PALAU GÜELL
PLAÇA REIAL
PLAÇA GEORGE ORWELL
ARTS SANTA MÒNICA
MUSEU DE LA CERA
LA MARE DE DÉU DE LA MERCÈ
MONUMENT A COLOM

LEFT: an overview of La Rambla, the most famous thoroughfare in Barcelona.
RIGHT: pigeons and tourists flock to the Plaça de Catalunya.

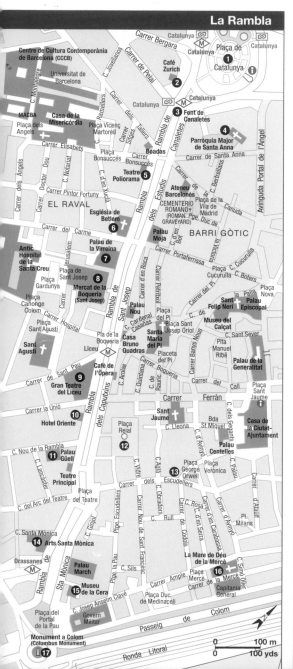

La Rambla

Centre de Cultura Contemporània de Barcelona (CCCB)

Universitat de Barcelona

MACBA
Casa de la Misericòrdia
Plaça dels Angels
Plaça Vicenç Martorell

Carrer Elisabets

EL RAVAL

Església de Betlem **6**

Palau de la Virreina **7**

Antic Hospital de la Santa Creu

Plaça de Sant Josep

Plaça Gardunya

Plaça Canonge Colom

Plaça Sant Agustí

Sant Agustí

Mercat de la Boqueria (Sant Josep) **8**

Palau Nou

Casa Bruno Quadras

Pla de la Boqueria

Liceu **M**

Cafè de l'Òpera

Gran Teatre del Liceu **9**

Carrer la Unió

Hotel Oriente **10**

C. Nou de la Rambla
Palau Güell **11**

Teatre Principal

Plaça del Teatre

C. Santa Mònica
Arts Santa Mònica **14**

Drassanes **M**

Palau March

Museu de la Cera **15**

Plaça del Portal de la Pau

Monument a Colom (Columbus Monument) **17**

Café Zurich **2**

Plaça de Catalunya **1**
Catalunya **i**

Font de Canaletes **3**

Parròquia Major de Santa Anna **4**

Boadas

Teatre Poliorama **5**

Ateneu Barcelonès

CEMENTERIO ROMANO* (ROMAN GRAVEYARD)

Palau Moja

BARRI GÒTIC

Plaça de la Vila de Madrid

Plaça Nova

Sant Felip Neri
Palau Episcopal

Museu del Calçat

Santa Maria del Pi

Placeta del Pi

Plaça Sant Josep Oriol

Pita Manuel Ribé

Palau de la Generalitat

Plaça Sant Jaume **i**

Carrer Ferràn

Sant Jaume

Casa de la Ciutat-Ajuntament

Palau Centelles

Plaça George Orwell **13**
Plaça Verónica

La Mare de Déu de la Mercè

Plaça Mercè **16**

Capitania General

Ronda Litoral

0   100 m
0   100 yds

Plaça de Catalunya's trees, or in the bright winter sunshine that fills it with a light and warmth which barely reaches the narrowest of the Old Town streets.

Pigeons flock here to be fed by children and old ladies. Tacky stalls sell plastic toys and caramelised nuts. Families wander around aimlessly, lovers meet beneath the gushing fountains and predatory youths lurk, with an eye on swinging handbags and cameras. Men gather to play chess beneath the monument to a much-loved Catalan leader, Macià, designed by contemporary sculptor Subirachs, and tourists in shorts and sun hats queue for the bus tour.

The *plaça*'s past

The square is more of a created centre than one with a real Catalan heart. Consider its history. When the medieval wall of Barcelona was demolished in 1854 to extend the city by making a new district, the **Eixample** *(see page 195)*, the *plaça* was a large field outside the city, traversed by a mountain stream (the stream bed later formed the founda-

Recommended Restaurants, Bars & Cafés on pages 108–9

tions of La Rambla) and connected to the inner city by means of an entrance called the Portal dels Orbs. The entrance was later renamed the **Portal de l'Angel** because, so the story goes, when Sant Ferrer crossed through this doorway with his followers, he was greeted by an angel. The 19th-century Plan Cerdà, a project for the redevelopment of Barcelona, called for the creation of a square a little further inland, at the junction of **Passeig de Gràcia** and the **Gran Via**.

Another rival project presented by Antoni Rovira i Trías proposed an enormous *plaça*, 800 by 400 metres (2,600 by 1,300 ft) to be called the "Forum Isabel II". Yet another plan for a *plaça* similar to that which we know today was designed in 1868 by Miquel Garriga.

While the authorities were trying to reach an agreement, the owners of the corresponding plots of land grew fed up with waiting and began to build. In 1902, Lord Mayor Ledesma ordered the demolition of all these buildings, but it was another quarter of a century before the *plaça* took on its current appearance. Based on a design by Francesc Nebot, the square was officially opened by King Alfonso XIII in 1927.

La Deesa *(Goddess) by Josep Llimona on the Plaça de Catalunya.*

Winds of change

Ever since this uneasy birth, the winds of change have swept through the square, taking away any vestiges of nostalgia and tradition. Now it is bordered by banks and giant shopping institutions that seem to have

FAR LEFT: taking a break in the square.
LEFT: the main branch of El Corte Inglés department store is on Plaça de Catalunya.
BELOW: fountains in the *plaça*.

As well as being the hub of Barcelona in terms of transport and city communications, Plaça de Catalunya is the centre of the city in a wider sense. If you look in the middle of the square itself you'll find paving stones arranged in the shape of a star which, they say, marks the centre of the capital of Catalonia.

ABOVE: street entertainment mixes with artists' wares.
BELOW: old meets new on La Rambla.

been transplanted from Madrid and elsewhere like some kind of late 20th-century colonisation.

On the corner now dominated by the Hard Rock Café and a branch of the El Corte Inglés empire, stood the legendary Maison Dorée café. Such was the character of this establishment that, when it closed its doors in 1918, another café of the same name opened at No. 6. "It was never the same," wrote Lluís Per-manyer, city historian, who relates that it was here that a tradition of "five o'clock tea" was introduced to Barcelona.

Another meeting point of intellectuals was the old Hotel Colón, which has since been a bank and is about to be reborn as luxury flats. Older generations of Republicans remember when the facade of the hotel was covered in portraits during the Civil War. With giant posters

Recommended Restaurants, Bars & Cafés on pages 108–9

SHOP

El Corte Inglés occupies the whole of the eastern side of Plaça de Catalunya. The department store is so named ("The English Cut") because its distant origins lie in a humble Madrid tailor's shop that specialised in the style, a far cry from today's exhausting air-conditioned expanse of goods and madding crowds.

of Marx, Lenin and Stalin, there was no mistaking that this was the headquarters of the Unified Socialist Party of Catalonia (PSUC), then the leading socialist group.

El Triangle

It's difficult to miss the monumental department store **El Corte Inglés**. On the opposite side is El Triangle, a commercial centre which is home to **FNAC**, a mega media store with several slick floors of books, music and technology. On the ground floor is a newsstand with an excellent range of magazines. The broad pavement here forms a tenuous link between La Rambla and the lesser known Rambla de Catalunya, an elegant boulevard which runs through the Eixample past *modernista* buildings to meet the Diagonal *(see page 200).*

Café Zurich ❷

At the point of the "triangle" where **Pelai** meets the top of La Rambla is **Café Zurich**, a replica of the original café which was demolished to build El Triangle. Thanks to its vantage point at a busy crossroads, and with the same old bad-tempered waiters, it has taken on the persona of the former

famous landmark, and remains a favourite rendezvous point.

Whether you are seated on Café Zurich's terrace, or emerging blinking from the metro exit, contemplate the panorama ahead.

LA RAMBLA

The city's main pedestrian street is one of the most famous boulevards in Europe, and for many people one of the distinguishing features of

ABOVE: newsstand on La Rambla. **BELOW:** feeding the pigeons on Plaça de Catalunya.

From River to Road – the History of La Rambla

Once lined with convents and then a fashionable promenade, today La Rambla offers something for everyone from opera-goers and children to tourists and thieves.

Originally, La Rambla was the river bed (the Latin name *arenno* was replaced by the Arab word *ramla*) that marked the exterior limits of the city fortified by King Jaume I. But when Barcelona expanded during the 15th century, La Rambla became part of the inner city. In due course, a number of religious houses were built in the surrounding areas and the river bed came to be known as the "Convent Thoroughfare". Only at the beginning of the 18th century did La Rambla become a more clearly defined street, after permission was granted to build on the ancient walls in the Boqueria area. In 1775 a section of the city walls was torn down and a central walkway built, lined with poplar trees and higher than the roadway that ran along either side.

Within the small and densely populated area of the ancient fortified city, La Rambla was the only street of any significance, and it became the city's focal point. Renovations were constantly under way during the 19th century, and the street settled down to become more exclusive and aristocratic; this change of status was aided by the disappearance of some of the surrounding buildings and convents, creating space for new squares and mansions.

La Rambla assumed its present shape between 1849 and 1856 when all the remaining fortifications were torn down. The first plane trees, brought from Devesa in Girona, were planted in 1851, and the street became "the fashionable promenade route, where the cream of Barcelona parades on foot, by carriage or on horseback", according to the 19th-century journalist Gaziel.

Today's promenaders are more mixed and more cosmopolitan, though the "cream" can still be spotted wrapped in furs on their way to the opera at the Liceu. Since the regeneration of the Old Town in the 1990s, more uptown residents are venturing down to these "lower" parts to visit art galleries and trendy boutiques or eat in the eclectic selection of new restaurants. They mingle with tourists, hen parties, pickpockets, petty criminals cheating at dice tricks and prostitutes assailing northern European businessmen. The local youth move in large crowds looking for cheap beer before going clubbing.

And while the fun continues, out come the municipal cleaners in force, like some kind of eco-angels, sweeping, collecting rubbish and vigorously hosing down the gutters in preparation for a new day. ❑

LEFT: a theatre poster dating from 1929.
ABOVE: La Rambla has long been a favourite meeting place.

Recommended Restaurants, Bars & Cafés on pages 108–9

DRINK

Tucked just inside Tallers, the first street on the right as you head down from Plaça de Catalunya, is Boadas, the oldest cocktail bar in town, with a 1930s interior and walls lined with caricatures of the original owner. The bar is known for its mojitos; the recipe was inherited from Boadas, who learnt his art in Cuba where, like so many Catalans in the 19th century, his parents had emigrated to.

Barcelona. This kaleidoscopic avenue throbs day and night, exerting an undeniable magnetism which attracts both visitors and locals, and which never fails to entertain.

The best advice is to plunge in, go with the flow and enjoy the constant weird and wonderful activity. Let yourself be carried past lottery ticket booths, shoe shiners, cheap *pensions*, human statues, northern Europeans in shorts in December, and locals in sharp suits. Let your senses be assailed by the perfumed air of the flower stalls, the chatter of the gossips and the yells of the porters delivering fruit to the market. Don't miss a thing, especially the gambling con artists and ubiquitous pickpockets who inevitably prey on such a bountiful crowd. After dark La Rambla loses none of its daytime energy, becoming the main artery for anyone going *de juerga* (out for a wild time) in the Old Town.

RAMBLA DE CANALETES

Between the top of La Rambla and the Columbus monument where it ends there are five different parts to the promenade. The first, **Rambla de Canaletes**, is named after the **Font de Canaletes ❸**, one of the symbols of Barcelona.

A small brass plaque at the foot of this 19th-century cast-iron fountain confirms the legend that all those who drink its waters will be enamoured of Barcelona and always return. It is a favourite meeting place, and posses of retired men regularly gather here for *tertúlies* (chatting in groups and putting the world to rights – often around a table after a large meal). The "font" is at its most jubilant when Barça football fans of all ages gather there to celebrate yet another victory for their successful team.

Shopping Streets

Just beyond the fountain, at the junction with Bonsuccés, is the splendid *modernista* pharmacy

ABOVE: Dr Masó's Farmacia Nadal has been here for decades.
BELOW: drinking from the Canaletes fountain.

Teatre Poliorama stages a variety of shows, including flamenco (see page 271 for contact details).

ABOVE RIGHT: the music shop next to the Palau de la Virreina has an attractive facade and a timeless interior **(BELOW).**

Nadal, and across La Rambla are the diverging streets Santa Anna and Canuda, both pedestrian shopping streets.

Parròquia Major de Santa Anna ❹

✉ Santa Anna ⏰ Mon–Sat 9am–1pm and 6.30–8pm; avoid weekends, the time for weddings and Masses ⓖ free 🅱 Catalunya

Hidden behind the busy shops of Santa Anna on the left is the **Parròquia Major de Santa Anna**, an oasis of peace. The Romanesque church and Gothic cloister are marvellous examples of the architecture of their time.

Return to La Rambla via **Plaça de la Vila de Madrid**, reached from the narrow street Bertrellans almost opposite the church: it is an attractive, landscaped square with some Roman graves dating from the 1st to 3rd centuries and a wonderful jacaranda tree. On the corner, at Canuda No. 6, is the **Ateneu Barcelonès**, a traditional cultural enclave dating from 1796. For members only, but you can steal a glimpse of the hushed library and magnificent interiors from the square.

RAMBLA DELS ESTUDIS

Back on La Rambla, the crowd gets denser and the noise level rises as it passes through a corridor of kiosks and human statues. This is the **Rambla dels Estudis**, so named because the 16th-century university was here.

The Reial Acadèmia de Ciències i Arts on the right also houses the **Teatre Poliorama ❺**, which has regular performances *(see page 271)*. On the exterior of the building, which was designed by Josep Domènech i Estapà, is the clock that has been the official timekeeper of the city since 1891. In *Homage to Catalonia* George Orwell recounts days spent on guard on this roof.

Of all the vast conglomeration of the former university, only the **Església de Betlem ❻** (beyond the smart 1898 hotel) remains, a long and rather depressing bulk. The Baroque facade on **Carme** was built in 1690 but the main structure was not completed until 1729.

Opposite is the **Palau Moja** (also known as the Marquis de Comillas Palace), an important 18th-century

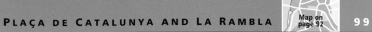
Recommended Restaurants, Bars & Cafés on pages 108–9

neoclassical building housing some offices of the Generalitat (the Catalan government) and occasionally open to show exhibitions. Under the arcades is the Generalitat bookshop, with a few titles of general interest amid weighty tomes of statistics on Catalonia.

BRIEF DETOURS

At the corner, **Portaferrissa** leads into a world of commerce and numerous fashion shops, cafés selling hot chocolate and sticky confectionery, and the central part of the **Barri Gòtic** *(see pages 111–25)*. To the right of La Rambla is Carme, an interesting street going into the heart of **El Raval**, worth a brief detour for **El Indio**, a textiles shop (at No. 24) founded in 1870 and little changed since. Inside there are long wooden counters for proper display of the cloth, and wooden chairs for stout ladies to rest their legs.

RAMBLA DE SANT JOSEP

Back on the **Rambla de Sant Josep** (better known as the **Rambla de les Flors**), the air smells sweet. During

the 19th century this was the only place where flowers were sold. The Catalan Impressionist artist Ramón Casas (1866–1932) picked out one of the flower sellers here to be his model, and she later became his wife.

Palau de la Virreina ➐

On the right is the **Palau de la Virreina**, a magnificent 18th-century Rococo building set back from the road for greater effect. In 1771 Manuel Amat, Viceroy of Peru, sent a detailed plan from Lima for the

Pretty bouquets for sale on one of the many flower stalls in the Sant Josep section of La Rambla.

BELOW: the courtyard of Palau de la Virreina.

construction of the house that he planned to build on La Rambla. The final building was not completed until 1778, and the viceroy died only a few years after taking up residence. It was his young widow who was left to enjoy the palace, which became known as the palace of the "Virreina" or vicereine.

Today it is an excellent exhibition venue specialising in photography and image-based art as well as being the official cultural information centre, and a booking office. Wander

RIGHT: fresh fruit to go in La Boqueria. **BELOW:** La Boqueria market occupies a grand 19th-century structure.

into its handsome courtyard: around fiesta time there is usually some *gegant* (giant) or *drac* (dragon) lurking, before being brought out on parade. Next to it is a music store with a charming *modernista* front.

Mercat de la Boqueria ⓫

✉ Mercat Sant Josep ⓒ Mon–Sat 7am–8pm 🚇 Liceu

Half a block further down is the entrance to the city's most popular and famous market, the **Mercat de la Boqueria**, or Mercat Sant Josep. The first stone was laid on 19 March 1840, Saint Joseph's day, to appease the saint whose convent on the same spot had been burnt down in the 1835 riots. Again, take plenty of time to enjoy shopping there, or simply to observe what's going on.

Discerning shoppers – restaurateurs early in the morning, housewives mid-morning and the men in charge of the Sunday paella on Saturdays – queue patiently for the best produce, bark their orders and refuse to be fobbed off with anything below par. The fishwives also shriek, trying to seduce passers-by into the day's best catch. It is a heady experience, despite the frantic crowds, as there is something quintessentially Mediterranean about the noise, human warmth and the serious business of buying and eating wonderfully fresh produce. It is at its best early in the morning before the spectators arrive.

On the opposite side of La Rambla is the **Palau Nou**. The total antithesis to La Boqueria, it is an ultra-modern building that is supposedly completely automated, including "robot parking" on nine levels underground. It also provides a short cut through to the **Plaça del Pi**, and effectively frames the beautiful Gothic tower of the *plaça*'s church, Santa Maria del Pi.

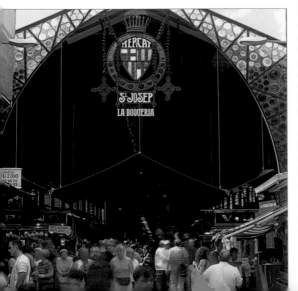

Recommended Restaurants, Bars & Cafés on pages 108–9

Pla de la Boqueria

Continuing on down, La Rambla enters the **Pla de la Boqueria** (marked only by a widening of La Rambla, and a break in the shady avenue of trees). This was the site of executions in the 14th century, when it was paved with flagstones. The name dates from the previous century, when tables selling fresh meat, *mesas de bocatería,* were erected

here (*boc* is the Catalan for goat's meat). In the 15th century the tables of gamblers and cardsharps replaced the meat stalls.

Today the flagstones have been replaced by a Joan Miró pavement created in the 1970s – look out for his signature. On one corner stands the **Casa Bruno Quadras**, built by Josep Vilaseca in 1891. The building's colourful, extravagant decoration includes umbrellas, fans and a great Chinese dragon, illustrating the oriental influence on the *modernista* designers.

An oriental dragon and parasols on the modernista *facade of the Casa Bruno Quadras on Pla de la Boqueria.*

BELOW: Miró's distinctive pavement on Pla de la Boqueria.

The Liceu theatre was beautifully renovated and much extended after a serious fire in 1994.

BELOW:
the facade of the Liceu.
BELOW RIGHT:
Cafè de l'Òpera, an old favourite.

RAMBLA DELS CAPUTXINS

At this point the **Rambla dels Caputxins** begins, so called because, until 1775, the left side was the site of the Capuchin Convent and its adjacent vegetable garden.

Gran Teatre del Liceu ❾

✉ La Rambla, 51–59; www.liceu barcelona.com ☎ 902 533 353 (bookings); 93-485 9900 (information) ⓒ tours (charge),

guided 10am; non-guided 11.30am, 12pm, 12.30pm and 1pm 🄴 Liceu

The mood changes slightly now, as this stretch is dominated by the **Gran Teatre del Liceu,** cathedral of the *bel canto* in Spain and launch pad for names such as Carreras and Caballé. The original building, dating from 1861, was badly damaged by fire in 1994, but has since been extravagantly restored to its former glory. New technology has been installed and a second stage added. The theatre season now covers a wide range of productions from classical to ambitious avant-garde opera, ballet and recitals.

Alongside the theatre, Sant Pau leads down to the Romanesque church of Sant Pau del Camp in El Raval *(see page 149).*

Cafè de l'Òpera

Opposite the opera house is the **Cafè de l'Òpera,** opened in 1929. It remains a good place to read the newspapers in the morning – subdued and peaceful – yet builds up to a giddy pitch late at night.

The Liceu

The Liceu, founded by philanthropist Manuel Gibert i Sans, staged its first opera in 1838. Construction of a bigger venue, on land acquired from a former convent on La Rambla, began in 1844. The project was second only to that of La Scala in Milan, with space for 4,000 spectators and every type of performance, from musical galas to operas and ballet. Stravinsky, de Falla, Caruso, Callas, Plácido Domingo and Pavarotti have all performed here, as well as Catalonia's own Pablo Casals, Montserrat Caballé and Josep Carreras. In 1994 a fire gutted the interior. City authorities announced that the opera house would be rebuilt, and architect Ignasi de Solà Morales doubled its size while conserving its original style. It reopened in 1999 to much public acclaim. In attempts to broaden its appeal, the programme includes cabaret sessions in the foyer, performances for children and opera film cycles. A shop and café are situated below street level.

Recommended Restaurants, Bars & Cafés on pages 108–9

Carrer Ferràn

The Gran Teatre del Liceu ends opposite **Ferràn**, one of the most elegant streets in Barcelona in the first half of the 19th century. Remnants of this time can still be seen despite the invasion of fast-food outlets and souvenir shops. Now pedestrianised, the street leads up to the Plaça Sant Jaume at the heart of the Barri Gòtic.

Hotel Oriente ⑩

The legendary Hotel Oriente, a little further down La Rambla, preserves the structures of the Collegi de Sant Bonaventura, founded by Franciscan monks in 1652. The cloister is the ballroom, surrounded by the monks' gallery. A wall plaque reminds guests that this was the first public place in Barcelona to use gas lighting. Once favoured by the likes of Ernest Hemingway, it has now been absorbed into a large hotel chain.

Palau Güell ⑪

✉ Nou de la Rambla 3–5; www. palauguell.cat ☎ 93-472 5775
🅒 Apr–Sept 10am–8pm, Oct–Mar 10am–5.30pm, closed Mon
🅒 charge 🅁 Liceu or Drassanes

Just off Rambla dels Caputxins as you continue down is the **Palau Güell**. Built by Antoni Gaudí between 1885 and 1889 as the home of his patron, Count Güell, it has recently reopened after lavish renovation.

With this early commission, the architect embarked on a period of fertile creativity. Gothic inspiration alternates with evident Arabic influence. The building is structured around an enormous salon, from which a conical roof covered in pieces of tiling emerges to preside over a landscape of capriciously placed battlements, balustrades and strangely shaped chimneys.

Plaça Reial ⑫

Back on the other side of La Rambla, an arcaded passageway leads to the infamous **Plaça Reial**, another Barcelona landmark and one of the most handsome yet decadent of its squares. Attempts to clean it up have done little to change its character, so tourists on terrace bars still jostle

On the roof of Palau Güell, you can admire Gaudí's fantastic ceramic chimneys, and enjoy great views over the city.

BELOW: Plaça Reial combines elegance and decadence in one square.

EAT

Restaurants and bars line the Plaça Reial. Glaciar is an old favourite, still full of life, and MariscCo is a stylish seafood restaurant. In the nearby streets too, try traditional Los Caracoles (with sizzling chickens on a blazing grill on the exterior wall), and La Fonda. The latter is related to Quinze Nits in the Plaça and has the same effective formula – reasonably priced Catalan food, served in an attractive interior of palms and pale wood.

RIGHT:
bar on Plaça Reial.
BELOW: street lamps in Plaça Reial designed by the young Gaudí.

with junkies, and backpackers share benches with tramps. Restaurants, bars and clubs predominate, like the well-established **Jamboree** jazz club, along with its sister club **Tarantos** for flamenco, both open after the shows for dancing. **Sidecar**, considered one of the most fashionable spots, has live music. The buzz never lets up.

On Sunday mornings, stamp and coin collectors gather around the **Font de Les Tres Gràcies** and the two *fanals* (street lamps) designed by a young Gaudí. Inspired by the French urban designs of the Napoleonic period, this is the only one of the many squares planned in Barcelona during the 19th century that was built entirely according to its original plan. Its uniform, arcaded buildings were constructed by Francesc Daniel Molina on the plot where the Capuchin Convent once stood. Return to La Rambla through Passatge de Bacardí (the Cuban rum was created by a Catalan).

Plaça del Teatre

The terraces that line La Rambla along this stretch are pretty well spurned by locals, but as long as you don't expect the ultimate culinary experience it is tempting to pull up a chair, order a cool drink and watch the world go by.

Where the promenade opens up again into the **Plaça del Teatre**, or **Plaça de les Comèdies**, another notorious street, **Escudellers**, leads off to the left. A kind of cross between ingrained seediness and up-to-the-minute trendiness, it is representative of many parts of Barcelona today. Walk along it to feel the pulse of the harsher elements of the city, and to observe its present evolution.

Plaça George Orwell

Escudellers opens up at the far end into a square, **Plaça George Orwell**, created in the 1980s as a result of dense housing demolition; trendy bars and restaurants have opened here, and a bike rental company has set up shop. The sculpture on the square is by Leandre Cristòfol.

Now return down Escudellers, passing small grocer's shops, falafel bars, discos and dives. Narrow streets lead off to the right and left, most hiding late-night bars (*see margin tip, left*).

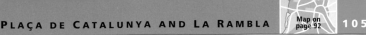
Recommended Restaurants, Bars & Cafés on pages 108–9

Teatre Principal

Back on La Rambla you reach the spot where, in the 16th century, the city's first theatre was built. The present **Teatre Principal** replaced the old wooden theatre that was for many years the only stage in Barcelona. A 2,000-seater, it was built on the site of the historical Corral de les Comèdies, a popular early theatre, although it never appealed to the bourgeoisie. Opposite the theatre is a monument to Frederic Soler "Pitarra", founder of the modern Catalan theatre.

RAMBLA DE SANTA MÒNICA

The few prostitutes remaining in this area choose the square surrounding the monument to offer their charms – a reminder of what used to be called the **Barrio Xino** (in Spanish Barrio Chino). A shadow of its former self, the area has been cleaned up in recent years, but the neon signs of sex shops and the like are still in evidence. The square marks the beginning of the **Rambla de Santa Mònica**, the last stretch of La Rambla before it reaches the harbour.

At this point the pace of the human river slows, as if reaching its delta, and the personality of La Rambla seems to fade. The Rambla de Santa Mònica is lined with caricaturists, portrait painters and artisans, and a craft market is held here at the weekend. This is where, in 1895, films were first shown publicly in Spain by the Lumière brothers. Some handsome buildings have been restored and new ones built, notably on the left for the university of Pompeu Fabra.

Arts Santa Mònica ❶

✉ La Rambla, 7; www.artssanta monica.cat ☎ 93-567 1110 🕐 Tue–Fri 2–9pm, Sat–Sun and holidays 11am–7pm ◎ free 🚇 Drassanes

On the right side as you continue towards the port is the **Arts Santa Mònica**, a former convent re-designed as an exhibition space by the highly regarded local architects Piñón and Viaplana, who have been instrumental in much of the new Barcelona. Now under new direction, it is an exciting space with

Stereotypical art for sale is plentiful along the lower reaches of La Rambla.

BELOW: the Arts Santa Mònica building.

KIDS

La Rambla is a great place to take children. From feeding pigeons in Plaça de Catalunya and posing with the human statues to persuading parents to buy them ice creams and being happily horrified by the models in the Wax Museum, there's plenty for them to enjoy.

ABOVE: the Wax Museum's ticket kiosk. **BELOW:** last refreshment stop at the foot of La Rambla.

interesting, experimental shows and accompanying activities. At street level an information centre provides details of cultural events in Catalonia. Opposite the centre is the **Palau March** (1780), today the Generalitat's Department of Culture.

Just before the Arts Santa Mònica, a narrow street, Santa Mònica, heads off into the former Barrio Xino, where you'll find a range of seedy and newly fashionable old bars. An evocative French atmosphere is on offer in the timeless **Pastis** at No. 4 Santa Mònica – except on tango nights, when the bar transforms itself into a corner of Buenos Aires.

Museu de la Cera ⑮

✉ Passatge de la Banca, 7; www.museocerabcn.com 📞 93-317 2649 🕒 mid-July–late Sept daily 10am–10pm; rest of year Mon–Fri 10am–1.30pm, 4–7.30pm, Sat–Sun 11am–2pm, 4.30–8.30pm 🎫 charge 🚇 Drassanes

Towards the end of La Rambla, on the left, an old-fashioned ticket booth sells tickets for the Museu de la Cera. The roof of Barcelona's wax museum sports Superman, poised to leap from the top of the building, and inside are more than 360 waxworks, giving an insight into some of Catalonia's historic personalities. Recent acquisitions include Prince Charles and Camilla.

Around this part of La Rambla you'll usually find a horse and car-

Recommended Restaurants, Bars & Cafés on pages 108–9

riage waiting to whisk tourists off for a trot around town.

Our Lady of Mercy ⑯

A long street on the left, Ample, leads to the 18th-century church of **La Mare de Déu de la Mercè**, usually known simply as **La Mercè**, the patroness of Barcelona, and the name given to many Catalan women. A dramatic statue of the Virgin and Child stands on the top of the church, creating a distinctive element on the waterfront skyline.

The square was one of the first urban spaces (1983) to appear as a result of the Socialist city council's long-term project of demolishing old buildings to open up dense areas. It is at its most festive on 24 September, the day of La Mercè, when *gegants* and *castellers (see pages 26–7)* greet the dignitaries coming out of Mass, before the main *festa major* of Barcelona takes off. It is also customary for every member of the Barça football team, whatever his creed, to come and pay his respects to the Virgin after important victories, before going off to parade the trophy in front of the fans in Plaça Sant Jaume.

The last building on the left side of La Rambla before you reach the Waterfront has a curious history. In 1778 the foundry of the Royal Artillery, as well as its workshop, were transferred to this building, known as **El Refino**. The foundry was one of the most renowned cannon factories of its time. From 1844 until 1920 it was occupied by the offices of the Banco de Barcelona and, since the Spanish Civil War (1936–9), it has been converted into the offices of the military governor.

Monument a Colom ⑰

☎ 93-302 5224 ⊙ daily 8.30am–8pm ⊚ charge 🅿 Drassanes

A challenging end to this long walk is the steep climb to the top of the Columbus Monument, in the **Plaça del Portal de la Pau**, built for the 1888 Universal Exposition. Fortunately, it also has an internal lift as well as a great view over the city and port. ❑

The Columbus statue is a useful landmark. A lift will take you to the top and save you a long climb.

BELOW: the superb view from the top of the Columbus Monument.

BEST RESTAURANTS, BARS AND CAFÉS

Restaurants

Prices for a three-course dinner per person with a bottle of house wine:
€ = under €25
€€ = €25–40
€€€ = €40–60
€€€€ = over €60

Consider La Rambla a colourful avenue to walk down and enjoy, rather than a place to eat. With just a few notable exceptions, the restaurants are low on quality and high on price, but there's plenty of choice nearby.

Amaya
La Rambla, 20–24 ☎ 93 302 6138 ◵ L & D daily. €€ (set menu Mon–Fri L €) [p304, A3]
This well-established Basque restaurant is a traditional treasure in the midst of the cheap

alternatives surrounding it. You can opt for a snack at the bustling bar or the more elegant dining room at the rear, where fish is the best option. Now run by the fourth generation of the same family.

ATN
Canuda, 6 ☎ 93 318 5238 ◵ L & D Tue–Sat, L only Mon. € [p304, B1]
Just off La Rambla in the atmospheric, literary surroundings of the Ateneu (cultural organisation), with an attractive terrace overlooking Plaça de la Vila de Madrid.

Attic
La Rambla, 120 ☎ 93 302 4866 ◵ L & D daily. €€ [p304, B1]
Part of a chain that produces authentic

Spanish cuisine on a large scale, but does so effectively, creating a good ambience. Popular with tourists. The tables overlooking La Rambla provide an irresistible floor show and the roof terrace is perfect.

Bar Cañete
Unió 17 ☎ 93 002 9425 ◵ L & D (tapas) Mon–Sat. €€ [p304, A2]
A slick new spot just off La Rambla serving well-prepared authentic tapas or platillos (small dishes) at their long, shiny bar.

Bar Lobo
Pintor Fortuny, 3 ☎ 93 481 5346 ◵ B, L & D daily. €€ [p304, A1]
The hippest member of the Tragaluz empire attracts a cool crowd with its slick interior, lounging terrace in a busy pedestrian street, and combination of light Mediterranean and Japanese dishes. Open late for drinks at weekends.

Can Culleretes
Quintana, 5 ☎ 93 317 3022 ◵ L & D Tue–Sat. L only Sun. €€ [p304, B2]
This is the second-oldest restaurant in Spain, founded in 1786 and full of character. Adorned

with paintings and photos of famous visitors, it mercifully remains authentically Catalan, serving the likes of wild boar stew and spinach canelones.

Drassanes
Avinguda Drassanes ☎ 93 317 5256 ◵ L Mon–Sat. €€ (set menu €) [p304, A3]
A part of the medieval building in which the Maritime Museum is housed, this is a delightful setting for lunch.

El Paraguayo
Parc, 1 ☎ 93 302 1441 ◵ L & D Tue–Sun. €€ [p304, A3]
A magnet for passionate carnivores, with daily deliveries of Argentinian and Uruguayan meat, duly grilled in the inimitable Argentinian style. Always has a lively atmosphere.

Fresc Co
Carme, 16 ☎ 93 301 6837 ◵ L & D daily. € [p304, A1]
Healthy fast food. Pile up your plates from a huge choice of salads, then gorge on the dish of the day, or pasta and pizza. Finish with fruit, or ice cream if you've had enough of eating healthily. A hit with kids and adults alike. There are branches all over town.

LEFT: appetising paella. **ABOVE RIGHT:** Kiosco Universal: fantastic seafood in the heart of La Boqueria market.

Irati
Cardenal Casañas, 17 ☎ 93 302 3084 🕐 L & D daily. €€ *Pintxos* all day. €
[p304, B2]
One of the first of a bevy of Basque bars that opened in the 1990s. Grab what you fancy from the great variety of *pintxos* (snacks on a toothpick) that emerge at regular intervals from the kitchen. It's best to go a bit earlier than Barcelonan lunch and dinner times, before they run out of food. Serious à la carte Basque dishes are served at the rear.

Kasparo
Plaça Vicenç Martorell, 4 ☎ 93 302 2072 🕐 L and all-day snacks Tue–Sat. Closed Jan. € [p304, A1]
A charming terrace bar in this secluded square just off La Rambla. Delicious and cosmopolitan light snacks and lunch dishes, the original creations of its Australian owners. There's a play area for children in the square.

Kiosco Universal
Mercat Sant Josep (La Boqueria), Parada 691 ☎ 93 317 8286 🕐 B & L Mon–Sat. € [p304, A2]
Pull up a stool at the bar amid the market's stallholders and eat the freshest of produce, cooked before your eyes.

La Xina
Pintor Fortuny, 3 ☎ 93 342 9628 🕐 L & D daily. €€ (set menu L €) [p304, A1]

Delicate amounts of Chinese food served with enormous style in attractive surroundings complete with lacquer finishes and a giant paper dragon. A mix of designer Chinese and Barcelonan styles.

Los Caracoles
Escudellers, 14 ☎ 93 302 3185 🕐 L & D daily. €€€ [p304, B2]
This old Barcelona favourite still oozes atmosphere, from the moment you walk in through the sizzling, busy kitchen and are settled in its labyrinthine interior, at a table with a crisp white cloth. Specialises in rich meat dishes like lamb and suckling pig.

Pinotxo
Mercat Sant Josep (La Boqueria), Parada 466 ☎ 93 317 1731 🕐 B & L Mon–Sat. €€ [p304, A2]
A high-profile market bar, where the uptown crowd pause from their Saturday shopping for cava and oysters, or whatever the charismatic owner has selected from the

season's produce at the neighbouring stalls.

Sagarra
Xuclà, 9 ☎ 93 301 0604 🕐 B, L & D Tue–Sat, L only Mon. € [p304, A1]
Don't be put off by the somewhat formal, conventional decor – this is a good, honest, local place serving traditional dishes with a touch of flare. Excellent value lunchtime menu too. Has tables on the small square.

Bars and Cafés

This is a good area for cafés and *xocolateries*, with legendary meeting place **Cafè Zurich** on Plaça de Catalunya a perfect starting point. Have a coffee at the *modernista* **Escribà** at La Rambla, 83, and you won't be able to resist an exquisite pastry. For real indulgence don't miss the oldest milk bar in town, **Granja Viader,** Xuclà, 4–6, a delightful spot where kids' favourite *cacao-lat* (chocolate milk) was invented. Or try **La Pallaresa**, Petritxol, 11, one of several *granjes* in this street, where the *xocolata desfeta,* Catalan drinking chocolate, is not for the faint-hearted. Halfway down La

Rambla the **Cafè de l'Òpera**, subdued in the morning but buzzing by night, retains its charm despite recent facelifts. Two essential night-time stops are **Boadas**, Tallers, 1, a classic cocktail bar straight from the 1930s, and **Pastis**, Santa Mònica, 4, a small corner of Marseille at the foot of La Rambla. **Castells**, Plaça Bonsuccés, has good *tapes* and cool beers to offer both day and night.

Recommended Restaurants, Bars & Cafés on pages 124–5

BARRI GÒTIC

There's no finer introduction to Barcelona's Golden Age
than a stroll around the warren of narrow streets
that constitutes the lovely Barri Gòtic,
the oldest part of the city

The jewel of the Old Town, the Gothic Quarter or Barri Gòtic is a dense nucleus of historic buildings that has formed the central part of the Old City since Roman times. Today it represents the centre of municipal administration and is home to the Catalan autonomous government.

The oldest part of the city, it is built around **Mont Tàber**, Taber Hill, a misnomer for what is little more than a mound. This section of the Old Town is surrounded by the remains of Roman walls clearly indicated with descriptive signs. Layer upon layer of different architectural styles illustrate the different periods of Barcelona's history, from remnants of the Roman city to contemporary architectural solutions seen in renovation work and extensions to old buildings. The Gothic period predominates, reflecting the glorious medieval period when Catalonia was at its height.

A TOUR OF THE BARRI GÒTIC

This route is designed to take in the key sites, and constitutes an enjoyable walk through the present-day Gothic Quarter with its residents, its street musicians, its cafés and commerce. Alternatively, you can simply absorb its atmosphere by wandering aimlessly around its narrow streets, feeling the sense of history and observing the day-to-day comings and goings of the local people.

Approach from Plaça de Catalunya down **Portal de l'Angel**, a wide paved street full of shoe shops, the major fashion chains and a branch of El Corte Inglés, which specialises in music, books, urban fashion, sport

Main attractions

PLAÇA NOVA
CASA DE L'ARDIACA
CATEDRAL
PLAÇA SANT FELIP NERI
MUSEU DEL CALÇAT
PLAÇA SANT JOSEP ORIOL
SANTA MARIA DEL PI
PLAÇA SANT JAUME
PLAÇA SANT JUST
PLAÇA DEL REI
MUSEU D'HISTÒRIA DE LA CIUTAT
PALAU DEL LLOCTINENT
MUSEU FREDERIC MARÈS
MUSEU DIOCESÀ

LEFT: walking through the atmospheric alleyways of the Barri Gòtic.
RIGHT: bustling Carrer Ferràn, leading from La Rambla to the heart of the Barri Gòtic.

Friezes designed by Picasso decorate the exterior of the Col·legi d'Arquitectes (Architects' Association).

and computers, and is housed in a grandiose building. The wide space lends itself to street performances. Bear left at the fork at the bottom, taking Arcs past a fine *modernista* building now housing a hotel, an Aladdin's cave of a toyshop, and the **Col·legi d'Arquitectes**, the Architects' Association, a 1960s building with friezes designed by Picasso, but executed by Norwegian Carl Nesjar.

Plaça Nova ❶

The street leads into Plaça Nova, and there, in front of you, is one of the main Roman gates to the old city, the **Portal del Bisbe** (Bishop's Gate). The towers date from the 1st century BC but the name came later, from the nearby 18th-century Bishop's Palace. The sculpted letters by Catalan artist Joan Brossa spell out "Barcino", the Roman name for the city.

Avinguda de la Catedral

Here Plaça Nova merges with **Avinguda de la Catedral**, a wide open space spreading out at the foot of the cathedral steps. The paving hides an underground car park and successfully highlights the drama of the ancient facades, rising theatrically above the Roman walls. Sit on one of the polished stone benches or the terrace of the **Hotel Colón** and take it all in: the constant movement of children, footballs and bicycles, the clicking of cameras, large groups off

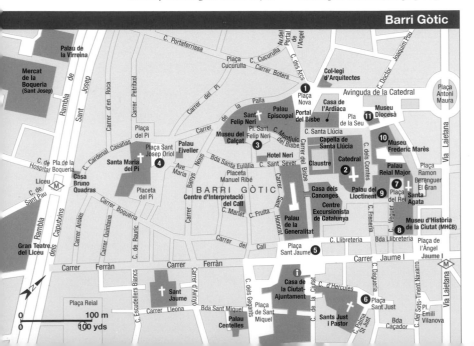

Recommended Restaurants, Bars & Cafés on pages 124–5

towards the cathedral. On the corner is a chapel dedicated to Santa Llúcia, patron saint of the blind and, curiously, of seamstresses. Built in 1268, it is one of the oldest parts of the cathedral and a fine example of Romanesque architecture, with images of the Annunciation and the Visitation decorating the facade capitals. The holy-water font inside the chapel is from the 14th century. A rear doorway leads into the cloister.

The **Fira de Santa Llúcia**, an atmospheric Christmas arts and crafts fair, fills the cathedral square for most of December. It also sells Christmas trees of all shapes and sizes, plus everything you could possibly need to make your own Nativity scene, from the Three Kings to the *caganer (see margin, right)*.

Wise men, the baby Jesus, donkeys and the caganer *are all essential figures in the Nativity scene. A curious Catalan tradition, the* caganer, *usually dressed as a local peasant – though sometimes as a star footballer or politician – is supposedly fertilizing the earth to bring good luck in the New Year.*

cruise ships, balloon vendors and beggars. An antiques market takes place here on Thursdays, and at the weekend the gatherings of *sardana* dancers form large, impenetrable bouncing circles (6.30pm on Sat, noon on Sun, 7pm on Wed). All this is played out against the surprisingly neo-Gothic front of the cathedral, which was tacked onto its 13th-century origins in the 19th century.

Through the Roman gate

Enter the Gothic Quarter through the Roman gate in Plaça Nova, up the slope into **Bisbe**. On the right is the **Palau Episcopal**, built in 1769 around a 12th-century courtyard, which is the only remaining evidence of the original palace after centuries of modifications. The frescoes on the façade (facing the Carrer Montjuïc del Bisbe) date from the 18th century, while the triple recess windows and large *flamígero* window in the courtyard are from the 14th century. It was the Pope's HQ when he visited in 2010.

Opposite the palace entrance a short street, **Santa Llúcia**, leads

The cathedral precincts

Opposite the Capella de Santa Llúcia, on the other corner, is the **Casa de l'Ardiaca** (Archdeacon's Residence), built in the 15th century on Roman ruins. It has one of the most evocative patios in the city. A tall, elegant palm tree rises high above a

LEFT: a palm tree gives shade in the cathedral cloisters (*see page 116*). **BELOW:** Carrer del Bisbe.

The cathedral's ornate choir pews were carved at the end of the 14th century.

BELOW: courtyard of the Casa de l'Ardiaca.

outer wall, with square towers and the remains of two aqueducts (which can be seen from Avinguda de la Catedral) is from the 4th century AD.

The Cathedral ②

✉ Pla Catedral de la Seu, 3; www.catedralbcn.org 📞 93 342 8260 🕒 daily 8.30am–12.30pm and 5.15–7pm; free; tourist visiting times: Mon–Sat 1–4.30pm, Sun 2–4.30pm; includes the church, choir stalls, roof, cloisters and museum in the Sala Capitular 💲 charge 🚇 Liceu/Jaume I

fountain, which is decorated with flowers at Corpus Christi and is the setting for a curious tradition, *l'ou com balla*, in which a fragile egg "dances" on the spouting water. The building contains the **Municipal History Archives,** a valuable collection of historical chronicles and documents. Extensions at the rear of the patio have opened up the building, revealing another angle on the Roman tower and part of the first city wall, dating from the 1st century BC. The

Enter the *catedral* by the main door. Its traditional, ornate chapels are a far cry from the simple majesty of Santa Maria del Mar *(see page 132)*. For any kind of spiritual peace it is essential to visit in off-peak hours, such as first thing in the morning, to avoid groups and the accumulation of human traffic; attending Mass is no solution, as the congregation chatters loudly and goes in and out at will.

The construction of the cathedral began in 1298 under the patronage

Recommended Restaurants, Bars & Cafés on pages 124–5

of Jaume II, on the spot where an early Christian church had been destroyed by the pillaging of Al-Mansur, the vizier of Córdoba, in 985. Some signs of it can be seen in the remarkable subterranean world beneath the present cathedral, which can be visited from the City History Museum (MHCB, *see page 120*).

The highlights

The main area consists of three naves and an apse with an ambulatory beneath an octagonal dome. Two 14th- and 15th-century towers rise at each end of the transept. Beneath the main altar is the crypt of Santa Eulàlia, and of particular note are the dome's multicoloured keystones. Some say that this is one of Catalonia's three "magnetic" points.

The tomb of Santa Eulàlia, behind the altar, is an important 14th-century work of art, executed in alabaster by a disciple of Giovanni Pisano during the same period as the episcopal cathedral. The most outstanding altarpiece is that of the Transfiguration, designed by Bernat Martorell in the chapel

dedicated to Sant Salvador, which was built in 1447.

The high-backed choir pews are by Pere Sanglada (1399), and the lower-backed benches were carved by Macià Bonafè towards the end of the same century. The retrochoir (the extension behind the high altar) was built in the early 16th century by Bartolomé Ordóñez. The Capella del Santo Cristo de Lepanto (Chapel of Christ Lepanto) contains the crucifix borne in the Christian flagship against the Ottomans in the battle of Lepanto. Built between 1405 and 1454, it is considered the finest example of Gothic art in the cathedral.

The oldest part is that of the Porta de Sant Ivo (St Ive's Door), where

TIP

Next to the entrance of the Casa de l'Ardiaca (see page 113), look out for the letterbox designed by the *modernista* architect Domènech i Montaner. The swallows suggest how fast the post should travel; the tortoise represents the reality.

LEFT: gilded altarpiece in one of the ornate side chapels in the cathedral. **BELOW LEFT:** the fountain in the cathedral cloister. **BELOW:** the imposing facade of the cathedral.

TIP

For a gargoyle's view of the city, take a lift to the rooftop of the cathedral (*see tourist visiting times, page 114*).

ABOVE: city view from the cathedral. **BELOW:** 13 geese live in the cathedral cloister.

some of the Romanesque windows and archways can still be seen. Most of the cathedral's more antique furnishings are in the MHCB, but there is a small collection in the **Sala Capitular** (Chapter House; opening times same as cathedral; charge, or as part of a tourist visit, *see page 114*).

A small pavilion beside the Porta de la Pietat shelters a 15th-century terracotta statue of St George by Antoni Claperós, and the door to the western end of the transept is made from marble taken from the earlier Romanesque cathedral.

The cathedral cloisters

On one side is the Santa Eulàlia Portal which leads to the **cathedral cloister**, a quiet haven and perhaps the most atmospheric part of the cathedral, with the sound of running water from the pretty fountain and a romantic garden of elegant palms, medlars and highly perfumed magnolia trees, all enclosed by 15th-century wrought-iron railings. Thirteen geese are the sole residents, symbolising the age of Santa Eulàlia, co-patron saint of Barcelona, when she died.

Plaça Sant Felip Neri ❸

Leave the cloister through the side door which gives on to **Plaça Garriga i Bachs**. To the left notice the picturesque bridge across the street (another neo-Gothic construction), linking two departments of the Generalitat. Cross the square to **Montjuïc del Bisbe**, a narrow street leading into **Plaça Sant Felip Neri**. This small square is a treasure, enclosed by heavy stone buildings and happily neglected, which increases its historic impact.

Adjoining the 18th-century church of Sant Felip Neri is a school, so if you coincide with playtime the peace will be shattered by shrieking children and stray footballs.

In fact, a large number of children were killed here when a bomb

Recommended Restaurants, Bars & Cafés on pages 124–5

dropped nearby during the Civil War. The pock-marked church façade tells the tale. The eccentric **Museu del Calçat** (Shoe Museum; Tue–Sun 11am–2pm; charge) was formerly in a street opposite the cathedral, **Corríbia**, cleared to make Avinguda de la Catedral, and was moved to this *plaça*, brick by brick. An enormous shoe made to measure for the Columbus statue in La Rambla and ex-President Jordi Pujol's shoes are among the curiosities.

You could contemplate the square from the shady terrace café of the exclusive boutique Hotel Neri, then take Sant Sever and go down **Baixada Santa Eulàlia** into a world apart, with hidden courtyards behind enor-

mous wooden doors and small dark workshops where furniture is polished and restored. At **Banys Nous** (New Baths), turn right past a shop selling embroidered antique nightdresses. On the wall opposite, a panel of ceramic tiles explains the origin of the street's name.

Plaça Sant Josep Oriol ❹

Where the street joins Palla (which, to the right, runs back to the cathedral past art galleries and antique shops), turn left towards **Plaça Sant Josep Oriol**. This lively square, where artists sell their work, is dominated by the sought-after terrace of the **Bar del Pi**, and is one of the most popular spots in the Old Town. Along with the adjoining Plaça del Pi and Placeta del Pi, it embraces the church of **Santa Maria del Pi**. Begun in 1322 and completed in the 15th century, this is a fine example of Catalan Gothic architecture, fortress-like on the exterior but ample and welcoming inside. The rose window is magnificent when lit from within. Local producers come in from the country

EAT

Recommended restaurants near the cathedral include La Cassola, with tasty Catalan home cooking, in Sant Sever, and El Portalón in Banys Nous. The latter, a timeless bodega, is a good bet in winter, when its warming bean stews go down well *(see pages 124–5)*.

LEFT: snails at the Catalan restaurant La Cassola in Sant Sever.
BELOW: Plaça Sant Felip Neri.

On Plaça del Pi, Ganiveteria Roca is a fascinating shop with a beautiful façade, crammed with thousands of knives and scissors of every kind (*ganivet* is the Catalan word for knife). Fashion victims will delight in Custo, a newcomer to this ancient square.

RIGHT: the Spanish and Catalan flags fly outside the Palau de la Generalitat. **BELOW:** Santa Maria del Pi is a prime example of Catalan Gothic. **BELOW RIGHT:** candles lit by the faithful.

to sell goat's cheese and honey at the market on the Plaça del Pi (first and third weekends of the month, Fri–Sun all day).

Buskers became so numerous here that local residents campaigned to have them banned, except between 6–8pm on Saturday and noon–2pm on Sunday. Guests of the popular Hotel Jardí no doubt appreciate the ruling. Before leaving the square check out the knife shop *(see margin)*, dating from 1911, and around the corner from it the very pretty street **Carrer Petritxol**.

The **Palau Fiveller**, at No. 4 in Plaça Sant Josep Oriol, is occupied by the Agricultural Institute. Take the narrow street **Ave Maria** that runs down its side and at the end turn right, back into Banys Nous. Traditional shops are giving way to more commercial enterprises, but at least one landmark, the wonderful **Obach** hat shop *(see page 67)*, remains unchanged. Turn left here and follow **Call**, the main street in Barcelona's Jewish Quarter until 1401 *(see page 123)*, as it winds up to Plaça Sant Jaume.

PLAÇA SANT JAUME ⑤

The area that today forms the **Plaça Sant Jaume** was inaugurated in 1823, at the same time as the streets **Ferràn** and **Jaume I**. It is the civic heart of the city, home to the **Ajuntament** (City Council), which runs Barcelona, and the **Generalitat** (government of Catalonia), although the Parliament building is in Parc de la Ciutadella *(see page 138)*. The current president of the Generalitat, since the end of 2010, is Artur Mas.

Recommended Restaurants, Bars & Cafés on pages 124–5

Palau de la Generalitat

The **Palau de la Generalitat** is guarded by the Mossos d'Esquadra, the autonomous police force. Opposite, the town councillors in the **Casa de la Ciutat** are protected by the Guàrdia Urbana. Demonstrations wind up in this square, as do festive parades, Barça fans and players after major football and basketball victories, and, of course, visiting dignitaries. This is where President Tarradellas was given a clamorous reception on his return from exile to attend the birth of the new democracy in 1977.

Both buildings are of Gothic origin and can be visited on key public holidays, such as Sant Jordi, 23 April, and La Mercè, 24 September. The Palau de la Generalitat can also be visited by booking online (www. gencat.cat) for the second or fourth weekend of the month. Each has some fine elements: the oldest part of the Casa de la Ciutat (Town Hall) is the **Saló de Cent**, created by Pere Llobet in 1373; the Gothic façade tucked down the side street **Ciutat** is the most delicate. The **Pati dels** Tarongers (a 16th-century courtyard full of orange trees) is the most famous part of the Palau de la Generalitat and the scene of many official photographs. From the square you can glimpse the painted ceilings of a large reception room.

Tourist Information

There is a tourist information office in the Town Hall, on the corner of Ciutat (Mon–Fri 8.30am– 8.30pm, Sat 9am–7pm, Sun 9am– 2pm). Take Ciutat out of the square and immediately turn left into Hercules, a quiet street leading to **Plaça Sant Just ❻**. This is an interesting, often overlooked corner of the Barri Gòtic with a strong sense of identity. The *plaça* has all the elements of a village: a church, a *colmado* (grocer's shop), a restaurant, a noble house, and children playing football.

The streets off here are also worth exploring, notably **Palma Sant Just** for the bodega and its breakfasts with wonderful omelettes, and **Lledó** for its medieval houses, some featuring trendy boutiques.

TIP

From early December until the fiesta of Els Reis (The Kings) on 6 January, the Plaça Sant Jaume is taken over by the largest Nativity scene in town – and the longest queues to visit it. Nativity figures are sold in the Cathedral Square throughout December.

BELOW: noisy festivities marking La Mercè in Plaça Sant Jaume.

BELOW: the Torre de Martí I. **BELOW RIGHT:** statue of the count-king Ramón Berenguer III (1082–1131).

The church of **Sant Just and Sant Pastor** was an ancient royal chapel until the 15th century. According to legend, it is built on the site of Barcelona's first Christian temple. The Cafè de l'Acadèmia spills out onto the square *(see page 124)*.

THE ROYAL QUARTER

Behind the cathedral, centring on the Plaça del Rei, is the Conjunt Monumental de la Plaça del Rei, the royal quarter of Barcelona's medieval count-kings. To get there from Plaça Sant Just, follow **Dagueria** past a cheese shop *(see margin)* and over Jaume I, turning right into Baixada Llibreteria and then left into Veguer. This leads to the Museu d'Història de la Ciutat (MHCB) and the Plaça del Rei at the end.

Plaça del Rei ➐

The **Plaça del Rei** is a fine medieval square, testimony to the nobility of the ancient city. It was here that all the flour brought into the city in payment of taxes was collected. The sculpture on the square is by the Basque artist Eduardo Chillida.

Entrance to the *plaça*'s former royal buildings, the Palau Reial Major, is from the Museu d'Història, accessed back on Veguer.

Museu d'Història de la Ciutat ➑

✉ Plaça del Rei, 7–9; www.museuhistoria.bcn.cat
☎ 93 256 2100 🕐 Tue–Sat 10am–7pm, winter until 5pm, Sun 10am–8pm 🎫 charge, free Sun from 3pm
🚇 Jaume I/Liceu

The museum's eclectic collection, not all on show, includes maps, models, Roman portraits, guild paraphernalia and an anarchist's bomb that damaged the Liceu opera house in 1893.

The museum also gives access to the excavations of the Roman city that flourished between the 1st and 7th centuries. Covering 4,000 sq metres (43,000 sq ft) beneath the Plaça del Rei, it offers an intriguing insight not only into Roman building methods, but also into commercial and domestic life.

A Royal City

The royal palace of the count-kings of Barcelona-Aragón, Palau Reial Major, begun in the 11th century, lies between the cathedral and the northern Roman wall. Its courtyard is now the Plaça del Rei, and beneath it you can see the foundations of the Roman episcopal palace from which it grew. At its core is the great hall, the Saló del Tinell, that has served as throne room, banqueting hall, Parliament and inquisitors' court. When the crown slipped from Barcelona's grasp and the palace decayed, Madrid's appointed viceroy had his residence built on the left side of the square, the Palau del Lloctinent *(see page 122)*. The 16th-century Gothic mansion, the City History Museum, was brought here brick by brick to house artefacts amassed for the 1929 Universal Exposition. While re-siting the building, the Roman city beneath was discovered, and since then the complex has been gradually restored.

Recommended Restaurants, Bars & Cafés on pages 124–5

Palau Reial Major

Also accessed from the museum is the **Palau Reial Major**, with vast vaulted ceilings, 13th-century triple-recess windows and 14th-century rose windows.

The main room of the palace, the great **Salò del Tinell**, was built by Guillem Carbonell, the architect to Pere III in 1359. Its six unreinforced arches span an unprecedented 15 metres (50ft). It was later converted to a Baroque church, only to recover its original appearance after restoration work during and after the Civil War. In the 15th century the Inquisition held court here. Legend has it that the walls of the tribunal cannot bear a lie to be told, and that if this occurred, the ceiling stones would move, adding further to the victims' terror.

Next door is the **Capella Reial de Santa Agata**, built for Jaume II (1302–12) using the Roman wall as its north side. The decorated ceiling timbers are by Alfonso de Córdoba, the beautiful Epiphany altarpiece painted by Jaume Huguet in 1465, and the Taule de Santa Agata in the Queen's Chapel from around 1500. It also houses the stone on which the saint's breasts were mutilated.

The **Torre de Martí I** is sometimes called a *mirador* because of its fine views over both the royal complex and the city. It was built by Antoni Carbonell and is named after Martí I ("the Humanist", 1356–1410), last in the 500-year dynasty of Barcelona count-kings. The silhouette of the box-shaped Renaissance tower built like a dovecote is an outstanding feature of the palace.

On the northern side of Santa Agata chapel, outside the Roman walls, is the Plaça Ramon Berenguer El Gran, distinguished by

The remains of the Roman city are accessed via the Museu d'Història de la Ciutat.

BELOW: you don't have to visit the Museu Frederic Marès to enjoy its pleasant courtyard and café.

Museu Frederic Marès has an excellent collection of Spanish sculpture.

ABOVE RIGHT: carving on a sarcophagus in the Museu Frederic Marès. **BELOW:** Palau del Lloctinent.

the statue of the king on his horse. It is well worth a detour to get a feel of the Roman past and see how the medieval city was built on the Roman walls. A metal panel explains which part of the Roman city it was and illustrates an itinerary around what remains of the walls and towers.

Palau del Lloctinent ❾

✉ Comtes, 2 🕐 daily 10am–7pm
🆓 free 🚇 Jaume I

Back in the Plaça del Rei, opposite the chapel is the Palau del Lloctinent, magnificently restored. Part of it is open to the public. When the kingdoms of Catalonia and Aragón were joined with that of Castile, Carlos V created the office of deputy *(lloctinent)* for the court's representative, and this palace, the official residence, was built in 1549 by Antoni Carbonell. The facade is Catalan Gothic, but the inner courtyard is one of the few examples of Renaissance architecture left in the city and has a wonderful carved wooden ceiling. Until recently it was the headquarters of the Arxiu de la Corona d'Aragó (Archive of the Crown of Aragon).

Museu Frederic Marès ❿

✉ Plaça de Sant Iu, 5–6;
www.museumares.bcn.cat 📞 93 256 3500 🕐 Tue–Sat 10am–7pm, Sun 11am–8pm 🅰 charge, free Sun from 3pm 🚇 Jaume I

Follow Comtes down the side of the cathedral to a tiny square, Sant Iu, which leads into the charming courtyard of the Museu Frederic Marès. This private collection, donated by the Catalan sculptor Marès in 1946, includes Spanish sculpture, with medieval pieces in the crypt. Upstairs, the Museu Sentimental gives an insight into life in the city in the 18th and 19th centuries.

Comtes leads out into the **Pla de la Seu**, in front of the cathedral. On the right is a beautiful Gothic building, the **Pia Almoina**, where 100 meals were once given to the poor daily. It now houses the **Museu Diocesà ⓫** (Tue–Sat 10am–2pm, 5–8pm, Sun 11am–2pm; charge), with a small collection of religious objects and paintings and which also holds temporary exhibitions. ❑

Recommended Restaurants, Bars & Cafés on pages 124–5

The Jewish City

In Catalonia the Jewish Quarter of a town or city is known as the *call*, meaning "narrow street" or "lane". A marked route leads visitors through Barcelona's *call*.

Situated west of the Roman metropolis in what is now the Gothic Quarter, the *call* reached its peak of importance during the Middle Ages and had a remarkable cultural reputation. For centuries the only university in Catalonia was the Universidad Judía or Escuela Mayor. This community also had a talent for finance, and monarchs were known to apply for loans. Their knowledge was so advanced that they were made ambassadors at court, but their display of wealth and their superior lifestyle created great jealousy.

The fortunes of the Jews began to decline in 1243 when Jaume I ordered the separation of the Jewish Quarter from the rest of the city and made Jews wear long hooded capes with red or yellow circles. Fights erupted, and worsened when a rumour spread that Jews were responsible for bringing the Black Death to Spain. Full-scale rioting in several cities in 1391 was provoked mainly by a group from Seville who encouraged the population to storm houses in the Jewish Quarter and murder the occupants.

The riots began in Valencia and spread to Mallorca, Barcelona, Girona, Lleida and Perpignan. Those in Barcelona were by far the most violent; the *qahqal* (the original Hebrew

for *call*) was virtually destroyed and about 1,000 Jews died. The survivors were forced to convert to Christianity or flee, despite the efforts of the national guard to defend the lives and properties of the persecuted.

Joan I ordered the arrest and execution of 15 Castilians responsible for the uprising, but despite this the *call* was never rebuilt. By 1395 the flow of anti-Semitism had reached such proportions that the synagogue on the street called Sanahuja was converted into a church (Sant Jaume, in Carrer de Ferràn). In 1396, the principal synagogue was rented to a pottery maker.

The *call* disappeared in 1401 when the synagogues were abolished and Jewish cemeteries destroyed. It was not until 1931 that the first new Spanish synagogue was established. It was shut down during the Civil War, reopened in 1948, and later moved to its present site in Carrer d'Avenir.

Today the only evidence of the prosperous era of the *call* is certain stretches of the Carrer de Banys Nous and the Carrer del Call. The City History Museum has signposted a route through the Jewish Quarter and opened a centre explaining its history: Centre d'Interpretació del Call (Placeta Manuel Ribé, Wed–Fri 11am–2pm, Sat 10am–7pm, winter until 5pm, Sun 10am–8pm; charge).   ❑

ABOVE: ceremony in the *call*. **RIGHT:** an illustration from the Barcelona Haggadah.

BEST RESTAURANTS, BARS AND CAFÉS

Restaurants

Prices for a three-course dinner per person with a bottle of house wine:
€ = under €25
€€ = €25–40
€€€ = €40–60
€€€€ = over €60

Modern restaurants designed within medieval buildings, fusion food in old local bars, one of the best Japanese restaurants in town, and economical family-run establishments – this historic quarter has it all.

Agut

Gignàs, 16 ⓒ 93 315 1709 ⓒ L & D Tue–Sat, L only Sun. €€ [p304, B3]
Bustling, noisy, traditional restaurant with heaps of atmosphere and walls lined with paintings. Good for getting the "Barcelona feel" and for succulent Catalan specialities.

Bosco

Capellans, 9 ⓒ 93 412 1370 ⓒ B, L & D Tue–Sat, L only Sun. € [p304, B1]
Hidden from the shopping crowds of Portal de l'Angel is this peaceful restaurant with a terrace on the quiet square. Fresh fish and seasonal vegetables from La Boqueria are on the lunchtime set menu.

Buenas Migas

Baixada de Santa Clara, 2 ⓒ 93 269 1287 ⓒ B, L & D daily. € [p304, B2]
This picturesque branch of the successful *focacceria* chain with branches all over town is tucked behind the cathedral in ancient premises. The savoury pies with spinach or artichoke are delicious. Good for a light lunch.

Café Babel

Correu Vell, 14 ⓒ 93 315 2309 ⓒ L & D daily. € [p304, B2]
Pocket handkerchief-sized bar big on atmosphere, with quiet terrace under one of the remaining Roman towers. All-day snacks and sandwiches and occasional live music.

Cafè de l'Acadèmia

Lledó, 1 ⓒ 93 315 0026 ⓒ B, L & D Mon–Fri. €€ [p304, B2]
Delicious new interpretations of classic Catalan dishes have made this low-key place one of the best options in town. Tables in the medieval square. Popular with politicians from nearby Plaça Sant Jaume. Book early for dinner. Closed at weekends.

Cafè d'Estiu

Plaça Sant Iu, 5–6 ⓒ 93 310 3014 ⓒ B, L, & D Tue–Sun, Mar–Sept. € [p304, B2]
Delightful café serving refreshments and light snacks in a courtyard next to the Museu Frederic Marès entrance.

Can Fly

Baixada de Viladecols, 6 ⓒ 93 snacks served all day Tue–Sun. € [p304, B2]
Attractive bar squeezed into a corner overlooking one of the Roman towers. Delicious snacks, unusual salads, *torrades* (toast rubbed with oil and tomato, served with cheese or ham), and the best olives ever.

El Gran Café

Avinyó, 9 ⓒ 93 318 7986 ⓒ L & D daily. €€ (set menu €) [p304, B2]
A classic old restaurant with Parisian overtones, but quite expensive unless you order the set-lunch menu.

El Portalón

Banys Nous, 20 ⓒ 93 302 1187 ⓒ L & D Mon–Sat. € [p304, B2]
Barrels, pitchers of wine, nicotine-stained walls and old men playing dominoes – this place oozes atmosphere, and the set menu chalked on a blackboard is good value. Don't miss their *potajes* (bean or chickpea stews) in winter.

LEFT: Els Quatre Gats. **RIGHT:** the enticing Bar del Pi.

Els Quatre Gats

Montsió, 3 ☎ 93 302 4140
Ⓒ B, L & D daily. €€ (set
menu Mon–Sat L €)
[p304, B1]
The house Puig i Cadal-
fach built, made famous
by Picasso and friends.
The food is very accept-
able but it's not a priority.

La Cassola

Sant Sever, 3 ☎ 93 318
1580 Ⓒ L Mon–Fri,
D Thur–Fri. € [p304, B2]
Family-run, with regular
clientele from nearby
offices who enjoy good
home-made food.

La Fonda

Escudellers, 10 ☎ 93 301
75 15 Ⓒ L & D daily. €
(set menu Mon–Sat D €)
[p304, A2]
The popularity of this
restaurant, part of the
Quinze Nits family,
comes from its appeal-
ing decor and reasonably
priced Catalan food.
Keep an eye on your
belongings as you stand
in the inevitable queue.

L'Antic Bocoi del Gòtic

Baixada de Viladecols, 3
☎ 93 310 5067 Ⓒ D Mon–
Sat. €–€€ [p304, B2]
Inspiring, delicious Catalan specialities plus
imaginative salads. A
warm and characterful
interior, incorporating
part of the old city wall.

Les Quinze Nits

Plaça Reial, 6 ☎ 93 317
3075 Ⓒ L & D daily. €
[p304, A2]
The only way to beat the
queues for this elegant

restaurant serving cheap
Catalan food is to follow
a northern European
timetable (lunch at 1pm,
dinner at 8.30pm).
Sitting on a terrace overlooking the majestic
square is a treat.

MariscCo

Plaça Reial, 8 ☎ 93 412
4536 Ⓒ L & D daily. €€
[p304, B2]
Stylishly renovated
premises that were not
too long ago a taxider-
mist's workshop, in
prime position in this
handsome square. Has
appealing outdoor tables
and specialises in
seafood and rice dishes.
This eaterie is some-
where you can eat at
northern European hours
as they do not close in
the afternoon.

Matsuri

Plaça Regomir, 1 ☎ 93 268
1535 Ⓒ D Mon–Sat. €
[p304, B2]
Filling a gap in the mar-
ket, this good-looking
restaurant specialises in
southeast Asian food,
which is given a personal
interpretation by its
creative chef.

Peimong

Templaris, 6 ☎ 93 318
2873 Ⓒ L & D Tue–Sat. L
only Sun. € [p304, B2]
A small, very simple
restaurant just behind
Plaça Sant Jaume, serv-
ing authentic *ceviche*
(raw fish marinated in
lemon juice with fresh
coriander and spicy pep-
pers) and other Peru-

vian specialities, including Peruvian beers and
Inca Kola.

Shunka

Sagristans, 5 ☎ 93 412
4991 Ⓒ L & D Tue–Sun.
€€ [p304, B1]
Tucked away in a quiet
street near the cathe-
dral, this hidden spot
ranks high among the
many Japanese restau-
rants in the city. Its
menu is impressive
enough for the renowned
chef Ferran Adrià (of el
Bulli fame) to be a regu-
lar customer.

Taller de Tapas

Plaça Sant Josep Oriol, 9
☎ 93 301 8020 Ⓒ L & D
daily. € [p304, B2]
A clever formula whereby
you can sit down to
tapas, instead of fighting
for space at the bar, has
turned this place into a
success story with sev-
eral branches around
town, including one at
Argenteria, 51 in the
Born and one on the
Rambla Catalunya,
49–51 in Eixample.
Perfect for light dinners.
The extensive menu
includes puddings.

Bars and Cafés

Favourite squares for
coffee or drinks are
the Plaça del Pi and
adjoining Plaça Sant
Josep Oriol, where
there are several
cafés, including the
enticing terrace of the
Bar del Pi. Serious coffee enthusiasts should
not miss the **Mesón
del Café**, Llibreteria,
16, something of a
curio in today's
designer city. Nearby
Can Conesa, Llibrete-
ria, 1, in a corner of the
Plaça de Sant Jaume,
is a traditional sand-
wich bar making some
of the best toasted
bocatas in town, as the
queue testifies. With
its cool music, stylish
interior and creative
tapes, **Ginger**, Lledó, 2,
has become an essen-
tial stop on the night
scene, while timeless,
cavernous **Glaciar** is

still one of the best
bars in Plaça Reial.
Taste the boutique
hotel experience with-
out the bill by having a
drink on the terrace of
the **Neri Hotel** in Plaça
Sant Felip Neri, or jos-
tle your way to the
counter to select *tapes*
in one of the many bars
in Carrer Mercè near
the port, like the Gali-
cian **Celta**, at No. 16.

Recommended Restaurants, Bars & Cafés on pages 140–1

LA RIBERA, BORN AND PARC DE LA CIUTADELLA

The narrow streets and grand mansions of La Ribera resound with reminders of medieval commerce, but the focus is switching to a vibrant bar and restaurant scene

The *barri* of La Ribera is loosely defined as that part of the Old Town that is separated from the Barri Gòtic by Via Laietana. There is a beaten track to the door of its star museum, the Museu Picasso, but the area has many other attractions, including the modish Born area, so take the long way round to get there and enjoy discovering its many contrasts, from the present-day rag trade to medieval merchants' houses, from new social and urban developments to the most beautiful church in Barcelona.

Palau de la Música Catalana ❶

✉ Carrer Palau de la Música, 4–6; www.palaumusica.org 📞 902-442 882 ⏰ guided tours daily 10am–3.30pm, Aug and Easter until 6pm ⓔ charge 🚇 Urquinaona

Like so many of the city's *barris*, La Ribera is a richly woven texture of contrasts. Nothing is more representative of this than the **Palau de la Música Catalana**, an extravaganza of a concert hall designed by leading *modernista* architect Domènech i Montaner in 1908 *(see pages 55 and 57)*, and declared a World Heritage

building by Unesco. The only concert hall in Europe to be naturally lit, in all its ornate splendour it was cramped uncomfortably between dull neighbours. However, in a major renovation plan by Oscar Tusquets, architect of an earlier extension, it has been liberated and now has a new space for chamber concerts, the Petit Palau, a rehearsal room and an elegant restaurant.

One of of the best ways to visit it is to take a guided tour. They are popular, so it is worth booking in

LEFT: Passeig del Born. **RIGHT:** a busker plays to an audience in La Ribera.

Details from a stained-glass window in the 10th-century church of Sant Pere de les Puel·les.

RIGHT: mosaic details on the facade of the Palau de la Música Catalana.

advance. Alternatively pop in for a coffee in its bar to sample the atmosphere and see plenty of *modernista* detail, or even better attend one of the concerts in its busy classical season, or during the International Jazz Festival *(see page 270)*.

Characterful squares

Continue along **Carrer Sant Pere Més Alt** through the heart of today's rag-trade district, the wholesale end of Catalonia's once great textile industry. On weekdays it buzzes with activity, particularly around the 19th-century arcades, like the Passeig Sert, birthplace of painter Josep Maria Sert (1876–1945), where old warehouses have been converted into lofts.

The street emerges into the comparative tranquillity of **Plaça Sant Pere ❷**, site of a much-renovated 10th-century church, **Sant Pere de les Puel·les**, a former Benedictine monastery. In the middle of this triangular square is a *modernista* drinking

fountain, designed by Pere Falqués, famed for his benches-cum-lampposts on Passeig de Gràcia.

Follow **Basses Sant Pere** down past a vintage shop and local bars, keeping a firm grip on your rucksack and camera, to **Plaça Sant Agustí Vell ❸**. Signs of urban cleansing are evident, but new social housing and created *plaças* have not wiped out local colour altogether. There are several terrace bars, but do not miss **Mundial**, a 1950s time warp, famed for its seafood *tapes (see page 141)*.

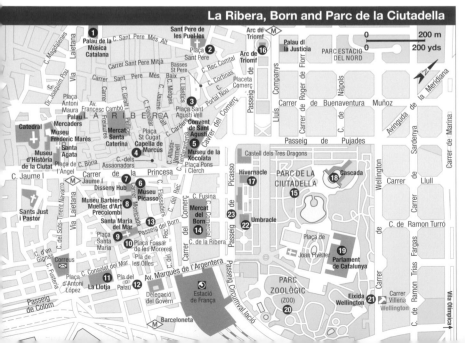

La Ribera, Born and Parc de la Ciutadella

Recommended Restaurants, Bars & Cafés on pages 140–1

EAT

For sweet treats, sample the wonderfully rich hot chocolate in the Museu de la Xocolata or visit Brunells *pastisseria* on the corner of Montcada and Princesa. If you are not tempted by the *pastisseria*'s meringue-like *roque de Montserrat*, inspired by the sacred mountain, there are plenty of other cakes and pastries to choose from.

From here, one option is to take Carrer Carders, with several interesting shops, to the delightful Romanesque chapel of **Marcús** ❹, where post horses were blessed on the main route out, being just beyond the city walls and the Portal Major. Turn left into Montcada for the Museu Picasso *(see pages 130–1)*. Alternatively, take one of the narrow alleys to the right, leading to the magnificent Santa Caterina market *(see page 69)*.

Another option from Plaça Sant Agustí Vell is to meander down Tantarantana, to the former **Convent de Sant Agustí** ❺ at Comerç, 36. Now a civic centre, you can wander through its 14th-century cloisters. It also houses the **Museu de la Xocolata** (Mon–Sat 10am–7pm, Sun 10am–3pm; charge), which may interest children and chocolate-lovers.

Assaonadors and Princesa

Just before Princesa, turn right into **Assaonadors**, which immediately on the right opens into a long *plaça*, **Allada-Vermell**, a typical Barcelona "hard" square. Created by the demolition of a row of housing, it brings light and space into the dense *barri*, providing a recreation area and several bars good for snacks.

Continue along Assaonadors, taking the first left which leads into **Princesa**. The Parc de la Ciutadella *(see pages 135–9)* is at the end of the road, but turn right towards the city

centre again. It is a busy, narrow street full of lorries unloading goods and taxis unloading tourists by Montcada. On the corner before turning into Montcada you might be tempted by Brunells *pastisseria (see margin, right)*.

STREET OF MUSEUMS

Montcada has become museum street supreme since the local authorities started renovating its medieval palaces in 1957, but it is a lot more besides and can be enjoyed on many levels. Named after members of a noble medieval family who

ABOVE: the Palau de la Música Catalana's café.
BELOW: statue of Catalan composer Luis Millet outside the Palau de la Música Catalana.

The **Museu Picasso** opened in 1963 and now occupies five palaces: Palau Berenguer d'Aguilar, Baró de Castel-let, Meca, Casa Mauri and Finestres. The last two, opened in 1999, are for temporary exhibitions; the main entrance is through the 15th-century Aguilar palace. Its beautiful court-yard, with a surrounding first-floor gallery and pointed archways resting on slender columns, was designed by Marc Safont, who is best known for the inner patio of the **Generalitat** building *(see page 119)*.

The museum has the most com-plete collection of Picasso's early works, including sketches in school books and a masterly portrait of his

died during the conquest of Mal-lorca (1229), it was the city's most elegant district from the 12th to the 18th century. It linked the water-front with the commercial areas, when Catalonia's trading was at its height. The merchants' palaces reflect this former prosperity.

ABOVE: the Picasso Museum is one of the city's major tourist attractions. **RIGHT:** the artist's familiar signature. **BELOW RIGHT:** Picasso postcards in the museum shop.

Museu Picasso ⑥

✉ Montcada, 15–23; www.museu picasso.bcn.cat ☎ 93-256 3000 ⏰ Tue–Sun including public holidays 10am–7.30pm ⓒ charge; free Sun from 3pm 🚇 Jaume I

Picasso in Barcelona

Pablo Ruiz Picasso was born in Málaga in southern Spain in 1881. His family soon moved to La Coruña in Galicia, then to Barcelona in 1895, where his father took up the post of painting professor at La Llotja School of Art. One department of this school can still be found in Carrer Avinyó, and the story goes that a brothel in this street inspired the title (and content) of Picasso's landmark painting *Les Demoiselles d'Avignon* (1906–7). The painting caused shock and outrage among art critics. Picasso's precocious genius is legendary: aged just 14, he entered his father's school, completing the month-long entrance exams in a single day. He repeated this feat two years later at the Royal Acad-emy in Madrid before abandoning his studies and setting out for Paris. He never again lived in Barcelona, but donated a considerable number of his works to the museum here.

Recommended Restaurants, Bars & Cafés on pages 140–1

SHOP

The gift shop in the Museu Barbier-Mueller is full of Latin-American colour from Mayan textiles to Colombian gold.

mother, done when he was only 16 years old. The Blue Period (1901–4) is also well represented, as are his ceramics. It is an absorbing collection, although there are only a few of Picasso's later works, including the fascinating studies of *Las Meninas* dating from the 1950s.

Disseny Hub Barcelona ➐

✉ Montcada, 12; www.dhub-bcn.cat
📞 93-256 2300 🕐 Tue–Sat 11am–7pm, Sun 11am–8pm 💶 charge; free Sun from 3pm; tickets cover entry to DHUB Pedralbes 🚇 Jaume I

Opposite is another noble Gothic palace, the Marquès de Lló, home to the new Disseny Hub Barcelona (DHUB), a new concept design museum which involves research as well as exhibitions. With links to the business world it aims to be a leader of its kind. The DHUB Montcada and DHUB Pedralbes, which houses the Textile, Graphic and Decorative Arts collections (*see page 214*), are the two temporary locations, which are due to move in 2012–13 to the much-vaunted Design Museum, under construction in Glòries.

Museu Barbier-Mueller d'Art Precolombí ➑

✉ Montcada, 14; www.barbier-mueller.ch/barcelone 📞 93-310 4516 🕐 Tue–Fri 11am–7pm,

Sat–Sun 11am–8pm 💶 charge; free Sun from 3pm 🚇 Jaume I

Adjoining it, in the Palau Nadal, is the **Museu Barbier-Mueller d'Art Precolombí**, which has a small but prestigious collection of pre-Columbian art, representing most styles of pre-Hispanic American civilisations. The gift shop has some beautiful pieces.

Shops and galleries

Continuing down Montcada you come to the Palau Cervelló, at No. 25, housing the art gallery **Galeria**

ABOVE: Museu Picasso.
BELOW: Carrer Montcada, also known as museum street.

EAT

For refreshments on Montcada, pop into the marble-and-tile haven El Xampanyet (No. 22) for a glass of sparkling wine and some anchovies. On Placeta Montcada, with its fine palm tree, is the authentic Basque bar Euskal Etxea. You must arrive at aperitif time (around 1pm or 8pm) to catch the best *pintxos*, or else you'll have to opt for a full meal in the restaurant.

RIGHT: an exhibit in the small but excellent Museum of Pre-Columbian Art.
BELOW: specialities at Euskal Etxea on Placeta Montcada.

Maeght (Tue–Fri 10am–2pm, 4–7pm, Sat 10am–2pm, free). Opposite is the Palau Dalmases where at a price you can sip a cocktail and hear live opera or flamenco. Bijou shops and fashion boutiques are multiplying here, replacing the traditional local shops.

On the right, just before the Passeig del Born, is **Sombrerers**, named, like many in the area, after the medieval guilds (in this case, 'the hatters'). Follow its shade, with the towering edifice of Santa Maria del Mar on the left, past Casa Gispert, an exquisite grocery specialising in nuts, to reach the **Plaça Santa Maria**, once the church's graveyard. The Gothic fountain is one of the oldest in the city, dating from 1402.

Santa Maria del Mar ❾

✉ Plaça Santa Maria ☎ 93-310 2390 🕐 Mon–Sat 9am–1.30pm and 4.30–8.30pm, Sun 10am–1.30pm and 5–8.30pm 🆓 free 🚇 Jaume I

On reaching the square, stand back and take in the Gothic facade of the Basílica de Santa Maria del Mar, con-sidered by many – and justly so – to be the city's most beautiful church.

The church was built relatively quickly, between 1329 and 1384, resulting in a purity of style which ranks it as the most perfect example of Gothic church architecture in Catalonia. All the local corporations collaborated in the building, and it became a symbol of the economic and political power of Catalonia during this period.

Main features

The facade exhibits all the characteristics of the Catalan Gothic style: "prevalence of horizontal lines; flat

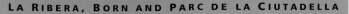

Recommended Restaurants, Bars & Cafés on pages 140–1

TIP

Santa Maria del Mar is a popular venue for concerts (as well as for fashionable weddings), so check local listings for a recommended opportunity to sit back and enjoy this sacred corner of Barcelona.

terraced roofing; wide open spaces; strong buttresses and octagonal towers ending in terraces", according to Alexandre Cirici, the Catalan art historian. It is a much more down-to-earth style than northern European Gothic, lacking the decorative filigree and pointed spires of the latter.

The rose window is 15th-century, the original having been lost in the earthquake of 1428. The interior is breathtaking in its elegance. The church is built in what is known as the "salon" design, with three lofty and almost identical naves, which contribute to the sense of space.

Ironically, the drama of more recent history has contributed to this purity: fire during the Civil War destroyed a great deal of the interior, which left it free of over-ornate decoration. The octagonal columns are 13 metres (43ft) apart, a distance no other medieval structure was able to achieve.

Leave through the side door of the church to see the **Plaça Fossar de les Moreres** ⑩, a memorial to the fallen in the 1714 siege of Barcelona *(see page 36)*, who are buried here in the former cemetery. Designed in 1986 by Carme Fiol, one of the leading architects in Barcelona's urban space programme, it is a venue for Catalan nationalists to meet on 11

September, La Diada, the day Barcelona fell and the Catalan national holiday.

THE OLD COMMERCIAL DISTRICT

Take d'Espaseria from this side of the church to Consolat del Mar. On one side is **La Llotja** ⑪, the former stock exchange (now in Passeig de Gràcia). Its core is from the 14th century, but the outer shell was completed in 1802. Part of the Acadèmia de Bellas Artes, where Picasso,

ABOVE: whiling away the evening on the Plaça Santa Maria.
BELOW: the facade of the lovely Santa Maria del Mar.

Gaudí and Miró studied, is still on
an upper floor.

The main facade of La Llotja
looks over **Pla del Palau** , where
a royal palace once stood. Now
devoted mostly to restaurants, it
was the political centre of town for
a period during the 18th and 19th
centuries under the dominant
viceroy. There are several good
restaurants to choose from and a
small playground in the square.

Keeping on the same pavement, walk
through to **Plaça de les Olles** (Square
of the Cooking Pots), a charming little square with pleasant terrace cafés.
One ordinary-looking bar is in fact
one of the city's best places to eat,
Cal Pep *(see page 140)*. In the far
corner turn into Vidrieria, another
street named after a medieval guild
('the glaziers', *see box*), to reach the
hub of the Born.

Passeig del Born

Glass and tin fairs used to be held in
the Passeig del Born, as well as jousts
and tournaments from the 13th to the
17th century. Take time to wander

along this boulevard and its adjoining streets, where the quirky bars,
shops and art galleries change hands
and style with remarkable frequency,
but where a few stalwarts remain.

At the end, in Plaça Comercial,
there are several good cafés and
restaurants, any of which would make
a fine place to contemplate the mag-

RIGHT: protecting La
Llotja. **BELOW:** the
wrought-iron facade of
Mercat del Born.

Medieval Guilds

Many of the streets in the *barri* of La
Ribera are named after trades, a
throwback to the medieval boom when
guilds were formed to look after the inter-
ests of craftsmen. At their height between
the 13th and 15th centuries, there were
135 *gremis* (guilds), and 52 streets still
carry their names. Watch out for Sombrerers (hatters), Flassaders (blanket
weavers), Mirallers (mirror makers),
Argenteria (silversmiths), Assaonadors
(tanners), Agullers (needlemakers) and
Semoleres (pasta makers). The Museu
del Calçat in Plaça Sant Felip Neri *(see
page 117)* is housed in the guildhall of the
shoemakers, the first guild to be formed
and the last to be disbanded in the 20th
century, when the Civil War broke out.

Recommended Restaurants, Bars & Cafés on pages 140–1

nificent wrought-iron **Mercat del Born ⑭**, designed by Fontseré and Cornet in 1873. The building functioned as Barcelona's central wholesale fruit and vegetable market from 1876 until 1971. Recent excavations revealed valuable archaeological remains of life before the citadel was built *(see box, page 136)*, which will be exposed when the building reopens as a cultural centre in late 2012.

PARC DE LA CIUTADELLA ⑮

✉ Passeig de Pujades/Passeig de Picasso ⓒ summer daily 8am–9pm, winter 8am–8pm ⓐ free ⓟ Jaume I/ Arc de Triomf

Just beyond this area is Barcelona's oldest and most visited park, the Parc de la Ciutadella, which is also one of the city's most attractive. It is easy to while away half a day here, simply walking in the fresher air, or enjoying some of the diverse activities on offer. Located between the Old Town and the new Vila Olímpica, it has two entrances on Passeig de Picasso.

However, one of the most interesting approaches, which also gives the park its historical perspective, is

from the northern end of Passeig de Lluís Companys, next to the Arc de Triomf (easily reached by the metro of the same name, or by bus).

Arc de Triomf ⑯

This enormous brick arch served as the entrance to the 1888 World Exposition site *(see page 37)*, which was held on the redeveloped land that was previously the site of the citadel of the occupying Spanish forces *(see box, page 136)*. From the top of Passeig de Lluís Companys you can look up **Passeig Sant Joan** – a typical Eixample street with architectural echoes

The rejuvenated area in and around the Passeig del Born is full of boutiques, speciality food shops, restaurants and bars.

BELOW: colourful street life in La Ribera.

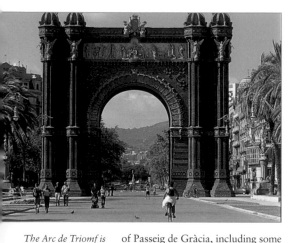

The Arc de Triomf is an imposing structure that was built as the entrance to the 1888 World Exposition.

palms are some of the most attractive of the many species growing in the city.

In front of the monumental Palau de la Justicia (Law Courts), old men play *petanca* (a southern European form of bowls), while cyclists vie for space with dog-walkers and retired couples who sit on pieces of cardboard playing card games. At the end is the main entrance to the Parc de la Ciutadella.

Park life

Interesting buildings remain from its military past *(see box, below)* and from its glorious time as the Exposition showground, but the most remarkable aspect of the park is its refreshing tranquillity. It is a real city park, full of skateboards and footballs, prams and toddlers. There are bicycles made for six for hire, as well as rowing boats on the lake. On Sunday large families parade in their best outfits before lunch, and New Age drummers meet for jam sessions. Yet it is still peaceful. Constantly tended by municipal gardeners, it is verdant, scented and shady.

of Passeig de Gràcia, including some fine *modernista* houses – towards the Collserola range.

The light and space around the Arc de Triomf are truly representative of Barcelona. Designed by Josep Vilaseca, the arch includes sculptures by Josep Llimona, among others. It is easy to imagine visitors to the Exposition sweeping down this thoroughfare to the showground, past the magnificent street lamps. Today's

Ciutadella's History

The name, La Ciutadella (which means citadel, or fortress), has its origins in the use to which Felipe V put this land. After the fall of Barcelona in 1714, following a siege by Franco-Spanish troops, he ordered the building of a fortress capable of housing 8,000 soldiers who would control the city in his name. To do this it was necessary to demolish 40 streets and 1,262 buildings. Remains have been discovered beneath the Mercat del Born. Barceloneta was built to accommodate the evicted residents.

In 1869 General Prim ceded the land to the city for conversion into a public park; the Town Hall issued a public tender for the landscaping, which went to Josep Fontseré. His plan was approved in 1873 but it was not until 1888, the year of the World Exposition, that the park began to be a reality, emerging in a shape later to be damaged by bombing in the Civil War.

Recommended Restaurants, Bars & Cafés on pages 140–1

On the right as you enter is the **Castell dels Tres Dragons** (Castle of the Three Dragons), designed by Domènech i Montaner. It was intended to be the restaurant of the 1888 Exposition, though it never opened as such. However, it was one of the first *modernista* projects in Barcelona and the architect's studio for years. Until 2010 it was the Zoological Museum, now moved to the Museu Blau in the Forum *(see page 171)*.

The Hivernacle 🔟

Behind the building is the beautiful Hivernacle, an elegant greenhouse bursting with tropical plants, due to be reopened after restoration work. Beyond it is a more classical-looking structure built to be a museum in 1878, the first public one in the city. More recently it has been the Geology Museum, but the collection is now in the Museu Blau *(see above)*.

The Cascada 🔟

Cross over the inner road and follow signs to the Cascada, the monumental fountain and artificial lake

designed by Fontseré in 1875; both the cascade and the lake were intended to camouflage a huge water deposit in the central section of the waterfall, which can be reached by two flanking, symmetrical stairways. Curiously, Gaudí worked on this project as a young architecture student. Something of a landmark and meeting place, its esplanade is often used for concerts, shows or fairs.

ABOVE: lounging and boating in the Parc de la Ciutadella. **BELOW:** families having fun.

Barcelona's zoo has a good reputation, particularly for its lowland gorillas and dolphin show.

RIGHT: the elegant Hivernacle.
BELOW: the Cascada, a monumental fountain designed in 1875.

Catalan Parliament

With your back to the Cascada, follow the boating lake round either way to the Plaça de Joan Fiveller, where there is a serene, oval formal garden designed by French landscape architect J.C.N. Forestier. The statue in the lake is *El Desconsol*, one of Catalan sculptor Josep Llimona's most highly regarded pieces.

This square is bordered by the remnants of the citadel era: the Governor's Palace, now a secondary school, the chapel and the arsenal.

This last is now where the **Parlament de Catalunya** ⑲ sits, guarded by the Catalan police, the Mossos d'Esquadra.

Parc Zoològic ⑳

✉ Parc de la Ciutadella; www.zoobarcelona.com ☎ 93-225 6780 ⏱ summer daily 10am–7pm, winter 10am–5pm ⓒ charge 🚇 Barceloneta/Arc de Triomf, Ciutadella Vila Olímpica

Follow the paved road towards the park gates to the Parc Zoològic, or Zoo, founded in 1892. Its most

famous inmate was Snowflake (Floquet de Neu), the only albino gorilla in captivity, who died amid much lamenting in 2003, and was succeeded by various non-albino descendants. Highlights include the Aquarama dolphin show (hourly at weekends).

Exiting from the zoo

From within the zoo the **Wellington exit** ㉑ leads to the street of the same name and takes you to the **Vila Olímpica** and its beaches *(see pages 164–5)*. A tram runs from here to Plaça de les Glòries, with another route down to Diagonal Mar and the Fòrum site with its beach *(see page 171)*. The metro is also close by, but for further exploration take **Avinguda Icària** into the Olympic Village, or head for the Hotel Arts (the right-hand skyscraper) passing through a small, modern park, **Parc Cascades**, above the Ronda Litoral, with a towering sculpture titled *David i Goliat* by Antoni Llena.

You might like to complete your day with a swim on Barceloneta beach and dinner in the Olympic Port. If this sounds appealing, but the zoo doesn't, there is another exit from the park on Pujades, behind the Cascade. Turn right and follow Wellington past the haunting brick structure, the **Diposit de les Aigües**, which once

Recommended Restaurants, Bars & Cafés on pages 140–1

stored water on its roof. Part of this building has been impressively restored as the library of the nearby University Pompeu Fabra.

The Umbracle 22

If you prefer to do full justice to the Ciutadella, from the main entrance to the zoo head up towards the Arc de Triomf and on your left is the **Umbracle**. This beautiful arched building, with fine iron columns and wooden-slatted roof, was also designed by Fontseré. It offers much-needed shade for the more delicate species in the park. The dim light inside is reminiscent of a jungle.

Passeig de Picasso 23

A small gate by the Umbracle leads out of the park to the Passeig de Picasso. The handsome arcaded apartment blocks here were designed by Fontseré as an integral part of his redevelopment plans. Some good bars and a bike-rental shop are located under the arches. Further up the road are the Aire de Barcelona Arab baths, perfect for weary limbs after an excess of sightseeing. A large modern

sculpture in a transparent cube on the park boundary is by leading Catalan artist Antoni Tàpies and was designed as a homage to Picasso.

Opposite the park entrance is the broad street **Marquès de l'Argentera**. Spain's first railway line was inaugurated here in 1848. The station, the **Estació de França**, was little more than a shack when it opened in 1929, yet was the largest in Europe. Renovated in 1992, it looks more like a grand hotel than a railway station. ❑

ABOVE: Parlament de Catalunya in the park. **BELOW LEFT:** a seal poses in the Parc Zoològic. **BELOW:** the splendid interior of the Estació de França.

BEST RESTAURANTS, BARS AND CAFÉS

Restaurants

Prices for a three-course dinner per person with a bottle of house wine:
€ = under €25
€€ = €25–40
€€€ = €40–60
€€€€ = over €60

At the hub of this area is the trendy Born district, whose recent rise to fame has resulted in a constant turnover of bars, cafés and restaurants, so there's plenty of choice and increasingly multicultural options. There are also many old, established favourites as well as new stars where you need to book, or join the queue, if visiting on a Thursday, Friday or Saturday.

Alsur Café

Sant Pere Més Alt, 4 ☎ 93-310 1286 🕒 B, L & D daily. € [p304, B1]
A laid-back café within earshot of the Palau de la Música, serving home-made snacks at any time of day. Try Argentinian specialities like empanadas or *alfajores* (a sublime biscuit that melts in the mouth). Free Wi-fi and a unique i-bar where you can watch films while munching or sipping a cocktail.

Bascula

Flassaders, 30 bis ☎ 93-319 9866 🕒 L & D Wed–Sat. € [p304, C2]
A new kind of restaurant, run as a co-operative by people from many

different countries, in a former sweet factory in the labyrinth of streets behind the Picasso Museum. Delicious snacks and wholesome meals using organic produce, mostly vegetarian.

Cal Pep

Plaça de les Olles, 8 ☎ 93-310 7961 🕒 L & D Tue–Fri, L only Sat, D only Mon. €€€ [p304, C2]
Jostle and queue to sit at the bar (avoid the dining room at the back), where you can witness the chefs tossing and flipping fat prawns and succulent squid. Mediterranean cooking at its simplest and very best, with atmosphere to match.

Comerç 24

Comerç, 24 ☎ 93-319 2102 🕒 L & D Tue–Sat. €€€ [p305, C2]
One of the leading lights in new-wave Catalan cooking, chef Carles Abellán, inspired by several years working in the laboratory-kitchen of El Bullí, has opened his own designer-smart restaurant where the tasting menu, the *Festival de Tapas,* is a trip for the taste buds.

Cuines Santa Caterina

Mercat Santa Caterina, Av. Francesc Cambó ☎ 93-268 9918 🕒 L & D daily. €–€€ [p304, B2]

The first market bar for beautiful people in a bustling designer space. Rub shoulders with them at long communal tables as the very visible kitchen whips up deliciously fresh Mediterranean dishes with a contemporary twist.

Dionisos

Av. Marquès de l'Argentera, 27 ☎ 93-268 2472 🕒 L & D daily. € [p305, C2]
A genuine taste of Greece in pleasant surroundings overlooking the Parc de la Ciutadella. Ideal for a light lunch after a walk or cycle ride in the park.

El Passadís del Pep

Pla de Palau, 2 ☎ 93-310 1021 🕒 L & D Mon–Sat. €€€€ [p304, C2]
This is a place for people "in the know", the kind of place you walk past if you are not. Be prepared to spend a lot, but otherwise relax; you don't even have to choose your food – it is simply brought to you.

Euskal Etxea

Placeta Montcada, 1–3 ☎ 93-310 2185 🕒 L & D & *tapes* daily. €€€ (*tapes* €) [p304, C2]
This is a stronghold of Basque cuisine just two minutes from the Picasso Museum, where you can be sure of a

good meal. Discover a range of Basque specialities by opting for *cazuelitas*, small portions served in casserole dishes. If you prefer *tapes*, it is advisable to get there early to catch the fresh *pintxos* at the bar.

La Candela

Plaça de Sant Pere, 12 ☎ 93-310 6242 ⏲ L & D daily. € [p304, C1] Delicious Mediterranean food with an exotic edge and good, plentiful salads in this minute restaurant which spills out into the surprisingly quiet square. A very attractive place to eat on summer evenings.

Mosquito

Carders 46, Baixos 2a ☎ 93-268 7569 ⏲ L & D Tue–Sun. € [p304, C2] The delightful English owners of Mosquito define their food as "exotic tapas", which is a modest assessment of the delicious, original Asian dishes they create personally. It's rare to find such good oriental cuisine in Barcelona. What's more, it's open from 7pm, which is handy if you are travelling with children and want an early dinner.

Mundial

Plaça Sant Agustí Vell, 1 ☎ 93-319 9056 ⏲ *Tapes* Tue–Sun. € [p304, C2]

May the Mundial never change. A stalwart of traditional Spanish bars, which are fast fading in this up-and-coming district, its solid marble bar is piled with fresh, simple and tasty seafood *tapes*.

Pla de la Garsa

Assaonadors, 13 ☎ 93-315 2413 ⏲ D only daily. €–€€ [p304, C2] This tastefully restored medieval stable with attractive decor is a peaceful option for an evening meal. Enjoy Catalan specialities, especially their range of cheeses, patés and *embotits* (cured sausages, ham and typical pork products).

Rodrigo

Argenteria, 67 ☎ 93-310 3020 ⏲ B, L & D Thur–Tue. € [p304, B2] Endearing, busy, family-run restaurant. Delicious food at very economical prices. Chaotic but fun, especially if you begin with the house *vermut* (vermouth).

Senyor Parellada

Argentería, 37 ☎ 93-310 5094 ⏲ L & D daily. €€ [p304, B2] A mixture of unusual and classic Catalan dishes in a sophisticated environment, run by the Parelladas, a well-known family of restaurateurs. Half-portions available.

Set Portes

Passeig Isabel II, 14 ☎ 93-319 3033 ⏲ L & D daily. €€ [p304, B3] Over 160 years old and still going strong. Sympathetically restored, this classic restaurant remains popular, especially for family Sunday lunches. Specialises in rice dishes, one for each day of the week. Also has the advantage of remaining open through the afternoon and evening until 1am.

Bars and Cafés

There are now numerous terraces on pavements and in small squares for cool drinks or coffee, plus an explosion of late-night bars – just follow the crowd. Don't miss La Ribera's gem though, **El Xampanyet**, Montcada, 22, a pretty, ceramic-tiled bar, with its intoxicating, fizzy white wine and house anchovies. From **La Vinya del Senyor**, Plaça Santa Maria, 5, a tiny, designer wine bar with an extensive choice of interesting wines by the glass, you can gaze at the wonderful Santa Maria del Mar church. **La Ciutadella**, Passeig Pujades, 5, is a typical Spanish cafeteria with a sunny terrace, ideal for a refreshment or snack after a long walk in the Ciutadella. Just by the park entrance is the pleasant terrace of **Drac Café**, with light snacks available all day.

LEFT: Mosquito's oriental take on tapas.
RIGHT: Senyor Parellada.

Recommended Restaurants, Bars & Cafés on pages 150–1

EL RAVAL

Contemporary art, music, design and cultural centres plus a new Rambla are rejuvenating the historic but long-neglected quarter of El Raval

The section of the Old Town to the west of La Rambla is known as El Raval. Enclosed by **Ronda de Sant Antoni** and **Ronda de Sant Pau**, in the 1930s this area was one of the most densely populated urban areas in the world, when it became derogatorily known as the Barri Xino (literally Chinese Quarter, but meaning "degenerate"). It is still given a wide berth by many of Barcelona's inhabitants. However, it is one of the districts of the city with the most potential, and a stimulating area to visit. Although some parts of El Raval are still fairly run-down, and can sometimes feel menacing, many of the city's most interesting cultural activities are now taking place here.

Religious past

In its medieval past the area was heavily populated by convents and other religious institutions. With the advent of industrialisation in the late 18th century the emphasis switched to factories, and dense urbanisation began. Relics of the religious past still stand out in today's bustling El Raval.

LEFT: a taste of North Africa – enjoying a pot of mint tea on the Rambla del Raval.
RIGHT: atmospheric bar on Doctor Dou, a busy street full of interesting venues.

Two pretty squares

Walking down La Rambla from Plaça de Catalunya, take the second road on the right, Bonsuccés, which opens into the **Plaça Bonsuccés** ❶. The large building dominating the square is a former convent dating from 1635, now district council offices. The adjoining modern archway leads into **Plaça Vicenç Martorell**, a square where the convent cloisters would have been. In the far corner of the arches, the popular bar **Kasparo** provides delicious

Main attractions

CASA DE LA MISERICÒRDIA
MUSEU D'ART CONTEMPORANI DE BARCELONA
CENTRE DE CULTURA CONTEMPORÀNIA DE BARCELONA
ANTIC HOSPITAL DE LA SANTA CREU
LA CAPELLA
RAMBLA DEL RAVAL
ESGLÉSIA DE SANT PAU DEL CAMP

TIP

If you look closely at the Casa de la Misericòrdia you will see a small wooden circle in the wall, where babies were pushed through and received by nuns on the other side, until as recently as 1931.

ABOVE RIGHT: skateboarders take advantage of the space outside MACBA. **BELOW:** the stunning structure of the museum.

alternative snacks, and a shady terrace on which to relax and watch children playing in the central park.

On one side of the square is the **Casa de la Misericòrdia** (1583), formerly a hospice for abandoned children. It has been cleverly restored, complete with interior palm tree, to make more council offices.

Elisabets

Return to Plaça Bonsuccés and turn into Elisabets, by the restaurant of the same name (good for hearty winter dishes and atmosphere), heading towards the **Convent dels Àngels**, a MACBA exhibition space, at the end of the street. There is a good bookshop, Central, in the lofty space of the Misericòrdia chapel and some wonderful tall palms, before you pass ultra-hip hotel Casa Camper *(see page 257),* discreet in its 19th-century shell. **Doctor Dou** on the left has some interesting bars, good-value restaurants and art galleries. After a couple of designer shops on Elisabets is another well-renovated chapel, part of an orphanage dating back to 1370.

Museu d'Art Contemporani de Barcelona (MACBA) ❷

✉ Plaça dels Àngels; www.macba.cat
📞 93-412 0810 🕐 Mon, Wed–Fri 11am–7.30pm, Sat 10am–8pm, Sun 10am–3pm 🄬 charge
🚇 Catalunya/Universitat

At this point you emerge into the **Plaça dels Àngels**, which opens up into the unexpected space dominated

Recommended Restaurants, Bars & Cafés on pages 150–1

by the breathtaking Museu d'Art Contemporani de Barcelona. Opened in 1995 and designed by US architect Richard Meier, the building is dazzling against the Mediterranean sky and gigantic in the context of the humble buildings beyond. The social and urban significance of the architecture in this once declining area has been as much of a talking point as the collection inside, which comprises Catalan, Spanish and some international art, mostly from the second half of the 20th century. The museum also hosts interesting temporary exhibitions.

Its large forecourt has evolved into a world-class space for skateboarding and is also a venue for local fiestas and music festivals, notably the Sónar Advanced Music Festival. The Filipino families who live in the narrow streets around **Joaquín Costa** often gather here on warm evenings: the square is a fascinating melting pot of local residents and cosmopolitan visitors.

The CCCB, a lively arts venue, occupies a renovated 18th-century hospice.

MACBA was built in the grounds of the enormous Casa de la Caritat (poorhouse), which once provided a home for thousands of children (part of it still stands around the corner in Montalegre). The former 18th-century hospice has now become a centre for contemporary culture.

ABOVE: style-conscious residents. **BELOW:** MACBA hosts cutting-edge exhibitions.

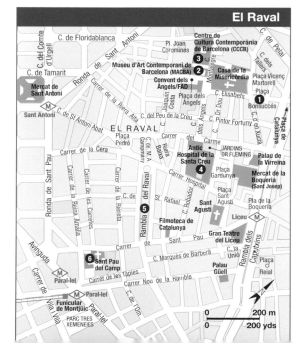

ABOVE: a decorative detail on the Centre de Cultura Contemporània.
BELOW: well-stocked bookshop in La Raval.

Centre de Cultura Contemporània de Barcelona ❸

✉ Montalegre, 5; www.cccb.org
☎ 93-306 4100 🕐 Tue–Sun 11am–8pm, Thur until 10pm
📷 charge 🚇 Catalunya/Universitat

The Centre de Cultura Contemporània de Barcelona (**CCCB**) is a brilliant centre with a stimulating programme of diverse cultural activities, including dance, music, film, video and seminars. It also has great views from its Sala de Mirador. The complex – a renovation of the old hospice by architects Piñón and Vilaplana – rivals MACBA for its architectural interest.

Plaça Joan Coromines

Go through the central Patí de les Dones of the CCCB, a courtyard often used for performances or film festivals, into the **Plaça Joan Coromines** which links it with the MACBA art museum. The C3 Bar, with a terrace overlooking the square, is a fashionable place to meet and have a snack, and it converts into a lounge bar at night. This area is a central part of the Sónar Festival every June, Barcelona's famed music festival.

Antic Hospital de la Santa Creu ❹

✉ Carrer del Carme, 47 🕐 daily 8am–9pm 📷 free 🚇 Liceu

Return to Plaça dels Àngels. The FAD design association on one corner of the square has occasional exhibitions. Continue along the tree-lined street of Àngels to Carme, turn left and cross the road into the Antic Hospital de la Santa Creu, a large Gothic complex that was a hospital until the 1920s. On the left is the 18th-century Academy of

Recommended Restaurants, Bars & Cafés on pages 150–1

La Capella

✉ Hospital, 56 🕐 Tue–Sat noon–2pm and 4–8pm, Sun 11am–2pm 💶 free 🚇 Liceu

As you emerge into the street, Carrer Hospital, check if there is an exhibition in La Capella, once the hospital's chapel, which promotes experimental artists and has interesting work on display.

MULTICULTURAL EL RAVAL

With your back to La Rambla, follow Carrer Hospital deeper into El Raval. This is a busy commercial street, even on Sunday, reflecting the increasing number of shops run by Pakistanis, who are the most recent immigrant group in the district. Tandoori restaurants sit side by side with halal butchers, Arabic pastry shops, kebab bars, bazaars crammed with cheap goods and long-established tailors selling uniforms for employees in the catering business. A sign above a narrow doorway, squeezed between two shops indicates the entrance to a *mezquita*, one of the city's mosques.

Medicine and Surgery, and on the right the **Institut d'Estudis Catalans** in the hospital's **Casa de Convalescència**. Wander through the atmospheric cloistered patio, a favourite meeting place for lonely down-and-outs but full of charm, and with a terrace café serving delicious light meals. The Biblioteca de Catalunya occupies much of the old hospital building, along with the Massana art school.

EAT

El Raval is a good neighbourhood for vegetarians, as there are a number of restaurants catering to their needs, some offering organic dishes (*see pages 150–51*).

LEFT: the inner patio of the Antic Hospital de la Santa Creu.
BELOW: film screening at the CCCB.

The new Rambla del Raval is a venue for cafés, concerts and markets.

ished to create this pleasant Rambla. Old residents and new immigrants are finally venturing out to enjoy the space, which is also used as a venue for lively outdoor markets and concerts. The prostitutes, thieves and junkies are still hovering but on the whole have retreated to the narrower streets behind, where the darker side of urban life is still evident.

The new Rambla is lined with restaurant terraces, kebab bars and the city's first authentic fish and chip shop. The cutting-edge five-star Barceló Raval hotel (see page

Urban regeneration

Trendy second-hand clothes shops are another new thread in this multicoloured fabric. **Riera Baixa**, a short pedestrian street on the right off Hospital, is full of them and has an outdoor market on Saturday.

Rambla del Raval ❺

Carrer Hospital then disgorges into the new broad **Rambla del Raval**, not to be confused with the famous Rambla, a model example of the city council's policy of urban regeneration. Old housing was demol-

BELOW AND RIGHT: multi-faceted Raval.

Recommended Restaurants, Bars & Cafés on pages 150–1

257), with its zany night-time lighting, towers over this new scene. Just opposite is the legendary restaurant Casa Leopoldo *(see page 150)*, which was once hidden down a seedy street.

Església de Sant Pau del Camp ❻

☒ Sant Pau, 101–103 ☎ 93-441 0001 ☯ Mon–Sat 10am–1.30pm, 4–7.30pm ☒ charge ☒ Paral·lel/ Liceu

A left turn on Sant Pau leads back to the Liceu on La Rambla past the Filmoteca de Catalunya (film library and theatre) newly housed in Plaça Salvador Seguí, another key piece in the urban regeneration scheme. Turn right to find the Romanesque church of **Sant Pau del Camp**, generally considered to be the oldest church in Barcelona. Surrounded by greenery, including an olive tree, a cypress and a palm, it is a true survivor in this long-beleaguered area.

Sant Pau del Camp is a fine example of Romanesque architecture, quite rare in the city. The present building dates from the 12th century, but it incorporates elements of an earlier church that was built in 912. Its small cloister, with unusual carvings, is a gem. On the exterior above the main door, look for the simple carving of the Hand of God and a winged creature, a symbolic representation of one of the Evangelists.

Much of the former industrial activity was in this lower part of El Raval – the new park behind the church was created after a fire burnt down a factory – and the park's tall chimney is a fitting memorial to the area's industrial past. A sports centre, Can Ricart (open to the public) has been built in a former textile factory.

Continue along the last block in Sant Pau, past the mirrored shopfront of **La Confiteria**, a pastry shop turned stylish bar.

At the end of Sant Pau is the metro Paral·lel where you can catch the funicular up to the Parc de Montjuïc, not far from the Fundació Joan Miró *(see page 186).* ❑

BELOW LEFT: the Romanesque doorway of Sant Pau del Camp, Barcelona's oldest church **(BELOW)**.

BEST RESTAURANTS, BARS AND CAFÉS

Restaurants

Prices for a three-course dinner per person with a bottle of house wine:
€ = under €25
€€ = €25–40
€€€ = €40–60
€€€€ = over €60

This once-forgotten neighbourhood is rapidly becoming fashionable. The only difficult aspect of finding a place to eat here is making the choice. There is a wide range of venues for all tastes, tending towards new ideas of fusion, or new concepts in eating, although there's no shortage of genuine local places, plus multi-cultural options, and several vegetarian choices.

Anima

Àngels, 6 ☎ 93-342 4912 Ⓒ L & D Mon–Sat. € [p303, E2]
Peaceful pavement tables plus a designer interior are a good setting for the delicious dishes presented like artworks by the young, creative chef. Good-value set menu at lunch. Tapas available from 7pm. Close to MACBA.

Biocenter

Pintor Fortuny, 25 ☎ 93-301 4583 Ⓒ L & D Mon–Sat, L only Sun. € [p304, A1]
This was one of the first vegetarian restaurants in the city. You can choose between an enormous, nutritious *menú del día*

(four courses) or a substantial *plato combinado* (one dish with accompaniment). Either way you will enjoy a hearty meal in soothing surroundings. Good value set menu in the evening.

Ca l'Isidre

Les Flors, 12 ☎ 93-441 1139 Ⓒ L & D Mon–Sat. €€€€ [p303, E2]
This is a family-run business that has grown into one of the city's best restaurants. The smart clientele appreciate the meticulous attention to detail in food, decor and service. Classic Catalan dishes exquisitely prepared, using whatever's in season from the nearby Boqueria market.

Can Lluís

Cera, 49 ☎ 93-441 1187 Ⓒ L & D Mon–Sat. € [p303, E2]
Can Lluís is the kind of genuine Catalan restaurant you would hope to find in a small village, so it's a pleasant surprise to encounter it in the heart of the city. Delicious food is served amid noise and bustle, and no pretensions. Excellent value for money.

Casa Leopoldo

Sant Rafael, 24 ☎ 93-441 3014 Ⓒ L & D Tue–Sat, L only Sun. €€€€ [p303, E2]
Just off Rambla del Raval, a family-run Barcelona classic with great atmosphere. Particularly known

for its fish and its own version of the Catalan staple, *pa amb tomàquet*.

Dos Trece

Carme, 40 ☎ 93-301 7306 ⓒ L & D daily. €–€€ [p304, A1]
Fashionable place with a laid-back attitude and good atmosphere. Unconventional dishes show the influence of the owner's Mexican/LA background.

El Fortuny

Pintor Fortuny, 31 ☎ 93-317 9892 ⓒ B & L daily, D Wed–Sat. € [p303, E2]
The atmosphere of a student café belies the high standard of the French-influenced dishes always made with what's fresh in the market.

Elisabets

Elisabets, 2 ☎ 93-317 5826 ⓒ L Mon–Sat, D Fri. € [p304, A1]
A bustling local bar, serving hearty winter stews and a good-value set menu. Only serves tapas in the evening except on Fridays.

En Ville

Doctor Dou, 14 ☎ 93-302 8467 ⓒ L daily, D Tue–Sat. €€ (set menu L & D €) [p304, A1]
Creative Catalan cooking with a French edge in charming, spacious surroundings. Marble tables, palms and gentle live music (Tue and Wed) complete the picture. Good value.

Fonda Espanya

Sant Pau, 9–11 ☎ 93-550 0010 ⓒ L & D Mon–Sat, L only Sun. €€€ [p303, E2]
Radical refurbishment in this legendary hotel has included installing Basque star chef Martín Berasategui in the kitchen. Top-notch cooking in a dining room decorated by *moderniste* architect Domènech i Montaner.

Juicy Jones

Hospital, 74 ☎ 93-443 9082 ⓒ L & D daily. € [p303, E2]
Latest branch of this vegan restaurant selling genuinely organic juices all day, as well as tasty Hindu and European dishes. Excellent value for money.

La Verònica

Rambla del Raval, 2–4 ☎ 93-329 3303 ⓒ L & D daily. €€ [p303, E2]
This ultra-trendy spot selling *pizzas del mercat* topped with whatever is in season has moved here from the Gothic Quarter, a sure sign of just how up-and-coming the new Raval really is. Eat al fresco on their terrace on the Rambla.

Maharaja

Rambla del Raval, 14 ☎ 93-442 5777 ⓒ L & D daily. € [p303, E2]
The ultimate in Spanish-Indian crossover has to be their biryani paella served on an open-air terrace in the middle of this new rambla. Their more traditional Indian dishes are good, too.

Organic

Junta de Comerç, 11 ☎ 93-301 0902 ⓒ L & D daily. € [p304, A2]
Good choice of wholesome organic food in an impressive space. A branch in La Boqueria market sells healthy take-away snacks.

Rita Blue

Plaça Sant Agustí, 3 ☎ 93-342 4086 ⓒ L & D Mon–Sat, L only Sun. €–€€ [p304, A2]
Serves "Tex-Med" fusion food featuring light snacks as well as more substantial mains. Serves good cocktails and has a popular terrace on the Square.

Romesco

Sant Pau, 28 ☎ 93-318 9381 ⓒ L & D Mon–Sat. € [p304, A2]
The fluorescent lighting and formica-topped tables deter no one. Romesco is famous for its *frijoles*: black beans, rice, minced meat, fried egg and fried banana, all on one plate. A favourite with students and anyone who appreciates simple grilled fish.

Silenus

Àngels, 8 ☎ 93-302 2680 ⓒ L & D Mon–Sat. €€ (set menu Mon–Fri L €) [p303, E2]
Comfortable and arty café/restaurant with an appetising selection of Mediterranean and international dishes, including plenty of seafood. In warm weather, tables are set up in the street.

Bars and Cafés

This area now buzzes day and night as more and more terrace cafés open in small squares, or wherever the pavement is wide enough to set out a few tables and chairs. The light, sunny space of Rambla del Raval is practically lined with bars and places for *tapes*, such as **Fragua**, at No. 15, or **La Paciencia**, a friendly local bar on the corner with Sant Pau. For sunset cocktails with a panoramic view head up to the rooftop terrace of the **Barceló Raval** hotel at No. 17.

The bars in the MACBA square always attract a colourful crowd. **Oliva**, Pintor Fortuny, 22, is a stylish café fitted out with pale wood, and **Iposa**, Jardins del Dr Fleming, has tables outside and lots of atmosphere inside.

The night scene in and around Joaquín Costa is popular, with a mixture of old favourites, like the *modernista* **Almirall**, at No. 33, and some trendy newcomers, among them **Betty Ford** at No. 56 and **Negroni** at 46.

LEFT: vegan restaurant Juicy Jones.

Recommended Restaurants, Bars & Cafés on pages 166–7

THE WATERFRONT

Rejuvenated for the Barcelona Olympics in 1992, the
waterfront area has added an exciting new dimension
to the city. Bold development is continuing, with the
creation of Diagonal Mar and the Fòrum on land
reclaimed from the sea

I t is ironic that Barcelona, a city on
the shores of the Mediterranean
with a large industrial port and
strong maritime tradition, gained a
"waterfront" only in the last decade
of the 20th century. As the popular
saying went, Barcelona lived with its
back to the sea.

Being bordered on one side by the
Mediterranean, the city's residential
and commercial areas expanded
inland, first with the construction of
the 19th-century Eixample and then
by moving further up the hill towards
Collserola during the 20th century.
Investment tended to be linked with
this movement, and as a result the Old
Town and Barceloneta were neglected.

Regeneration

The rediscovery of the waterfront
began in the 1980s as part of the
Socialist city council's vision, but the
1992 Olympics were the vital catalyst.
The development, perhaps the most
radical transformation of any city in
Europe, represented an investment of
400 billion pesetas (3 billion). Some
5km (3 miles) of beaches were renovated or newly created, landscaped
and equipped with facilities. The Vila
Olímpica was built, creating what is
now a new residential district and its

port. The old city wharves, once
hidden under tumbledown sheds,
emerged, blinking, into the sun.
Barceloneta was transformed. Since
1992 the momentum has been sustained with projects like Maremàgnum and, more recently, Diagonal
Mar and the Fòrum area *(see page
165)*, and, for better or worse, there
are more to come. The port area
beyond the W hotel is due for major
development.

For energetic walkers or cyclists,
this route could be one long itinerary

Main attractions

MUSEU MARÍTIM
LAS GOLONDRINAS
PORT VELL
MAREMÀGNUM
AQUÀRIUM
MUSEU D'HISTÒRIA DE CATALUNYA
BARCELONETA
BEACHES
PORT OLÍMPIC
VILA OLÍMPICA
FÒRUM

LEFT: Port Vell, Barcelona's old port.
RIGHT: on the waterfront.

The base of the Monument a Colom, built in 1888 to honour Christopher Columbus.

RIGHT: a wooden submarine designed by Catalan Narcís Monturiol.

right along the front. However, to be able to enjoy the walk and fully appreciate the extensive renovations, to take in the many colourful details and have time to pause in the right places (such as the fish restaurants in Barceloneta), the route should be split into two (or more) days. What's on offer on Barcelona's waterfront is something quite extraordinary for a large cosmopolitan European city.

Museu Marítim ❶

✉ Av de les Drassanes, s/n; www.mmb.cat ☎ 93-342 9920
🕒 daily 10am–8pm ⓒ charge
🚇 Drassanes

A good place to begin is the Maritime Museum, which brings to life Catalonia's seafaring past. Housed in the massive **Drassanes Reials** (Royal Shipyards), at the foot of La Rambla just before it meets the port, the building alone makes a visit worthwhile – the magnificent Gothic

shipyards dating from the 13th century are a fine and rare example of civic architecture from that period. The art critic Robert Hughes described this stunning building as "perhaps the most stirring ancient industrial space of any kind that has survived from the Middle Ages: a masterpiece of civil engineering".

The entrance to the museum is along the side, where there is an inviting terrace café in a shady garden with a lily pond. Due to major renovation work the permanent collection

Recommended Restaurants, Bars & Cafés on pages 166–7

is closed, but temporary exhibitions and the schooner *Santa Eulàlia (see page 157)* can be visited.

Exhibits

The collection includes real fishing boats from the Catalan coast, representing the importance of both fishing and boatbuilding in the country's history, and models of vessels from all ages. Also on display is a modern Olympic winner, a model-making workshop, maps, instruments and other sea-related artefacts. The highlight is the full-scale replica of the 16th-century galley in which Don Juan of Austria led the Christian fleet to defeat the Turks in the battle of Lepanto in 1571. Like so many vessels over the centuries, it was built here in one of the slipways then on the water's edge.

THE PORT OF BARCELONA

Today you have to cross a wide road, full of traffic leading to the Ronda Litoral, before reaching the water. Leaving the **Monument a Colom** *(see page 107)* to your left, go down the side of the rather overbearing former **Duana Nova** (New Customs House), built between 1895 and 1902 from a project drawn up by Enric Sagnier and Pere García. Crowned by a massive winged sphinx and other mythical flying beasts (Barcelona's port buildings seem to specialise in fine rooftop silhouettes), the Duana Nova is designed in the form of the letter "H", the most practical design for processing cargoes.

To the left of the Columbus statue as you look out to sea is the **Junta d'Obres del Port** (Port Authority Building), designed by the engineer Julio Valdés and built in 1907. Its original use was as the reception for passengers arriving in the city from the sea. The interior is somewhat eclectic in style, while the exterior of the building is impressively ornate.

To the right, the **Moll de Barcelona ❷** and, beyond it, the **Moll de Sant Bertran** are the centre for ferry services to the Balearic Islands. This quay also has the 119-metre (390ft) -high **Torre de Jaume I**

The bow of Santa Eulàlia *overlooks Port Vell (above), and a model of Magellan's* Santa María de la Victoria, *the first ship to circumnavigate the world (1519–1522), is on display at the Maritime Museum (above left).*

BELOW: view over Monument a Colom and Junta d'Obres del Port.

Passeig Marítim is hugely popular with afternoon strollers, cyclists and rollerbladers.

BELOW: the ornate Port Authority Building.

link for the cross-harbour cable car, which comes from Montjuïc and goes to the tower on the other side of the harbour, the **Torre de Sant Sebastià** (an alternative route to the beach). The cable car has hardly changed since its introduction in 1931 – unlike the spectacular views it affords of the city and port, which are constantly changing.

World Trade Center ❸

At the end of the quay stands the **World Trade Center**, designed by the architect I.M. Pei (who also designed the Louvre glass pyramid); it makes a loud statement in the middle of the port, looking remarkably like the luxury cruisers moored alongside it. Unlike most waterfront developments, this building is not used for social or leisure activities: it is a commercial centre with offices, a smart restaurant and a very grand hotel.

Las Golondrinas ❹

✉ Moll de Drassanes; www.las golondrinas.com ☎ 93-442 3106 🕐 summer daily 11.30am–8.30pm, winter hours vary @ charge 🚇 Drassanes/Barceloneta

Capital of the Med

The port of Barcelona plays an important commercial role, covering a huge area winding south towards the airport. Recent expansion involved diverting the River Llobregat and current construction work will double its size. The authorities' much vaunted aim is to establish it as "Europe's southern port", tying in with the city's aspiration to be regarded as the "capital of the Mediterranean". While massive container ships line the docks beneath the Castell de Montjuïc, enormous white cruise ships moored against the Moll Adossat are now part of the landscape. As the largest cruiser terminal in Europe, it regularly disgorges hundreds of passengers into La Rambla for sightseeing.

Recommended Restaurants, Bars & Cafés on pages 166–7

A popular way of seeing the harbour is to take a ride on one of the Golondrinas, or ferries, which are moored on the Moll de Drassanes. Apart from a pause during the Civil War, they have been plying these waters since the 1888 Exhibition. Half-hour trips in the older pleasure boats take you out to the new entrance to the port and back past the fishing boats.

More modern catamarans head out of the harbour and along the coast to the Olympic port and the Fòrum, taking around 90 minutes.

PORT VELL ❺

Just beyond the Golondrinas is Port Vell, the old port, now a yacht harbour. A sleek, sinuous walkway and footbridge, the **Rambla de Mar**, leads across the water to Maremàgnum *(see right)*, on the **Moll d'Espanya**, Port Vell's main quay.

Moored alongside the palm-lined **Moll de la Fusta** ("Wood Quay", where it was stored in the past) is the *Santa Eulàlia* (Tue–Fri noon–5.30pm, Sat–Sun 10am–5.30pm, later in summer; charge, or free with ticket to Museu Marítim). Restored

to its original glory, this schooner dates from the beginning of the 20th century when it took cargo to the Americas. Its moment of glory is on 5th January when it brings in the three Wise Kings to parade around the city *(see page 269)*.

Maremàgnum ❻

✉ Moll d'Espanya; www.maremag num.es ☎ 93-225 8100 🕒 daily, shops 10am–10pm, restaurants until 1am 🚇 Drassanes/Barceloneta

Crowds head over the Rambla de Mar footbridge to Maremàgnum, the Aquàrium and the IMAX cinema. The complex has a wide range of shops and places to eat and a cinema with eight screens. The bars and restaurants are dominated by fast-food outlets but there are some exceptions, like **L'Elx al Moll**, with an irresistible terrace overlooking the fishing boats *(see page 166)*. Despite the commercial context, a few *tapes* while watching the yachts or looking across the harbour to Barcelona's Gothic towers and 19th-century chimneys takes some beating.

KIDS

There's plenty to keep children distracted around the port. The wavy design of the Rambla de Mar footbridge appeals, especially when it opens up to let yachts through. Once across the bridge, there's the Aquarium, an IMAX cinema and a replica of the world's first combustion-powered submarine.

BELOW LEFT: the Rambla de Mar footbridge leading from the mainland to Maremàgnum. **BELOW:** the World Trade Center, designed by I.M. Pei.

The Maremàgnum shopping complex is popular with locals and tourists alike.

BELOW: inside the Maremàgnum leisure complex.

With 11,000 animals and 450 different species, the colourful marine communities of the Mediterranean and the tropical seas are shown off in all their glory. A glass tunnel leads visitors through the sharks and rays, while experienced divers can book to swim amongst them.

Around Passeig d'Isabel II

Pass the historic submarine, a reproduction of the *Ictineo II*, invented by Catalan Narcís Monturiol, and follow the path that leads up to the **Mirador del Port Vell** (a slightly raised lookout point). On Moll de la Fusta is American pop artist Roy Lichtenstein's *El Cap de Barcelona* (*Barcelona Head*), a striking sculpture made in 1992 to commemorate the Olympics; the mosaic of stoneware shows Gaudí's influence. On the corner of Via Laietana is the headquarters of **Correus** (the post office), a very grand building completed in 1927. The enormous vestibule was decorated by the prestigious *noucentiste* artists (from the 1900s) Canyellas, Obiols, Galí and

Aquàrium ❼

✉ Moll d'Espanya; www.aquarium bcn.com ☎ 93-221 7474 🕒 daily 9.30am–9pm, until 11pm in July and Aug 🅖 charge 🚇 Drassanes/ Barceloneta

Since opening in 1995 the Aquàrium, one of the largest in Europe, has become the most successful crowd-puller in Barcelona, beating the Sagrada Família into second place.

Recommended Restaurants, Bars & Cafés on pages 166–7

Museu d'Història de Catalunya ❽

✉ Plaça de Pau Vila 3; www.mhcat.net
☎ 93-225 4700 🕐 Tue–Sat 10am–7pm, Wed until 8pm, Sun 10am–2.30pm 💶 charge Ⓜ Barceloneta

Labarta. It is easier to buy stamps in an *estanc* (the tobacconists' shops found in every district) but not nearly as interesting. It is not hard to see why the facade has been used by film-makers as a stand-in for American law courts.

With your back to Correus, walk towards the sea. On the left is **Reina Cristina**, a street full of cheap and cheerful electro-domestic shops. At No. 7 is Can Paixano, a popular cava bar selling sparkling wine and hefty sandwiches at rock-bottom prices, frequented by locals and tourists alike. Nearby is the first Galician seafood restaurant to open in Barcelona, **Carballeira** *(see page 166)*. If you are passing when the *arròs a la banda* (a delicious rice dish) is coming out of the kitchen, cancel all other plans: stand at the bar and request a portion with *alli-oli* (garlic mayonnaise) and a glass of Galician *vino turbio*.

Back on the quayside, the promenade sweeps on round, past a floating bar, to the **Moll Dipòsit** and the **Moll de la Barceloneta**. These once busy working quays now shelter the **Marina Port Vell**, where some of the most exclusive motor and sailing yachts in the Mediterranean winter or pass through on their way to the Balearics or the Caribbean.

This fascinating museum is housed in the Palau de Mar, a former warehouse complex (the Magatzem General de Comerç, 1881, the last one in the area), beautifully renovated in 1992. True to its name, the museum elucidates Catalan history, but also looks at it from a wider historical perspective, with various bits of technical wizardry and plenty of interactive spaces – try walking in a

For a bird's-eye view of Port Vell and the length of the waterfront, take the cable car, which runs between Montjuïc and the Torre de Sant Sebastià, or just go as far as the Torre de Jaume I.

ABOVE LEFT: Roy Lichtenstein's sculpture, *Barcelona Head.*
BELOW: up close and personal with the sharks at the Aquàrium.

EAT

The Museu d' Història
de Catalunya is a good
place for lunch or dinner.
The restaurant on the
top floor, Restaurant
1881, offers Mediter-
ranean dishes and fine
views over the harbour
(tel: 902-520 522).

ABOVE: you can hire a
bike to explore the
waterfront. **BELOW:** the
new Hotel W.

suit of armour, or building a Roman
arch – which kids of all ages love.

BARCELONETA 9

Beyond the museum is Barceloneta,
once home to the city's fishing community. The main focus here, along
the quayside, is on leisure and eating
out. Sunday lunch at one of the
restaurants in front of the Palau de
Mar has become a regular pastime
for those who can afford it. This is an
attractive place to sit and watch the
world go by, and is sheltered even in
winter. The charms of outdoor eating
often outweigh the gastronomic
shortcomings, so as long as you don't
expect haute cuisine you will be spoilt

for choice along the whole length of
Passeig Joan de Borbó. Even for
Barcelona residents it is a thrill to eat
on a pavement in the December sun.

Fishermen's Wharf

At the end of the promenade is an
expensive but excellent fish restaurant called Barceloneta *(see page 166)*;
it features in Woody Allen's film
*Vicky Cristina Barcelona (see box,
page 161)*. Just beyond are glimpses
of the hard-working fishing boats
moored up against the **Moll dels
Pescadors** (Fishermen's Wharf). The
distinctive clock tower, **Torre del Rel-
lotge** (closed to the public), started life
as a lighthouse. Close by is the fish

Recommended Restaurants, Bars & Cafés on pages 166–7

market (*mercat de peix*, first opened in 1924), where the boats come in twice a day (from 6.30am and 4.30pm) to supply the fishmongers.

Towering above the scene is the **Torre de Sant Sebastià**, whose 78-metre (257ft) height marks the end, or the beginning, of the route of the cable car, which completes its 1,300-metre (4,200ft) journey on Montjuïc.

At the foot of the tower, **Club Nataciò Atlètic Barceloneta** (also known as Banys Sant Sebastià) has an excellent heated outdoor pool (tel: 93-221 0010; Mon–Sat 6.30am–10.30pm, Sun 8am–7.30pm, winter Sun 8am–4.30pm). It also has a large indoor pool and small spa area and overlooks the beach of Sant Sebastià.

The landscape has changed here recently as the promenade has been developed to reach the domineering new landmark of the Hotel W Barcelona, designed by local architect Ricardo Bofill. If your budget does not run to the €10,000 Extreme Wow suite you may at least be able to have a *copa* in the Eclipse bar on its 26th floor. The sea wall beyond the hotel is free, giving a great new perspective on both port and city. Some feel, though, that the intelligent town planning of the 1980s is now being compromised.

Origins of Barceloneta

Town planning in the 18th century was also of questionable merit. The streets behind the quayside are in a grid formation, the pattern of which was born of a military decision. It was to Barceloneta that the inhabitants of La Ribera were relocated when their homes were demolished to make way for the building of the fortress La Ciutadella, after the siege and conquest of Barcelona by Felipe V. The streets were built in a series of narrow, rectangular blocks all facing in the same direction (towards La Ciutadella), facilitating easy military control (volleys from the castle could be directed down the streets).

This residential area is now an appealing mix of traditional and modern; washing hangs along the narrow balconies, while the bars and restaurants have become popular night spots, and apartments are being restored and let to tourists.

The Museu d'Història de Catalunya is full of fascinating historical artefacts.

BELOW: outdoor pool on the waterfront.

Vicky Cristina Barcelona

When Woody Allen came to town in 2007, supposedly in love with its Mediterranean charms, the feeling was mutual. Red carpets were rolled out to greet him and local politicians rushed to shake his hand and open their coffers, causing some controversy. It became commonplace to run into the inimitable director, in his trademark cap, putting his stars through their paces on the Waterfront and other emblematic locations around the city, like La Rambla or Park Güell. Starring Javier Bardem, Penélope Cruz, Scarlett Johansson and Rebecca Hall, *Vicky Cristina Barcelona* has met with mixed reviews, but the postcard scenes of Barcelona have spread its fame further than ever around the globe.

Behind the beach scenes lie the characterful streets of Barceloneta.

BELOW:
a waiter at work on the Passeig Marítim.

Mercat Barceloneta

In the square in the middle of Barceloneta is the **Mercat Barceloneta** (Plaça Font; tel: 93-221 6471), built in *modernista* style in 1884 but recently renovated and given the designer treatment. Inside, along with the fish, meat, fruit and vegetable stalls is Lluçanès *(see page 69)*, a restaurant which in the short time it's been open has already won a Michelin star, the first to be awarded to a restaurant in a market.

Platja Barceloneta ⑩

By cutting through the streets of Barceloneta to the **Passeig Marítim**, or wandering along from Platja Sant Sebastià, you arrive at Platja Barceloneta (*platja* means beach), with wooden walkways, palms and designer showers as part of the post-Olympic seafront. The beaches along this stretch are easily accessible by public transport, and both the sand and the water's surface are cleaned daily, with weekly sanitary checks on top of that.

It's clear that the people of Barcelona, as well as tourists, derive enormous pleasure from these wide open beaches. Every morning, locals come down in their towelling dressing gowns to swim in all weathers, play cards, gossip and get fit. In summer the beaches get very crowded and noisy by midday, but then comes the lunchtime exodus. If you can't make it in the early morning, wait until the early evening sun brings a new tranquillity – an eight o'clock swim here is sheer bliss.

Recommended Restaurants, Bars & Cafés on pages 166–7

The beaches are now an essential part of Barcelona's famed nightlife. New *xiringuitos* or beach restaurants serve drinks and snacks by day, but at sunset the DJs start spinning, young people come out to play and a cool scene emerges.

Part of Barceloneta beach has been renamed Somorrostro in homage to the shanty town and its inhabitants who were there until the mid-1960s. The famous and much-loved gypsy flamenco dancer, Carmen Amaya, was born there.

Parc de la Barceloneta and onwards

On the eastern edge of Barceloneta is the Parc de la Barceloneta, a fine setting for the *modernista* water tower, **Torre de les Aigües**, by Josep Domènech i Estapà (1905), virtually the only original industrial building left in this area.

It stands in dramatic contrast to the avant-garde Gas building, **Torre del Gas**, on one side of the park and the gleaming Hospital del Mar on the other. The formerly gloomy hospital underwent a metamorphosis for the Olympics and is now more reminiscent of an international airport than a major public hospital.

Along the promenade at beach level are several hip bars and one of the best restaurants on the beach, Agua *(see page 166)*.

PORT OLÍMPIC ⓫

You can't miss the Port Olímpic: two skyscrapers tower above a huge woven copper fish sculpture (*Pez y Esfera*, meaning "fish and sphere") by Frank Gehry, who is best known as the architect of the Guggenheim Museum in Bilbao.

The first skyscraper is the luxurious **Hotel Arts** *(see page 258)*, designed by Bruce Graham (architect of Chicago's Sears Tower and the Hancock Centre). You can wander beneath Frank Gehry's awesome fish sculpture and imagine the heady view from the exclusive suites high up in the Arts, favoured by rock stars, actors and jet-setters. At ground level is the **Barcelona Casino**. The other building is the MAPFRE tower, housing offices.

Here, bars and restaurants pro-

Rebecca Horn's Estel Ferit (Wounded Star) *pays homage to Barceloneta's traditional beach restaurants, now demolished.*

BELOW: *Homenatge a la Natació* by Alfredo Lanz, on Sant Sebastiá beach.

Barcelona's casino is next to the Hotel Arts, which towers over the Port Olímpic.

BELOW: Frank Gehry's fish sculpture.

liferate, with entrances on the promenade overlooking the strikingly modern marina. If you don't mind paying extra for the location, this is a colourful place to stop and eat, watching the yachts and dinghies coming and going. If you want a quiet drink, though, think again. At night the clubs and cocktail bars seem to attract the whole of Barcelona.

At the end of the **Moll de Gregal**, jutting out to sea, is the municipal sailing school, offering courses for the public and short trips along the seafront with a skipper (book on www.barcelonaturisme.com).

Vila Olímpica ⑫

It is worth taking time to go inland a block or two, to see the feats of architecture that comprises the Olympic Village. On the way you'll come to the **Parc del Port Olímpic**, behind the towers. In the **Plaça dels Campions** (Champions' Square) are listed the names of the 257 gold medallists of the 1992 Olympics, as well as the handprints of Pele and cyclist Eddie Merx, along with numerous other sporting heroes. The Vila Olímpica was built according to a master plan developed by architects Mackay, Martorell, Bohigas and Puigdomènech, on land formerly occupied by 19th-century ramshackle warehouses and tumbledown factories.

The flats accommodated athletes in 1992 and since then have been gradually sold. The development was a major undertaking, and a vital part of Barcelona's wider plan of achieving long-overdue improvements to the city's infrastructure. It involved major changes, like moving the railway lines into Estació de França underground.

Recommended Restaurants, Bars & Cafés on pages 166-7

bridges that connect with the residential areas behind. The promenade is popular with joggers, skaters, cyclists and walkers.

The waterfront ends with the **Fòrum** area, legacy of a world symposium in 2004 and now used for large-scale events like music festivals and the Feria de Abril, the traditional annual celebration of the Andalucian community in Catalonia. A huge solar panel marks the spot. It also has a swimming area without sand, an enclosed area landscaped into the sea.

The 200 buildings cover 74 hectares (183 acres), and are in 200 different designs. The area did not become a new neighbourhood of Barcelona overnight, but it is now looking more established, has become a desirable place to live, and is beginning to merge with the remaining buildings of Poble Nou that surround its outer limits. In the midst of a clinical shopping mall is one of the few magnetic points that attracts people in the evenings: the 15-screen cinema complex, Icària Yelmo, which specialises in *v.o.* (original-language) films.

This part of the city, along with the former industrial area of Poble Nou (inland from Bogatell and Mar Bella beaches), has been the scene of frenetic construction in recent years. Dubbed as speculation by many, in theory a new residential area, Diagonal Mar, is being created, as is a new hi-tech business district *(see page 168.)*

From here one could wander inland to get a taste of the latest developments, walk back along the ever exhilarating seaside or catch a tram, metro or bus back into the centre. ❏

This is Marc, *by Robert Llimós (1997), who welcomes you to the Parc del Port Olímpic.*

LEFT: juggling on Sant Sebastià beach.
BELOW: the distinctive style of the Hotel Arts.

THE BEACHES

Return to the front to walk along the series of beaches after the Port Olímpic. Tons of sand were imported to create **Platja Nova Icària** (named after the original industrial neighbourhood), **Bogatell, Mar Bella, Nova Mar Bella** and, most recently, **Llevant**, reclaiming a seafront that had been cut off by railway lines, yards and warehouses. The strategic Ronda Litoral (ring road) runs all along here but at a lower level, and is cleverly hidden beneath parks, playgrounds and

BEST RESTAURANTS, BARS AND CAFÉS

Restaurants

Prices for a three-course dinner per person with a bottle of house wine:
€ = under €25
€€ = €25–40
€€€ = €40–60
€€€€ = over €60

The 4km (2½ miles) of waterfront makes an endlessly tempting place to walk, eat and drink, especially in the winter when there is nothing like the luxury of eating a paella outdoors. Sea views are a treat that sometimes requires a sacrifice, either financially or in food quality, but is often worth it. However, don't miss some of the best options hidden in the back-streets of Barceloneta.

Agua
Passeig Marítim, 30 ☎ 93-225 1272 Ⓒ L & D daily. €€ [p305, D4]
This stylish, relaxed restaurant, serving modern Mediterranean food, is virtually in the sand near the Vila Olímpica. The combination is bliss,

especially at lunchtime, so book days in advance, especially at weekends.

Arola
Marina, 19-21 ☎ 93-221 1000 Ⓒ L & D Wed–Sun. €€€€ [p305, D3]
In the luxurious surroundings of the Hotel Arts, overlooking Gehry's sculpted fish and the Olympic Port, is one of top Catalan chef Sergi Arola's restaurants. For the ultimate indulgence book the Chef's Table near the kitchen where you can have a personalised menu. A snip at €150.

Barceloneta
L'Escar, 22 ☎ 93-221 2111 Ⓒ L & D daily. €€€ [p304, B4]
Barceloneta's outdoor terrace in a privileged position, jutting out above the fishing boats and super yachts of the marina Port Vell, makes this one of the most delightful places to enjoy high-quality seafood dishes.

Bestial
Ramón Trias i Fargas, 2–4 ☎ 93-224 0407 Ⓒ L & D daily. €€ [p305, D4]
Sea views, minimalist interior, multilevel outdoor terrace, beautiful clientele – this is more of a place to be seen in than to eat in, though their unusual risottos and Italian-inspired pasta dishes are good. Reasonably priced set menu Mon–Fri.

Can Majó
Almirall Aixada, 23 ☎ 93-221 5455 Ⓒ L & D Tue–Sat, L only Sun. €€€ [p304, C4]
This is one of the best and most established of the Barceloneta fish restaurants, where it's worth paying a bit extra to be sure of a good paella.

Can Solé
Sant Carles, 4 ☎ 93-221 5012 Ⓒ L & D Tue–Sat, L only Sun. €€ [p304, C4]
In the heart of Barceloneta, literally and metaphorically, and a favourite with local people, it has been cooking great seafood and fish since 1903.

Carballeira
Reina Cristina, 3 ☎ 93-310 1006 Ⓒ L & D Tue–Sat, L only Sun. €€€ [p304, B3]
Excellent Galician fish dishes in old-style restaurant. At lunchtime

try a simple *tapa* of *arròs a la banda* (delicious rice cooked in fish stock) at the bar. Accompany it with a glass of Ribeira (Galician white wine), in particular, the cloudy variety, *turbio*.

L'Elx al Moll
Local 9, Maremàgnum ☎ 93-225 8117 Ⓒ L & D daily. €€ [p304, B4]
As a close relative to the Elx in the Paral·lel, known for its rice dishes since 1959, you can be sure of a good rice dish here. Try the *pica-pica* (assorted starters), followed by the rice of your choice. A cut above most of the other eating options in this commercial centre, with a quayside terrace and great views of the port.

La Oca Mar
Espigó Bac de Roda, Platja Mar Bella ☎ 93-225 0100 Ⓒ L & D Wed–Sat, L only Sun–Tue. €€ [off map]
At Oca Mar you can wine and dine virtually in the sea. This spectacular restaurant, jutting out to sea on the breakwater, serves an extensive range of well-prepared seafood and local seasonal dishes.

Puda Can Manel
Passeig Joan de Borbó, 60–61 ☎ 93-221 5013 Ⓒ L & D Tue–Sun. €

[p304, B4]
A good, middle-range fish restaurant on this parade bursting with restaurants, many of which are probably best avoided. This eaterie is well established, with a pretty terrace overlooking Port Vell.

Sal Café

Passeig Marítim [93-224 0707 © summer L & D daily, winter L only Sun–Tue. € [p305, C4]
Down on the Barceloneta beach near the climbing frame is this slick restaurant-cum-bar, the trendiest *xiringuito* around, serving exotic flavours. A resident DJ presides over the relaxed scene until 3am on Friday and Saturday, but stops earlier on other nights.

El Suquet de l'Almirall

Passeig Joan de Borbó, 65 [93-221 6233 © L & D Tue–Sun. €€€ [p304, B4]
This comfortable, tastefully decorated restaurant with a small terrace overlooking Port Vell is in a different league to its numerous neighbours. Chef Quim Marqués has given new interpretations to traditional Mediterranean favourites such as rice dishes and *suquet* (fish stew).

Torre d'Altamar

Passeig Joan de Borbó, 88 [93-221 0007 © L & D Tue–Sat, D only Mon. €€€€ [p304, B4]
Perched 75 metres (250ft) above the port in Torre Sant Sebastià, this smart restaurant is in competition with L'Orangerie *(see page 222)*

for the title of "best dining room with a view". The gourmet experience does not quite measure up to such heights, but the panorama is spectacular.

Xiringuito Escribà

Avinguda del Litoral, 42 [93-221 0729 © summer L & D daily, winter L only Tue–Sun. €€ [p305, E3]
One of the more elegant *xiringuitos* (beach bars), serving good fish and other dishes on its terrace. Fab desserts as you'd expect from this famous pastry maker.

Bars and Cafés

There are bars and cafés galore along the waterfront, in the streets behind and even in the sea, like the comfortable floating bar **Luz de Gas Port Vell**, Moll del Dipòsit. **Can Paixano**, Reina Cristina, 7, with its cheap cava and tasty sandwiches, is a popular student dive, while nearby **Vaso de Oro**, Balboa, 6, serves beer chilled to perfection and excellent *tapes* to the crowd crammed into its long, narrow

space. The **Fastnet Bar**, Passeig Joan de Borbó, 22, is popular with sports fanatics for its televised events.

LEFT: Agua has a good terrace. **ABOVE:** night-time view of the port from the terrace at L'Elx al Moll. **RIGHT:** seaside seafood, a great way to lunch.

21ST CENTURY BARCELONA

Never content to sit on its laurels, Barcelona launched itself into the new millennium with an ambitious goal of creating a new knowledge-based business district in an industrial wasteland. Its evolution makes fascinating viewing.

Main attractions
TORRE AGBAR
CAN FRAMIS
CA L'ARANYÓ
RAMBLA DE POBLE NOU
PARC CENTRAL
MUSEU BLAU
PARC DIAGONAL MAR

BELOW: Torre Agbar rises amongst the new cityscape.

The area which stretches from Plaça de les Glòries, the arterial roundabout at the extreme right of the Eixample, down to the Fòrum and Diagonal Mar and between Avinguda Diagonal and the waterfront is a curious landscape of 19th-century industrial land morphing into a high-tech business district with pockets of residential zones and green spaces. This is the **22@ Innovation district** which has merged with the original community of **Poble Nou** and the new residential district **Diagonal Mar** to give a new dimension to the city and is an area worth exploring for locals and visitors alike. This is an ever-changing panorama as waste land transforms into star architect-designed skyscrapers, and red-brick former factories find new life as cultural centres or university faculties.

The story goes that after the highly successful Olympic Games and consequent urban regeneration programme the city authorities invented another challenge, a new goal to generate work, investment and vital infrastructure. The idea of creating a new knowledge-based industrial district was agreed in 2001. Ten years on, despite world recession, huge strides have been made, although there are still forests of cranes, placards promising new energy-efficient buildings and a supposed completion date of 2020. Many key companies in ICT, medical technology, energy and media have bought into it and are established in state-of-the-art skyscrapers, graduates stream into their brand new faculties and locals have been re-housed in sustainable buildings.

DHUB to Ca l'Aranyó

A good starting point is **Glòries** ❶ metro. As you emerge from the station two loud statements herald

Recommended Restaurants and Bars on page 171

what's to come. The imposing **DHUB** (Disseny Hub), a new design museum (due to open in 2012, *see page 131*), straddles the road and Jean Nouvel's **Torre Agbar**, the new landmark on the city skyline, rises high above you. Stretching down to the sea is the redeveloped Avinguda Diagonal with different lanes for different means of transport, including some of the new 30km (18½ miles) of bicycle lanes.

Turn right off Diagonal down Roc de Boronat where local architect Enric Ruiz Geli's **Media-TIC** building, clad in energy-saving material, houses part of the distance learning UOC (Open University). Opposite is **Can Framis 2** (Roc Boronat, 116–126; tel: 93-320 8736; Tue–Sat 11am–6pm, Sun 11am–2pm, closed Aug; charge), an award-winning conversion from ruined wool factory to contemporary art museum, housing the Fundació Vilacasas' private collection. The juxtaposition of the

old factory chimney against the surrounding steel, concrete and glass is the leitmotif in this area, repeated in the magnificent **Ca l'Aranyó 3** in Llacuna, a former textile factory now housing the faculty of Communication of the University of Pompeu Fabra. Buildings like this explain why the nineteenth **Poble Nou** (New Town) was nicknamed the Catalan Manchester, not just because of the textile industry that dominated but because of the style of industrial architecture, a fusion of Manchester-style iron structures with Catalan vaulting.

The old community

Follow any of the streets on the left into the **Rambla del Poblenou 4**, and turn right towards the sea. Still the heart of the old community which grew up in the area's industrial heyday, this is like a thread of real life in the midst of the high-tech environment. Here in the shade of the

EAT

The striking contrasts in this area are also echoed in its restaurants, from lofty gourmet cuisine with a view at the Torres twins' Dos Cielos restaurant, high in the ME hotel, or the more down-to-earth endearing bars of the Rambla del Poblenou.

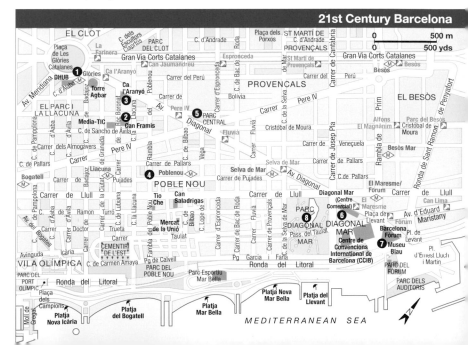

21st Century Barcelona

plane trees normal *barrio* life goes on: babies in prams, kids playing football, old ladies gossiping over their shopping trolleys as they return from the market and retired gents sipping their pre-lunch *vermuts*. There are numerous bars and restaurants running its length with terraces on the rambla, but an essential stop is **Tio Che** at No. 44, for a cool *orxata* or ice-cream, a favourite with local families on Sundays. Meander through the side streets that cross the rambla and you'll be rewarded with small squares and narrow streets with one-storey *modernista* houses and shops that seem timeless.

You can either continue down to the beach at the end of the rambla,

ABOVE AND BELOW: exhibits and hands-on entertainment at the natural science museum, Museu Blau.

or head back up towards Avinguda Diagonal along a parallel street like Bilbao, where the local library is located in another former textile factory, the imposing **Can Saladrigas**. Cross over Diagonal to Jean Nouvel's **Parc Central ❺**, a designer green space surrounded by modern blocks and some still empty cement skeletons. Beyond it is **Can Ricart**, where artists' studios will hopefully be salvaged to cohabit with an ambitious project to turn this former fabric printing factory into Linguamón, a cultural centre for languages.

The Fòrum

Catch a tram down Diagonal, running between original housing for migrant workers from other parts of Spain in the 1950s and '60s on one side and towering new builds like the 29-storey, luxurious ME hotel on the other. Travel as far as **Diagonal Mar ❻** where there is a large shopping centre, several hotels and a conference centre, the CCIB. Jutting into the sea is the **Fòrum** area, legacy of a world symposium in 2004 and now used for large-scale events like music

Recommended Restaurants and Bars below

festivals and the April Fair, the annual celebration of Catalonia's Andalucian community. The original Fòrum building designed by Herzog and de Meuron has just been adapted to house the **Museu Blau** ❼ (Plaça Leonardo da Vinci, 4–5; Tue–Sun 10am–7pm; charge, free from 3pm Sun), the natural science museum formerly in the Ciutadella Park. It has a permanent exhibition of planet earth and its history as well as a section entitled *Laboratorios de la vida*, exploring life from microbes to reproduction.

Beyond the museum is the **Parc del Fòrum** which has a sense of no-man's land under the shadow of an enormous solar panel. However its marina, landscaped bathing pool and other facilities may develop in the next few years, as more locals start to come to the area and the proposed new Diagonal-Besòs (CIDB) university campus building, centred on Zaha Hadid's Spiralling Tower, starts to take shape.

This is all work in progress and fascinating to watch, albeit a regular source of controversy and slowed down by the current economic climate. Meanwhile another project regarded as a white elephant a few years ago, the residential area and its **Parc Diagonal Mar** ❽ designed by the late Enric Miralles, is beginning to take root and look more established. This inspired park with creative games for kids and landscaped lakes is a pleasant oasis amid the high rises. Return to the centre on the 41 bus to complete the tour as it follows the newest part of the waterfront and then passes through the **Vila Olímpica**, which 20 years ago was itself a brainchild of the enterprising municipal authorities. ❑

ABOVE: Parc Diagonal Mar is divided into seven areas linked by one theme: water.

RESTAURANTS & BARS

Bar Llacuna
Llacuna, 88 📞 93-300 8957 🕐 L Mon–Fri, D only Fri. € [off map]
A great find amid the high-tech 22@ blocks, this is a local corner bar with a difference. Subtly spruced up by its young Catalan owners, it still welcomes the old clientele while serving traditional dishes with a modern twist. Offering excellent value and a good atmosphere, it's best to get there early for lunch to beat the office crowd.

Barlovent
Rambla del Poblenou, 21 📞 93-225 2109 🕐 B, L & D Tue–Sun. € [off map]
A great corner bar, located just inland from the waterfront on the bustling Rambla Poble Nou. The *tapes* are genuinely home-cooked and are good enough to meet with local residents' approval.

Els Pescadors
Plaça Prim, 1 📞 93-225 2018 🕐 L & D daily. €€€ [off map]
This charming restaurant specialising in seafood and game is a complete surprise. Find it tucked onto a pretty square amid the former textile factories and new developments of Poble Nou. Worth tracking down.

● ● ● ● ● ● ● ● ● ● ● ●
Prices for a three-course dinner per person with a bottle of house wine: € *under* €25, €€ €25–40, €€€ €40–60, €€€€ *over* €60

BESIDE THE SEASIDE

Few cultural capitals visited for their history, architecture, art or gourmet restaurants can also boast a seashore with boardwalks and palm trees

It was the acclaimed '92 Olympics that transformed Barcelona's heavily industrial coastline into today's glamorous waterfront. Until then people had little contact with the Mediterranean on their doorstep. Essential work in preparation for the Games rewarded its inhabitants with a string of golden beaches and a long, landscaped promenade to jog, cycle or dog-walk along.

Today these beaches are a well-established summer playground for Barcelonans and visitors, thronged with kids, grandparents and the bronzed and beautiful who flop from sun lounger to beach bar as the sun sets. By nightfall the DJs start spinning, making the beach a cool place to be on a summer night.

The Essentials

✉ *www.bcn.cat/platges* 📞 *010 (general info line)*
🚇 *L4 Barceloneta; Ciutadella; Bogatell; Llacuna; Poble Nou; Selva de Mar; El Maresme*
🚌 *6, 14, 17, 36, 41, 45, 59, 64, 71, 92, 141*

TOP: the beaches get incredibly crowded in the summer, but are still enjoyed by locals in the winter.

ABOVE: in nearby Sitges you can combine time on the beach with exploring this pretty whitewashed town with its shops, restaurants and museums.

ABOVE LEFT: it's worth observing the flags: green is fine, yellow suggests swimming with caution and the red flag means don't go in the water. The sea may be flat but it could be polluted or infested with jellyfish.

CITY BEACHES

Sant Sebastià

Southernmost beach sheltered beneath the skyscraper Hotel W (aka "The Sail", *see right*), quieter than Barceloneta beach. Disabled swimming service (daily July– early Sept; weekends in June).

Nova Icària

Attractive beach with the municipal sailing school and facilities for various other water sports. Disabled swimming service.

Mar Bella

Newly created in 1992, this beach is full of fun for kids, with a skateboarding area in the park just behind. Also has a nudey section.

A SHORT TRAIN RIDE AWAY

Sitges

Only 40 minutes by train but a world apart, often with better weather than Barcelona. Several beaches to choose from and the pretty town to explore.

Montgat Nord

The furthest point you can get to on the Maresme coast using the basic T10 transport ticket (Zone One). Long, open sandy beach popular with surfers. A mere 15 minutes from Plaça de Catalunya.

Caldes d'Estrac

Also known as Caldetes, this charming spa town has a long peaceful beach overlooked by *modernista* villas. A pleasant 45-minute train ride along the coast.

LEFT: Frank Gehry's giant sculpture *Pez y Esfera* overlooks Platja Somorrostro and pinpoints the Olympic Port and Village.
BELOW: for some members of the family the beach is a perfect antidote to monuments and museums.

Recommended Restaurants, Bars & Cafés on page 191

MONTJUÏC

The lofty setting for the 1992 Olympic Games has superb views of the city, two world-class museums, an inspiring cultural centre, gardens, and the entertaining Poble Espanyol, "Spanish Village"

The small hill of Montjuïc is only 213 metres (699ft) high, but it has an undeniable physical presence that is noticeable from most parts of the city. From along the waterfront it marks the end of the leisure port, and from the Ronda Litoral it acts like a barrier between the inner residential area of the city and the industrial sprawl of the Zona Franca, the gateway to the south.

From high points around Barcelona you can see how densely packed a city this is – the result of its growth having been contained within the natural limits of the River Besòs, the Collserola range, the Mediterranean and Montjuïc.

Montjuïc past and present

The rocky promontory of Montjuïc has also featured in some of the key events in Barcelona's history. A pre-Roman civilisation made a settlement here, preferring its rough heights to the humid plain that the Romans later opted for. The Romans did, however, build a temple to Jupiter here, which is thought to explain the origin of the name: Mons Iovis eventually evolved into Montjuïc.

In 1929 the hill was landscaped and used as the grounds of the Universal Exposition. More recently, it was seen by millions of people worldwide as it hosted the opening and closing ceremonies and core events of the 1992 Olympic Games. It was regarded as the "nerve centre" of the Games.

Today it is a large city park offering a wide range of cultural, leisure and sporting activities – a playground used by both residents and tourists. It is a wonderful space for walking dogs

Main attractions

FONT MÀGICA
PAVELLÓ MIES VAN DER ROHE
CAIXAFORUM
POBLE ESPANYOL
MUSEU NACIONAL D'ART DE CATALUNYA
MUSEU D'ARQUEOLOGIA DE CATALUNYA
ESTADI OLÍMPIC
PALAU SANT JORDI
PARC DEL MIGDIA
JARDÍ BOTÀNIC
FUNDACIÓ JOAN MIRÓ
CASTELL DE MONTJUÏC

LEFT: escalators were installed on Montjuïc for the 1992 Olympic Games.
RIGHT: open-air concert in Poble Espanyol.

*Plenty of help to find
your way around.*

and allowing children to run wild, or just for clearing the head and getting a bird's-eye view of Barcelona, especially its maritime area. Apart from the cable car that crosses the harbour, this is the only place where you can piece together the waterfront at a glance, and watch the comings and goings of the busy industrial port.

PLAÇA D'ESPANYA ❶

One of the best approaches to Montjuïc is from **Plaça d'Espanya**, which has good metro and bus connections. (If you are heading for a specific destination, such as the Fundació Joan

Miró or the castle, the funicular from Paral·lel metro station is a better option.) Plaça d'Espanya is a large, noisy junction at the southern end of town. It is glaring and hot, surrounded by an incoherent mixture of buildings and, with little or no shade, is not a place to linger.

Spare a brief moment, however, to look at the statue to Spain in the middle of the square's roundabout, commissioned for the 1929 Universal Exposition. The most intriguing thing about it is that Josep Jujol was the sculptor; it is difficult to reconcile this monumental piece with the same

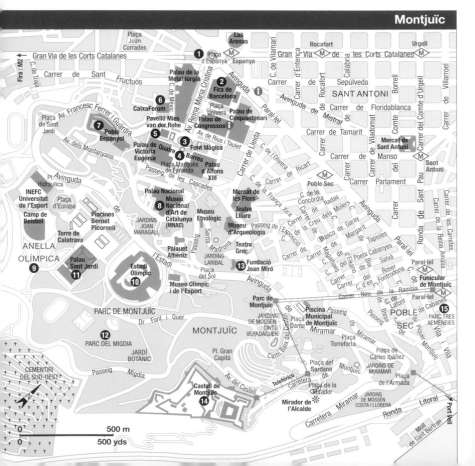

Recommended Restaurants, Bars & Cafés on page 191

artist's brilliant ceramic serpentine bench in Park Güell *(see pages 224–5)*, built at least 15 years earlier. The explanation for the two opposing styles was that the Primo de Rivera dictatorship in Madrid controlled the design of Jujol's monument to Spain.

Las Arenas

The disused bullring, **Las Arenas**, on the other side of the square opened in 1900 with a capacity for 15,000 spectators. It has been converted into a huge commercial centre after standing empty for years. In 2004, city councillors became the first in Spain to declare their opposition to bullfighting, and in 2010 the Parliament of Catalonia passed the law prohibiting it in Catalonia. The last *corridas* were in the Monumental bullring, near Plaça de les Glòries in 2011.

HEADING UP THE HILL

Turning your back on the roundabout, head past the twin Venetian-style towers, designed by Ramón Reventós, that formed the main entrance to the Universal Exposition of 1929. Most of the buildings here

were designed for this event, with a sweeping vista up to the **Palau Nacional**, the enormous, rather overbearing building at the top of the steps. The Exposition, opened by King Alfonso XIII, had as its themes industry, art and sport, and was a political *tour de force* for the Primo de Rivera dictatorship. The hillside was landscaped in accordance with a plan drawn up by Forestier and Nicolau Maria Rubió i Tudurí. Some 15 palaces were built, as well as national and commercial pavilions, a stadium, a swimming pool,

Detail on the staircase of the Palau Nacional.

BELOW: the Palau Nacional, designed for the Universal Exposition of 1929, houses a wonderful art museum *(see pages 181–2 and 192–3).*

The Font Màgica really does look magical during the son et lumière shows, held several evenings a week.

BELOW: statuary decorating the Plaça d'Epanya.
BELOW RIGHT: view from Mirador del Palau Nacional.

two congress centres. If a trade fair is being held, you may be diverted, but there will be a way to reach all the different activities.

The upper esplanades are reached by escalator; the system of escalators was created for the 1992 Olympics, the next major event after the Exposition to bring enormous change to this district.

ornamental fountains, the Poble Espanyol (Spanish Village), the Greek amphitheatre, several towers and the access avenue.

Fira de Barcelona ❷

It still looks very much like a showground, and today acts as the main headquarters of the Barcelona Trade Fair organisation, the **Fira de Barcelona**. The showground has additional premises on Gran Via, the total amounting to 295,000 sq metres (3,175,000 sq ft), including

Font Màgica ❸

🏛 010 ◉ *Son et lumière* shows May–Sept Thur–Sun every half hour from 9–11.30pm, Oct & mid-Dec–Apr Fri–Sat 7–9pm, closed late Oct–mid-Dec for maintenance Ⓜ Espanya

The imposing Font Màgica, designed by Carlos Buïgas for the Exposition in 1929, has been restored. The dancing fountain, creatively lit, delights thousands of visitors during the *son et lumière* shows.

Four barres ❹

Just behind the fountain four very symbolic columns have been erected. Representing the stripes on the Catalan flag, they were originally installed

by Puig i Cadafalch in 1919, but demolished by the Primo de Rivera regime in 1928. Their reinstatement has been a moral victory for the Catalan independent movement.

Pavelló Mies van der Rohe ❺

✉ Av. de Francesc Ferrer i Guàrdia, 7; www.miesbcn.com ☎ 93-423 4016 🕒 Tue–Sun 10am–8pm, Mon 4–8pm 💲 charge 🚇 Espanya

Before going up, don't miss the Pavelló Mies van der Rohe across the esplanade. Built by Ludwig Mies van der Rohe as the German Pavilion for the 1929 Exposition, it was later dismantled, but, at the instigation of some leading architects, rebuilt in 1986 to celebrate the centenary of the architect's birth. Its clean lines are quite breathtaking, and help one understand the beauty of minimalism *(see picture on page 49)*. The contrast with some of the other, pompously ornate, buildings of the same time is extraordinary. Van der Rohe's professor wrote at the time: "This building will one day be remembered as the most beautiful of those built in the 20th century."

CaixaForum ❻

✉ Av. de Francesc Ferrer i Guàrdia, 6–8; www.fundacio.lacaixa.es ☎ 93-476 8600 🕒 daily 10am–8pm 💲 free 🚇 Espanya

Across the road is a fascinating former textile factory, Casaramona, built by Puig i Cadafalch in 1911. Another gem of *modernista* industrial architecture, it has been converted by the cultural organisation Fundació "la Caixa" into its centre, the CaixaForum, a wonderful space with an entrance designed by Arata Isozaki. Apart from its own

TIP

The Olympic swimming pools on Montjuïc will hold the FINA World Aquatic Championships in 2013.

ABOVE LEFT: puppet show during the Festa de la Tolerancia, Poble Espanyol. **BELOW:** Passeig de la Cascades, on the approach to MNAC.

EAT

During the Grec Festival in June and July an attractive open-air restaurant operates near the Greek amphitheatre (*see page 182*).

contemporary collection, it holds temporary exhibitions, concerts, debates and music festivals. It's always worth checking what's on in this inspiring space, and the building itself is worth a visit.

Poble Espanyol ❼

✉ Av. de Francesc Ferrer i Guàrdia, 13; www.poble-espanyol.com ☎ 93-508 6300 ◷ Sun 9am–midnight, Mon 9am–8pm, Tue–Thur 9am–2am, Fri 9am–4am, Sat 9am–5am ⓔ charge 🅿 Espanya

Just along the road is the Poble Espanyol, also built for the 1929 Exposition. The shady green of **Avinguda de Francesc Ferrer i Guàrdia** is

ABOVE RIGHT, RIGHT AND BELOW: sculpture garden, puppet show and sumnmer concert, all at Poble Espanyol.

a welcome relief after the exposed areas of the Fira. The Poble Espanyol has reinvented itself recently and now provides many diversions both day and night, from well-organised activities for kids including treasure hunts in English and arts and crafts workshops, to a *tablao*, where you can watch flamenco dancing. It is not just "family" entertainment: young people flock here for the buzzy night scene, especially in summer. The village is one of the most popular venues in Barcelona.

It was built as a showpiece for regional architecture, handicrafts, and cultural and gastronomic styles from all over Spain. It has a Plaza Mayor, typical of many squares you might find in any part of the country, where popular fiestas take place. The square is at its best when it stages jazz and rock concerts during the summer months.

Innovations in the village

The entrance is through San Vicente de Avila Portal. Javier Mariscal, one of Barcelona's most popular designers (he was responsible for the Olympic mascot), put the Poble Espanyol into the limelight in the early 1990s by creating a trendy bar within the gateway, the **Torres de Avila**. One of the city's most popular open-air clubs, La Terrazza, opens here in the summer. The vil-

Recommended Restaurants, Bars & Cafés on page 191

lage has also opened some new spaces for contemporary art like the Fundació Fran Daurel, with more than 300 pieces including works by Picasso, Barceló, Miró and Tàpies, and a sculpture garden.

Approaching the Palau Nacional

From here, you can either walk up the hill, following signs to the **Palau Nacional,** or take a longer walk up Avinguda de l'Estadi straight to the Olympic Stadium. The easiest route, however, is to go back down to the Font Màgica and take the escalator.

In some lights, or at a distance, the Palau Nacional can look imposing and quite dramatic, but on the whole it looks somewhat out of place in Barcelona. However, the museum in this massive building should not be missed.

Museu Nacional d'Art de Catalunya (MNAC) ❶

✉ Parc de Montjuïc; www.mnac.cat
📞 93-622 0376 🕐 Tue–Sat 10am–7pm, Sun 10am–2.30pm 💶 charge
🚇 Espanya

Since 1934 the Palau Nacional has housed the Museu Nacional d'Art de Catalunya (MNAC), which has the most important Romanesque art collection in the world, including murals that were peeled from the walls of tiny churches in the Pyrenees in the province of Lleida and brought down by donkey. There is also an excellent Gothic collection and a selection of Renaissance and Baroque art *(see photo feature, pages 192–3).*

ABOVE LEFT AND RIGHT: lots to look up to in the Palau Nacional. **BELOW:** the Baroque art section of MNAC in the Palau.

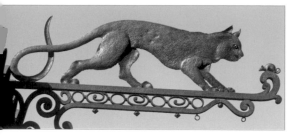

The sign of the cat at the Font del Gat in Jardins Laribal.

However, after major renovation work under the direction of the Italian architect Gae Aulenti, it also now houses a complete collection of Catalan art, ranging over a millennium. The original collection has been complemented by the 19th- and 20th-century works from the former Museu d'Art Modern, which includes work by Casas, Rusiñol, Nonell and Fortuny, and the decorative arts, including pieces by Gaudí and Jujol.

The museum also holds a part of the Thyssen collection of paintings, a coin collection, drawings, engravings and photography. From the steps of the Palau turn right if you fancy a detour to the museums of

BELOW AND BELOW RIGHT: a Greek figure and floor mosaic in the Museu d'Arqueologia.

archaeology and ethnology on Passeig Santa Madrona. The former Throne Room houses a restaurant.

Museu Etnològic

✉ Passeig Santa Madrona, 16–22; www.museuetnologic.bcn.cat
📞 93-424 6807 🕒 summer Tue–Sat 10am–6pm; winter Tue, Thur 10am–7pm, Wed, Fri, Sat 10am–2pm, Sun 10am–2pm and 3–8pm
🎫 charge, free Sun from 3pm
🚇 Espanya/Poble Sec

The Museu Etnològic has collections from all over the world, notably Latin America and the Philippines. A section on Japan, the *Espai Japó*, is an indication of the new cultural (and commercial) exchange between Catalonia and Japan. The museum will close for renovation work in 2012.

On the same street and in the midst of lovely gardens (the **Jardins Laribal**), is a small, pretty café and restaurant, La Font del Gat. Further down the hill is the **Teatre Grec** (Greek amphitheatre, *see margin note, opposite*).

Recommended Restaurants, Bars & Cafés on page 191

Museu d'Arqueologia de Catalunya

✉ Passeig Santa Madrona, 39–41; www.mac.cat ☎ 93-423 2149
🕑 Tue–Sat 9.30am–7pm, Sun 10am–2.30pm 💶 charge
🚇 Espanya/Poble Sec

Just beyond the Teatre Grec is the recently renovated Museu d'Arqueologia de Catalunya, with finds relating to the first inhabitants of Catalonia, including those in the Greek and Roman periods.

From here, the route will take you down the hill as far as the complex of theatres including the **Teatre Lliure** and the **Mercat de les Flors**, which specialises in contemporary dance and movement featuring many top-level international companies, and the **Institut del Teatre**, a drama school. The

productions here are generally interesting and of a good standard. However, if your main goal is to check out the Olympic legacy on Montjuïc, this detour should be left for another day as it takes you a long way downhill.

ANELLA OLÍMPICA ❾

The Anella Olímpica (Olympic Ring) is spread across the hillside behind the Palau Nacional and easily accessible from there by escalator. The buildings here appear to be sculpted out of the ridge, with open views to the south dropping down behind them. Despite the passage of time, they are dazzling in the abundant light of Montjuïc.

There are eight Olympic-standard sports centres and three athletics tracks in the area, but if you stick to the road you will see only a fraction of what was created. Fortunately, a walkway on the inland (downhill) side of the main stadium gives access to the central square.

Estadi Olímpic ❿

✉ Av. de l'Estadi, s/n 🕑 summer daily 10am–8pm, winter 10am–6pm
💶 free 🚇 Espanya/Paral·lel funicular

TIP

On the way down the hill from La Font del Gat is the Teatre Grec, also built for the 1929 Exposition. Inspired by a model of Epidaurus, the theatre's backdrop is a solid wall of rock which was part of an old abandoned quarry. During the Grec summer festival it is an important venue for plays and concerts, a magical place to see a good show on a hot summer night.

LEFT: colourful tiles on the café La Font del Gat. **BELOW:** inside the Teatre Lliure.

The Piscina Munici-
pal de Montjuïc was
used for diving
events in the 1992
Olympics.

BELOW: outside the
Olympic Stadium.

The Estadi Olímpic was actually built for the 1929 Universal Exposition, following a design by Pere Domènech. Its opening football match was a victory for the Catalan side against Bolton Wanderers – a little-known fact. It remained open until the Mediterranean Games in 1955, then fell into disrepair. Extensive works for the 1992 Olympics involved lowering the arena by 11 metres (36ft) to create the extra seating needed for 55,000 spectators.

Most of the track events and the opening and closing ceremonies were held here.

Just outside the stadium a new museum has opened, the **Museu Olímpic i de l'Esport** (summer Tue–Sat 10am–8pm, winter Tue–Sat 10am–6pm, Sun 10am–2.30pm; charge). It's the first in Europe giving a global view of sports with interactive exhibits, multimedia installations and, of course, coverage of the 1992 Games.

The Barcelona Olympics

Being awarded the 1992 Olympics was a huge boost to Barcelona and Catalonia in the post-Franco years. Seeing it as a golden opportunity to attract investment, update long-neglected infrastructures and reinvent Barcelona as a major player on the European scene, both city and citizens rose to the challenge. After six years of tremendous upheaval, a spectacular inauguration in the renovated stadium on Montjuïc marked the beginning of probably the first "designer-Olympics". Vast crowds passed through the new glass and marble airport, the world's top athletes settled into brand-new housing in the Olympic Village built on derelict industrial land, and 3.5 million viewers focused on this hitherto overlooked Mediterranean city. What they saw was striking architecture, breathtaking settings for the different events and a city of new urban spaces, renovated facades and public art, to say nothing of new stadiums and sports facilities. It was considered one of the most successful Games in recent times.

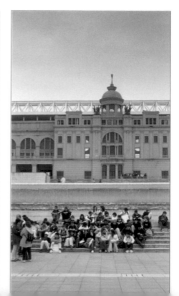

Recommended Restaurants, Bars & Cafés on page 191

Olympic installations

Below and west of the stadium stretches the immense **Olympic Terrace**, lined with pillars. In the middle of the main terrace is a lawn with an artificial stream flowing through it; on the left is a small forest of identical sculptures. The terrace drops down to a second level in the middle distance, and then to a third – the **Plaça d'Europa** – a circular colonnaded area built on top of a massive water tank containing 60 million litres (13,200,000 gallons) of drinking water for the city. The whole has the atmosphere of a recreated Roman forum.

On each side of the terrace are key installations: to the left the **Palau Sant Jordi**, to the right the **Piscines Bernat Picornell**. In the far distance is the **INEFC Universitat de l'Esport**.

Torre de Calatrava

There is one highly visible landmark here that caused great controversy at the time, not least with the architects who created the whole Olympic Ring: the great white **Torre de Calatrava** communications tower (188 metres/616ft), designed by Spanish architect Santiago Calatrava, known for his elegantly engineered bridges. Olympic architects Frederic Correa, Alfonso Milá, Joan Margarit and Carles Buxadé hated the tower project, and rallied dozens of intellectuals to their cause. Nevertheless, the Telefònica tower went ahead, and the result is stunning.

Palau Sant Jordi ⓫

📞 93-426 2089 ⓒ Sat–Sun 10am–6pm, except when hosting an event 🚇 Espanya

Other than the stadium itself, the installation most in the public eye is the **Palau Sant Jordi**, an indoor stadium designed by Japanese architect Arata Isozaki. The ultramodern design in steel and glass can seat 15,000, with not a pillar in sight.

Since the Olympics, the Palau has proved popular for concerts and exhibitions as well as sporting events.

Parc del Migdia ⓬

Just beyond the stadium is an expanse of hillside known as the

The roof of the Palau Sant Jordi measures 160 metres (525ft) by 110 metres (360ft), and was built on the ground in situ, covered in ceramic tiles then raised slowly using hydraulic pistons. It took 10 days to reach its final height of 45 metres (148ft).

BELOW: the Olympic Stadium lit up for the closing ceremony of the 1992 Games.

Parc del Migdia, a great spot for picnics. The beautifully landscaped botanical garden, **Jardí Botànic** (June–Aug daily 10am–8pm, Sept–May 10am–6pm; charge, free Sun from 3pm), is a sustainable garden in keeping with Barcelona's aspirations for the new century, and is well worth visiting.

Palauet Albéniz

Returning to Avinguda de l'Estadi, opposite the stadium are the smaller, more peaceful and elegant gardens of Joan Maragall surrounding the **Palauet Albéniz**. This "little palace"

RIGHT: a walk in the Parc del Migdia.
BELOW: the Palau Sant Jordi, Torre de Calatrava and Olympic Terrace.

is now the official residence of visiting dignitaries to Barcelona. It was built as a royal pavilion for the 1929 Exposition, and during the years of self-government in Catalonia – from 1931 until the end of the Civil War – it was a music museum.

Fundació Joan Miró ⓰

✉ Parc de Montjuïc, s/n;
www.fundaciomiro-bcn.org
📞 93-443 9470 ⏰ Tue–Wed, Fri–Sat 10am–7pm, summer until 8pm, Thur 10am–9.30pm, Sun 10am–2.30pm
💶 charge 🚇 Paral.lel + funicular

With the stadium on your right, follow the main road until it becomes **Avinguda de Miramar**. On the left is the **Fundació Joan Miró**, an understated yet powerfully impressive gem on this sporting hill. Designed by Josep Lluís Sert, eminent architect and friend of Miró, the gallery has been open since 1974 *(see pictures on page 61)*.

A Mediterranean luminosity floods the striking building and shows

Recommended Restaurants, Bars & Cafés on page 191

Joan Miró was born in Barcelona in 1893 and studied here, but in 1920 he went to Paris, where he was influenced by the Surrealists. He spent the latter years of his long life – he was 90 when he died – in Palma de Mallorca, home of his wife, Pilar. For more on Miró's life and work, see pages 60–61.

Miró's work in its best light. One of the largest collections in the world of Miró's work, it includes paintings, drawings, sculptures and tapestries as well as his complete graphic work. It also contains the mercury fountain designed by Alexander Calder for the Spanish Republic's Pavilion in the 1937 Paris Exhibition. It seems fitting that this should be here now: the Spanish Pavilion was intended as a political statement, coinciding as it did with the Civil War, was designed by Sert and included Miró's work and Picasso's *Guernica* (see box on page 50). Contemporary exhibitions and concerts are also held here regularly.

Montjuïc gardens

Just before the municipal swimming pool on the left, scene of Olympic diving in 1992, is the funicular station, Parc de Montjuïc, with the **Jardins de Mossèn Cinto Verdaguer** close by.

Continue along the road for magnificent views of the port from the **Jardins de Miramar**, where there are

several bars serving food and refreshments, and the impressive **Jardins de Mossèn Costa i Llobera**. Once a strategic defence point, the Buenavista battery, this is now a cactus garden, described by the *New York Times* as one of the best gardens in the world. It has cacti from

ABOVE AND BELOW: exhibits at the Fundació Miró.

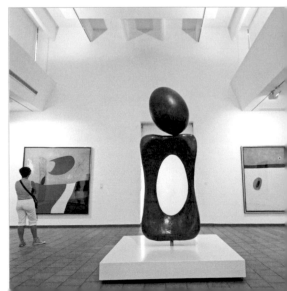

Views across the port from the Castell de Montjuïc.

The Castell de Montjuïc was built in the 17th century during the battle between Catalonia and Spain's Felipe IV, known as the War of the Reapers. At the beginning of the 18th century Bourbon troops ransacked the castle; it was rebuilt between 1751 and 1779. The new fortress was in the form of a starred pentagon, with enormous moats, bastions and buttresses. It has little appeal for Catalans, as it represents oppression by the central government in Madrid, and is a place where torture and executions took place over many years.

Mexico, Bolivia, Africa and California. A 5-star hotel has also opened here, with extraordinary views of the port *(see page 259)*.

Alternatively, you could catch the funicular back down to Paral·lel metro station, or complete the Montjuïc experience and take the cable car up to the Castell de Montjuïc for an even better view.

Castell de Montjuïc

✉ Carretera de Montjuïc, 66
☎ 93-256 4445 ◷ winter daily 9am–7pm, summer until 9pm ⓒ free
🚇 Paral·lel + funicular, cable car

RIGHT: a garden cherub. **BELOW:** the castle battlements.

Recommended Restaurants, Bars & Cafés on page 191

It was here that **Lluís Companys**, Catalan Nationalist leader and president of the Generalitat, was shot in 1940. A statue of Franco was removed from the castle courtyard soon after his death in 1975. The castle has finally been ceded to the city by central government in Madrid and there are various proposals for its future, including becoming an International Centre for Peace.

The citizens of Barcelona are now enjoying reclaiming their castle and it is being used more for leisure activities. An open-air cin-ema in its grounds is a popular event during the Grec festival held in the summer, and keen climbers spend their weekends abseiling down the castle walls.

THE ROUTE DOWNHILL

Descending the hill on foot, you pass through the **Plaça del Sardana** with its circle of stone dancers, sculpted by Josep Cañas in 1966. Nearby is the **Mirador de l'Alcalde** (the Mayor's Lookout Point), with panoramic views over the waterfront. A new walkway, the Camí del Mar, runs from here to the Mirador de L'Anella Olímpica, giving a new perspective southwards over the delta of the River Llobregat.

Return to Plaça d'Espanya by the escalators, or from the castle take the scenic route down by catching the cable car from the Plaça de l'Armada, in the area known as Miramar, and cross to the port.

There is a pleasant walking route down the hill beginning opposite the Plaça Dante near the Fundació Miró, and leading down steps into Poble

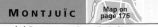

TIP

A cool tip for summer nights: take a picnic up to Sala Montjuïc, an open-air cinema at Montjuïc castle from July to early August (www.salamontjuic.org; tel: 93-302 3553).

ABOVE LEFT: the Jardins de Mossèn Cinto Verdaguer.
BELOW: *sardana* dancers sculpture, Plaça del Sardana.

WHERE

Paral·lel is a good departure point for heading into the Old Town through El Raval, going down to the water-front or returning to the centre by metro.

Sec, the unspoilt neighbourhood that slopes down the hill. Follow the steep street Margarit and make a detour into Plaça Sortidor, which has an attractive old bar where they do a set lunch menu. Meander down-wards through this bustling district, a genuine neighbourhood, where pedestrianized street Blai is full of unusual and attractive bars and restaurants, making it a good nightlife spot.

Alternatively wander down through the Mirador del Poble Sec, a newly landscaped park, or opt for the funicular, which you can board near Plaça Dante. The rail descends a distance of 760 metres (2,500ft) and disembarks at Avinguda Paral·lel, not far from the church of Sant Pau *(see page 149)*.

Avinguda Paral·lel

Avinguda Paral·lel was originally called Calle Marqués del Duero, until in 1794, a Frenchman, Pierre François André Méchain, discov-ered that the avenue's pathway coin-cided with the navigational parallel 44°44'N.

This neighbourhood has always been known as the centre of variety theatre and vaudeville. Its most famous theatre was El Molino, a colourful music hall which, after being closed for years, reopened in 2010 after major refurbishment. It now offers lunch and dinner shows with content ranging from vaude-ville to tango, burlesque to fla-menco. Its reopening is bringing life back to what used to be known as the "Broadway of Barcelona". Even the world's most famous chef, Fer-ran Adrià, has made a serious invest-ment in the area by opening Tickets, arguably the most expensive tapas bar in town.

Parc Tres Xemeneies ⓯

Parc Tres Xemeneies, just down the avenue towards the sea, is domi-nated by three enormous 72-metre (235ft)-high chimneys. This is a fine example of a "hard" urban park, with interesting design ideas. The chimneys are the remains of the "Grupo Mata", an electricity-producing plant dating from the turn of the 20th century. ❑

BELOW: performers in the 'Made in El Molino' show, El Molino theatre.

BEST RESTAURANTS, BARS AND CAFÉS

Restaurants

Prices for a three-course dinner per person with a bottle of house wine:

€ = under €25
€€ = €25–40
€€€ = €40–60
€€€€ = over €60

This is more an open space for picnics than somewhere for dinner, but the cultural centres have attractive cafés and there are several *xiringuitos* (kiosks) in the parks serving snacks. Down the hill in the Paral·lel and Poble Sec districts, options range from corner bars to state-of-the-art tapas.

Barramón

Blai, 28–30 ☎ 93-442 3080 🄮 L & D Sat–Sun, D only Mon–Fri. € [p303, D2]
Bar-cum-restaurant with great young atmosphere in Poble Sec, serving varied risottos among other good things. One of the few places in Barcelona where you can try the Canary Island speciality *papas arrugadas*, "wrinkled potatoes".

La Caseta del Migdia

Parc del Migdia ☎ 693 992760 (mobile) 🄮 summer L & D Wed–Sun, winter L Sat–Sun. € [p302 B4]
Al fresco rustic eating with an amazing view, hidden away in the pine

trees. One of the few spots you can watch the sun set in the city. Try sardines accompanied by rumba on summer nights, or take a picnic and buy drinks at the bar.

Elche

Vila i Vilà, 71 ☎ 93-441 3089 🄮 L & D daily. €€–€€€ [p303, D3]
Famous for its paella and other rice dishes since 1959, when the parents of the present owners brought the recipes from Valencia.

Fundació Joan Miró

Avingunda de Miramar, 1 ☎ 93-329 0768 🄮 L only Tue–Sat. €–€€ [p303, C3]
Select menu of pasta, wok and Indian dishes in the luminous setting of the Miró museum.

Quimet i Quimet

Poeta Cabanyes, 25 ☎ 93-442 3142 🄮 L & D *(tapes)* Mon–Fri, L only Sat. € [p303, D2]
Wall-to-wall wine bottles (unusually wide choice by the glass) and excellent *tapes* in this tiny, authentic bar run by the third generation of "Quims".

Rías de Galicia

Lleida, 7 ☎ 93-424 8152 🄮 L & D daily. €€€€ [p303, C1]
A well-known,family-run

Galician restaurant with fresh, top-quality seafood delivered daily.

Tablao de Carmen

Poble Espanyol, Av. de Francesc Ferrer i Guàrdia, 13–27 ☎ 93-325 6895 🄮 D Tue–Sun. €€€€ (includes show) or tapas menu €€€ [p302, B1]
One of several restaurants in the Spanish Village. Touristy but can be fun. This one has a good flamenco show twice a night, with a set dinner.

Tickets

Av. Paral.lel 164 ☎ 93-292 4254 (booking only on www.ticketsbar.es) 🄮 L Sat–Sun, D Tue–Sat. €€€–€€€€ [p303, D1]
Word has spread so fast about Ferran Adrià's spherical olives and hot cheese and ham airbags that you need to book months in advance to get a look in at this tapas bar with staff in circus garb.

La Tomaquera

Margarit, 58 🄮 L & D Tue–Sat, L only Sun. €€

[p303, D2]
No phone, no reservations, no credit cards, but always packed. A rough-and-ready restaurant where large portions of grilled meat are served with the essential dollop of *allioli* and house wine. Snails are the speciality.

Bars and Cafés

One of the city's most famous *orxaterias* is the **Sirvent**, at Parlament, 56. Join the crowds to try this refreshing (non-alcoholic) drink made from *xufas* (tiger nuts). Amid a rather dreary selection of cafeterias along the Paral·lel it's a relief to stumble upon **La Confiteria**, Sant Pau, 128, an attractive bar with well-preserved *modernista* fittings. In the heart of Poble Sec don't miss a Sunday lunchtime *vermut* (vermouth) with cabaret in the colourfully redecorated old bar, **Gran Bodega Saltó**, Blesa, 36.

ABOVE RIGHT: restaurant in the Fundació Joan Miró.

THE HOME OF CATALAN ART

The Palau Nacional is home to the Museu Nacional d'Art de Catalunya (MNAC), which brings together collections spanning 1,000 years of Catalan art

At the end of 2004, after a decade of refurbishments, the Palau Nacional opened its doors for the first time to the fully integrated collections of Catalan art in the city.

The original collection of the umbrella museum, MNAC, runs from Romanesque through to Baroque and has the finest assemblage of medieval art in Europe. To this has been added various collections, including that of the Museu d'Art Modern that until recently had its own home next to the Parlament de Catalunya in the Parc de la Ciutadella. The Palau Nacional was redesigned after relinquishing its function as host centre for the Universal Exposition of 1929.

Unmissable above the exhibition halls and shooting fountains of Montjuïc, the imposing neo-Baroque "palace" is lit up at night by nine searchlights. Check out the architecture, especially the Sala Oval, and the impressive art collections.

The Essentials

✉ *Palau Nacional, Parc de Montjuïc; www.mnac.es*

📞 *93-622 0376*

🕐 *Tue–Sat 10am–7pm, Sun and public hols 10am–2.30pm*

💶 *charge, but free first Sunday of every month*

Ⓜ *L1 and L3 Plaça d'Espanya*

ABOVE: 13th-century retable depicting *The Martyrdom of St James.*
ABOVE LEFT: *Annunciation and Epiphany,* a church panel dating from *c.*1350.

THE HIGHLIGHTS

Romanesque The greatest collection of Romanesque art in Europe includes many wall paintings from churches in the Pyrenees, rescued from decay at the beginning of the 20th century. Dating from the 11th to the 13th centuries, these paintings, along with altar screens, chests, madonnas and crucifixes, are brightly coloured and executed with a powerful simplicity that has inspired many modern Catalan painters.

Gothic Catalonia's exceptional period of architecture was also rich in fine art. From the 13th to the late 15th centuries, religious paintings by Jaume Huguet, Bernat Martorell and many others in the collection are complemented by sculpture, metal and enamel work and other decorative arts.

Renaissance and Baroque Between the 14th and the 19th centuries, Catalonia had no artists of international standing. This is a European collection, with works from Italy and the Netherlands as well as from Spain, with paintings by El Greco, Goya, Velázquez and Zurbarán.

Modern Art The collection of modern Catalan art runs from the early 19th century until the Civil War (1936), and is important for anybody who wishes to understand *modernisme* and *Noucentisme*, the driving art forces of the modern city. *Modernista* furniture, decorative arts and interiors can also be seen.

Other Collections MNAC also oversees a collection of coins, prints and drawings from the 17th to the 20th centuries, and has a department of photography. Its temporary exhibitions are top-quality.

TOP: the formidable Sala Oval has been splendidly restored and is often used for events.

ABOVE: depiction of the 13th-century *Assault on the City of Mallorca.*

LEFT: a golden casket, one of many magnificent chests, caskets, screens and crucifixes.

TOP: *Poble Escalonat* (Terraced Village, 1909) painted by Joaquim Mir (1873–1940).

LEFT: one of Ramón Casas's most famous paintings, *Ramón Casas y Pere Romeu en Tàndem.*

Recommended Restaurants, Bars & Cafés on pages 206–7

THE EIXAMPLE

Cerdà's 19th-century grid system of streets allowed the city's wealthy elite to commission some of the most innovative buildings of the age, including Gaudí's fabulous Sagrada Família

The Eixample is one of the most characteristic districts of Barcelona, and has some of its most distinctive elements, such as the Sagrada Família and much of the city's famed *modernista* architecture. It stands as a symbol of the 19th-century boom that initiated the city's modern era, and today is the most populated district in the city.

Layout of Eixample

After the narrow, irregular streets of the Old Town, where history has left layer upon layer of building styles, the Eixample can feel like a new town. Its regular structure forms a repeated pattern. Traffic roars down one street and up another in a well-structured one-way system, all the way from its southern boundary by Plaça d'Espanya to its northern limit leading up from Plaça de les Glòries.

Plaça de les Glòries is the axis for three main roads crossing the city: La Meridiana, Gran Via and Avinguda Diagonal. From here the tram goes through Diagonal Mar and the Fòrum, and heads out to Sant Adrià, a suburb on the other side of the River Besòs.

Plaça de les Glòries is pinpointed by the **Torre Agbar**, headquarters of a water company. Designed by the French architect Jean Nouvel, it has an outer casing of glass vents reflecting 40 colours and is spectacular by night *(see picture, page 51)*.

An expanding city

The Eixample is broken into two halves, *la dreta* (right) and *l'esquerra* (left) on either side of **Balmes** as you look inland towards the summit of Tibidabo. Within the two halves are

Main attractions

PASSEIG DE GRÀCIA
ILLA DE LA DISCÒRDIA
CASA BATLLÓ
RAMBLA DE CATALUNYA
PALAU ROBERT
LA PEDRERA
SAGRADA FAMÍLIA
PARC JOAN MIRÓ

LEFT: Gaudí's magnificent Casa Batlló.
RIGHT: lamp designed by Pere Falqués in the Passeig de Gràcia.

In the Eixample, be sure to look up to admire the wealth of architectural details.

residential. Since the 1960s *la dreta* has undergone a profound transformation. With the earlier inhabitants moving to uptown districts, the larger houses have been converted into offices and flats.

The best way to appreciate the Eixample is to wander aimlessly. Peep into doorways to see *modernista* lamps and ceramic tiles, look up at balconies and stained-glass *tribunes* (enclosed balconies), notice the decorative facades, as well as the plants, washing and other elements of real life that go on inside these museum pieces. Take time to visit the art galleries that abound, to notice old shop signs, to shop in ancient *colmados* (grocer's stores).

Whenever possible, catch a glimpse of the inner patios of these *illas*, the name of each four-sided block of buildings: sadly not used for the greater good, as Cerdà, the brilliant town planner behind this scheme, would have wished *(see*

well-defined neighbourhoods, such as those of the **Sagrada Família** and **Fort Pienc** (on the right) and **Sant Antoni** (on the left).

Most of Barcelona's *modernista* landmarks can be found in *la dreta*, while *l'esquerra* is more modern and

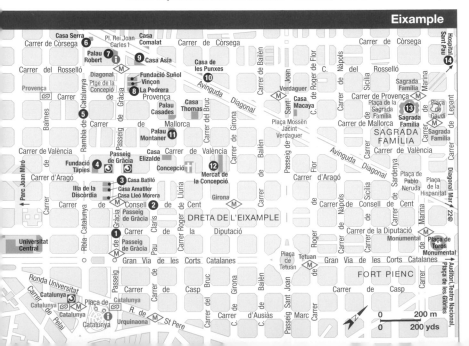

Recommended Restaurants, Bars & Cafés on pages 206–7

box, below), but mostly for car parks, commercial or private use. They still make fascinating viewing though, particularly the backs of the elegant houses and some well-established private gardens.

PASSEIG DE GRÀCIA ❶

The tour outlined here will focus on the central area and some key areas leading off it. Using Plaça de Catalunya as a pivotal point, cross over to Passeig de Gràcia. This wide, tree-lined avenue originally linked

the Old City and the village neighbourhood of Gràcia even before the ancient walls of the city were torn down. Cerdà increased its width to 60 metres (200ft), which makes it distinctive from the uniform streets of the rest of the Eixample; more recently, the pavements have been widened. The beautiful wrought-iron street lamps, which are incorporated with mosaic benches, were designed by Pere Falqués in 1906.

Notice the hexagonal pavement tiles designed by Gaudí and unique to the Passeig de Gràcia. Everywhere you look there are fascinating details.

Junction with Gran Via

This is a broad, busy thoroughfare that brings traffic from the airport and the south right through town to the motorways heading north and up the coast. The fountains in the middle and the impressive buildings around it prevent it from being merely a major through-road, however. As you cross over, don't miss a fine example of 1930s architecture by Sert, prestigious architect of the Fundació Miró, now taken over by Tous jewellers.

 SHOP

On the *xamfrà* (street corner) of Passeig de Gràcia and Diputació you will find Adolfo Domínguez, top Spanish designer for men and women, and on the junction with Gran Via, the flagship premises of Zara. Above Gran Via is Bel, selling timeless, classic tailored fashion for men and women.

LEFT: shopping on Passeig de Gràcia.
BELOW LEFT: aerial view of the Gran Via.

Cerdà

Barcelona recently celebrated the 150th anniversary of the enlightened town plan designed by liberal-minded civil engineer Ildefons Cerdà i Sunyer. When the Old Town could no longer be contained by the city walls, Cerdà's radical proposal for its extension *(eixample)* was adopted in 1859. He planned a garden city in which each block *(illa)* of housing would have a huge central open space, and there would be shady squares, as well as public facilities. In contrast to the dark lanes of the dense Old Town, his wide streets and geometric layout would let light and air into the city. Cerdà's plan was not adopted in its entirety. His "utopian socialism" did not appeal to the more conservative elements in the city, and speculation inevitably reared its ugly head. However, its spirit has informed the strong sense of urbanism visible in Barcelona today.

TIP

The Centre del Modernisme has information on a do-it-yourself tour of *modernista* buildings in the city including discounts on entrance charges (basement of the Tourist Office, Pl. de Catalunya 17; www.rutadel modernisme.com).

RIGHT: Zara's flagship store is on Passeig de Gràcia. **BELOW LEFT AND RIGHT:** up-market dining and shopping In Eixample.

Consell de Cent ❷

Continue up Passeig de Gràcia to Consell de Cent, which demands a detour. Cross Passeig de Gràcia and wander a block or two, to see some of the city's best art galleries as well as the shop of **Antonio Miró**, one of the first designers to bring fame to Catalan fashion in the 1970s. Apart from his twice-yearly collections, he is often brought in to advise on institutional fashion decisions: he designed the uniforms for the *Mossos*, the Catalan police force, and various Olympic and Fòrum uniforms. Even the Liceu opera house *(see page 102)* has a Miró label on its velvet designer stage curtain.

Illa de la Discòrdia

The most famous, and no doubt most visited, block on Passeig de Gràcia is between Consell de Cent and Aragó. The block, known as the **Illa de la Discòrdia** (the "Block of Discord") gained its name because of the juxtaposition of three outstanding buildings, each of which is in a conflicting style, although they are all categorised as modernist *(see*

picture on pages 54–5).

Casa Lleó Morera, designed by Lluís Domènech i Montaner and decorated with the sculptures of Eusebi Arnau, is on the corner, with an exclusive leather shop occupying the ground floor. Slightly further up is the **Casa Amatller** by Josep Puig i Cadafalch, and next door to it is Casa Batlló. Unfortunately, the first cannot be visited, but take a peek at the extraordinary ceramic work inside its entrance. The Casa Amatller is being renovated but should open in 2013 offering guided tours.

Recommended Restaurants, Bars & Cafés on pages 206–7

Casa Batlló ❸

✉ Passeig de Gràcia, 43; www.
casabatllo.es ☏ 93-216 0306
🕐 daily 9am–8pm 💰 charge
🚇 Passeig de Gràcia

Casa Batlló, remodelled by Gaudí in 1906 and considered the ultimate Gaudí masterpiece, has recently opened to the public for the first time in its history, despite the upper floors being occupied. The visit includes the main ground floor, the attic, and the rooftop with its extraordinary chimneys.

Declared a World Heritage site in 2005, the Casa Batlló is perhaps the most dazzling of the architect's buildings. At any time of day or night there is a small crowd on the pavement staring up at its facade. The pale stone, extracted from quarries on Montjuïc hill, is delicately sculpted and, together with the balconies, almost bone-like.

The extraordinary decoration continues inside, from the grand public rooms, including furniture designed by Gaudí for the Batlló family, to areas not normally seen by visitors, like the light well, the chimney pots and the rear facade. Batlló recommended his architect to Milà, and so began La Pedrera three blocks up *(see page 202)*.

Just around the corner on busy Aragó is another Domènech i Montaner work, built in 1886 for the publishers Montaner i Simón and now the Fundació Tapies.

Fundació Tàpies ❹

✉ Aragó, 255; www.fundaciotapies.
org ☏ 93 487 0315 🕐 Tue–Sun
10am–7pm 💰 charge 🚇 Passeig de
Gràcia/Catalunya

Observe this extraordinary building from across the street to get the full perspective, and pick out the chair in the Tàpies sculpture which crowns it, *Núvol i Cadira* (Cloud and Chair.)

Reputedly the first *modernista* building, it reflects the more rationalist ideas of Domènech i Montaner compared with Gaudí's expressionism in the ornate facade of Casa Batlló. The interior spaces make a good setting for the large collection of work by

Inside the curvaceous Casa Batlló, a house that Gaudí remodelled for José Batlló y Casanovas, a Barcelonan textile merchant.

BELOW LEFT: Casa Batlló illuminated at night. **BELOW:** Casa Batlló interior.

The Núvoli i Cadira *(Cloud and Chair) sculpture crowning the Fundació Tàpies.*

BELOW: *modernista* pharmacy facade.

Antoni Tàpies, who is considered to be Spain's greatest living artist. Excellent temporary exhibitions of modern art are also held here.

RAMBLA DE CATALUNYA ❺

After the Tàpies museum, continue to the next corner and turn right into Rambla de Catalunya, which runs parallel with Passeig de Gràcia, one block away. It is like an elongation of the Old Town's La Rambla through the central part of the Eixample. The atmosphere, though, is quite different: the central boulevard is quiet and sedate, the pavement cafés are patronised by smart, middle-aged Catalans or their offspring, and the shopping is sophisticated and expensive, as are the elegant galleries.

REACHING THE DIAGONAL

At the end of Rambla de Catalunya, the Eixample meets the Diagonal, where there is more high-end shopping. On the right is **Casa Serra ❻**, built by Puig i Cadafalch in 1908. It was controversially adapted to accommodate the **Diputació de Barcelona**, the central government body which occupied the Palau de la Generalitat in Plaça Sant Jaume during the Franco regime, and had to be relocated with the return of democracy. In the complex designed by Milà and Correa the new steel building seems like a large shadow of the older one.

Palau Robert ❼

✉ Passeig de Gràcia, 107; www.gencat.cat/palaurobert 📞 93-238 8091 🕒 Mon–Sat 10am–7pm, Sun 10am–2.30pm 💶 free
🚇 Diagonal; FGC Provença

Recommended Restaurants, Bars & Cafés on pages 206–7

SHOP

A visit to Vinçon, Barcelona's high temple of interior design, can easily swallow up a morning. Its gallery, La Salon Vinçon, stages exhibitions on graphic and industrial design.

and some international artists. It is housed in a magnificently redesigned building now open to the public. It also has a space called "Nivell Zero" which shows the work of emerging young artists.

More *modernista* creations

After this, turn right into Rosselló and pass the back of Puig i Cadafalch's Palau Baró de Quadras, turning into Diagonal to reach its splendid entrance. Built in 1904, it is now the headquarters of **Casa Asia** ❾ (Av. Diagonal 373; Tue–Sat 10am–8pm, Sun 10am–2pm; free; metro: Diagonal, FGC: Provença), a cultural centre linking Spain with oriental countries. It holds exhibitions, conferences and has a restaurant named Azafrán. It provides a good opportunity to see the detailed interior of a *modernista* house.

Walk down the Diagonal a short way to see another building by Puig i Cadafalch, the **Casa Terrades** (1903–5), also known as the **Casa de les Punxes** ❿, at Nos 416–420. Sadly, it is not possible to go inside, but the exterior is impressive enough. Like Casa Quadras and Casa Serra, it displays Nordic neo-Gothic influences.

At this point delve deeper into everyday Eixample and see how

these architectural gems form part of a normal neighbourhood. Follow Bruc and turn right into Mallorca to **Casa Thomas** (No. 293), designed by Domènech i Montaner. At the end of the block on the opposite corner is the **Palau Montaner** ⓫ (No. 278; tel 93-256 2504; Sat–Sun 10.30am–12.30pm; discount with Centre del Modernisme, *see margin page 198*), a grand work by the same architect. Its lavish interior can be visited at weekends in a guided tour.

ABOVE: fireplace in Vinçon. **BELOW:** Fundació Suñol.

Fresh produce at the Mercat de la Concepció between Carrer d'Aragó and València.

BELOW: the towers and cranes of the Sagrada Família.

Go down Roger de Llúria and on the next corner left again into València. On the opposite *xamfrà* (the typical chamfered corner designed by Cerdà) is **J. Múrria**, an exceptional delicatessen frozen in time, which is worth visiting for the sheer aesthetics of the place, to say nothing of is mouth-watering display of hams, cheeses and fine wines. Walk along València, past **Navarro's**, the best flower shop in town and which never closes, until you reach the **Mercat de la Concepció ⑫** (www.laconcepcio.com). This is a fine example of a 19th-century market,

remodelled in late 20th-century style with striking results.

From here zig-zag block by block until you reach Mallorca and see the towering spires (and cranes) of the Sagrada Família. If you get footsore hail a yellow and black cab to complete the journey. They are never too pricey for short rides.

SAGRADA FAMÍLIA ⑬

✉ Mallorca, 401; www.sagradafamilia.cat 【 93-207 3031 ⓒ daily Apr–Sept 9am–8pm, Oct–Mar 9am–6pm ⓒ charge 🚇 Sagrada Família

Here, in this ordinary neighbourhood, the symbol of Barcelona for many, and the reason the name Antoni Gaudí spread around the world, is a staggering sight.

The temple was actually begun in 1882 as a neo-Gothic structure under the direction of the architect Francesc P. Villar. Gaudí took over the project a year later, using Villar's plans as a starting point, but greatly expanding their scale and originality. It became Gaudí's main

 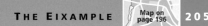

Recommended Restaurants, Bars & Cafés on pages 206–7

Parc Joan Miró

Venturing beyond the central part of the Eixample is a good way to complete the picture of Barcelona from the mid-19th century to the present day. On the extreme left of the Eixample is one of the first urban parks created in the 1980s. Covering four Eixample blocks above Plaça d'Espanya where Diputació and Aragó meet Tarragona (metro Espanya or Tarragona), is the **Parc Joan Miró**. It is a great area for kids to run wild in. The 22-metre (70ft)-high Miró statue *Dona i Ocell* (Woman and Bird) is striking in its simple setting on a small island in the middle of a pool. One of Miró's last works, it was unveiled in 1983, just a few months before he died.

You could link a visit to the park with a trip to Montjuïc *(see pages 175–91)*. Alternatively, combine it with a walk along Gran Via or a parallel street to get a sense of the day-to-day life of the city. The apartment blocks along this route follow the Cerdà plan, even though, on the whole, they grew up later and are more modest than earlier buildings in the Eixample. ❑

Parc Joan Miró is also known as the Parc de l'Escorxador, because it was the location of the municipal slaughter-house until 1979.

project for the rest of his life. He realised long before he died that he would not live to see its completion, admitting: "It is not possible for one generation to erect the entire temple."

At the time of his death in 1926 only the crypt, apse, part of the Nativity facade and one tower had been completed. Today, some 80-plus years after Gaudí's death, work progresses well under Jordi Bonet Armengol, the son of one of Gaudí's long-standing aides. By 2010 the naves were completed and Pope Benedict XVI came to dedicate them, granting the church the status of basilica.

This extraordinary building is best tackled in the morning rather than at the end of a long day's sightseeing, as there is much to see. *(For more information on its main features, see pages 208–9.)*

Along Avinguda de Gaudí is the less well-known *modernista* complex, the **Hospital Sant Pau ⓮** (1902–12), a fascinating World Heritage site. Made up of over 20 buildings, it is the work of the prolific Domènech i Montaner. A public hospital until 2009, it is now being renovated but can be visited on a guided tour (English tours daily 10am, 11am, noon, 1pm with discounts; *see page 198*).

LEFT: *Dona i Ocell* (Woman and Bird) in the Parc Joan Miró.
BELOW: Hospital Sant Pau, by Domènech i Montaner.

BEST RESTAURANTS, BARS AND CAFÉS

Restaurants

Prices for a three-course dinner per person with a bottle of house wine:
€ = under €25
€€ = €25–40
€€€ = €40–60
€€€€ = over €60

Alkimia

Industria, 79 ☎ 93-207 6115 ◉ L & D Mon–Fri. €€€€ [p307, D2]
A shining example of the new talent in Catalan cuisine, young chef Jordi Vilà is the alchemist in question, working wonders on ordinary Catalan dishes and converting them into something quite delicious. With its Michelin star it is one of Barcelona's leading restaurants.

La Bodegueta

Rambla de Catalunya, 100 ☎ 93-215 4894 ◉ L & D *(tapes)* Mon–Sat. D only Sun. € [p306, B3]
Spain was once full of bodegas like this one, with massive old fridges, barrels and marble tables where you can accompany the rough red wine with olives, *tacos de manchego* and a plate of *jamón serrano*. Happily, here you can still do so. It now has tables on Rambla de Catalunya, but the atmosphere inside is better.

El Caballito Blanco

Mallorca, 196 ☎ 93-453 1033 ◉ L & D Tue–Sat, L only Sun. €€ [p306, A3]

Casa Amalia

Passatge Mercat, 4 ☎ 93-458 9458 ◉ L & D Tue–Sat, L only Sun. €€ (set menu L Tue–Fri €) [p306, C3]
This bustling, local spot serves the freshest food sourced from the Concepció market nearby. Excellent-value *menú del día*.

Casa Calvet

Casp, 48 ☎ 93-412 4012 ◉ L & D Mon–Sat. €€€€ [p306, C4]
Satisfy gourmet and culture-vulture needs in one fell swoop at this top-class restaurant, housed in former textile offices designed by Gaudí and full of his characteristic details.

Cata 1.81

València, 181 ☎ 93-323 6818 ◉ D (from 6pm) Mon–Sat. €€ [p306, A3]
The main point of this is an old-fashioned, popular place that always has traditional Catalan dishes from which to choose. The fresh ingredients are selected according to what is in season. It's a relief to find places like this have escaped being redesigned and relaunched in 21st-century Barcelona.

sophisticated little bar is to taste an excellent range of different wines (*cata* is a tasting), served in quarter-litre decanters. However, the tiny accompanying dishes have taken on equal importance and come in a wild mixture of flavours in true new-Catalan style.

Cervecería Catalana

Mallorca, 236 ☎ 93-216 0368 ◉ *Tapes* daily. € [p306, B3]
You may have to queue to get a place at the bar in this popular, unpretentious spot that serves some of the best classic tapas like *tortilla de patatas, pimientos de Padron* or *pulpo* (octopus), but it's worth it. And being a *cervecería* the perfect accompaniment is a cool draught beer.

Cornelia & Co

Valencia, 225 ☎ 93-272 3956 ◉ B, L & D daily. €€ [p306, B3]
Aka "The Daily Picnic Store", this good-looking place is a new concept in Barcelona. It's like an enormous delicatessen, where you can either shop or sit down and eat at one of their long tables, rubbing shoulders with uptown folk. Excellent produce and friendly, helpful staff.

LEFT: Moo, in fashionable Hotel Omm. **RIGHT:** Tragaluz.

place to eat *bacalao a la vizcaína* (salt cod with red pepper sauce) and other Basque dishes.

Jaume de Provença
Provença, 88 ■ 93-430 0029 © L & D Tue–Sat, L only Sun. €€€ [p301,D3]
This establishment rose to fame in the 1980s with Jaume Bargués's inspired interpretations of classic Catalan and international dishes, and is still regarded as one of the city's best restaurants.

José Luis
Diagonal, 520 ■ 93-200 7563 © B, L & D daily. €€ [p306,A1]
Elevated prices that are worth paying for sophisticated *tapes* eaten in the company of an uptown crowd. A classic *cervecería* more in keeping with Madrid's style.

Koyuki
Còrsega, 242 © 93-237 8490 © L & D Tue–Sat, D only Mon. €–€€ [p306,A2]
This is one of the simplest but best Japanese restaurants in the city, less expensive than most and frequented by comic-reading Japanese.

Mauri
Rambla de Catalunya, 102 ■ 93-215 1020 © B, L & T Mon–Sat, B Sun only. € [p306,B2]
A classic establishment selling pastries and ready-made dishes for elegant locals who are not inclined to cook, or who meet up with friends

Drolma
Hotel Majestic, Passeig de Gràcia, 68 ■ 93-496 7710 © D Mon–Sat, L Sat. €€€€ [p306,B3]
One of the first Barcelona hotels to place due importance on its dining room, the Majestic launched the highly regarded Drolma with its equally respected chef, Fermin Puig, only a few years ago. It has risen rapidly and is now one of the most luxurious restaurants in Spain. This is top-notch international cuisine at heady prices.

Gorría
Diputació, 421 ■ 93-245 1164 © L & D Tue–Sat, L only Mon. €€€€ [p307,D4]
As genuine as the first day the Gorría family opened this Basque restaurant over 30 years ago. Daily deliveries of fish make it the perfect

for cakes and coffee in the afternoon. Good-value set lunch if you feel like mingling with an uptown crowd.

Moo
Hotel Omm, Rosselló, 265 ■ 93-445 4000 © L & D Mon–Sat. €€€€ (midday menu €€€) [p306, B2]
Top restaurant in the very fashionable Hotel Omm. Sleek surroundings and delectable modern cuisine. Supervised by the Roca brothers.

Ponsa
Enric Granados, 89 ■ 93-453 1037 © L & D Mon–Sat, L Sun. €–€€ [p306, A2]
A highly polished classic. Old-fashioned good taste and great food, in one of the most attractive streets of the Eixample.

Taktika Berri
València, 169 ■ 93-453 4759 © L & D Mon–Fri, L only Sat. € *tapes* €€ à la carte. [p306, A3]
High-standard authentic Basque *tapes* (known as *pinchos*) and à la carte menu in a *modernista* building that was once a textile workshop.

Tragaluz
Passatge de la Concepció, 5 ■ 93-487 0621 © L & D daily. €€–€€€ [p306, B2]
The flagship of this unfailingly successful group, this place shot to fame in the early '90s as one of the first designer restaurants. It has recently been brought up to 21st-century speed,

but retains its original charms and excellent Mediterranean cuisine. The eponymous skylight (*tragaluz*) is bigger than ever so you feel as if you are on a sunlit terrace. On the ground floor is Tragafishhh for oyster lovers.

Txapela
Passeig de Gràcia, 8–10 ■ 93-412 0289 © *Tapes* daily. € [p306, B4]
This place seems to be from a do-it-yourself kit for Basque restaurants, but nevertheless it has a surprising range of tasty hot and cold *pinchos* (snacks on toothpicks), and is in a convenient location for shoppers. Open until 2am at weekends.

Bars and Cafés
Pavement cafés are everywhere in this busy district, but Passeig de Gràcia and Rambla de Catalunya are best for people-watching.

For a more business-like shot of coffee, **Bracafé**, Casp, is a classic, or try the more leisurely **Laie Libreria Café**, Pau Claris, 85, where the abundance of reading matter slows you down. This bookshop also has an attractive dining room with salad buffet.

Dry Martini, Aribau, 162, is *the* place to be at cocktail hour, and **Xixbar**, Rocafort, 19, is a tiny, very pretty spot specialising in gin and tonics.

ANTONI GAUDÍ'S MASTERPIECE

The Sagrada Família, unofficial symbol of the city, was dreamed up by a religious patriot with astonishing vision

Antoni Gaudí i Cornet was born in Reus in 1852 and studied in Barcelona's School of Architecture. His principal patron was the industrialist Eusebi Güell i Bacigalupi, for whom he designed Palau Güell *(see page 103)*, the would-be garden suburb of Park Güell *(see page 211)* and the crypt at Colònia Güell, an industrial estate outside the city. La Pedrera, his best-known town dwelling, is a Unesco Monument of World Interest *(see page 202)*.

Undoubtedly Gaudí's greatest work, however, was the Temple Expiatori de la Sagrada Família (Expiatory Temple of the Holy Family), which he embarked on at the age of 31. Deeply religious and a passionate Catalan, Gaudí spent the last 27 years of his life living in a hut on the site. When he was fatally injured by a tram in 1926, the only parts of the church completed were the Nativity facade, one tower, the apse and the crypt, where he is buried. Today the work continues, with an optimistic completion date of 2026, the centenary of the great architect's death.

ABOVE: when finished, the basilica will have 18 towers representing the 12 Apostles, the four Evangelists, the Virgin Mary and Jesus.
LEFT: Antoni Gaudí (1852–1926) spent most of his career in Barcelona. He has been described as "the Dante of architecture".
BELOW: the Pasión (Passion) facade, with sculptures of gaunt, tormented characters by Josep Maria Subirachs.

The Essentials

✉ Mallorca, 401;
www.sagradafamilia.cat
☎ 93-207 3031
🕐 Apr–Sept 9am–8pm,
Oct–Mar 9am–6pm;
*guided visits in English
available four times a day*
💶 entrance charge
Ⓜ Sagrada Família

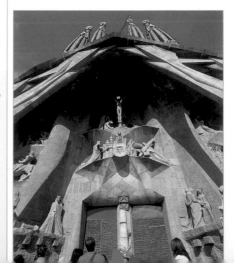

THE HIGHLIGHTS

Passion Facade Visitors enter through a door in the west face of the building where angular figures of Christ's Passion have been sculpted by the Catalan artist Josep Maria Subirachs, an avowed atheist.

The Nave Running north–south, the nave has a forest of tree-like pillars. Gaudí eschewed straight lines. His original design for the 1,300 bench seats was to have them so close together that slovenly worshippers would be unable to cross their legs. After the nave was completed in 2010, it was dedicated by Pope Benedict XVI.

The Towers For a view over the church, you have to take a lift to the top of one of the spindly towers that rise above the east and west facades, sparkling with Venetian mosaics and tinkling with bells. Four more will rise above the Glory (south) facade. Gaudí also envisaged a giant central tower, much taller than Barcelona Cathedral's.

Nativity Facade On the east side of the building is the only facade completed by Gaudí, in 1904. Beautifully and ornately carved and dripping with symbolism, its doorways represent Faith, Hope and Charity.

Ambulatory This external cloister will provide a sheltered walkway all the way round the outside of the building.

The Crypt and Museum The crypt is by the original architect, Francesc de Paula Villar i Lozano, who was employed for just one year, and this is where Gaudí is buried. Here too are models of the church, and a collection of artefacts, but most of Gaudí's plans were destroyed during the Civil War.

LEFT: with the help of young apprentices, skilled craftsmen and new technology, work on the nave was completed in 2010 so that services can be held.
RIGHT: one of the mosaic-encrusted spires of the Sagrada Família.

Recommended Restaurants, Bars & Cafés on pages 221–3

ABOVE THE DIAGONAL

Avinguda Diagonal effectively cuts the city in two. In the little-explored area above this divide are some of the city's most distinctive districts and worthwhile excursions

The Diagonal is the name of the arterial road that slices through the city at an angle, from its western boundary in the Les Corts district right down to where it meets the sea. Two well-worn clichés about the city are that it has traditionally turned its back to the sea, and that people who live above the Diagonal never venture below it. Neither are now true. The development of the waterfront in the 1990s succeeded in dispelling the former and, along with the whole urban-renewal programme, has drawn uptown people downtown.

Many visitors to Barcelona never make it above the Diagonal, but the Park Güell is among the few isolated pockets here that are well trodden.

PARK GÜELL ❶

✉ Olot 1–13 🕒 park daily, May–Sept 10am–9pm, Apr and Oct 10am–8pm, Mar and Nov 10am–7pm, Dec–Feb 10am–6pm 🎟 free for park, charge for the Casa-Museu Gaudí
🚇 Vallcarca or Lesseps

Designed by Antoni Gaudí, Park Güell is the second-most visited park in Barcelona after the Ciutadella. It

was planned as a garden suburb on the estate of the industrialist Eusebi Güell, who went on to commission Gaudí for several other projects.

The estate was to encompass 60 building plots, but only five buildings were completed: the two pavilions flanking the entrance, both designed by Gaudí, and three others inside the park, one of which is today the Casa-Museu Gaudí. One of the pavilions is now open to the public (charge).

(For more information on Park Güell, see pages 224–5.)

Main attractions
PARK GÜELL
GRÀCIA
TURÓ PARC
PALAU REIAL DE PEDRALBES
DHUB & MUSEU DE CERÀMICA
MONESTIR DE PEDRALBES
PARC DE COLLSEROLA
TORRE DE COLLSEROLA
TIBIDABO AND THE PARC D'ATRACCIONS
COSMOCAIXA

LEFT: view from the summit of Tibidabo.
RIGHT: the Ferris wheel in the Parc d'Atraccions, Tibidabo.

Getting to the main sites above the Diagonal is easy. For Park Güell take metro line 3 to Lesseps and walk, or Vallcarca and take the escalators up to a side entrance. The Palau Reial de Pedralbes is also on metro line 3.

RIGHT: mosaic detail, Park Güell.

GRÀCIA

The Park Güell is in the upper part of the district of **Gràcia ❷**, also "above the Diagonal" but without the connotations described on the previous page. On the contrary, it is a neighbourhood with its own history and distinctive personality, preserved in the narrow streets and squares, which have managed to keep out large-scale projects and expensive residential developments.

Traditionally Gràcia was a *barri* of artisans. Generations of families remain loyal to the district, and since the 19th century a strong gypsy community has been well integrated here. There are few newcomers, apart from a small number of young

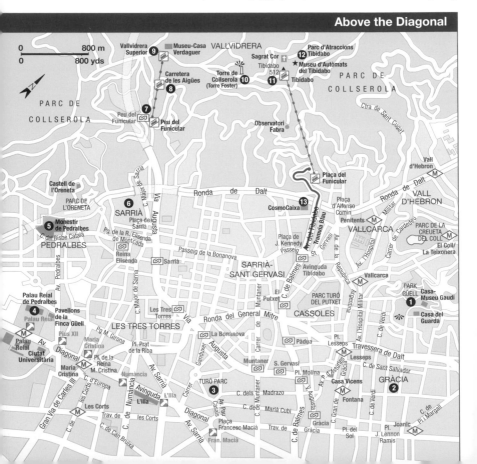

Above the Diagonal

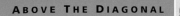

Recommended Restaurants, Bars & Cafés on pages 221–3

people, students and a sprinkling of foreigners charmed by the district's down-to-earth character.

The *vila* (a cut above "village") of Gràcia was once reached from Barcelona by a track through open fields (today's Passeig de Gràcia, *see page 197*). Its established buildings imposed the upper limit on the Eixample, Cerdà's 19th-century expansion plan for Barcelona; the streets of Còrsega and Bailèn were built right up to its sides. The upper boundary is loosely Travessera de Dalt, and on the western side Príncep d'Astúries, although the official municipal district extends a little further.

Gran de Gràcia

The main route into Gràcia is along Gran de Gràcia, the continuation of Passeig de Gràcia, but it is also well served by the metro (Fontana and Lesseps L3; Joanic L4; Gràcia FGC line). Gran de Gràcia is a busy but elegant street full of shops and *modernista* apartment blocks. It also has one of the best and most expensive fish restaurants in the city, the Galician Botafumeiro (*see page 221*).

Walking up the hill, take any of the turnings to the right and zigzag up through streets bustling with small businesses, workshops, wonderfully dated grocer's shops and trendy fashion shops. At night, shuttered doors open to reveal an array of bars and restaurants, ranging from typical Catalan to Lebanese.

You need to visit Gràcia both during the day and in the evening to appreciate its charms fully.

Plaça del Sol

The whole area is dotted with attractive *plaças*; look out for the lively Plaça del Sol, which functions as an unofficial centre for the district. Nearby is the Verdi multiscreen cinema in a long street of the same name; it always shows *v.o.* (original version) films.

There is an early Gaudí house, Casa Vicens (closed to the public) in Carolines, a street on the other side of Gran de Gràcia, just above metro Fontana. It is worth a quick detour to see the facade of this striking house, which Gaudí built for a tile manufacturer.

TURÓ PARC ❸

By contrast with Gràcia, a classic example of residential life "above the Diagonal" is the area around Turó Parc, pinpointed by the roundabout Plaça Francesc Macià (on many bus routes), where one begins to leave the 19th-century Eixample

TIP

If you visit Barcelona in August you may coincide with the Festa Major de Gràcia, the main festival of the district. For at least a week around 15 August, the patron saint's day and a national holiday, the narrow streets are extravagantly decorated, music fills the squares both day and night, and everyone has a wild time. It is well worth going along.

ABOVE: Casa Vicens, an early Gaudí building.
BELOW: Plaça del Sol.

and enter the upper reaches of the Diagonal. Modern office blocks, hotels, smart shops and expensive properties are the trademark. In the park, just at the end of **Pau Casals** (a monument to the famous Catalan cellist is at the entrance), it is not uncommon to see children playing under the watchful eye of a fully uniformed nanny.

Also known as **Jardins Poeta Eduard Marquina**, the park was a project of landscape architect Rubió i Tudurí, and has two distinct areas. One is made up of lawn, hedges and flowerbeds laid out in a classic geometric pattern, the other contains children's playgrounds, a small lake and an open-air theatre. Sculptures by Clarà and Viladomat, among others, dot the interior of the park.

ABOVE AND RIGHT: items in the Museu de Ceràmica in the Palau de Pedralbes. **BELOW:** Palau Reial de Pedralbes.

From Plaça Francesc Macià the Diagonal is wider and the traffic faster, revving up for one of the main routes out of town. Walk, or catch a bus or tram, to the gardens of the Palau Reial de Pedralbes, passing the shopping centre L'Illa on the left.

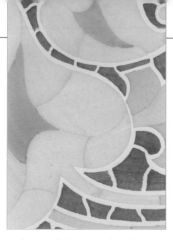

Palau Reial de Pedralbes ❹

✉ Diagonal 686; www.dhub-bcn.cat; www.museuceramica.bcn.es
📞 93-256 3465 ⏰ grounds daily 10am–nightfall, DHUB Pedralbes and Museu de Ceràmica Tue–Sun 10am–6pm 💶 free, charge for the museums, except Sun from 3pm
🚇 Palau Reial

The Royal Palace is the result of a 1919 conversion of the antique Can Feliu into a residence for King Alfonso XIII during his visits to Barcelona. It is elegant, and the classical garden peaceful, but it has little sense of history.

Only the museums housed in the palace can be visited. It is temporarily home to the **Textile Museum**, the **Museum of Decorative Arts** and the **Graphic Collection**, which come under the DHUB umbrella. There is an interesting new permanent exhibition of the textile collection, while the Decorative Arts includes Spain's only industrial-design collection. However these are due to move to the Design museum in Glòries in 2012–13 *(see page 169)*. The **Ceramics Museum** includes some interesting pieces by Miró and Picasso.

The grounds

The garden, built to a "geometric decorative outline" in the 1920s, also by Rubió i Tudurí, integrated

Recommended Restaurants, Bars & Cafés on pages 221–3

the stable block. The lodge interior is simple but with the distinct stamp of Gaudí, particularly the use of brightly coloured ceramic tiles. Built between 1884–7, this was one of his earlier commissions.

Monestir de Pedralbes ➎

✉ Baixada del Monestir, 9; www.museuhistoria.bcn.es
☎ 93-256 3434 🕒 summer Tue–Sat 10am–5pm, winter until 2pm, Sun 10am–8pm, winter until 5pm
🎟 charge (combined ticket with MHCB available, *see page 120*), free Sun from 3pm 🚇 Palau Reial; FGC Reina Elisenda

Chalice in the Monestir de Pedralbes, where you can also see the nuns' cells and refectory.

At the top of Avinguda Pedralbes, by the Creu (cross) de Pedralbes, are the welcomingly old stones of the Monestir de Pedralbes. This is one of the most peaceful corners of the city.

The monastery was founded in 1326 by Queen Elisenda de Montcada, widow (and fourth wife) of King Jaume II. She herself took the vows of the Order of St Clare, and today some 20 nuns are still in residence. The fine Gothic architecture,

the existing palace garden with land ceded by Count Güell. What remains of his neighbouring estate are the lodge and gates, the **Pavellons de la Finca Güell** (Avinguda Pedralbes, 7; Fri–Mon 10am–2pm; guided tours Sat–Sun am; charge), designed by Gaudí. Guarded by an awesome iron dragon gate, also created by Gaudí, one building was the caretaker's lodge and the other was

LEFT: statue of Isabel II presenting her son Alfonso XII, outside the Palau de Pedralbes. **BELOW:** the Monestir de Pedralbes.

RIGHT: Parc de Collserola is popular with cyclists.
BELOW: soaking up the far-reaching views of the city.

most notably the unusual three-tiered cloister, evokes the spiritual side of monastic life, while the rooms that are open to the public provide an insight into the day-to-day life of the monastery's inhabitants. There are some remarkable 14th-century murals by the Catalan artist Ferrer Bassa.

SARRIÀ

While up here, take the opportunity to visit **Sarrià** ❻ by taking Passeig Reina Elisenda de Montcada, which leads straight into **Plaça Sarrià** (also reached in under 10 minutes from Plaça de Catalunya and other central stations on the FGC line). Recognisable as a former village, despite being a sought-after city residence today, it is more charming than Pedralbes, and the wealth more discreet.

This is a real neighbourhood with a market, old ladies in cardigans queuing for lottery tickets, local bars, and the attractive church of **Sant Vicenç** at the centre of things. The main street leading down from the church, **Major de Sarrià**, encourages strolling. The pastry shop **Foix de Sarrià**, founded in 1886, makes an elegant corner. **Casa Joana**, another old established business and little changed, still serves good home cooking at a reasonable price.

Parc de Collserola

From Sarrià you can get a taste of the **Parc de Collserola** by taking a walk on the city side of the hill, overlooking the whole of Barcelona *(see box, below)*. The trip is equally manageable from the centre with the efficient and frequent FGC train service from Plaça de Catalunya.

Recommended Walk

If you take the funicular, or "funi", up to Vallvidrera, consider getting off at the Carretera de les Aigües, a track cut into the side of the hill that winds around to beyond Tibidabo. Popular with joggers, cyclists, ramblers and dog-walkers, it is perfect for stretching city legs, particularly on bright blue, pollution-free days, when the views are breathtaking. For an enjoyable round trip, walk as far as the point where the track crosses the Tibidabo funicular, where a badly indicated footpath leads down to the Plaça del Funicular. Once here catch the tram, or walk to Avinguda Tibidabo FGC station, which will return you to the city centre.

Recommended Restaurants, Bars & Cafés on pages 221–3

The Parc de Collserola is a green belt measuring 17 by 6km (11 by 4 miles), which is on the city's doorstep. Its 8,000 hectares (20,000 acres) of vegetation border the Ronda de Dalt ring road, and spread over the Collserola range of hills to Sant Cugat and beyond.

This easily accessible area is a bonus to city living. It is best known for its highest peak, Tibidabo (512 metres/1,680ft) and its distinctive skyline, with the Sagrat Cor church, a 20th-century confection, and the Torre de Collserola communications tower forming a dramatic backdrop to Barcelona.

The funicular

Reach the Parc by taking the FGC train to **Peu del Funicular ⑦** ("foot of the funicular"), which leads up to Vallvidrera, a suburban village on the crest of the hill where the desirable homes come with a spectacular view. There are frequent services from this station which, by particular request (at the press of a button), will stop halfway to Vallvidrera at **Carretera de les Aigües ⑧** *(see box,*

opposite), where you may want to continue on foot.

Alternatively, take the funicular as far as **Vallvidrera Superior ⑨**, an attractive *modernista* station in this pleasant village, evocative of the days when city dwellers would spend the summer up here for the cooler air. The air still feels a few degrees cooler, even in the height of summer, and definitely cleaner.

Torre de Collserola ⑩

✉ Carretera Vallvidrera–Tibidabo, 8–12; www.torredecollserola.com
☎ 93-211 7942 ⊙ July–Aug Wed–Sun noon–2pm, 3.15–8pm, Mar–June and Sept–Dec Sat–Sun noon–2pm, 3.15–8pm, check website for earlier closing times off season
ⓒ charge ⏹ No. 111

The No. 111 bus will take you to the striking communications tower, the **Torre de Collserola**, designed by Norman Foster for the Olympics and sometimes known as the **Torre Foster**. Up close it is even more impressive than from afar, with giant stays anchoring it to the hill.

View from the Torre de Collserola.

BELOW LEFT AND RIGHT: the Torre de Collserola, also known as the Torre Foster.

The blue wooden tram, the Tramvia Blau, has been plying the route to the base of the Tibidabo funicular since 1901.

BELOW: high flying at the Parc d'Atraccions.

Catalunya). The contrast of the pine-scented cooler air that hits you as the train doors open is quite extraordinary. Walk up a path to the information centre, the **Centre d'Informació del Parc de Collserola** (daily 9.30am–3pm), a helpful base with an exhibition about the park's wildlife, maps and a bar/restaurant.

Close to it is **Villa Joana**, also known as the Museu-Casa Verdaguer (Carretera de l'Església, 104; Sat–Sun 10am–2pm; free; FGC: Baixadoir de Vallvidrera), an atmospheric 18th-century house. This is where the much-loved Catalan poet Jacint Verdaguer lived until his death in 1902. It is now a museum dedicated to the poet, with some rooms preserved from the year he died. Various footpaths lead off into the woods of pine and cork oak to *fonts* (natural springs) and picnic spots. After several days in the steamy city, this area is the answer.

A lift will take you up to the observation deck on the 10th floor for a panoramic view 560 metres (1,837ft) above sea level. On clear days you can see as far as Montserrat.

The other side of the hill

The Collserola park on the other side of the hill is another world, yet a mere train ride through the tunnel after the Peu del Funicular stop to **Baixador de Vallvidrera** station (just 13 minutes direct from Plaça de

TIBIDABO ⓫

The best-known summit of the Collserola range is Tibidabo, with its legendary funfair. Its popularity

Recommended Restaurants, Bars & Cafés on pages 221–3

means moving in large crowds and queuing, but it still has its charms. You can reach the summit from Sarrià, by walking along Bonanova, which leads to Avinguda del Tibidabo, becoming Passeig Sant Gervasi at the end. It is a tiring street to walk along as it is always congested. The bus journey is more pleasant and offers an interesting slice of life.

However, a trip to Tibidabo is more likely to be a day's or half-day's excursion directly from the centre of town. The FGC train goes to Avinguda Tibidabo station. Coming out in **Plaça de John Kennedy**, pause a moment to take in the colours of La Rotonda, a *modernista* house opposite, which is due for renovation.

The Tramvia Blau

At the base of Avinguda Tibidabo, the ancient Tramvia Blau (blue tram), rattles up the hill, passing beautiful *modernista* houses. The avenue's former elegance is now diminished, many of the large houses having been converted into institutions, advertising agencies or flats.

The tram stops at the **Plaça del Funicular**, where there are attractive bars and **La Venta**, a good restaurant with a pretty terrace *(see page 223)*.

The Top of Tibidabo

From Plaça del Funicular you can catch the funicular to the funfair at the summit. This lofty playground has been a popular tradition since the turn of the 20th century. It tends to look more interesting from a distance, but the views are spectacular – and children love it. The church, the **Sagrat Cor**, topped by the figure of Christ, has little charm, but this doesn't prevent the crowds flocking to it. Floodlit at night, it forms a dramatic part of the Barcelona skyline.

Parc d'Atraccions ⑫

✉ Plaça del Tibidabo; www.tibidabo.cat
📞 93-211 7942 🕓 Mar–Apr Sat–Sun noon–8pm, May–June & Sept Sat–Sun noon–9pm, July Wed–Fri noon–9pm, Sat noon–11pm, Sun noon–10pm, Aug Mon–Thur noon–10pm, Fri–Sun noon–11pm, Oct Sat noon–9pm, Sun noon–8pm, Nov–mid-Dec and mid-Jan–Feb Sat–Sun noon–6pm

ABOVE: stained-glass window and exterior of the Sagrat Cor church on the top of Tibidabo. **BELOW:** retro fun at the Parc d'Atraccions.

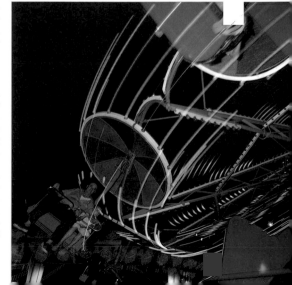

Find a planetarium and giant Pirarucu fish at CosmoCaixa.

BELOW: the Flooded Forest, a recreation of the Amazon rainforest at CosmoCaixa.
BELOW RIGHT: hands-on fun at the science museum.

ⓔ tickets allow unlimited access to the rides; cheaper tickets for just six rides are also available
🚋 Tramvia Blau/funicular from Plaça del Funicular or Tibibus from Plaça de Catalunya

This funfair has a wonderful retro air. Some of its attractions date back to 1901, when the funicular first reached the top, and some are from renovations that took place in 1986. There is also a museum of automatons, the **Museu d'Autòmats**, displaying pieces made between 1901 and 1954. The

tram, funicular and bus run in conjunction with the opening times.

CosmoCaixa ⑬

✉ Isaac Newton, 26; www.obrasocial.lacaixa.es 📞 93-212 6050
🕐 Tue–Sun 10am–8pm, also Mon during late June–Sept ⓔ charge
🚆 FGC Avinguda Tibidabo 🚌 196

A few minutes' walk from Plaça John Kennedy (walk up Avinguda Tibidabo from the FGC station and turn left onto Teodor Roviralta) is one of the most exciting science museums in Europe, the CosmoCaixa, with plenty of hands-on exhibits and interesting temporary exhibitions for all ages. Even 3–6-year-olds are catered for in the "Clik dels Nens", a space to play and learn in created by the high-profile designer Javier Mariscal.

There are many other innovative ways to enlighten the public on the subjects of science and technology. Among the highlights is the Flooded Forest, a recreation of part of the Amazon rainforest. The museum is funded by the affluent cultural foundation of La Caixa savings bank. ❑

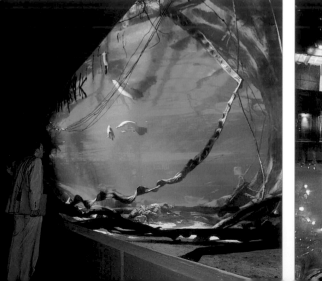

BEST RESTAURANTS, BARS AND CAFÉS

Restaurants

Prices for a three-course dinner per person with a bottle of house wine:
€ = under €25
€€ = €25–40
€€€ = €40–60
€€€€ = over €60

This area covers a lot of ground, so it has an equally broad range of restaurants, cafés and bars, from inexpensive student haunts and "ethnic" restaurants in the Gràcia neighbourhood to top-notch Michelin-starred restaurants in the smarter zones and rustic outdoor restaurants in Collserola Park.

A Contraluz
Milanesat, 19 ☏ 93-203 0658 ⓒ L & D daily. €€€ (set menu €) [off map]
Located in a quiet street in the smart residential Tres Torres area (en route to the Monestir de Pedralbes), this house and garden is a relaxing place to dine, and frequented by a fashionable clientele. The reasonably priced lunchtime menu is a good option.

Abac
Av. Tibidabo, 1 ☏ 93-319 6600 ⓒ L & D Tue–Sat. €€€€ [off map]

Now under the Michelin star of young chef Jordi Cruz, this exclusive restaurant in its own garden has 15 hotel rooms and a spa. An indulgent night for travelling gourmets is guaranteed.

Amir de Nit
Plaça del Sol, 2 ☏ 93-218 5121 ⓒ L & D daily. € [306, B1]
There are quite a few Lebanese places in Barcelona now, but this has always been a firm favourite. It has a large choice of well-prepared, delicious dishes, and its location in one corner of this popular square in Gràcia is perfect, especially for eating alfresco on a summer evening.

La Balsa
Infanta Isabel, 4 ☏ 93-211 5048 ⓒ L & D Tue–Sat, L only Sun, D only Mon. €€€ [off map]
Prize-winning design of wood and glass with views of greenery. There are terraces for eating alfresco. International and Catalan cuisine served.

Bilbao
Perill, 33 ☏ 93-458 9624 ⓒ L & D Mon–Sat. €€ [p306, C2]
Find an animated atmosphere in this tradi-

tional eatery in Gràcia, frequented mainly by journalists, artists and writers. Especially busy at lunchtime.

Botafumeiro
Gran de Gràcia, 81 ☏ 93-218 4230 ⓒ L & D daily. €€€€ [p306, B1]
This smart Galician restaurant, haunt of the rich and famous, has a long-running reputation as *the* place to eat seafood in Barcelona. Oysters are served at the bar.

Can Tomás
Major de Sarrià, 49 ☏ 93-203 1077 ⓒ L & D until 10pm Thur–Tue. € [off map]
People come to Sarrià from all over town for

Tomás' renowned *patatas bravas* (fried potatoes served with spicy sauce and/or mayonnaise), made according to his own secret recipe.

Casa Joana
Major de Sarrià, 59 ☏ 93-203 1036 ⓒ L & D Mon–Sat. € [off map]
Very good value for this generally expensive part of town, especially the midday menu. A cosy, family-run restaurant where it's good to choose traditional dishes like *canelons*.

Casa Trampa
Pl. de Vallvidrera, 3 ☏ 93-406 8051 ⓒ L Tue–Sun, D Fri–Sat. € [off map]

RIGHT: a classic Barcelonan bar.

Prices for a three-course dinner per person with a bottle of house wine:
€ = under €25
€€ = €25–40
€€€ = €40–60
€€€€ = over €60

Traditional, homely Catalan restaurant with food to match, right in the centre of this charming "village" that is part of the city. Their *croquetas* are a must. It is just a funicular ride away and well worth the trip. Combine a meal here with a walk in the Collserola park.

El Jardí de l'Abadessa
Abadessa d'Olzet, 26
93-280 3754 L & D Mon–Fri. €€ [off map, FGC Reina Elisenda]
A very attractive uptown spot in a large garden, ideal for a peaceful lunch after a visit to the Monestir de Pedralbes, or to

possibly rub shoulders with a Barça star on a summer evening. Serves light Mediterranean dishes. A great place to sip a glass of cava.

Envalira
Plaça del Sol, 13 93-218 5813 L & D Tue–Sat, L only Sun. €€–€€€ [p306, B1]
A classic in the heart of Gràcia whose decoration does not seem to have changed in all the years the family has run it, but where you can be sure of an excellent *arroz* (rice dishes including paella). The house speciality is *arroz a la milanesa*. This is Spanish cooking at its most genuine.

Flash-Flash
Granada del Penedès, 25
93-237 0990 L & D daily. €–€€ [p306, A1]
Almost a period piece

now, this bar was super-trendy in the 1970s. Its wonderful white leatherette seating and black-and-white Warhol-type prints on the walls still have a lot of style and it's a great place for tortillas (there are over 70 varieties to choose from), sandwiches and snacks.

Hisop
Passatge Marimon, 9
93-241 3233 L & D Mon–Fri, D only Sat. €€€ [p306, A1]
Two young Catalan chefs practise the latest culinary art of deconstructivism with amazing results in this minimalist restaurant, much acclaimed by foodies.

Neichel
Beltrán i Rózpide, 1–5
93-203 8408 L & D Tue–Sat. €€€€ [off map]

A prize-winner for its modern, stylish design and two Michelin stars, Neichel looks onto a garden of lemon trees. The owner describes the food as "avant-garde Mediterranean", and there is a special "tastes and aromas" menu.

L'Orangerie
Hotel La Florida, Carretera Vallvidrera–Tibidabo, 83–93
93-259 3000 L & D daily. €€€€. Brunch Sun. €€€ [off map]
The ultimate indulgence for Sunday brunch is this 5-star Grand Luxe hotel on top of Tibidabo. Sip cava while overlooking the most panoramic view of Barcelona.

Roig Robí
Sèneca, 20 93-218 9222 L & D Mon–Fri, D only Sat. €€€€ [p306, B2]

Mercè Navarro's famed restaurant is a beautifully subtle, elegant space with a terrace, and food and service to match the high standard of the surroundings. A favourite with locals in the know.

La Rosa del Desierto

Plaça Narcís Oller, 7 ☎ 93-237 4590 ☺ L & D Tue–Sat, L only Sun. €€ [p306, B2]
A pioneer of Moroccan cooking in Barcelona, this well-established restaurant has had a facelift and put up its prices, but it remains one of the best places to have couscous, offering a choice of 10 different ones, all delicious.

Roure

Riera Sant Miquel, 51 ☎ 93-237 7490 ☺ L & D

Mon–Sat. € [p306, B1]
This is a classic Barcelona corner bar that is always bustling. Popular with a strong band of regulars, it serves *tapes* all day long and meals at lunchtime (worth coming for the paella on Thursday). Good value in every sense.

La Singular

Francisco Giner, 50 ☎ 93-237 5098 ☺ L & D Mon–Fri, D only Sat. € [p306, B1]
This is a wonderful little Gràcia restaurant with a warm, friendly atmosphere and great cooking, using seasonal local produce but giving it an edge.

La Venta

Plaça Doctor Andreu, 1 ☎ 93-212 6455 ☺ L & D Tue–Sat. €€€ [off map]

One of the prettiest restaurants in the city, at the foot of the funicular to Tibidabo. High-class Mediterranean food – the perfect setting for springtime lunches or summer nights on the leafy terrace. Their recently opened *mirador* is more exclusive, with magnificent views over the city.

Bars and Cafés

Gràcia is full of old neighbourhood cafés, new trendy bars and ever-popular terrace cafés, especially in its many squares. In particular, try **Café del Sol** in the Plaça del Sol, or the **Virreina** in the Plaça de la Virreina. **Salambó**, Torrijos, 51, is a bit more sophisticated, and **Sol Soler,** Plaça del Sol, 21, is charming and serves delicious *tapes*. **La Cervesera Artesana**, Agustí, 14, brews its own beer.

By contrast, the cafés further up the Diagonal are full of expensively dressed residents. **Sandor**,

Plaça Francesc Macià, 5, is an elegant classic from the 1940s.

The recently opened **Café Vienés**, in the Hotel Casa Fuster *(see page 259)*, Passeig de Gràcia, 132, is at the top of the range in the magnificently restored Domènech i Montaner building. It is well worth a visit in itself.

LEFT: retro chic at Flash-Flash.
ABOVE: La Venta is a great place for lunch.

PARK GÜELL

A high point in the city is the park designed by Antoni Gaudí to be an avant-garde suburb

The "park" of Park Güell is officially spelt the English way because its developer, the industrialist Eusebi Güell, intended it to be a suburban "garden city" along the then fashionable English lines. Sixty houses were planned to benefit from a 15-hectare (38-acre) environment designed by Antoni Gaudí, and although only five were completed, the park remains one of the architect's most appealing works.

Always aware of the struggle between man and nature, Gaudí used shapes which harmonised with the landscape, building a complex of staircases, zoomorphic sculptures, sinuous ramps and viaducts. The most important single element of the park is a two-tiered plaza; the lower part is the Sala Hipóstila, a hypostyle of Doric columns leaning inwards and with hollow central cores to collect water from the terrace above. This was designed to be the estate's market-place. The overhead terrace is an open area with wonderful views, surrounded by an undulating bench of mosaics by Josep Jujol.

Built between 1900 and 1914, the park was taken over by the city council in 1918 and is today a Unesco World Heritage Site.

The Essentials

✉ *Carrer d'Olot, s/n*
☎ *010*
🕐 *daily 10am to 6–9pm, depending on time of year*
💰 *free. Charge for Casa-Museu Gaudí and Casa del Guarda, the lodge*
Ⓜ *Lesseps, then 20-minute walk or Vallcarca; buses 24, 92*

ABOVE: Jujol's bright ceramic serpentine bench outlines the terrace – a popular place to sit and relax or take stock of the city which stretches out below.
BELOW: it's also easy to spend time gazing at the endlessly fascinating details of the ceramic decorative work.

CASA-MUSEU GAUDÍ

Park Güell's original showhouse was the work of a collaborating architect, Francesc Berenguer. Gaudí himself moved into this house, which he called Torre Rosa, in 1906 after no buyers were found, and it remained his home until his death in 1926. Today the three-storey **Casa-Museu Gaudí** *(pictured above)* contains his bed, prie-dieu and crucifix, as well as drawings and a collection of furniture designed by him and taken from different parts of the city. Although Gaudí was the mastermind of the proposed "garden city", it was never intended that he should be the architect of the 60 houses. Plots were to be sold with the provisos that buildings took up no more than one-sixth of the ground area, and garden walls should be no more than 40cm (16 inches) high. A second house, Casa Trias, was built by Juli Batllevell in 1903 for a lawyer, Martín Trias Domènech, and it remains in the Trias family hands.

Count Güell died in Casa Larrard, the original house on the estate, in 1918, knowing that nobody else wanted to share his dream.

ABOVE: The method of decoration using broken glazed ceramics (incorporating old crockery and bottle bottoms at times) is a hallmark of Gaudí buildings, known as *trencadís*.
LEFT: Gaudí designed two Hansel and Gretel-like pavilions with fantastical roofs to flank the park entrance. The Casa Guarda, open to the public, has a small but interesting exhibition.
RIGHT: inside the park entrance a double staircase leads up to the market hall and, above it, the terrace intended to stage concerts and theatrical events, which extends on to level land behind.

Recommended Restaurants on pages 242–3

AROUND BARCELONA

The Catalonian hinterland as far as the Pyrenees and long stretches of coastline on either side of Barcelona provide exceptional opportunities for excursions from the city, most of which are possible on public transport

Barcelona

arcelona is a great city to be in, but there are also beaches, mountains, wine country, religious retreats and historic provincial cities all within relatively easy reach. Travelling to and from the city by hire car is best avoided in weekday rush hours, Sunday evening, all weekend in summer, and at the start and end of Christmas, Easter and August holidays. Visitors who travel outside these times will enjoy straightforward, stress-free journeys. Travelling by train and bus is also manageable from the city.

EXCURSIONS

Some of those excursions are day trips but it would be worth taking two or three days for the longer ones.

There are two options for journeys to the south of Barcelona (Sitges and Tarragona), two to the west (Sant Sadurní and Montserrat), three inland to the north (Montseny, Vic and the Pyrenees), two up into the province of Girona (Figueres and Girona), one to the Maresme coast just north of Barcelona (Caldetes), and one to the Costa Brava.

Sitges, Caldetes and the Costa Brava all have fine beaches;

Montserrat, Montseny and the Pyrenees are mountain-top retreats; Vic, Tarragona, Figueres and Girona are historic provincial centres.

Colònia Güell ❶

✉ Santa Coloma de Cervelló; www. elbaixllobregat.net/coloniaguell
📞 93-630 5807 🕓 summer Mon–Fri 10am–7pm, winter until 5pm, Sat–Sun 10am–3pm 💶 charge for church 🚉 FGC trains from Plaça d'Espanya to Colònia Güell station

Main attractions

COLÒNIA GÜELL
SITGES
TARRAGONA
SANT SADURNÍ D'ANOIA
VILAFRANCA DEL PENEDÈS
MONTSERRAT
PARC NATURAL DE MONTSENY
VIC
AIGÜESTORTES
GIRONA
FIGUERES
CALDES D'ESTRAC
BLANES
BEGUR

PRECEDING PAGES: Girona Old Town.
LEFT: Sitges beach below the church.
RIGHT: family fun on the Costa Brava.

TIP

Using a T10 metro card
(zone 1) you can travel
up the coast on a train
as far as Montgat Nord
(a favourite for surfers)
or down to Platja de
Castelldefels (and even
the airport).

One easy trip that can be done in half a day or less is to Santa Coloma de Cervelló to Colònia Güell, a 19th-century textile-industry estate with a church crypt designed by Antoni Gaudí. It is a fascinating place, and the crypt, named a World Heritage site in 2005, is a must for Gaudí enthusiasts.

SITGES ②

A smooth 40-minute train ride or a quick drive through the Garraf tunnels on the C32 motorway will whisk you south to **Sitges**, the closest clean and uncrowded bit of the Mediterranean coast. Sand and sun can be enjoyed at Castelldefels, 20 minutes from Barcelona, but the whitewashed houses and flower-festooned balconies of Sitges are worth the extra journey time, making you feel a world away. A day on the beach, with a paella for lunch, is a great idea. What's more, the weather is reputed always to be better in Sitges, so you could leave Barcelona in cloud and arrive to find glorious sunshine.

An international party atmosphere pervades Sitges in summer, and the town has a full calendar of festivals year round, including a

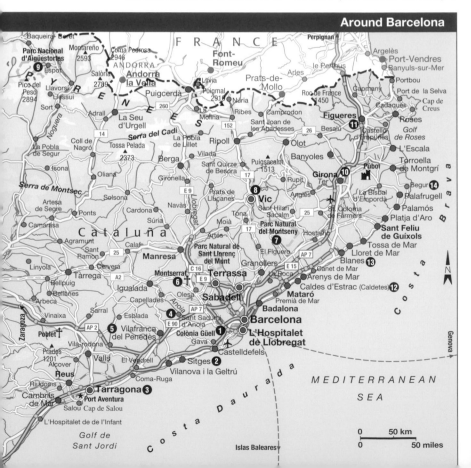

Around Barcelona

Recommended Restaurants on pages 242–3

notoriously wild Carnival, thanks to its gay community, and an International Film Festival in October.

The beaches are fringed by palms and an elegant promenade. They start on the other side of the 17th-century Església Sant Bartomeu i Santa Tecla, on the headland, and extend south past the Hotel Terramar.

Museu Romàntic Can Llopis

✉ Sant Gaudenci, s/n 🕒 summer Tue–Sat 9.30am–2pm, 4–7pm, winter Tue–Sat 9.30am–2pm, 3.30–6.30pm, Sun (all year) 10am–3pm

The Museu Romàntic Can Llopis gives a good insight into 19th-century living conditions and houses the **Lola Anglada** antique-doll collection.

TARRAGONA ❸

Around 90 minutes from Barcelona by train or car, **Tarragona** still has the feel of a provincial capital of the Roman Empire. Captured by Rome in 218 BC and later the capital of the Spanish province of Tarraconensis under Emperor Augustus, the town was the major commercial centre until Barcelona and Valencia over shadowed it following the Christian Reconquest in the early 12th century.

Rich in Roman ruins still being unearthed and stunningly beautiful ancient buildings, it was declared a World Heritage site in 2000.

The cathedral

Tarragona's **cathedral**, the centre-piece of the top part of the city, has been described by Catalonia's own travel writer Josep Pla as "easily and serenely mighty, solid as granite, maternal – a cathedral redolent of

ABOVE: life's a beach on Sitges's Platja d'Or.
BELOW: Tarragona's Roman amphitheatre.

Carvings on the door of Tarragona's splendid cathedral.

BELOW: Tarragona's atmospheric Passeig Arqueològic.
BELOW RIGHT: Corinthian pillars in the ancient Forum.

rounding the city, and finally east to the coastline and sea.

Below the walls is the middle section of Tarragona, with the wide and stately **Rambla** ending in the **Balcó del Mediterrani** (Mediterranean Balcony) looking over the beach, port and impressive Roman amphitheatre. The city's luminosity at this point has been much commented on and is indeed remarkable: a crisp elegance and clean air shimmer over the golden sandstone of 2,000-year-old Roman structures.

The port

The **Serrallo** section of the port is the main attraction in the lower part of the city, the multicoloured fishing fleet unloading their catch every afternoon, the fish auctioned off within minutes. A lunch at a dockside restaurant – featuring fine Tarragona wines and seafood just out of the nets – makes a delicious end to a visit.

Salou and Port Aventura

Just 8km (5 miles) south of Tarragona is the seaside resort of **Salou** and its neighbouring theme park

Roman virtues projected onto carved stone – a lion in repose, drowsy, unabashedly powerful."

Passeig Arqueològic

Explore the walled upper part of the city surrounding the cathedral, then tour the wall itself, the Passeig Arqueològic (Archaeological Promenade). It offers views south over the city, west out to the mountains, north to the hills and trees sur-

Recommended Restaurants on pages 242–3

Port Aventura, the largest in Europe after Disneyland Resort Paris (end Mar–end Oct daily, Nov–Dec Fri–Sun only; see www.portaventura.es to confirm opening times; charge). People travel for miles to experience the thrills and spills it offers. There are several hotels on the site and a new golf course.

SANT SADURNÍ D'ANOIA ❹

If you wish to experience the more indigenous pleasures of Catalonia, a trip to **Sant Sadurní d'Anoia,** a small town responsible for 80 percent of cava production, is recommended. Sparkling wine made in Catalonia is not champagne – it is cava.

A 45-minute train ride from Sants or Plaça de Catalunya stations in Barcelona will drop you in Sant Sadurní, right next to Freixenet, the world's leading producer of cava, with vineyards in California and operations in China.

Cava has been produced in Sant Sadurní since 1872 by Josep Raventós, founder of the Codorníu empire, who studied the *méthode champenoise* of Dom Pérignon and made Catalonia's first bottle of cava. It is an important part of life in Catalonia: baptisms, weddings, even routine Sunday lunches are occasions for popping corks. On 20 November 1975, the day Franco died, cava was given away free in Barcelona.

VILAFRANCA DEL PENEDÈS ❺

About 14km (8 miles) from Sant Sadurní is **Vilafranca del Penedès.** The Penedès region has more than 300 wine and cava-producing companies, most of which can be visited, including the winery and extensive vineyards of the world-famous Torres, which dominates the region. Information is centralised through the tourist office in Vilafranca (tel: 93-818 1254). Around Sant Sadurní even children have opinions on *bruts, secs* and *brut natures.*

Vinseum: Museu de les Cultures del Vi de Catalunya

✉ Plaça Jaume I, Vilafranca del Penedès; www.vinseum.cat ☎ 93 8900 582 ⏱ Tue–Sat 10am–2pm and 4–7pm, Sun 10am–2pm 💳 charge

One of Europe's best wine museums is being modernised to include the history of wine in Catalonia and is due to move into a renovated 13th-century palace. In the meantime, a temporary exhibition is on display and the visit ends with a wine tasting.

MONTSERRAT ❻

✉ www.montserratvisita.com ⏱ daily 6am–8pm, museum Mon–Fri 10am–5.45pm, Sat–Sun 10am–7pm

Freixenet offers a spectacular tour, including a screening of its famous Christmas advertisements, featuring stars such as Shakira, Penélope Cruz and more recently a short directed by Martin Scorsese. A glass of cava is presented to guests as a finale.

BELOW:
Sant Sadurní d'Anoia produces 80 percent of Spain's cava.

EAT

Sant Sadurní offers excellent gastronomic opportunities at local restaurants well known for fine cava and seafood. Between late January and mid-March, the *calçotada* is a traditional feast starring long-stemmed *calçots* (something between a spring onion and a leek), dipped in a romesco sauce of oil, peppers, garlic and ground nuts. Cava flows freely at these rustic banquets, accompanied by lamb or rabbit grilled, as are the *calçots*, over coals.

ABOVE AND BELOW: the Vinseum, Vilafranca del Penedès.

🔲 FGC from Plaça d'Espanya plus cable car or zip-train

Situated 48km (30 miles) west of Barcelona, and looming 1,236 metres (4,055ft) over the valley floor, Montserrat, the highest point of the lowlands, is Catalonia's most important religious site *(see pages 244–5)*. Here athletes pledge to make barefoot pilgrimages if their prayers are answered and vital competitions

won. Groups of young people from all over Catalonia make overnight hikes at least once in their lives to watch the sunrise from the heights.

"La Moreneta" (the Black Virgin), said to have been made by St Luke and brought to Barcelona by St Peter, resides in the sanctuary of the Mare de Deu de Montserrat. There is a separate door at the front of the basilica for people wanting to see and touch this statue of Madonna and Child, but be prepared to queue.

It can be reached easily and spectacularly by train, but the advantage of going by car is the opportunity of seeing it from different angles. In the words of Catalan poet Maragall, from varying perspectives Montserrat resembles "a bluish cloud with fantastic carvings, a giant's castle with 100 towers thrown towards the sky… above all an altar, a temple".

The basilica is packed with works by prominent painters and sculptors, including paintings by El Greco in the sanctuary's museum. Catalan poets have dedicated some of their most inspired verse to Montserrat, while maestros such as Nicolau and

Recommended Restaurants on pages 242–3

Millet have composed some of their finest pieces in its honour. Goethe is said to have dreamed of Montserrat, and Parsifal sought the Holy Grail here in Wagner's opera.

Excursions

There are several excursions to be made from the monastery. Via Crucis, the Way of the Cross (behind Plaça de L'Abat Oliba) leads to the hermitage of **Sant Miquel**. From Plaça de la Cru a cable car runs down to **Santa Cova**, a chapel in a grotto where the Virgin is said to have been hidden during the Moorish occupation.

On a clear day it is worth taking the funicular (plus a 20-minute walk) up to **Sant Joan**, one of the 13 *ermitas* inhabited by hermits until Napoleon's troops hunted them down and killed them. Montserrat's highest point is **Sant Jeroni**, from where Catalonia spreads out before you – sometimes as far as Mallorca.

Montseny hills ❼

Montserrat and the Montseny range of mountains in the **Parc Natural de Montseny** (www.turisme-montseny. com) occupy polar extremes in Catalonian spiritual life. Montserrat is vertical, acute and passionate, Montseny is smooth, horizontal, massive and placid. *Seny* in Catalan means sense, patience, restraint, serenity, and is a byword for a description of the national characteristics.

Best explored by car, this monumental mountain forest is presided over by four peaks: Turó de l'Home, Agudes, Matagalls (all around 1,500 metres/5,000ft) and Calma i Puigdrau, a lower peak at 1,215 metres (4,050ft). Lesser terrain features and watercourses connect and define these pieces of high ground, tracing out an autonomous geographical entity which always appears mistenshrouded on the horizon, often confused with cloud formations.

The village of **Montseny** can be reached via Santa Maria de Palautordera and Sant Esteve de Palautordera on the BV-5301. This road continues on to Brull, through the pass at Collformic and over to Tona, near Vic *(see page 236)*, traversing the entire Montseny massif. The road up from Sant Celoni, just off the *autovia*

BELOW LEFT: exquisite stained glass in the Montserrat basilica.
BELOW: looking down on the monastery at Montserrat.

ABOVE LEFT AND RIGHT: inside the basilica at Montserrat.
BELOW: the Parc Natural de Montseny.

towards France, via Campins and Fogars de Montclus, arrives at the **Santa Fe** hermitage, a vantage point which seems only a stone's throw from Montseny's highest points. The oaks and poplars are colourful in autumn, which is an unusual sight in Catalonia, where forests of deciduous trees are uncommon.

VIC ⑧

An easy hour's journey north by train or car, **Vic** (www.victurisme. cat) is an elegant market town with interesting medieval buildings, sophisticated shops and good food. It is the meeting place of industry, commerce and agriculture and a mixture of rural and urban life. With a strong ecclesiastical and cultural tradition, the town is an entity quite distinct from Barcelona, and the Vic accent is unmistakable.

Cathedral

Vic's **cathedral**, a neoclassical structure completed in 1803 and with a graceful 11th-century Romanesque bell tower, is best known for Josep Maria Sert's epic murals covering the interior walls. Sert left his personal vision in the voluptuous, neo-Baroque figures performing colossal deeds. His triptych on the back of the western door depicts the injustices in the life of Christ and, by association, in the history of Catalonia. With the cathedral in ruins as his background, Jesus expels the moneylenders from the temple and is, in turn, condemned to be crucified while Pilate washes his hands and Barabbas, the thief, is cheered by the crowd. Certain faces (Pilate, Barabbas) are said to be those of Franco's lieutenants, but El Generalísimo himself, visiting while Sert's work was in progress, did not see the resemblance.

The philosopher Jaume Balmes (1810–48), a native of Vic, is buried in the cloister, as is Sert.

Museu Episcopal

✉ Plaça Bisbe Oliba, 3 🕒 Tue–Sat 10am–7pm, closed lunchtime Mon–Fri in winter, Sun 10am–2pm 💶 charge

The museum has a large, impressive collection of Romanesque and Gothic pieces, including altarpieces and sculpted figures collected from local chapels and churches.

Recommended Restaurants on pages 242–3

Its treasures have now been re-housed in a new building designed by leading Barcelona architects Correa and Milà. Note especially the Romanesque textiles and *El Davallament de la Creu* (The Descent from the Cross), an especially fine 12th-century sculptural work in polychrome wood.

The magnificent **Plaça Major**, surrounded by low arcades, has a lively Saturday market and is a pleasant place to have a drink.

AIGÜESTORTES ❾

Although many parts of the Pyrenees can be visited in a day from Barcelona – keen skiers dash up to La Molina for as many downhill runs as they can pack in before returning for dinner on the coast – the **Parc Nacional d'Aigüestortes i Estany de Sant Maurici** (www.gencat.cat/parcs/aiguestortes), in the province of Lleida, deserves at least two or three days. An easy three to four hour car journey from the city, Catalonia's only national park is stunningly beautiful and a stimulating antidote to the city. It has some two hundred lakes, dramatic peaks, walks for all ages and a rich cultural heritage. Many of the Romanesque pieces of art in the MNAC in Barcelona *(see page 181)* and the Museu Episcopal in Vic came from 11th-century churches that can still be visited in this area.

ABOVE: Aigüestortes National Park.
BELOW: golden buildings in the elegant market town of Vic.

Baroque doorway in Girona, a city known for its fine Ciutat Antiga *(Old City).*

ABOVE RIGHT: one of Girona's typical stairways, Carrer Sant Llorenç. **BELOW:** the Old City rises on the banks of the River Onyar.

Espot

The village of **Espot** makes a good base. It is just outside the Parc, and easily reached on the C13 following the roaring Noguera Pallaresa river, a favourite for white water rafting. It has several hotels and some good restaurants serving hearty mountain fare like *estofat de porc senglar* (wild boar stew). There are easy trails straight from Espot, or from the car park beyond the village. Alternatively catch a four-wheel drive taxi to take you deeper into the park before you start walking. Seriously keen hikers can stay in one of several *refugis* (shelters), so as to cover as much of

this extensive 14,000 hectare (34,594 acre) national park as possible.

During the skiing season there is a small resort nearby, **Espot Esqui**, or you could opt for **Port Ainé**, slightly closer to Barcelona, which has a hotel at the foot of the slopes.

Another approach to Aigüestortes is through the **Boí Valley**, reached through El Pont de Suert on the N230. This valley has been made a World Heritage Site for the wealth of its Romanesque architecture. Don't miss the churches of Sant Climent and Santa Maria in **Taüll**, Sant Joan in **Boí** itself and Santa Eulàlia in **Erill la Vall**. Avoid rush hour and try and find a solitary moment in any one of these simple but majestic mountain churches. Catalans and people from other parts of Spain tend to flood into the main tourist centres in the Pyrenees in August, but there are still plenty of river banks and woods far from the madding crowd.

GIRONA ⑩

Girona and Figueres can be combined for a memorable excursion from Barcelona. **Girona**, the provincial capital, is a most attractive city (www.girona.cat/turisme), full of history, tasteful shops and high-class restaurants, and only an hour's drive

Recommended Restaurants on pages 242–3

or train ride from Barcelona. It is known for its **Ciutat Antiga** (Old City), especially the 13th-century **Jewish Quarter**, the **Call**, considered one of the two most important and best preserved in Spain (the other is Toledo's). The River Onyar separates the Old City from the modern section, which lies west of the river.

The footbridges over the Onyar provide some of Girona's most unforgettable views, including reflections of the colourful buildings on the banks of the river. The 12th-century **Església de Sant Pere de Galligants** is one of the city's oldest monuments, with a delightful Romanesque cloister built before 1154. From here you can walk around the city walls as far as Plaça de Catalunya.

Girona's Old City, built on a hill, is known for its lovely stairways, such as those up to the **Església de Sant Martí**, or the Baroque *escalinata* of 96 steps leading up to the cathedral.

Santa Maria Cathedral

Ⓒ Visit includes the museum; summer Mon–Sat 10am–8pm, winter 10am–7pm, Sun all year

10am–2pm, Treasury and Cloisters only Ⓒ charge (free on Sun)

Described by Josep Pla as "literally sensational", Girona's cathedral was built by Guillem Bofill, who covered the structure with Europe's largest Gothic vault. It includes several treasures, the most notable being the *Tapis de la Creació*, a stunning 12th-century tapestry depicting God surrounded by all the flora and fauna, fish and fowl of Creation. Equally impressive is Beatus's *Llibre de l'Apocalipsi* (Book of the Apocalypse), dated 975.

The **Església de Sant Feliu**, the **Arab Baths** and the Call with its **Museum of Jewish History** (summer Mon–Sat 10am–8pm, Sun 10am–2pm, winter Tue–Sat 10am–6pm, Sun–Mon 10am–2pm; charge) are other important landmarks of this ancient city.

FIGUERES ⑪

Figueres, another half-hour north on the AP7 motorway, is the major city of the **Alt Empordà**. The **Rambla** is the scene of the traditional *passeig*, the midday or evening stroll.

EAT

Figueres has many good restaurants. Hotel Empordà, on the outskirts of town, has one of Catalonia's most famous restaurants *(see page 242).*

BELOW LEFT: ceiling fresco in the Teatre-Museu Dalí, Figueres.
BELOW: Surrealist artist Salvador Dalí.

Salvador Dalí

Through the endeavours of the Gala-Salvador Dalí Foundation, the surreal world of Dalí now includes his home in Port Lligat, his wife Gala's castle in Púbol and the museum in Figueres. To get a broad view of the art and a vivid idea of the man, the best introduction is the **Teatre-Museu Dalí**. Thirty km (20 miles) away on the coast, near Cadaqués, is the **Casa-Museu Salvador Dalí**, a fascinating glimpse of Dalí's life. These old fishermen's cottages have limited space, so small groups are admitted every 10 minutes. It is essential to book in advance and obey strict rules (summer daily 9.30am–9pm, winter Tue–Sun 10.30am–6pm, closed Jan–early Feb; tel: 97 225 1015). Bought by Dalí for his wife in 1970, the **Castell Gala Dalí** is atmospheric, set in a landscaped garden in Púbol in the Baix Empordà district (summer daily 10am–8pm, winter Tue–Sat 10am–5pm, closed Jan–mid-Mar).

Teatre-Museu Dalí

✉ Plaça Gala-Salvador Dalí, 5; www.salvador-dali.org ⏱ July–Sept daily 9am–8pm, Oct–May Tue–Sun, times vary so check website 💲 charge

ABOVE: the sandy beach at Sant Pol.
BELOW: the attractive seaside village of Cadaqués.

Figueres is best known as the birth-place of the Surrealist artist Salvador Dalí, whose museum is aptly located in the former municipal theatre. This is one of the most visited museums in Spain and has a wide range of Dalí's work, including the *Poetry of America*, painted in 1943, a portrait of his wife Gala as *Atomic Leda*, and the huge ceiling fresco dominating the Wind Palace Room on the first floor. Whether you regard him as a genius or not, there is no denying that this museum, with its tricks and illusions, provides an entertaining show.

A new space, **Dalí.Joies** (entrance charge, or entry with ticket to main museum), in an annexe, exhibits 37 pieces of jewellery by Dalí and sketched designs.

Figueres is a good base for Dalí tourism in the region: both Dalí's house in **Port Lligat**, near Cadaqués, and the castle he bought for his wife, in **Púbol**, are open to the public *(see box, page 239)*.

COSTA DEL MARESME

The beaches just north of Barcelona have a much lower profile than Sit-ges, and are much maligned for the railway line that runs alongside them. As a result, they are often less crowded. In recent years most have been overhauled, with some beaches

Recommended Restaurants on pages 242–3

being widened, promenades land-scaped and marinas built. It is worth travelling beyond Badalona, though its promenade is a pleasant place for lunch. However, if you only have half a day, both Masnou and Vilassar de Mar are very acceptable, with *xiringuitos* (snack bars) on the beach.

Caldes d'Estrac ⑫

One of the most attractive resorts is **Caldes d'Estrac**, also known as **Caldetes**. The slightly longer journey – about 40 minutes from Barcelona by car on the speedy C32 and about 45 minutes on the train from Plaça de Catalunya – is well rewarded. Caldetes is a spa town – several hotels have thermal baths – and it has many pretty *modernista* houses. The long, sandy beaches never get too crowded, and the sea is usually clear.

Early evening is a particularly pleasant time, when families dress up in smart-casual clothes to promenade and have a drink on the esplanade, or an ice-cream on the seafront. You can enjoy all this, have dinner and get back to Barcelona for the night without too much effort.

Seaside villages

The beaches of Caldetes merge with those of **Arenys de Mar**, known for its attractive fishing port and famous restaurant, the **Hispania**, favoured by King Juan Carlos *(see page 243)*.

The next town north, **Canet de Mar**, has a refurbished waterfront and interesting 19th-century architecture, notably the home of Lluís Domènech i Montaner *(see page 54)*, one of the leading *modernista* architects in Barcelona. His studio can be visited (Tue–Sun 10am–2pm; charge).

Just beyond Canet de Mar is **Sant Pol**, a pretty, whitewashed village.

THE COSTA BRAVA

To get away entirely from city beaches it is worth going as far as the Costa Brava. The southernmost

parts of this rocky coastline *(brava)* can be reached in a day, like **Blanes** ⑬ where it officially begins. However, with more time you can get further north to the really magical parts, from **Tossa de Mar** up to the French border. Most of these places can be reached by bus from Estació del Nord bus station, though it is well worth renting a car to allow maximum freedom to explore.

The beaches and medieval inland villages of the area known as El Baix Empordà were until recently a well-kept secret. Some of the villages have been prettified, their honey-coloured houses tastefully renovated by middle class weekenders from Barcelona, but they remain endlessly charming. A good base could be **Begur** ⑭, a pretty hilltop village with a cosmopolitan edge, just inland from some of the prettiest *calas* (sandy inlets) that punctuate the rocky coastline. You will be spoilt for choice between the sheltered cove of **Tamariu**, lined with seafood restaurants, the clear azure of the different bays of **Aigua Blava** or the atmosphere of generations of family summers in **Sa Riera**.   ❏

BELOW: the church of Santa Maria in Arenys de Mar.

BEST RESTAURANTS

Restaurants

Prices for a three-course dinner per person with a bottle of house wine:
€ = under €25
€€ = €25–40
€€€ = €40–60
€€€€ = over €60

In rural areas all over Catalonia you'll find well-kept roadside restaurants, popular for weddings, baptisms and other family occasions, where you can be sure of a good, traditional meal, with *pa amb tomàquet* and pork dishes as staples, as well as the regional or seasonal speciality. There is also an increasing number of restaurants where creative young chefs are

practising their art (advance booking essential), as well as village bars, where a wholesome dish of the day, unpretentious and delicious, may have been cooked for local workers. Eating hours tend to be earlier than in the city.

Baro
El Carro
La Vinya s/n 🕻 97 366 2148 🕙 L & D daily early July–early Sept, rest of year weekends. €€
Succulent local meat cooked in a wood-burning oven, or *a la brasa* (charcoal grilled), and served in the shade of the garden close to the Noguera Pallaresa river is an experience not

to be missed. In a small village en route to the Aigüestortes National Park, though better to do the hiking before lunch.

Begur
La Pizzeta
Ventura i Sabater, 2 🕻 97 262 3884 🕙 D June–Sept daily, May–Oct Thur–Mon, Mar–Apr Fri–Sun. Closed Nov–Feb. €
Much more than pizzas in this creative, trendy restaurant in the garden of an old village house. Charming and cheap, so book early.

Cambrils
Joan Gatell
Passeig Miramar, 26, Cambrils Port 🕻 97 736 0057 🕙 L & D Tue–Sat, L only Sun. Closed May, Dec. €€€
This is the place to come if you are passionate about fish. Famed for choosing the freshest of the catch in this fishing village near Tarragona, and frying, grilling or baking it to perfection. The simpler the better, but if you go for rich sauces don't miss the *bullabesa de la casa*, which you may have to order in advance.

Castelldefels
Patricio
Carrer Onze, 9 🕻 93-636 6650 🕙 L Sun–Tue,

L & D Thur–Sat. €€
Bulldozed from the beach to make way for a promenade, like many charming restaurants around Catalonia, this old favourite is now in new premises one block in from the waterfront. However, its charcoal-grilled specialities, including *calçots* when in season (early in the year), are still as tasty. And the long beach is nearby to walk it all off afterwards.

Figueres
Hotel Empordà
Av. Salvador Dalí, 170 🕻 97 250 0562 🕙 L & D daily. €€€
Its founder, the late Josep Mercader, has become a legend, much like his fellow citizen Dalí. One of the first chefs to reinvent Catalan dishes back in the 1950s, his charisma and inspiration remain in this well-established and unpretentious restaurant.

Girona
El Celler de Can Roca
Can Sunyer 48 🕻 97 222 2157 🕙 L & D Tue–Sat. €€€€
One of the most established of the new wave of avant-garde restaurants

LEFT: cava accompanies a perfect Sunday lunch.
RIGHT: a café in Figueres.

in Catalonia, this is regarded by many as one of the best. Run by the three well-known Roca brothers: Joan is the chef who conjures up dishes like a carpaccio of pigs' trotters with vinaigrette, Josep advises expertly on wines and Jordi concentrates on the exotic desserts.

Maresme
Fonda Manau
Sant Josep, 11, Caldes d'Estrac 93-791 0459 L & D June–Sept Wed–Mon, Oct–May L Wed–Mon, D Fri–Sat. €
This small *fonda* (inn) serves good, simple food in its pretty courtyard, although the creative flair of Xavi Manau, son of the former owner, is now coming to the fore, resulting in delicious dishes like squid tossed with wild mushrooms.

Hispania
Reial, 54, Carretera N11, Arenys de Mar 93-791 0306 L & D Mon, Wed–Sat, L only Sun. Closed Oct. €€€€

A classic of Catalan cuisine, which has been in the same family for 50 years. The king is said to be a regular. Known for their seasonal dishes using fresh local produce, such as peas from Llavaneres or fresh clams from the port of Arenys. Their *crema catalana*, the national dessert, is legendary.

Petit Moll
Platja l'Espigó de Garbí, Vilassar de Mar 600-520 000 L & D daily mid-May–early Sept. €–€€
Very charming *xiringuito* (beachside restaurant) amongst the fishing boats, great for fresh sardines and salad after a swim. About a 20-minute train ride from Barcelona.

Pizzeria Estrac
Camí Ral, 5, Caldes d'Estrac 93-791 3188 L & D Sat–Sun, D only Mon–Fri July–mid-Sept. €
Pasta and particularly good home-made pizzas in an attractive restaurant in the heart of this pretty village. Pizzas can also be taken away.

Penedès
El Mirador de les Caves
Carretera Sant Sadurní–Ordal, Subirats 93-899 3178 L daily. €€
When visiting cava country, this is a good spot to sample the end product – and indulge in a good meal – while gazing across the vineyards that have produced it.

Sant Celoni
Can Fabes
Sant Joan, 6 93-867 2851 L & D Tue–Sat, L only Sun. €€€€
Chef Santi Santamaria is another star in Catalonia's culinary constellation. Like Ferran Adrià, founder of the now-closed El Bulli which was hailed as the world's best restaurant in 2009, his fame has spread abroad. People come from far and wide to enjoy his creations in the attractive setting of this country restaurant. He is faced with more competition now, but he still has three Michelin stars. There is a choice of tasting menus and a tiny Relais & Châteaux hotel attached.

Sitges
The temptation to eat a paella overlooking the sea is irresistible, and there are several places along the seafront to choose from. You'll be able to find more unusual options in the narrow streets leading up to the centre.

Al Fresco
Pau Barrabeig, 4 93-894 0600 D only Tue–Sun. €€€
Excellent fusion between Mediterranean and the Far East results in delicious food, served in a pretty courtyard.

La Santa Maria
Passeig de la Ribera, 52 93-894 0999 L & D daily. Closed mid-Dec–Feb. €€
La Santa Maria is a traditional restaurant where large families meet for Sunday lunch. Overlooking the main promenade, it's a good spot for paella.

Vilanova i la Geltrú
La Fitorra
Hotel César, Isaac Peral, 4–8 93-815 1125 L & D Tue–Sat, L only Sun. €€
Delicious food at a reasonable price, with immaculate and friendly service in this delightful hotel with a personal touch. The lunchtime buffet can be eaten in the shady garden, bursting with hibiscus flowers.

Vic
Ca L'U
Riera, 25 93-889 0345 L & D Thur–Sat, L only Sun, Tue, Wed. €€
Ca L'U is just the kind of place you'd hope to find in this market town. A 100-year-old family restaurant serving excellent local food, it attracts plenty of regular customers. An essential part of any visit to Vic.

MONTSERRAT

Catalonia's sacred monastery is a great day out for families, hikers, picnickers and pilgrims

La Moreneta, the Black Virgin of Montserrat, is the patron saint of Catalonia, and her statue is the object of pilgrimage for every Catalan Catholic. Reached by cable car or the Cremallera rack-and-pinion railway, the mountain-top monastery caters well for the hundreds of visitors who come every day, not just to see the Virgin in the basilica but to enjoy walks and picnics in the stunning, scented, flower-strewn hills. Try to avoid weekends if you can.

The whole complex is geared for visitors: sellers of local cheese and honey set up their stalls, restaurants and cafés make sure nobody goes hungry, and shops guarantee you will take home some souvenirs. An excellent audio-visual show explains the daily lives of the Benedictine monks, who offer accommodation (see page 262). The museum's art collection, with icons, masterpieces and modern Catalan art, as well as archaeological artefacts from the Bible Lands, should not be missed.

ABOVE: Plaça Santa Maria, the main square, with the entrance to the basilica through the five arches to the right. The art museum lies beneath the square. **LEFT:** pilgrims queue to see their beloved La Moreneta (the Black Virgin) and touch her golden orb, although she remains behind protective glass.
BELOW: a late 16th-century depiction of the Virgin of Montserrat.

The Essentials

✉ *01899 Montserrat;*
www.montserratvisita.com
📞 *93-877 7701*
🕐 *daily 6am–8pm;*
museum 10.30am–5.45pm
Mon–Fri, 1–7pm Sat–Sun
ℹ *free; charge for museum*
🚈 *FGC Plaça Espanya to*
Aeri de Montserrat (for
cable car) or Monistrol de
Montserrat for Cremallera.

MONASTERY MILESTONES

880 Image of the Virgin Mary found in cave.
1025 Oliba, Abbott of Ripoll, founds monastery.
12th–13th centuries Romanesque church built, current carving of Virgin Mary made.
1223 Mention of boys' choir, Europe's first.
1409 Pope grants the monastery independence.
1476 Gothic cloisters built.
1490 Printing press installed. Library becomes famous. Books are still published here today.
1493 Bernal Boïl, a local hermit, sails with Columbus; an Antilles island is named Montserrat.
1592 Present-day church consecrated.
1811–12 Napoleonic forces destroy monastery.
1844 Monks return and monastery is rebuilt.
1939–74 Monastery becomes symbol of Catalan resistance to Franco regime.
1982 Museum of Catalan painting opened.
1987 Mountain designated a national park.

ABOVE: the pope grants the monastery independence, from the 15th-century *Llibre Vermell de Montserrat*.

ABOVE RIGHT: the monastery before its destruction by the French in 1812.

RIGHT: the famous Escolonia boys' choir sings at 1pm and 6.45pm on weekdays and at noon and 6.45pm on Sundays. There is no choir on Saturdays or from 24 June to mid-August. A CD of their singing is an evocative souvenir.

INSIGHT GUIDES

BARCELONA
Travel Tips

TRANSPORT

GETTING THERE AND GETTING AROUND

Getting to Barcelona from most parts of Europe is easy and relatively inexpensive, and trains are now offering a viable alternative to flying. Once there, you will find public transport is efficient and affordable, and taxis can also be a good option. If you are going to be travelling much outside Barcelona, it's a good idea to hire a car, but it will be more of a disadvantage than an asset in the city itself, where traffic is heavy and parking is expensive and in short supply.

GETTING THERE

By Air

Iberia (www.iberia.com), the national carrier, and other major airlines connect with most parts of the world, sometimes via Madrid. There are numerous low-cost airlines flying to Barcelona from European cities. Among the most popular from the UK are **easyJet** (www.easyjet.com), **Monarch** (www. monarch.co.uk), **British Midland** (www.bmibaby.com) and **Jet2** (www. jet2.com). Spanish low-cost airline **Vueling** (www.vueling.com) is good for onward destinations in Europe.

Ryanair (www.ryanair.com) flies to Girona (90km/56 miles from Barcelona) and Reus (80km/50 miles from Barcelona) from several UK cities and has a few flights to El Prat, the main Barcelona airport. There are shuttle-bus connections to Barcelona from Girona, tel: 902-361 550, www.sagales.com and Reus, tel: 902-

447 726, www.hispanoigualadina.net. Tickets (around €14 single, €24 return) are available at the airports; the journey takes 60–90 minutes depending on traffic.

Direct flights from the US are operated by **Delta** (from Atlanta and New York; www.delta.com), **Continental** (from Newark; www. continental.com), **Iberia** (from several US cities; www.iberia.com) and **Air Europa** (www.aireuropa.com). **Air Canada** (www.aircanada.com) flies from Toronto and Montreal, while **Singapore Airlines** fly directly from Singapore to Barcelona.

Advance passenger information: Since 2007 Spain has demanded that all air carriers supply passport information about passengers flying into the country, prior to travel. Check with your airline before travelling; more details on www.dft.gov.uk.

Barcelona Airport

Barcelona Airport (El Prat, tel: 902-404 704; www.aena.es) is 12km (7 miles) south of the city. There

are two terminals T1, the new one, and T2 which mostly handles budget flights. (For information on transport to and from the airport, *see Getting Around.*)

Airlines flying out of Barcelona to other parts of Spain include:
Iberia: tel: 902-400 500
Air Europa: tel: 902-401 501

DISTANCES

Distances to other cities in Spain by road from Barcelona:
Tarragona: 98km (60 miles)
Girona: 100km (62 miles)
La Jonquera (French border): 149km (93 miles)
Valencia: 349km (217 miles)
San Sebastián: 529km (329 miles)
Bilbao: 620km (385 miles)
Madrid: 621km (386 miles)
Salamanca: 778km (483 miles)
Málaga: 997km (620 miles)
Sevilla: 1,046km (650 miles)

Air Nostrum: tel: 902-400 500
Spanair: tel: 902-131 415
Vueling: tel: 807-200 100

By Train

A more eco-friendly option from other parts of Europe is to take the **Trenhotel**, which runs daily from Paris to Estació de França in Barcelona, and several days a week from Zurich, Geneva and Milan (www.elipsos.com). The **Talgo** runs twice daily between Montpellier and Barcelona, to either Sants or Estació de França. Montpellier connects with the TGV, the French high-speed train. All other international connections involve a change at the French border, in Port Bou on entering Spain and Cerbère when leaving. These trains have few facilities. There is also a line from Barcelona to La Tour de Carol on the French border, further west in the Pyrenees, from Sants and Plaça Catalunya.

For international train information and reservations, tel: 902-243 402. A helpful website is www.seat61.com.

Most national long-distance trains terminate in Estació de Sants, some in Estació de França. For national train information, tel: 902-240 202, www.renfe.es. The AVE high-speed train to Madrid is one option.

TAKING TAXIS

All Barcelona taxis are black and yellow, and show a green light when available for hire. There are taxi ranks at the airport, Sants station, Plaça de Catalunya and other strategic points, but taxis can be hailed on any street corner.

Rates are standard and calculated by meter, starting at a set rate and clocking up at a rate governed by the time of day: night-times, weekends and fiestas are more expensive. Travelling by taxi is still affordable here compared to many European cities. If you travel outside the metropolitan area, the rate increases slightly.

Drivers do not expect a tip, but a small one is always appreciated. An extra charge is made for luggage per piece.

Taxis equipped for wheelchairs are available (tel: 93-420 8088).

By Bus

Eurolines (tel: 902-405 040; www.eurolines.com) offer a service from London which may involve a change in France. Most arrive at the bus station Barcelona Nord (tel: 902-260 606), but some go to Estació d'Autobusos Sants (tel: 93-490 4000). More information and timetables on www.barcelonanord.com. In the UK, contact National Express (tel: 08717 818 178; www.national express.com).

By Car

Barcelona is 149km (93 miles) or 1½ hours' drive from La Jonquera on the French border and can be reached easily along the AP7 (or E15) motorway (*autopista*, toll payable, around €13 from the border to the city) and then, nearer Barcelona, the C33. Alternatively, the national route N11 is toll-free but tedious.

Be careful when you stop in service stations or lay-bys: professional thieves work this territory. If you stop for a drink or a meal don't leave the car unattended.

The worst times to travel, particularly between June and September, are Friday 6–10pm, Sunday 7pm–midnight or the end of a bank holiday, when tailbacks of 16km (10 miles) are common. Normal weekday rush hours are 7–9am and 6–9pm.

The ring roads *(cinturones)* surrounding the city can be very confusing when you first arrive; it is worth studying a road map beforehand. The Ronda de Dalt curves around the top part of the city, and the Ronda Litoral follows the sea.

GETTING AROUND

From the Airport

Barcelona is only 12km (7 miles) from El Prat airport and is easily reached by train, bus or taxi.

Trains to Sants and Passeig de Gràcia depart every 30 minutes from 6am–11.38pm and take about 25 minutes. The approximate cost is €3, but the best value is a T10 card for

BELOW: the T1 terminal at Barcelona's airport.

TRANSPORT

ACCOMMODATION

SHOPPING

ACTIVITIES

A – Z

LANGUAGE

Zone 1 which can be shared between travellers, and can be used on the metro and buses in the city. It costs about €8. A shuttle bus connects Terminal 1 with the train station. The **Aerobús**, an efficient bus service, runs to Plaça de Catalunya from each terminal every 5 minutes, stopping at strategic points en route. It operates from 6am–1am; a single fare is about €5.30, a return €9.15. Note that the return ticket is only valid for up to nine days after purchase.

From Plaça de Catalunya the buses run from 5.28am–12.30am. Be sure to get on the one for your terminal when returning to the airport. A night-bus, the N17, runs from Plaça de Catalunya/Ronda Universitat from 11pm–5am.

To reach most central parts of Barcelona by taxi will cost about €25–30 plus an airport supplement and a token amount for each suitcase. To avoid misunderstandings, ask how much it

TOURIST BUSES

A convenient way of getting an overall idea of the city is to catch the official city Tourist Bus (**Barcelona Bus Turístic**), which takes in the most interesting parts of the city. You can combine three different routes, and get on and off at the 44 stops freely. It also offers discounts on entrance charges.

The buses operate year-round with frequent services, the first leaving Plaça de Catalunya at 9am. The fleet includes buses equipped for wheelchairs and open-air double deckers.

For information and tickets ask at a tourist information

will cost before getting into the taxi: *"Cuánto vale el recorrido desde el aeropuerto hasta …* (e.g.) *Plaça de Catalunya?"* Get the taxi driver to write down the answer if necessary.

office such as the one on Plaça de Catalunya, or book online at www.barcelonaturisme.com. The two-day ticket is better value.

An alternative tourist bus, Barcelona City Tour, run by Julia Tours, covers roughly the same route. Its main advantage is that there are fewer queues.
Julia Tours
Tel: 93-317 6454
www.barcelonacitytour.cat

Public Transport

Barcelona is a manageable city to get around, whether on foot or by public transport. The latter is efficient and good value.

Metro

The metro has eight colour-coded lines but the main ones are 1, 2, 3, 4 and 5. Some are equipped for wheelchairs and prams, with lifts. Trains are frequent and cheap, with a set price per journey, no matter how far you travel. It is more economical to buy a card that allows 10 journeys (Targeta T10), available at stations, banks and *estancs* (tobacconists). It can be shared and is valid for FGC trains, RENFE trains within Zone 1 *(see right)* and buses. If you change from one form of transport to another within 1 hour and 15 mins, the ticket will still be valid, so you won't be charged again. Trains run 5am–midnight Mon–Thur and Sun, 5am–2am Fri and all night Sat.

FGC

The local train service, Ferrocarrils de la Generalitat de Catalunya (FGC), interconnects with the metro, looks like the metro and

BELOW: along the Passeig de Colom near the waterfront.

functions in the same way, but extends beyond the inner city to towns on the other side of Tibidabo, such as San Cugat (from Plaça de Catalunya) and to Manresa and Montserrat (from Plaça d'Espanya). It is a useful service for reaching the upper parts of Barcelona and for parts of Tibidabo and the Parc de Collserola.

The metro ticket is valid on this line within Zone 1, but travel beyond is more expensive. The FGC lines can be recognised on the metro map by their distinctive logo. Within the city the timetable is the same as the metro, but beyond it varies according to the line. Check in a station or call 010 for information. FGC, tel: 93-205 15 15; www.fgc.cat.

Bus

The bus service is good for reaching the areas the metro doesn't, and for seeing more of Barcelona. Single tickets are the same price as metro tickets and can be bought from the driver, or a multiple card (Targeta T10) of 10 journeys can be punched inside the bus, but not bought on the bus (see Metro left). Most buses run from 4.25am–11pm. There are night services (the **Nit bus**) that run from Plaça de Catalunya, but lines vary, so check on the map or at bus stops.

The **Tibibus** runs from Plaça de Catalunya to Plaça del Tibidabo (on the top of the hill).

Cycling

Barcelona is now a cyclist-friendly city, with over 156km of bike lanes, parking facilities and many great traffic-free places to cycle, such as the port, marinas, and along the beachfront from Barceloneta to Diagonal Mar. Bikes can be taken on trains free of charge, and a useful map of the cycle lanes can be found at www.bcn.cat/bicicleta.

Bicing

The red-and-white bikes parked at strategic points all over town are unfortunately not for rent. These "Bicing" bikes are exclusively for resident/long-term use: membership is paid annually, and any use over 30 minutes is charged to a credit card. The idea is to complement the public transport system, to get you to the metro or station and not for touring, so maximum use is two hours. Luckily though, there are plenty of enterprising companies that rent bikes and organise cycling tours by day and night (see page 275).

Barcelona on Foot

Walking is one of the best ways of getting around Barcelona – despite the traffic fumes. It is ideal for seeing the many details that cannot be charted by maps or guidebooks – modernista doorways, ancient corner shops, roof gardens and balconies.

The tourist office Turisme de Barcelona (Plaça de Catalunya, tel: 93-285 3832, www.barcelonaturisme.com) offers the following guided walking tours:
Barcelona Walking Tours Gothic Quarter: daily in English at 10am.
Picasso Route: a glimpse of the artist's life in Barcelona ending with a tour of the museum. There are also **Modernista**, **Gourmet**, **Literary** and **Marina** routes to name a few.

The **Route of Modernism**: A do-it-yourself route using a book available from the Centre del Modernisme (www.rutadelmodernisme.

These have been fluctuating recently in an attempt to reduce petrol consumption, but as a general rule:
• Urban areas: 50kph (30mph)
• Roads outside urban areas: 80–110kph (50–68mph)
• Dual carriageways outside urban areas: 110kph (68mph)
• Motorways: 110kph (68mph)

In case of breakdown on the road, call the general emergency number **112**, which has a foreign-language service and can connect you with the relevant service. On motorways and main roads there are SOS phone boxes.

com), the tourist office in Plaça de Catalunya, or bookshops.
Guided Tours of Palau de la Música Catalana: best to purchase in advance at the concert hall (10am–3.30pm; tel: 902-475 485; www.palaumusica.org).

Travelling outside Barcelona

By Train

The following stations currently function as described, but before planning any journey it is advisable to call **RENFE** (the national train network) for the latest information and ticket deals, tel: 902-240 202. It is wise to buy long-distance tickets in advance (on this number), especially at holidays. If you pay by credit card, tickets can be collected from machines at Sants and Passeig de Gràcia stations.

Estació de Sants, in Plaça Països Catalans, is for long-distance national and international trains, including the AVE high-speed train to Madrid. Some of these will also stop in **Passeig de Gràcia** station, which is convenient for central parts of town. Confirm beforehand that your train really does stop there.

Regional trains leave Sants for the coast south and north of Barcelona, including a direct train to Port Aventura theme park and the high-speed Euromed to Valencia and Alicante, which makes a few stops in between. In Sants station, queues can be long and ticket clerks impatient.

Estació de França, Avinguda Marquès de l'Argentera: international and long-distance national trains.

Plaça de Catalunya: apart from the metro and Generalitat railways (FGC), RENFE/Rodalies de Catalunya has a station in Plaça de Catalunya, where trains can be caught to Manresa, Lleida, Vic, Puigcerdà, La Tour de Carol, Mataró (Maresme Coast) and Blanes.

Plaça d'Espanya: FGC trains to Montserrat, Igualada and Manresa.

By Long-Distance Bus

There are regular long-distance bus lines running all over Spain which leave from the Estació d'Autobusos Barcelona Nord, Alibei 80, or Sants bus station. For information, tel: 902-260 606, www.barcelonanord.com.
Bus services to other parts of Catalonia are operated by:
Costa Brava: Sarfa
Tel: 902-302 025
Costa Maresme: Casas
Tel: 93-798 1100
Montserrat: Autocares Julià.
A daily bus leaves Sants bus station (c/Viriato) at 9.15am. Buy tickets on the bus.
Pyrenees: Alsina Graells
Tel: 902-422 242
Catalunya Bus Turístic offers day trips to different parts of Catalonia, such as Figueres and Girona (to the north), including the Dalí

BELOW: biker takes a break.

Museum, or Sitges (to the south), Montserrat and a wine producer in the Penedès from Apr–Oct. Also to Vic and Manresa. Information available from tourist offices, or tel: 93-285 3832.

By Sea

There is a regular passenger and car service between Barcelona and Mallorca, Menorca and Ibiza, as well as Morocco, with the **Acciona Trasmediterránea** company, based at the Estació Marítima, Moll de Barcelona (tel: 902-454 645; www.trasmediterranea. es). It also has a service to Italy in conjunction with **Grimaldi Ferries** (www.grimaldi-ferries.com).
Baleària has a regular service to the Balearics and in the summer a fast service – four hours as opposed to the usual eight. For information and bookings, tel: 902-160 180, www.balearia.com.

Driving in Catalonia

Driving is the most flexible way to see the rest of Catalonia, but cars are better left in a parking place while you are in the city. Avoid parking illegally, particularly outside entrances and private garage doors: the police tow offenders away with remarkable alacrity, and the charge for retrieval is heavy. If this happens, you will find a document with a triangular symbol stuck on the ground where your car was. This paper will give details of where you can retrieve your vehicle. Street parking, indicated by blue lines on the road and a nearby machine to buy a ticket, is limited. Convenient (but expensive) car parks are in Plaça de Catalunya, Passeig de Gràcia, and Plaça de la Catedral.

Drivers are supposed to stop for pedestrians at zebra crossings and when the green man is illuminated on traffic lights, but often they don't. Be sure to lock all doors when driving in town – thieving is common at traffic lights. Beware of anyone asking directions or saying you have a puncture. It is probably a trap.

Car Hire/Rental

Hiring a car is a good way to explore the area around Barcelona. It may be cheaper to make arrangements before you leave home as there are some good deals on the internet. The main companies are based in the airport and in central locations in the city.
Avis: tel: 902-180 854, www.avis.es
Europcar: tel: 902-105 055, www.europcar.es
Hertz: tel: 902-402 405, www.hertz.es
National-Atesa: tel: 902-100 101, www.atesa.es
Over: Josep Tarradellas, 42, tel: 902-410 410, www.over-rentacar.com. Good-value local company.
Vanguard: Viladomat, 297, tel: 93-439 3880, www.vanguardrent.com. Scooters also for hire.
www.pepecar.com is a good option if you book well in advance on the internet, but beware of added extras. The office is in Plaça de Catalunya.

Scooter Rental

A popular way of visiting the city. Several companies rent out scooters or give tours. Explore different options via the tourist office (www.barcelonaturisme.com).

Licences and Insurance

Citizens of the EU can use their national driving licence. Those from outside the EU need an international driving licence. Most UK insurance firms will issue a Green Card (an internationally recognised certificate of motor insurance) free of charge.

GoCars

A new transport option in Barcelona is sightseeing by GoCar. Guided by a GPS system and a recorded voice, these hazardous-looking vehicles are no doubt fun.
Local GoCar
Freixures 23 (outside Santa Caterina market), tel: 93-269 1792; www.gocartours.es

A CCOMMODATION

SOME THINGS TO CONSIDER BEFORE YOU BOOK A ROOM

The range of accommodation options in Barcelona has improved dramatically over the past few years, with the greatest change being the number of luxury hotels and up-market choices. As a reaction to the increased number of tourists, opportunist residents have been quick to see a gap in the market and provide alternative forms of accommodation. Self-catering has become a new phenomenon, with developers renovating whole buildings in the Old Town to offer as tourist lets.

Accommodation

Following the surge in tourism in post-Olympic Barcelona, fuelled by budget flights, there was a dearth of hotel rooms, but over the past few years there has been feverish building and renovation work to provide more accommodation in the city. There are now over 400 hotels and guesthouses *(pensions)*, ranging from basic rooms accommodating three or four beds to 5-star GL (Gran Luxe) sumptuous hotels.

At the top end of the scale establishments are suitably indulgent, in avant-garde or historic buildings, with privileged views and impeccable service at a very high price. Boutique hotels, with exquisite interior design and a more intimate feel, are on the increase.

In the moderate range there is a wide choice with an equally diverse price range according to the services offered or the location. Further away from the centre, better deals are available, and these are a good option considering the city's efficient public transport system which can whisk you to the centre in a matter of minutes.

The inexpensive range is most problematic. The few good hotels and *pensions* in this bracket are sought after, so they get booked up months in advance, especially over busy periods like holidays and half-terms. *Pensions* range from basic to decent, with just a few notable exceptions where an effort has been made to modernise or give some extra value. There are plenty in the centre, mostly in the Old Town, particularly in the streets leading off La Rambla. Some do not accept bookings in advance, so be prepared for dragging suitcases around, but at least that gives you the advantage of checking out the rooms first.

Rates vary dramatically, mostly on a supply and demand basis. Now that there are more rooms available, the client has more chance of getting a rate way below the standard price quoted, especially at weekends or off-peak times of the year. However, if there is a trade fair or large congress taking place, Barcelona still seems to be short of rooms. Ironically – and fortunately for the many northern European and American travellers who take their holidays in midsummer – July and August are not considered peak times, whereas September and October are high season. Good deals can also be found through internet booking, directly with the hotel or through the many booking services on the web. Special offers are advertised, often with bargains for families. There are several new hotels along the recently developed waterfront near Diagonal Mar where high-standard accommodation can be found at a reasonable price. As they are a taxi or metro ride from the centre they are less popular, but the advantages of sea views and more peaceful nights, not to mention speedy access to the beach, are well worth considering.

A quick search on the internet comes up with several agencies that have a range of flats on their books like www.flatsbydays.com, www.therooftops.org or www.oh-barcelona.com. At the luxurious end is www.cru2001.com, consisting of two buildings, one of which contains flats that each have an individual design based around a literary theme. Self-catering has

become a popular choice in the city as it offers the opportunity to select the area you wish to stay in and to buy fresh food from the local market, as well as giving favourable rates.

Bed and breakfast accommodation is also widely available now, and has the advantage of friendly local advice and a closer insight into Barcelona life. One agency with a wide choice of rooms is www.bcn rooms.com.

If you are a smoker, be aware that there are strict rules governing smoking in public places, and you should specify if you want a room where smoking is allowed.

Hotel Chains

Aside from the recommended hotels listed below, you could also contact the central offices of the following hotel chains to see what they have available when you are planning to travel.
Derby Hotels
Tel: 93-366 8800
www.derbyhotels.com
Group H 10
Tel: 902-100 906
www.h10hotels.com
Hoteles Catalonia
Tel: 900-301 078
www.hoteles-catalonia.com
NH Hotels
Tel: 902-115 116
www.nh-hotels.com

ACCOMMODATION LISTINGS

LA RAMBLA

1898
La Rambla, 109
Tel: 93-552 9552
[p304, A1] €€€€
www.hotel1898.com
A major renovation of the Philippines Tobacco Company headquarters produced this smart, comfortable hotel with a suitably colonial air in its

decor and indulgences, which include a personal shopping service, two year-round pools and top-floor suites with private garden and Jacuzzi.
Bagués
La Rambla, 105
Tel: 93-343 5000
[p 304, A1] €€€€
www.derbyhotels.com

The latest jewel in the Derby Hotels crown is, fittingly, a former jewellery shop in prime position on La Rambla, right next to La Boqueria market. It's all about attention to detail and elegant finishes using gold leaf and ebony. Even the swimming pool on the roof is slimline.
Catalonia Plaza Cataluña
Bergara, 11
Tel: 93-301 5151
[p304, B1] €€€
www.hoteles-catalonia.com
The magnificent late 19th-century entrance hall inevitably gives way to modernised bedrooms, but the place still has charm and is well located just off Plaça de Catalunya. Surprisingly, it has a small pool and terrace.
Catalunya Plaza
Plaça de Catalunya, 7
Tel: 93-317 7171

[p304, B1] €€€
www.h10hotels.com
On the square itself, so about as central as you can get. Standard hotel comfort behind an attractive facade, with a few of the original 19th-century features remaining.
Citadines Barcelona-Ramblas
La Rambla, 122
Tel: 93-270 1111
[p304, B1] €€€
Good value for money. Food shopping can be done at the Boqueria market or local supermarket. Pleasant breakfast buffet bar and good views from the rooftop.

BELOW: the Catalonia Plaza Cataluña.

Comercio
Escudellers, 15
Tel: 93-445 1530
[p304, A2] €€
www.hotel-comercio.com
All the basic comforts, and it's just off La Rambla. Rooms have en suite bathrooms, and some have three, four or five beds available.

Continental
La Rambla, 138
Tel: 93-301 2570
[p304, B1] €€€
www.hotelcontinental.com
This historic hotel's individual character is a welcome change. Swirling carpets and floral decor can be forgiven when you can sit on a balcony watching the world go by on the famous Rambla – and at a reasonable price. Ask for a room at the front if you don't mind the noise.

Ginebra
Rambla de Catalunya, 1
Tel: 93-317 1063
[p306, B4] €€
www.hotelginebra.net
This is on the basic side; not all rooms have en suite bathrooms. However, it is very clean, staff are friendly and the location is as central as it comes, with views of Plaça Catalunya from some rooms. All windows are double glazed.

Kabul
Plaça Reial, 17
Tel: 93-318 5190
[p304, A2] €
www.kabul.es
Long-established youth hostel in a privileged position on this magnificent square just off La Rambla. Rooms extend to dorms for up to 20. Renowned for a party atmosphere.

Le Meridien Barcelona
La Rambla, 111
Tel: 93-318 6200

ABOVE: the exclusive 1898, on La Rambla.

[p304, A1] €€€€
www.lemeridienbarcelona.com
A large, plush hotel, well positioned on La Rambla, born again after major renovations. The Presidential Suite, with a 360-degree view of the Old Town, can be yours for €2,000.

Onix Liceo
Nou de la Rambla, 36
Tel: 93-481 6441
[p304, A2] €€€
www.hotelonixliceo.com
This eco-friendly hotel just off the lower part of La Rambla has a minimalist style showing off the handsome decorative details of the grand building it occupies.

Oriente
La Rambla, 45
Tel: 902-100 710
[p304, A2] €€–€€€
www.hotelhusaoriente.com
Once a charismatic old favourite, the Oriente, in the heart of La Rambla, has been through a low period. However, after refurbishment it has recovered some of its former glory, including the splendid ballroom, but at the expense of some of its personality.

Pension Teruel
Plaça Bonsuccés, 6, 3°
Tel: 93-302 6120
[p304, A1] €€

Clean and in an excellent position overlooking a small, tree-filled square, it is only five minutes from Plaça de Catalunya and half a minute from La Rambla, which makes up for the basic rooms.

Pulitzer
Bergara, 8
Tel: 93-481 6767
[p304, B1] €€€
www.hotelpulitzer.es
The latest in this street of classy hotels is sleek, smooth and wonderfully luminous for such a central location. A cocktail on the roof terrace is a must.

Regina
Bergara, 4
Tel: 93-301 3232
[p304, B1] €€€
www.reginahotel.com
After recent renovation, this well-established hotel offers high-quality rooms and service in a central location just off Plaça de Catalunya.

Rivoli Ramblas
La Rambla, 128
Tel: 93-481 7676
[p304, B1] €€€
www.hotelrivoliramblas.com
Behind the elegantly cool 1930s facade is a modern hotel with tasteful rooms. The barman of the cocktail bar downstairs plays great music, which makes a refreshing change from musak.

Roma Reial
Plaça Reial, 11
Tel: 93-302 0366
[p304, B2] €€
www.hotel-romareial.com
Set in a corner of this stunning square. The rooms are basic but acceptable.

Royal Ramblas
La Rambla, 117
Tel: 93-304 1212
[p304, B1] €€€
www.royalramblashotel.com
The rather mediocre 1970s exterior gives way to a recently refurbished interior. Considering its position on La Rambla, it is good value.

Silken Ramblas
Pintor Fortuny, 13
Tel: 93-342 6180
[p304, A1] €€€
www.hoteles-silken.com
Comfortable rooms and a small rooftop pool make a pleasant retreat from the bustle.

PRICE CATEGORIES

Prices for a standard double room without breakfast or IVA (VAT):
€ = under €50
€€ = €50–€100
€€€ = €100–€200
€€€€ = over €200

TRANSPORT
ACCOMMODATION
SHOPPING
ACTIVITIES
A – Z
LANGUAGE

BARRI GÒTIC

Catalonia Portal de l'Àngel
Portal de l'Àngel, 17
Tel: 93-318 4141
[p304, B1] €€€
www.hoteles-catalonia.com
Many vestiges of its former life as a palace remain, including the splendid staircase and tiled floors. Combined with modern details and tasteful decor this is a really good option, well situated between the Gothic Quarter and the Eixample.

Colón
Avinguda Catedral, 7
Tel: 93-301 1404
[p304, B2] €€€
www.hotelcolon.es
A classic, in the centre facing the cathedral. Bedrooms in their floral style seem more English than Spanish. Request a room with a view of the cathedral square.

Denit
Estruc, 24–26
Tel: 93-545 4000
[p304, B1] €€€
www.denit.com
A new concept in B&B, this functional but very stylish hotel has the advantage of being associated with the Hotel Majestic so clients can use some of its facilities, like the luxurious spa. Very central, near the airport bus stop.

Duc de la Victoria
Duc, 15
Tel: 93-270 3410
[p304, B1] €€€
www.nh-hotels.com
Reasonably priced for what it offers, this modern hotel in a quiet location between La Rambla and the cathedral is surprisingly friendly.

Gran Hotel Barcino
Jaume I, 6
Tel: 93-302 2012
[p304, B2] €€€
www.hotelbarcino.com
A bit expensive for what it is, but there's no denying the luxury of being a stone's throw from Plaça Sant Jaume, the seat of government and nucleus of all fiestas.

Grand Hotel Central
Via Laietana, 30
Tel: 93-295 7900
[p304, B2] €€€
www.grandhotelcentral.com
As grand as they come, this luxurious hotel has a 1930s Manhattan feel, a restaurant run by Michelin-starred chef Ramón Freixa and one of the city's slickest rooftop swimming pools.

Hostal Lausanne
Portal de l'Àngel, 24,1º,1ª
Tel: 93-302 1139
[p304, B1] €
www.hostallausanne.es
A dream location for shoppers in this pedestrian street between Plaça de Catalunya and the cathedral. Some of the 19th-century elegance of the building remains.

Jardí
Plaça Sant Josep Oriol, 1
Plaça del Pi
Tel: 93-301 5900
[p304, B2] €€
www.eljardi-barcelona.com
An extremely popular hotel with no frills, but overlooking two of the most attractive squares in the Barri Gòtic. Book well in advance.

Neri
Sant Sever, 5
Tel: 93-304 0655
[p304, B2] €€€€
www.hotelneri.com
Barcelona's first boutique hotel. In a 17th-century palace giving on to Sant Felip Neri, one of the most atmospheric squares in the Gothic Quarter. Only 22 rooms, so early booking needed.

Nouvel
Santa Anna, 20
Tel: 93-301 8274
[p304, B1] €€€
www.hotelnouvel.es
Located in a pedestrian street, this attractive old building has a modern interior and comfortable, spacious rooms.

Racó del Pi
Pi, 7
Tel: 93-342 6190
[p304, B2] €€€
www.hotelh10racodelpi.com
Small hotel built within an 18th-century palace in a pretty pedestrian street in the heart of the neighbourhood. Only 37 rooms, so book early.

Rialto
Ferrán, 42
Tel: 93-318 5212
[p304, B2] €€
www.hotel-rialto.com
Modernised and straightforward, located in an interesting street just off Plaça Sant Jaume and near La Rambla.

Suizo
Plaça de l'Àngel, 12
Tel: 93-310 6108
[p304, B2] €€€
www.hotelsuizo.com
Lost some of its personality when renovated but in a great location. Request a room on Baixada Llibreteria for more peace.

BELOW: the lobby of the Grand Hotel Central.

LA RIBERA

Banys Orientals
Argenteria, 37
Tel: 93-268 8460
[p304, B2] €€
www.hotelbanysorientals.com
Still one of the best options in town, with impeccable slick interiors and stylish details, and it's in the hottest spot for shopping, wining and dining. Unbeatable value, so book well in advance.

Chic&basic
Princesa, 50
Tel: 93-295 4652
[p304, C2] €€
www.chicandbasic.com
In an elegant 19th-century building close to the Parc de la Ciutadella and the buzz of the Born, this utterly

chic hotel is so fashion-conscious that even the rooms come in XL, L or M. The basic bit is the astonishingly low price.

Park Hotel
Avinguda Marquès de l'Argentera, 11
Tel: 93-319 6000
[p304, C3] €€€
www.parkhotelbarcelona.com
An overlooked gem of 1950s architecture, quite rare in Barcelona, opposite the Estació de França and near the Parc de la Ciutadella. It is on the edge of the Born district, which is awash with cafés, restaurants and bars and within walking distance of the beach. Well-designed rooms.

Pensió 2000
Sant Pere Més Alt, 6, 1°
Tel: 93-310 7466
[p304, B1] €€
www.pensio2000.com
A noble marble staircase leads to this friendly family guesthouse, which is a cut above the average *pensión* and right opposite the Palau de la Música. Great value.

Pension Ciudadela
Comerç, 33, 1°,1a
Tel: 93-319 6203
[p304, C2] €€
www.pension-ciudadela.com
Opposite the Estació de França, this humble guesthouse has decent rooms at a very reasonable price, and is within staggering distance of the Born nightlife.

Triunfo
Passeig de Picasso, 22
Tel: 93-315 0860
[p305, C2] €€
www.atriumhotels.com
A simple, clean, recently modernised *pensión* in a wonderful location on an elegant avenue, on the edge of the trendy Born, overlooking the Parc de la Ciutadella. A convenient and reasonably priced place to stay.

EL RAVAL

Barceló Raval
Rambla del Raval, 17–21
Tel: 93-320 1490
[p304, A2] €€€
www.barceloraval.com
This cutting edge, 11-storey hotel in the middle of what's still a fairly shady area is typical of the city's urban regeneration policies. Striking design with panoramic views from every room, rooftop pool and terrace bar.

Casa Camper
Elisabets, 11
Tel: 93-342 6280
[p304, A1] €€€€
www.casacamper.com
The famed Majorcan shoemakers' first venture into hotel management, incorporating the aesthetics of design mecca Vinçon, has created an eco-friendly

boutique hotel as revolutionary as a Camper shoe. Stylish, functional rooms all have their own mini lounge across the corridor.

España
Sant Pau, 9–11
Tel: 93-550 0000
[p304, A2] €€€
www.hotelespanya.com
Reopened in 2010 after extensive renovation work, which has stripped some of the old faded charm but added welcome comforts and highlights the *moderniste* details which are the legacy of architect Domènech i Montaner's original decoration. The legendary dining room is now in the hands of Michelin-starred chef Martín Berasategui.

Gaudí
Nou de la Rambla, 12
Tel: 93-317 9032
[p304, A2] €€€
www.hotelgaudi.es
A modern hotel without much personality, but the treat is the view: get a room at the front, so you can feast your eyes on Gaudí's Palau Güell opposite. The top-floor rooms have small terraces which are worth fighting for.

Hosteria Grau
Ramelleres, 27
Tel: 93-301 8135
[p304, A1] €€
www.hostalgrau.com
Book early for this popular *pensión*, which is in a good position for shopping and visiting the Eixample and Old Town. Excellent breakfasts in the adjoining bar.

Inglaterra
Pelai, 14
Tel: 93-505 1100
[p304, A1] €€€
www.hotel-inglaterra.com
A good-looking hotel within an old facade,

equally well located for the bohemian Raval or the elegant Eixample. Stands out from the crowd in this price range.

Mesón de Castilla
Valldonzella, 5
Tel: 93-318 2182
[p304, A1] €€€
www.mesoncastilla.com

Furniture is old-fashioned and rustic in style. A bit quirky, but at least it's individual. Very good location near CCCB, university and shops. The owners are friendly and helpful.

Peninsular
Sant Pau, 34
Tel: 93-302 3138
[p304, A2] €€
www.hotelpeninsular.net
In a former convent, with rooms around an inner courtyard. An impressive lobby and dining room, and basic but clean rooms. A one-off and excellent value.

Sant Agustí
Plaça Sant Agustí, 3
Tel: 93-318 1658
[p304, A2] €€€
www.hotelsa.com
This historic hotel overlooks a quiet square. It is worth paying more for one of the luxury rooms on the fourth floor.

THE WATERFRONT

Arts
Passeig de la Marina, 19
Tel: 93-221 1000
[p305, D3] €€€€
www.hotelartsbarcelona.com
Its ranking as the hotel with the highest profile on the seafront has been challenged by the new W hotel but it is still a favourite with celebs. Rooms with panoramic views and every indulgence.

Duquesa de Cardona
Passeig Colom, 12
Tel: 93-268 9090
[p304, B3] €€€€
www.hduqesadecardona.com
A classically elegant hotel, in one of the handsome buildings

giving onto the original waterfront and the old harbour. The pool and terrace on the roof are a hidden treasure. Luxurious details at a moderate price.

Equity Point Sea Hostel
Plaça del Mar, 4
Tel: 93-224 7075
[p304, B4] €
www.equity-point.com
An unbeatable spot for a youth hostel right on Barceloneta beach. Branches in La Ribera, Gothic Point and Passeig de Gràcia.

Grand Marina
World Trade Centre
Moll de Barcelona, 1
Tel: 902-932 424

[p304, A4] €€€€
www.grandmarinahotel.com
You feel as if you are aboard a luxurious cruise ship. Some of the bedrooms, with hydro-massage baths, jut out into the port, while those at the rear have a panoramic view of the city.

Hotel 54
Passeig Joan de Borbó, 54
Tel: 93-225 0054
[p304, B4] €€€
www.hotel54barceloneta.com
A modern hotel in an extraordinary location in Barceloneta overlooking the port and city, so you can enjoy the sea, but still easily walk to the

centre. Once the fishermen's headquarters.

Marina Folch
Mar, 16, pral (1st floor)
Tel: 93-310 3709
[p304, C3] €€
www.hotelmarinafolchbcn.com
This is a family-run gem. There are only 11 rooms, and even company directors like staying here, so booking is essential.

21ST CENTURY BARCELONA

Barcelona Princess
Avinguda Diagonal, 1
Tel: 93-356 1000
[off map] €€€€
www.hotelbarcelonaprincess.com
On the cutting edge in all senses: designed by leading Catalan architect Oscar Tusquets, situated in Diagonal Mar, and offering all possible facilities. Prices are subject to radical cuts, too, so it is worth trying to bargain to sleep at this giddy height with views of sea and city.

Diagonal
Avinguda Diagonal, 205
Tel: 93-489 5300
[off map] €€€
www.hoteldiagonalbarcelona.com
Designed by award-winning Barcelona architect Juli Capella, this eye-catching new hotel rubs shoulders with the Torre Agbar in Plaça de les Glòries and the 22@ business district.

Front Marítim
Passeig García Faria, 69–71
Tel: 93-303 4440
[off map] €€

www.gbbhotels.com
One of the hotels on the waterfront between Vila Olímpica and Diagonal Mar. Being just a taxi ride away from the inner-city buzz can be advantageous, especially if you wake up to sea views.

Urbany Hostel
Av. Meridiana, 97
Tel: 93-245 8414
[off map] €
www.barcelonaurbany.com
High-tech youth hostel, with roof terrace overlooking the Torre Agbar,

swimming pool and Wi-fi. With twin-bed rooms at only €25 per person the appeal goes wider than "youth". For real budget travellers there are 8-bed dormitories for much less.

MONTJUÏC

Acta Milleni
Ronda Sant Pau, 14
Tel: 93-441 4177
[p303, E2] €€€
www.hotel-millennibarcelona.com
Though officially situated in the Raval, this modernised hotel is within easy reach of Montjuïc and the trade fair site. Good deals for family rooms.

Catalonia Barcelona Plaza
Plaça d'Espanya, 6–8
Tel: 93-426 2600
[p300, C4] €€€
www.hoteles-catalonia.com
A modern hotel popular with business clientele due to its location near the trade fairs. Situated at the foot of Montjuïc, it is easy to

reach from the airport.

Hotel Miramar
Plaça Carlos Ibáñez
Tel: 93-281 1600
[p303, D3] €€€€
www.hotelmiramarbarcelona.es
In prime position on the hilltop, these former TV studios have been transformed by local star architect Tusqets into a luxury hotel.

THE EIXAMPLE

Actual
Rosselló, 238
Tel: 93-552 0550
[p306, B2] €€€
www.hotelactual.com
A really welcome newcomer on the hotel scene. It has attractive minimalist decor yet maintains a warm, personal atmosphere. Book early.

América
Provença, 195
Tel: 93-487 6292
[p306, A2] €€€
www.hotelamericabarcelona.com
On a quiet corner of the Eixample, this hotel prides itself on being different from the average chain hotel. Offers excellent service and facilities for guests.

Avenida Palace
Gran Via, 605–607
Tel: 93-301 9600
[p306, B4] €€€
www.avenidapalace.com
Classic old-world gilt and chandeliers at new-world prices. You can even stay where The Beatles slept on their one visit to the city in 1965.

Casa Fuster
Passeig de Gràcia, 132
Tel: 93-255 3000

ABOVE: the ultramodern Diagonal.

Booking: 902-202 345
[p306, B2] €€€€
www.hotelcasafuster.es
A 5-star "Monument" hotel, this grand hotel is located in the magnificent Casa Fuster, built by Domènech i Montaner in 1908, with all its *modernista* splendour carefully restored.

Catalonia Berna
Roger de Llúria 60,
Tel: 93-272 0050
[p306, B3] €€€
www.hoteles-catalonia.com
In the heart of the Eixample, this pretty hotel will transport you back to the heyday of this 19th-century district. The

ornamental facade with painted frescoes has been carefully recovered.

Claris
Pau Claris, 150
Tel: 93-487 6262
[p306, B3] €€€€
www.derbyhotels.com
Well positioned in the middle of the Eixample, the Claris's strikingly designed interior was built behind the original facade of the Palace of Vedruna and is crammed with valuable art work.

Condes de Barcelona
Passeig de Gràcia, 75
Tel: 93-445 0000
[p306, B3] €€€

www.condesdebarcelona.com
Contemporary elegance in two *modernista* buildings facing each other in the Quadrat d'Or. Rooms available with private balcony; roof terrace with mini pool.

Cram
Aribau, 54
Tel: 93-216 7700
[p306, A3] €€€
www.hotelcram.com
High design, impeccable style and all the latest mod cons in the warm interiors of this renovated, handsome 19th-century building.

PRICE CATEGORIES

Prices for a standard double room without breakfast or IVA (VAT):
€ = under €50
€€ = €50–€100
€€€ = €100–€200
€€€€ = over €200

ABOVE: lobby of the Omm, the height of cool.

Legendary Barcelona restaurant Gaig is now part of the hotel.

Diplomatic
Pau Claris, 122
Tel: 93-272 3810
[p306, B3] €€€
www.marriott.co.uk
Sleek and crisp minimalist design with a spacious downstairs lounge. Amazing views from the roof terrace, which also has a gym and outdoor pool. Good value.

Gallery
Rosselló, 249
Tel: 93-415 9911
[p306, B2] €€€
www.galleryhotel.com
Well situated between Passeig de Gràcia and Rambla de Catalunya. Very pleasant bar on the first floor overlooking the street, and a restaurant that has tables outside in the garden.

Gran Hotel Havana
Gran Via, 647
Tel: 93-341 7000
[p306, C4] €€€€
www.granhotelhavana.com
The rooms here have been renovated and are stylish and pleasant. Attractive, luminous interior. Good location.

Granados 83
Enric Granados, 83
Tel: 93-492 9670
[p306, A2] €€€

www.derbyhotels.com
One of the latest to come from this chain of smart hotels, this is in possibly the prettiest street of the Eixample.

Granvía
Gran Vía, 642
Tel: 93-318 1900
[p306, B4] €€
www.nnhotels.com
Faded Old Spain splendour, which can be a welcome change from the pervading designer modernity of the city. Interior rooms are preferable, to avoid the traffic noise from Gran Via. Downstairs there is a large, restful lounge leading to a spacious terrace.

Hostal Cèntric
Casanova, 13
Tel: 93-426 7573
[p306, A4] €€
www.hostalcentric.com
New-generation guesthouse, fresh, clean and modern. Excellent value and within walking distance of the Old Town and the Eixample.

Hostal Ciudad Condal
Mallorca, 255
Tel: 93-215 1040
[p306, B3] €€
www.hostalciudadcondal.com
Very clean, respectable little *pensión* in the heart of the best part of the Eixample. All rooms with en suite bathroom.

Majestic
Passeig de Gràcia, 68
Tel: 93-488 1717
[p306, B3] €€€€
www.hotelmajestic.es
This warm, sophisticated classic was recently elected Spain's leading hotel and has opened a luxury spa on its top floor. Has two restaurants, including the famed Drolma, with only 10 tables where gourmets can sample an exquisite menu by well-known chef Fermí Puig.

Market
Passatge Sant Antoni Abat, 10
Tel: 93-325 1205
[p303, D1] €€
www.markethotel.com.es
Probably the best value place in town, with an attractive neo-colonial theme running through restaurant, bedrooms and indulgent bathrooms. A stylish find tucked behind bustling Sant Antoni market.

Omm
Rosselló, 265
Tel: 93-445 4000
[p306, B2] €€€€
www.hotelomm.es
This designer hotel is seriously cool and *the* place to be seen. It has slick, light rooms and a rooftop lap pool with views of the Sagrada Família. Whether you're

in the Moo restaurant, or chilling out in the Omm Session club you'll feel like you're in a fashion shoot.

Palace
Gran Via, 668
Tel: 93-510 1130
[p306, C4] €€€€
www.hotelpalacebarcelona.com
No longer part of the Ritz group but still eminently high-class, Palace has reopened after major refurbishment, making it even more sumptuous. Dalí had a permanent suite here.

Paseo de Gràcia
Passeig de Gràcia, 102
Tel: 93-215 0603
[p306, B2] €€
www.hotelpaseodegracia.es
Recently renovated in a simple manner but very effectively. Ask for a room on the eighth floor. Prime location and good value.

Praktik Rambla
Rambla Catalunya, 27
Tel: 93-343 6690
[p306, B4] €€€
www.hotelpraktikrambla.com
An amazingly stylish, fairly new hotel, making the most of the building's *modernista* features but mixed with fresh, clean design. Has an attractive terrace in typical Eixample interior patio. Great location.

Regente
Rambla de Catalunya, 76
Tel: 93-487 5989
[p306, B3] €€€
www.hcchotels.es
Pleasant hotel in an excellent position with some attractive original *moderniste* features. Rooftop pool open in summer.

Sant Moritz
Diputación, 264
Tel: 93-412 1500
[p306, B4] €€€
www.hcchotels.es

TRANSPORT

More of interest for its location than its style. On the ground floor are rooms for guests with disabilities.

Sixty Two
Passeig de Gràcia, 62
Tel: 93-272 4180
[p306, B3] €€€€
www.sixtytwohotel.com

Low-key elegance in this stylish newcomer. Their claim to individuality is the "Ask Me" service: a team of switched-on

young people who can answer your cultural, gastronomic or shopping queries. Small, oriental-style garden.

ABOVE THE DIAGONAL

ACCOMMODATION

Aparthotel Atenea
Joan Güell, 207–211
Tel: 93-490 6640
[p300, B1] €€€
www.city-hotels.es
Well-designed mini apartments in a classy part of the city, close to the Plaça Francesc Macià.

Aparthotel Bonanova
Bisbe Sevilla, 7
Tel: 93-253 1563
[off map] €€€
www.aparthotelbonanova.com
In a quiet residential area a short train ride from the centre. Reserve a room with a terrace if you can.

Casa Dover
Còrsega 429, pral. 1a
Tel: (mobile) +34 672 250 387
[p307, C2] €€
www.casadover.com
High class B&B with a stylish café on the

ground floor. Well-designed and decorated rooms in a perfect location on the edge of Gràcia with Gaudí monuments close by. A great newcomer to the accommodation scene.

Gran Hotel La Florida
Carretera Vallvidrera–Tibidabo, 83–93
Tel: 93-259 3000
[off map] €€€€
www.hotellaflorida.com
This Grand Luxe hotel is the ultimate in luxury, perched high on Tibidabo hill. Brought back to life from its former glory in the 1940s when the likes of Ernest Hemingway and James Stewart were clients, it has impeccable service and unbeatable views.

Hostal Lesseps
Gran de Gràcia, 239
Tel: 93-218 4434
[off map] €
www.hostallesseps.com
Owned by the same family as the Hostal Ciudad Condal (see page 260) and similar in style. Near the metro in Gràcia, making it a good base in a great area.

Hotel Tres Torres
Calatrava, 32–34
Tel: 93-417 7300
[off map] €
www.husatrestorres.com
The Tres Torres is a small hotel, very reasonably priced for this smart residential area. It's nothing spectacular, but it sits in a quiet leafy street and the centre of town is only minutes away on the FGC

trains. A good-value, peaceful option.

Melia Barcelona
Avinguda Sarrià, 48–50
Tel: 93-410 6060
[p301, D2] €€€
www.melia-barcelona.com
You could easily forget you're in Barcelona in this hotel and be anywhere in the world. Near the business district.

Rey Juan Carlos I
Avinguda Diagonal, 661–671
Tel: 93-364 4040
[off map] €€€
www.hrjuancarlos.com
A vast construction of glass and steel at the upper end of Diagonal and therefore a taxi ride away from everything. It offers maximum comfort and security, which may be why it is favoured by royalty and politicians. Stunning gardens and pool.

SHOPPING

ACTIVITIES

A – Z

BELOW: Gran Hotel La Florida.

LANGUAGE

FURTHER AFIELD

Efficient and frequent suburban train lines *(Rodalies)* make staying out of town a good option. A cool, comfortable 45-minute train ride will take you from a quiet beach-side hotel to the centre of Barcelona. Rooms are usually easier to book and rates better value.

There are several top-quality hotels, including *paradores*, and an increasing number of self-catering options and rural guesthouses, which range from simple rooms in a traditional farmhouse to more exclusive country houses. An internet search will throw up contacts, but a good start is the Catalan tourist office: www.gencat.cat/turistex.

Badalona

Hotel Miramar
Santa Madrona, 60
Tel: 93-384 0311 €
www.hotelmiramar.es
A traditional beach side hotel, fairly recently renovated with all mod cons included. Quirky but fun choice as it's only 10 minutes from Plaça de Catalunya by train, and a pleasant walk along Badalona's elegant promenade.

Caldes d'Estrac

Kalima
Passeig de les Moreres, 7
Tel: 93-791 4890 €€–€€€
www.kalima-caldes.com
Charming B&B in a small *modernista* villa on the promenade overlooking one of the less

frequented beaches. The devoted owners take care of every small detail. A gem at a reasonable price.

Capellades

Hostal Can Carol
Font de la Reina, 5
Tel: 93-801 0330 €€–€€€
www.hostalcancarol.com
Only half an hour inland from Barcelona near the Penedès wine region and Montserrat, this small hotel gives a warm welcome with its attractive, individually decorated bedrooms and rural surroundings. Wine tastings and other activities can be organised.

Espot

Hotel Saurat
Plaça San Martí, 1
Tel: 973-624 162 €€
www.hotelsaurat.com
A comfortable family-run mountain hotel, right in the heart of the village, it is a perfect base for all the different activities in the Aigüestortes national park and surrounding area. Now run by the fifth generation, its restaurant serves traditional, home-made cooking.

Girona

Aiguablava
Platja de Fornells, Begur
Tel: 972-622 058 €€€
www.aiguablava.com
A stylish, historic, traditional hotel. It overlooks one of the prettiest beaches on this spectacular coastline.

Bellmirall
Bellmirall, 3
Tel: 972-204 009 €
www.bellmirall.cat
Friendly and charming, this family-run bed and breakfast betwixt cathedral and city walls is a perfect base for discovering this historic city.

Montserrat

Cel·les Abat Marcet
Montserrat
Tel: 93-877 7701 €€
www.montserratvisita.com
The perfect way to capture the peace of Catalonia's sacred mountain – spend the night in a former monk's cell and avoid the busloads which descend in daytime. Good-value self-catering ranging from one-person studios to four-person apartments.

Palamós

Trias
Passeig del Mar, s/n
Tel: 972-601 800 €€€
www.hoteltrias.com
A once typical beach side hotel, it has reinvented itself into an extremely stylish, attractive place to stay with a good restaurant and swimming pool, all at a very moderate rate.

Ripoll

Mas El Reixac
Sant Joan de les Abadesses
Tel: 972-720 373 €
www.elreixac.com
Self-catering accommodation in tastefully restored farm buildings just outside a historic village. Walks on the

Barcelona

doorstep and skiing 30 minutes away. Log fires and duvets make it cosy in winter.

Sitges

Hotel Subur Marítim
Passeig Marítim, s/n
Tel: 93-894 1550 €€€
www.hotelsuburmaritim.com
Sitting right on the seafront, this attractive hotel has personality, plus a lovely pool in the garden. It's within walking distance of the centre, but at a peaceful distance. Good deals available out of season.

Vic

Parador de Vic-Sau
Paraje el Bac de Sau
Tel: 93-812 2323 €€€
www.parador.es
Traditional *parador* outside Vic, on the edge of a huge reservoir.

Vilanova i la Geltrú

Hotel César
Isaac Peral, 8
Tel: 93-815 1125 €
www.hotelcesar.net
A delightful hotel run by two sisters, one creative in interior design, the other in the kitchen. It has a tiny pool in a shady garden a stone's throw from the beach, and is full of personal charm.

S HOPPING

BEST BUYS

With the march of globalisation, the bargain that cannot be found back home is a rarity. However, for certain products the choice is much wider, and in some cases much better value. If you can't face trudging home with virgin olive oil, or fear your holiday budget will disappear if you venture into Loewe for leather, it is still worth seeing the colourful displays at the food markets and doing some serious window-shopping. Besides, Barcelona's combination of style and history makes strolling into shops a pleasure.

SHOPPING AREAS

The entire length of Passeig de Gràcia, Rambla de Catalunya and the interconnecting streets provide enjoyable shopping, ranging from chain stores to top international fashion and Spanish designers. The Ciutat Vella (Old Town) is now studded with artisanal shops, galleries and trendy souvenirs, and bursting with hip boutiques, particularly in the Born area. In the Gothic Quarter Portal de l'Àngel and Portaferrisa are best for young fashion chains and shoe shops, while the Raval has more quirky shops and vintage. The Avinguda Diagonal, from the top of Rambla de Catalunya up to the roundabout which forms Plaça Francesc Macià, and the streets behind are good for fashion, but they are expensive.

The upper parts of town have their own local district atmosphere and make a refreshing change. Try

Carrer de Muntaner, around the FGC station. Further up at No. 385 is Groc, Toni Miró's original shop. If you need a break, good wines by the glass accompany delicate snacks in the Tivoli at No. 361. Gràcia is a relaxed and charming place to shop, with young designer fashion and jewellery.

DEPARTMENT STORES AND SHOPPING MALLS

The largest department store is **El Corte Inglés**, with two branches in Plaça de Catalunya, one in nearby Portal de l'Àngel specialising in urban wear, music, books and sports, and others in Avinguda Diagonal. All branches are open Monday–Saturday 10am–10pm. The Plaça de Catalunya and Diagonal (No. 617) branches have excellent supermarkets.

The main shopping centres and malls are:

Barcelona Glòries, Plaça de les Glòries.
Bulevard Rosa, Passeig de Gràcia, 55. Smaller, more individual shops and boutiques.
Diagonal Mar, Avinguda Diagonal, 3. A huge complex in a new residential district by the sea, with Catalonia's first Primark. Large play area for kids.
Galeries Maldà, Portaferrissa, 22. Small local shops.
Gran Via 2, Avinguda Gran Via 75 L'Hospitalet. A new mega-centre with all facilities. Take FGC Pl. Europa from Pl. d'Espanya.
L'Illa, Avinguda Diagonal, 545. Superior shopping centre for the uptown crowd with upmarket cafés and a large supermarket.
Maremàgnum, Moll d'Espanya. A good range of shops open until 10pm every day. The only place you can shop on Sundays.
El Triangle. A large development in Plaça de Catalunya including

SHOPPING HOURS

Most small shops open between 9 and 10am and close between 1 and 2pm, opening again from 4 or 5pm to 8pm. Many clothes and food shops close at 8.30 or 9pm. Department stores, chain stores and shopping centres remain open through lunchtime. In the summer, smaller shops may close on Saturday afternoon. Only bakeries, pastry shops and a few grocers' shops are open on Sunday (until 3pm), with the exception of Maremàgnum *(see page 263).*

ABOVE: leather is expensive but of high quality.

Habitat, Sephora, an emporium of perfume and cosmetics for men and women, and FNAC (a huge book, computer and music store).

For out-of-hours grocery shopping the best bet is the Raval area, though most districts now have late opening mini-supermarkets opened by enterprising immigrants.

MARKETS

There are covered markets in every district of the city selling fruit, vegetables, meat and fish. A trip to Barcelona would be incomplete without visiting at least one of them. Markets open every day except Sunday from early morning until around 3pm. Avoid Monday; the selection is poor because the central wholesale market does not open and there is no fresh fish.

The largest and most colourful market is the Boqueria on La Rambla, which stays open until 8pm Monday–Saturday. The most exotic and expensive fare is in the entrance; the bargains are to be found in the maze of stalls behind, especially in the adjoining Plaça Sant Galdric which is a farmers' market.

Most of the municipal markets are being renovated gradually

and given the designer treatment: don't miss the Mercat Santa Caterina and Barceloneta market, with excellent specialist shops selling oil and wine, and good restaurants.

Book and antiques fairs are held with great regularity in Barcelona: look out for posters or announcements in the press.

Other regular markets of interest are:
Coin and stamp market, Plaça Reial. Sunday 9am–2.30pm. A timeless gem worth visiting.
Coin, video games and book market, Mercat Sant Antoni. Sunday 9am–2pm. Attractive market building on the junction of Carrer de Tamarit/Comte d'Urgell. Undergoing renovation but still operating in Ronda Sant Antoni.
Els Encants, Plaça de les Glòries. This is a genuine flea market. There are some expensive antiques, some old clothes, and a lot of trash, but among it all bargains can still be found. It gets very hot in the summer, so early morning is better for both bargains and comfort. Monday, Wednesday, Friday and Saturday 8am–7pm (winter), until 8pm in summer.
Mercat de Concepció, València, between Carrer de Bruc and Carrer de Girona. In this neighbourhood market you can see how

Barcelona mixes new design with old. Two blocks along València is Navarro, a legendary flower shop that never closes.
Mercat Gòtic d'Antiguitats, Avinguda Catedral. Antique market every Thursday. Some interesting collections.
Mercat Obert Raval. Colourful, creative market in the Rambla del Raval selling original fashion. There's a Moroccan tea tent selling delicious snacks too. Saturday and Sunday.
Moll de Drassanes. Weekend bric-a-brac market, by the sea.

CLOTHES

Leather

It is questionable whether leather garments are still worth buying in Spain, except perhaps at the top end of the market, where design and quality are outstanding. But shoes, handbags and suitcases are worth considering. The best in clothes, bags and accessories is **Loewe**, based in Madrid but with an important and sumptuous branch in Casa Lleó Morera (Passeig de Gràcia, 35).

There are other shops specialising in leather, the cheaper ones being found particularly in and around La Rambla and Portal de l'Àngel, some of them in strange first-floor surroundings and selling at factory prices.

Shoes

These are good value. Look out for Catalan and Spanish designers such as **Farrutx** (Rosselló, 218) who trade on sophisticated elegance, **Lotusse** (contemporary classical and very well made) and **Camper** (trendy, comfortable). Camper has branches all over town such as on Carrer Pelai, València, Passeig de Gràcia and Carrer Elisabets in El Raval. Another local designer, **Vialis**, makes creative, comfortable shoes in gorgeously soft leather (shops in Elisabets, Vidrieria, Verdi and Arenas shopping centre). **Tascón** has a good selection of these brands and others in their various branches (Passeig de Gràcia, the Born, Diagonal Mar, at the airport). The best areas for shoes and bags are Portal de l'Àngel, Rambla de Catalunya, Passeig de Gràcia, Diagonal and the malls. *(See also page 267.)*

Top Fashion

Toni Miró is by far the most famous Catalan designer of men's and women's wear, and his clothes are somehow representative of how the middle classes like to dress. They are characterised by their clean lines and subtlety (verging on the inconspicuous or sombre).

He has just opened a flagship store called **Salón Miró** (Rambla de Catalunya, 125) stocking his latest fashion collection as well as household items he has designed. Intended to be a multifunctional space.

Other designer names are:
Adolfo Domínguez, Passeig de Gràcia, 32 and 89.
Armand Basi, Passeig de Gràcia, 49.
José Tomas, Mallorca, 242.
Lydia Delgado, Minerva, 21.
Purificación García, Passeig de Gràcia, 21.
Sita Murt, Passeig de Gràcia, 11.
Shops selling national and international designer wear:
Jean Pierre Bua, Avinguda Diagonal, 469.
Noténom, Pau Clarís, 159.
On Land, Princesa, 25.
Paco Rueda Shop, Passeig de Picasso 36.
New local designers are emerging with tiny boutiques, mostly in the Born and Raval districts:
Cortana, Flassaders, 41. Stylish, comfortable clothes for women from this Mallorcan designer.
Miriam Ponsa, Princesa, 14. Up-and-coming Catalan designer with striking shop near the Picasso Museum.

In the growing street/urban wear category the city has its own, extremely successful names like **Custo Barcelona** and **Desigual**, both with shops all over town and spreading across the globe.

Cheaper Fashion

The two biggest fashion stores are **Zara**, with its many offshoots like Bershka, Oysho, and Pull & Bear, and **Mango**, with branches all over the city, closely followed by **H&M**. In the Old Town, Portaferrissa and Portal de l'Àngel are good streets for young fashion. On and around Carrer Avinyó are a lot of trendy shops, such as **American Apparel**, and El Born is brimming with boutiques. El Raval is catching up fast: **Caníbal** (Carmé, 5) has fun, one-off designs, and Riera Baixa is full of second-hand clothes boutiques.

In **El Mercadillo** and **Gralla Hall**, both on Portaferrissa, you can spend some happy hours flitting from shop to shop. The former is cheaper and more alternative, the latter geared more towards smarter, or club clothing. Both places were old palaces and are fun to visit whether you buy or not. When you've had enough, go for a drink or meal on the terrace upstairs at the back of El Mercadillo – such inner patios are a rare treat.

THE BEST OF BARCELONA DESIGN

Much of Barcelona's stylish image rests upon its reputation for design. To get an idea of how trendy Barcelonans decorate their homes, all you need do is take a trip around the first floor of **Vinçon**, considered the temple of interior design, at Passeig de Gràcia, 96.

Other design shops in the Eixample include:
Biosca & Botey, Rambla de Catalunya, 129. Noteworthy among hordes of lighting shops.
Dos i Una, Rosselló, 275.

Smaller lines include Mariscal earrings and gimmicks to help solve gift problems.
Pilma, just around the corner in Avinguda Diagonal, 403. Understated style for the home and excellent kitchen ware.
Zara Home, Rambla Catalunya and Passeig de Gràcia, 19. Not exactly born in Barcelona, but inspired ideas at reasonable prices.
Among the design shops in the Old Town are:
DHUB, Disseny Hub, Montcada

12, Until it all moves to Plaça de les Glories, the shop in this design centre is worth stopping at for inspiring gifts.
Gotham, Cenvantes, 7. Period pieces from the 1960s, furniture and lights.
Matirile, Passeig del Born, 24. Sells one-off lamps made to order, from new and recycled materials.
Vaho Gallery, Bonsuccés 13. Bags and other items are ingeniously designed from recycled PVC publicity banners.

FOOD

A taste of Spain back home always extends the holiday. Olives marinated in garlic direct from the market, spicy, cured sausages *(chorizo, fuet* and *sobrasada),* ham *(jabugo* is the best), cheese (Manchego, Mahon, Idiazabal), saffron, herbs, nuts, dried fruit and handmade chocolates are all easy to carry. Virgin olive oil, wine, cava and *moscatel* are less portable, but still worth the effort. Buy from the markets or *queviures* (grocers' shops). Some prime sites are:

Casa Gispert, Sombrerers, 23. Lovely old shop selling dried fruits, grains and coffees in sacks, as well as preserves and delicacies.
Colmado Quilez, Rambla de Catalunya, 63. Another well-stocked and gorgeous old shop full of delicacies, where men in blue smocks tend to your every need.
Escribà, La Rambla, 83. The family of the late Antoni Escribà, the famous chocolate "sculptor", continue his tradition in this beautiful shop. Have a coffee and pastry on the terrace and check out the window display.
Fargas, Boters, 2 (corner of Pi and Cucurulla). For chocolates, sweets and *turrones (see Planelles Donat).* Decorative old shop.
J. Múrria, Roger de Llúria, 85. This is where you will find the most exquisite selection of foodstuffs in the prettiest *modernista* building. Worth a visit just to observe.
Orolíquido, Palla 8. An exquisite array of olive oil and olive-based products, ranging from the finest DO virgin oil to soap.
Planelles Donat, Portal de l'Àngel, 27 (and other branches). Specialists in *turrón* (a sticky nougat-type delicacy traditionally eaten at Christmas). Good ice cream in summer.
La Seu, Dagueria, 16. Seasonal additive-free farmhouse cheeses from all over Spain. The Scots owner allows you access to the walk-in fridges. What you purchase

will be packed specially for travel. She also sells the best, most natural olive oils, and occasionally does cheese and wine tastings.
Xocoa, Vidriera, 4. Innovative contemporary chocolates, made in Catalonia, with flavours like "five peppers" or "thyme".

DRINK

As Spanish and Catalan wines become more competitive it is worth seeking the experts' advice to get to know new wineries and lesser-known DOs *(see page 78).*
L'Anima del Vi, Mariana Pineda, 3 bis. Small shop in Gràcia selling pure, natural wines.
El Celler de la Boqueria, Plaça Sant Josep, 15-B. In the side alley of the market. An interesting range from different regions at economical prices.
Vila Viniteca, Agullers, 7–9. A magnificent range of fine wines and spirits and helpful staff.
Xampany, València, 200. For serious purchasers of cava, with more than 100 types. Also cava accessories and memorabilia.

BOOKSHOPS

Altair, Gran Via, 616. Travel specialists.
BCN Books, Roger de Llúria, 118. English books.
Central, Elisabets, 6. Atmospheric bookshop in a former chapel. Small English section, but great for browsing. Another branch in Mallorca, 237 has an appealing café.
Col·legi d'Arquitectes, Plaça Nova, 5. Well-supplied and specialising in architecture and design.
FNAC, El Triangle, Plaça de Catalunya. Has stocks of English books for adults and children.
Kowasa, Mallorca, 235. Stocks photography books only, but a wide selection in a charming space with a rear garden. Also holds exhibitions.

Laie Llibreria Cafè, Pau Claris, 85. A good-looking bookshop selling mostly literature, art and media books, with a good café/restaurant upstairs. Also has a branch in the CCCB (Contemporary Culture Centre).
Quera, Petritxol, 2. Maps of Catalonia and walking books.

TRADITIONAL CRAFTS

Barcelona has many small shops specialising in traditional crafts. Whether you are looking for lace, feathers, fans or religious artefacts, there is sure to be someone somewhere making it. The best areas to try are the Barri Gòtic, around the Born, the Raval, Gràcia and Eixample.

The Generalitat runs the **Artesania Catalunya** (Banys Nous, 11), an exhibition centre with permanent displays, temporary shows, information and a shop.

Antiques and Old Books

There are many expensive antiques shops in the Eixample and the Barri Gòtic, notably on the streets Banys Nous and Palla. Prints and antique books are also a feature of Barcelona,

EXPORT PROCEDURE

Anyone resident outside the EU is exempt from IVA (Value Added Tax) on purchases worth more than €90. The IVA rate is 8 or 18 percent, according to the goods. The relevant forms to fill in for customs on leaving and on entering one's own country will be provided by the store. Ask for details at the time of purchase. Note that the goods may be subject to an even higher tax on return home. You can also ring Global Refund Information on 900-43 54 82. Large stores such as El Corte Inglés have a packing/despatch service.

SHOPPING ◆ 267

TRANSPORT
ACCOMMODATION
SHOPPING
ACTIVITIES
A – Z
LANGUAGE

particularly around the cathedral. **Librería Violán**, just off Plaça del Rei. Unusual books, prints and striking Art Deco posters.

Candles

Candles are quite a speciality of Barcelona. There are several shops near the cathedral, notably **Cereria Subirá**, Baixada Llibreteria, 7, founded in 1762.

Ceramics

Pots, tiles, plates... ceramics can be found all over the city, particularly in the Old Town. **La Caixa de Fang** in Carrer de Freneria has a huge range. Traditional ironmongers *(ferreterías)* usually have a good collection of classic brown earthenware cooking pots at non-tourist prices, as well as wonderful cooking utensils. Try **Targa**, Plaça de Palau 5.

Gloves, Shawls and Fans

Almacenes del Pilar, Boqueria, 43. Traditional *mantillas* (lace head scarves) and embroidered shawls.
Alonso, Santa Anna, 27. Leather (and other) gloves in the winter; fans in the summer. A beautiful little treasure trove.
Flora Albacín, Canada 3. Flamenco dress heaven for girls of all ages, plus shoes, earrings and fans.
Guantes Victoriano, Mallorca 195. A family-run business selling made-to-measure gloves of the finest leather.

Hats

Mil, Fontanella, 20. Supplies of old and new types of headdress.
Sombreria Obach, Call, 2. Hats of many descriptions, mainly traditional (e.g. berets). This timeless shop has to be visited.

Jewellery

For more conventional or very pricey pieces, look on Passeig de Gràcia, Rambla de Catalunya or other Eixample streets. In the Old Town you can find numerous tiny jewellery shops; often they occupy only the entrance of a building, with most of their wares in the window display. For something a bit different, try: **Joaquín Berao**, Rambla de Catalunya, 74. Designer items with a very individual stamp: smooth and chunky. Only the best materials used.

Knives

Ganiveteria Roca, Plaça del Pi. Impressive window displays. Inside you will find virtually every kind of cutting instrument for domestic use, and Spanish-style penknifes for outdoor use.

Lace and Fabrics

Casa Oliveres, Dagueria, 11. Full of antique treasures. Specialises in lace and will produce to order.
Coses de Casa, Plaça Sant Josep Oriol, 5. Fine Mallorcan fabrics.
Dona, Provença, 256. Embroidery and embroidery kits.
El Indio, Carme, 24. Magnificent *modernista* shop with huge rolls of fabric.
Rosemary, Calaf, 46. White linen, bedclothes, tablecloths and towels with elaborate details.

Taller de Lencería, Rosselló, 271. Linen with handmade lace borders.

Paper

Papirum, Baixada Llibreteria, 2. Sell handmade paper and notebooks of all sizes. They are not cheap but are beautiful and make great gifts.
Tarlatana, Comtessa de Sobradiel, 2. Marbled papers and bookbinding.

Shoes (Hand-Crafted)

Calçats Solé, Ample, 7. Come here for really original footwear, sturdy leather boots, Mallorcan sandals and rustic shoes from different parts of Spain.
La Manual Alpargatera, Avinyó, 7. A huge variety of *alpargatas*, the classic rope-soled canvas shoes of Old Spain. Here you can see them being made and choose your preferred design.

Toys

A cluster of toy shops can be found leading off either side of Plaça del Pi. The most original of these is **El Ingenio**, at Carrer Rauric, 6–8.
Xalar, Baixada, Llibreteria, 4. Wooden dolls' houses and other choice toys.

BELOW: urban street wear on a Barcelona back street.

ACTIVITIES

THE ARTS, FESTIVALS, NIGHTLIFE, SPORTS AND CHILDREN'S ACTIVITIES

Barcelona offers the best of both worlds: a dynamic cultural scene and colourful nightlife in a city rich in history and tradition. There is so much to do here: whether you plan carefully or just take pot luck something interesting will be happening. The city's calendar of festivals is one of the most extensive and varied in Europe, taking in every branch of the performing arts. If you can, time your visit to coincide with a local festival, as it is at the grassroots level that the vibrancy and vitality of Barcelona are best expressed.

THE ARTS

Cultural Events

The combination of Catalonia's rich cultural heritage and the dynamism of contemporary movements has made Barcelona one of Europe's cultural capitals. Apart from its architecture and more than 50 museums, there is a busy calendar of music and arts festivals, opera, visiting exhibitions and constant activity in design, theatre, dance and the arts in general, to say nothing of daily performances from street artists in the Ramblas and small squares of the Barri Gòtic.

Posters, banners, the daily and weekly press and multiple websites all herald what's on in Barcelona. The city council has a cultural information centre in the Palau de la Virreina, Rambla, 99 *(see page 269)*, which is very helpful, has leaflets and

information on nearly all cultural activities, and sells tickets. Also check the city's website www.bcn.cat. The Generalitat has a cultural information centre (closed at lunchtime) at the base of the Arts Santa Mònica *(see below)*. The tourist information office in Plaça de Catalunya sells two-for-the-price-of-one tickets on the day of a performance. Two of the savings banks also have an efficient system for ticket sales:
CXTelentrada of the CatalunyaCaixa, tel: 902-101 212; www.telentrada.com.
ServiCaixa of La Caixa, in most branches of the bank, tel: 902-332 211; www.servicaixa.com.

Cultural Centres

The following centres regularly hold temporary exhibitions of the visual arts, festivals and other events. Consult local press for details:
Arts Santa Mònica
Rambla Santa Mònica, 7

Tel: 93-567 1110
www.artssantamonica.cat
Born again into an exciting new space. No charge.
CaixaForum, the cultural centre of La Caixa Foundation
Av. Francesc Ferrer i Guàrdia, 6–8
Tel: 93-476 8600
http://obrasocial.lacaixa.es
Exciting space holding exhibitions of contemporary art, historical heritage, concerts and talks.
Centre de Cultura Contemporània de Barcelona (CCCB)
Montalegre, 5
Tel: 93-306 4100
www.cccb.org
Hosts seminars and a range of activities as well as installations, exhibitions of contemporary art, and film and music festivals.
CX La Pedrera
Provença, 261
www.catalunyacaixa/obrasocial.com
Apart from the Gaudí architecture itself, and the Espai Gaudí permanent exhibition on the man

and his work, there are free temporary shows on totally different themes in the exhibition space on the first floor.

Fundació Antoni Tàpies
Aragó, 255
Tel: 93-487 0315
www.fundaciotapies.org
Permanent collection of work by the artist himself plus very good shows by other internationally acclaimed artists. Beautiful art library upstairs.

Palau de la Virreina
Rambla, 99
Tel: 93-316 1000
www.bcn.cat/virreinacentredelaimatge
Cultural information centre run by the city council. Exhibition spaces devoted to photography and the moving image.

Art Galleries

Art galleries are usually open Tue–Sat 10.30am–1.30pm and 4.30–8.30pm. They tend to be concentrated in three areas of the city.

In the Eixample: Passeig de Gràcia, Rambla de Catalunya and on interconnecting streets (notably Consell de Cent):

Carles Taché, Consell de Cent, 290.

Galería Alejandro Sales, Julian Romea, 16.

Galería Estrany·De la Mota, Passatge Mercader, 18.

Galería Senda, Consell de Cent, 337.

Joan Prats, Rambla de Catalunya, 54.

Sala Dalmau, Consell de Cent, 349.

In the Old Town around Plaça Sant Josep Oriol, in the Born and in El Raval district, near the MACBA:

Angels Barcelona, Pintor Fortuny 27.

Artur Ramon Art, Palla, 10.

Ras, Doctor Dou, 10.

Sala Pares, Petrixtol, 5.

Trama, Petritxol 5, first floor.

In the streets behind Plaça Francesc Macià:

Fernando Alcolea, Plaça Sant Gregori Taumaturg, 7.

Music and Dance

Classical Music

A busy season of concerts by the Orquestra Simfònica de Barcelona i Nacional de Catalunya (OBC) and visiting orchestras and soloists runs from September to early July. The Festival de Música Antiga is held in April and May, and various international music festivals take place outside Barcelona in July and August, including the notable Festival de Peralada in Girona

TRADITIONAL FESTIVALS

Every district *(barri)* of the city has its own annual fiesta, known as the Festa Major, centred on its own patron saint. Giants (*gegants*, see picture) and comic characters parade the streets and *castellers* perform during fiestas. These troupes, made up of local people, erect human towers capped with the youngest and smallest. The *sardana*, the national dance of Catalonia, can also be seen every Sunday in Plaça Sant Jaume (at 7pm (6.30pm in winter), and in the Plaça de la Catedral on Sundays at noon.

Christmas. In early December the Santa Llúcia Fair of arts and crafts plus Christmas trees is held around the cathedral.

Sant Esteve (St Stephen's Day), 26 Dec. Families meet for an even larger meal than on 25th.

Reis Mags, Epiphany, 6 Jan. Children receive presents from the Three Kings, though modern commerce now indulges them with presents at Christmas as well. In Barcelona the Kings arrive from the Orient by boat the evening before and parade around the city.

Carnival (Carnestoltes), Feb or Mar. Wild pre-Lent celebrations close with the "Burial of the Sardine" on Ash Wednesday, a riotous mock funeral. The most extravagant Carnival parades are at Sitges, on the coast.

(www.festivalperalada.com).

Barcelona's arts festivals also include classical music. Among them is one for 20th-century music in October and the Festival de Guitarra de Barcelona in March–June. For information on all musical activities, check www.bcn.cat/cultura or the websites of the different venues.

The main places to hear classical music are:

L'Auditori
Plaça de les Arts, tel: 93-247 9300; www.auditori.cat

Sant Jordi, 23 April. A Catalan festival, St George's Day is also World Book Day, on which men give a rose to their lady, and receive a book in return.

Fira de Sant Ponç, 11 May. Aromatic and medicinal herbs, crystallised fruit and honey are sold in Carrer de l'Hospital.

Sant Joan, 23–4 June. Midsummer's Night, the eve of the Feast of St John, is a big event in Catalonia. It is celebrated with fireworks, cava and *coca*, a Catalan cake.

Diada de Catalunya, 11 Sept. Catalonia's national day is less a traditional fiesta than an occasion for political demonstrations and national anthems.

The Feast of La Mercè, 24 Sept. Barcelona's main fiesta is held in honour of the city's patroness. A week of merriment is crowned by the *correfoc*, a nocturnal procession of devils and fire-breathing dragons.

MUSIC HALL AND CABARET

Barcelona has a long and colourful tradition of show business, centred on the Paral·lel area, with the more decadent shows in the dark alleys of what was the Barri Xino, much of which has disappeared with the new urban planning. After a period of decline there is a revival of this kind of entertainment, stimulated by the reopening of **El Molino** (Vila i Vila, 99, www.elmolinobcn.com), the most famous and colourful. Find vaudeville burlesque, tango and

a weekly flamenco night with the option of dinner. Alternative cabaret can be found at:
Café Concert Llantiol, Rierita 7
Tel: 93-329 9009
Circol Maldà, Pi, 5, Pral. 2b
Intimate space in old palace for theatre, music and cabaret.
Gran Bodega Saltó, Blesa, 36
Tiny and colourful with a bohemian crowd.
Tinta Roja, Creu dels Molers, 17
Tel: 93-443 3243
Cabaret plus tango and Argentinian flavours.

A huge music auditorium which includes a Music Museum and now hosts the major concerts.
CaixaForum *(see page 268)*
Palau de la Música Catalana
Palau de la Música, 4–6
Tel: 93-295 7200/902-442 882
www.palaumusica.cat
If you have an opportunity to go to a concert in this extravagant *modernista* concert hall by Domènech i Montaner, then you should. Its programme includes flamenco, guitar, jazz and more popular concerts.

Contemporary Music

CCCB
Montalegre, 5
Tel: 93-306 4100
www.cccb.org *(see page 146)*
Fundació Miró
Montjuïc
Tel: 93-443 9470
This gallery hosts a season of 20th-century music, with particular emphasis on Catalan composers. L'Auditori *(see page 269)* also has a programme of contemporary music.

Jazz

The Terrassa Jazz Festival in the spring and the International Jazz Festival in the autumn gather together some leading names. In addition there is a jazz festival in the Old Town (Ciutat Vella), from mid-October to mid-December, and regular jazz and

blues sessions in an ever-increasing number of venues. To name a few:
Bel-luna, Rambla Catalunya, 5.
Harlem Jazz Club,
Comtessa de Sobradiel, 8.
Jamboree Jazz and Dance Club,
Plaça Reial, 17
www.masimas.com/jamboree
Jazz Sí Club, Requesens, 2
Jazzman, Roger de Flor, 238
www.jazzmanbcn.com

Rock/Pop

Barcelona is on the itinerary of most major international tours. Booking for these is usually

online or through music shops, notably in Carrer de Tallers, just off La Rambla. FNAC in the Triangle shopping centre at Plaça de Catalunya sells tickets for most of the well-known groups performing. On a smaller scale, some interesting offbeat musicians and eternal old timers often pass through. Check the listings. Some key venues:
Bikini, Diagonal 547;
www.bikinibcn.com. A well-loved club that was born again in this new venue in the 1990s. It has a well-selected, varied programme of live music, as well as a nightly disco of rock, funk and reggae.
Luz de Gas, Muntaner, 246;
www.luzdegas.com. Formerly a music hall, this is a pretty place for concerts of many descriptions: jazz, ethnic, rock, soul. It turns into a dance place later on, but by then you can consider going elsewhere – it's not their forte.
Palau Sant Jordi and Sant Jordi Club, Montjuïc. The former Olympic venue is a favourite for huge concerts.
Razzmatazz, Almogàvers, 122; www.salarazzmatazz.com. One of the best for hot-tipped international bands or old legends. Different spaces for different moods with a range of DJs and VJs.

BELOW: Jamboree, one of several jazz clubs in the city.

TRANSPORT

Sala Apolo/Club Nitsa, Nou de la Rambla, 113; www.sala-apolo. com. Once a music hall, now a trendy club with music from visiting DJs as well as live events. Different spaces have different styles, from the latest techno to jazz-swing. Always worth checking what's on.

Celtic

The city's Irish pubs nearly all have live music sessions. Check the local listings.

Opera and Ballet

Gran Teatre del Liceu
Rambla, 51–59
Iel: 93-485 9900/902-533 353 (tickets)
www.liceubarcelona.cat
Barcelona's opera house reopened in 1999 having been rebuilt after a devastating fire. Despite better technology and more productions, it is still difficult to get tickets. The repertoire has been broadened to have popular appeal, and avant-garde productions are on the rise. Good ballet season.

Contemporary Dance

Local companies and visiting groups perform in the city throughout the year.
Mercat de les Flors
Lleida, 59
Tel: 902-101 212
www.mercatflors.org
This venue is the former flower market converted into a theatre complex which specialises in dance and movement. A busy programme of national and international cutting-edge performers.

In addition there are dance seasons at the Liceu (see above), the Teatre Nacional (see right) and at outdoor locations during festivals.

Salsa

Some key venues:
Antilla BCN Latin Club, Aragó, 141–143
Sabor Cubano, Francisco Giner, 32
Samba Brasil, Lepant, 297

ABOVE: amphitheatre where the Grec festival is held *(see page 272)*.

Theatre

Most theatre productions are in Catalan or Spanish, but for true enthusiasts the theatrical experience should compensate for language problems.

Among the main theatres are:
Lliure
Plaça Margarida Xirgu
Tel: 93-228 9747
www.teatrelliure.com
Good contemporary productions.
Poliorama
Rambla, 115
Tel: 93-317 7599
Accessible theatre performances, including flamenco spectacles. Hosts occasional productions in English.
Romea
Hospital, 51
Tel: 93-301 5504
Teatre Nacional de Catalunya
Plaça de les Arts
Tel: 93-306 5700
www.tnc.cat
Ricardo Bofill's neoclassical building is located next to the auditorium near Plaça de les Glòries. It has the space to stage large-scale productions and smaller workshops.
Victoria
Avinguda Paral·lel, 67
Tel: 93-443 2929
Often stages musicals and ballet performances as well as flamenco shows.

Cinema

Barcelona has a great cinemagoing tradition. The following usually show *versió original* films (*v.o.* in listings) – foreign films that have been subtitled rather than dubbed.

Most showings begin around 4pm. The last and most popular screening will be around 10.30pm, although sometimes at weekends there will be a very late-night show, called the *sesión de madrugada*.
Boliche, Avinguda Diagonal, 508. A cinema with four screens.
Casablanca, Passeig de Gràcia, 115.
Filmoteca de la Generalitat de Catalunya, Avinguda Sarrià, 33. A film theatre showing less commercial films and retrospectives. Due to move to Plaça Salvador Seguí in 2012.
Icària Yelmo, Salvador Espriu, 61. Fifteen screens in the Vila Olímpica.
Méliès Cinemas, Villaroel, 102. Golden oldies.
Renoir-Les Corts, Eugeni d'Ors, 12. Six screens.
Renoir Floridablanca, Floridablanca, 135. Same chain, more conveniently located. Seven screens.
Verdi (Verdi, 32), and, around the corner, **Verdi Park** (Torrijos, 49). Together they have nine screens. Interesting and reliable selection.

ACCOMMODATION

SHOPPING

ACTIVITIES

A – Z

LANGUAGE

CASINOS

The Spanish are avid gamblers, and playing the various lotteries is a favourite pastime. If you want to do more serious gambling you have the following waiting for you:
Casino Castell de Perelada
Perelada
Tel: 972-53 8125
In the province of Girona, 20km (13 miles) from the French border.
Gran Casino Costa Brava
Lloret de Mar
Tel: 972-361 166
Gran Casino de Barcelona
Marina, 19–21
Tel: 93-225 7878
www.casino-barcelona.com

Arts Festivals

The Grec festival, held from mid-June to the end of July, is Barcelona's biggest summer cultural event. It brings together a high standard of national and international talent in theatre, music and dance. Performances take place all over the city, but one of the most impressive and appealing venues on a summer night is the Grec Theatre itself, an outdoor amphitheatre on Montjuïc. For information and booking: Palau de la Virreina, Rambla, 99, tel: 902-101 212, www.bcn.cat/grec.

Barcelona holds several film festivals throughout the year such as DocsBarcelona, In-Edit and the International Women's Film Festival. The **Sitges Festival Internacional de Cinema Fantàstic de Catalunya** (www.sitgesfilmfestival.com) is a well-established annual event every October specialising in fantasy.

The **Sonar Festival** of advanced music and multimedia arts in mid-June is an essential in the electronic music calendar, drawing an international crowd (www.sonar.es).

NIGHTLIFE

Barcelona is internationally known as being the city that never sleeps. Wander down La Rambla and through the squares of Gràcia after midnight or drive across the city and it becomes obvious why. The streets are buzzing, and this is just the beginning: lounge bars are slowly filling and clubs have hardly opened their doors. Most people are still finishing dinner (restaurants tend to open from 9pm) having had a cocktail before, or they are having an after-dinner drink before finding a place to dance. When the clubs close between 3 and 5am there are still the "Afters", bars where the die-hards can continue until 8 or 9am.

BELOW: Metro, one of Barcelona's best-known gay clubs.

ABOVE: Bar Marsella.

This is the usual programme from Thursday to Saturday, though there is still plenty happening on other days of the week. It's easy to understand, especially in summer when 2am is the most cool and comfortable time of day, and the party spirit is infectious. Amazingly, the hard-working Catalans still make it to their offices bright and early the next day.

Bars

The range is infinite, from neon-lit local bars to the designer bars of the 1980s and 1990s, from milk bars (*granja*) and New Age cafés serving juices and infusions to *cocteleries* (cocktail bars) and *xampanyeries* (champagne bars). In addition, there are bars with live music, dance halls, chill-out lounges, restaurants which transform into bars when the DJs move in after dinner and *xiringuitos* along the waterfront. The only problem is making the choice, so it's best to follow the crowd who usually lead to the latest, most fashionable place of the week. Here are some recommendations of old stalwarts mixed with new hot spots.

Almirall, Joaquim Costa, 33. Dark, enticing old *modernista* bar in a street that is suddenly hip.
Berimbau, Passeig del Born, 17. Brazilian bar with stunning *caipirinhas* – the Brazilian cocktail you will never forget.
Boadas, Tallers, 1. A classic Barcelona cocktail bar. The cartooned figure of the original owner watches from highly polished walls while elegant waiters mix the snappiest Martinis. Their *mojito*, Hemingway's Cuban favourite, is recommended.
Café del Sol, Plaça del Sol. Terrace on the square. A good start to an evening in the Gràcia district, with its many alternative bars and restaurants.
La Confiteria, Sant Pau, 128. Relaxed atmosphere and good sounds in this pretty bar housed in a former pastry shop.
Dry Martini, Aribau, 162. A large, traditional cocktail bar in which to ensconce yourself; choose between the green room or the red. Serves excellent Martinis.
Gimlet, Rec, 24. Very cool, small cocktail bar in the Born.
Ginger, Lledó, 2. Stylish cocktail bar in the heart of the Gothic quarter, with cool decor, intimate lighting and high-class tapas.
London Bar, Nou de la Rambla, 34. Popular both with resident

ABOVE: Café del Sol's terrace.

PUBS

Highly successful among expats and Catalans alike is the new wave of pubs, mostly Irish. Many have large-screen TVs for showing major sporting events.
The Clansman, Vigatans, 13. Scottish pub with the malts to prove it.
The Fastnet, Passeig Joan de Borbó, 22. Well positioned in Barceloneta, with football, Guinness and English pub food.
The Quiet Man, Marquès de Barberà, 11. An Irish pub selling draught Guinness. Good atmosphere and live music.

foreigners and a local crowd, this *modernista* bar with a marble counter and chandeliers gets more crowded the deeper you venture inside. Regular live music on the tiny stage at the back provides entertainment.
Margarita Blue, Josep Anselm Clavé, 6. You can eat Mexican food here both day and night, but also come for evening drinks when the place will be buzzing.
Marsella, Sant Pau, 65. This was probably the last old bar with "No spitting and no singing" signs on the walls. It was popular with local people until some years ago, when it underwent changes. As the old locals expired it has found new life with a young, international crowd. Beware the absinthe. Shades of what the infamous Barri Xino used to be like.
Mirablau, Plaça Dr Andreu (at the foot of the Tibidabo funicular). Has a spectacular view over Barcelona day and night, as well as a dance floor.
Nick Havanna, Rosselló, 208. Once famed for its design and the in-crowd it attracted, this is no longer the most fashionable place in town to go, but it's good value and gives an idea of the Barcelona "design bars" of the 1980s.

Pastis, Santa Mònica, 4. More than 40 years old, this small corner of Marseille at the bottom of La Rambla offering *pastis* to the strains of Brel and Piaf, is a welcome alternative to the high-design and high-tech bars throughout the city. Tango and live music some nights.
Els Quatre Gats, Montsió, 3. A *modernista* landmark, famous thanks to the artists, including Picasso, who frequented it at the turn of the 20th century. You can eat in the restaurant or just have drinks at the front.
Rita Blue, Plaça Sant Agustí. Even buzzier than its older sister, Margarita Blue, it serves Tex-Med food and has a large, pleasant terrace.
Snooker Club, Roger de Llúria, 42. An elegant, modern snooker club, good for a cool cocktail or an after-dinner drink.
Torres de Avila, Poble Espanyol. An extravaganza created by designers Arribas and Mariscal (of Olympic mascot fame), showing Barcelona 1990s design. It's been reborn, after temporary closure, as a chill-out bar.
XiX bar, Rocafort, 19. Small, prettily tiled bar with big atmosphere, and not just because they specialise in gin and tonics.

ABOVE: for an Andalucian flamenco show, go to a *tablao*.

Clubs

Club venues are ever-changing. Check in the local listings for what's current, or better still, ask around. The bars lining the Plaça Reial make a good starting point.

Club Ommsession, Rosselló, 265. If you can't stay in the trendiest hotel in town, at least enjoy its club. A seriously cool place to see and be seen in.

Dot, Nou de Sant Francesc, 7. Small and very popular. In-house and visiting DJs play the best of current styles every night of the week. You can drink, dance and watch films all at the same time.

Eclipse, Hotel W, Plaça de la Rosa dels Vents, 1. Way up on the 26th floor you'll find the latest cool venue, where the view (and probably the cost of a cocktail) will take your breath away.

KGB, Alegre de Dalt, 55. An old favourite going through a revival, with live music sessions on Friday.

Moog, Arc del Teatre, 3. Found down an alleyway off La Rambla. A small place but very good for techno/electronic. You can dance until 5.30am if you so desire,

and even later at weekends.

The One, Poble Espanyol. A popular club with a lot of action located in a mock palace in the Spanish Village on Montjuïc.

Otto Zutz Club, Lincoln, 15. One of the first designer discos. Best after 2am. Occasional live music.

Rosebud, Adrià Margarit, 27. If you want a taste of the high life, this sophisticated place has magnificent views and a garden.

Universal, Marià Cubí, 184. Striking decor on three floors. Dance to house music downstairs, funk, pop and '80s sounds upstairs, or just drink in plush surroundings.

La Terraza, Avinguda Francesc Ferrer i Guàrdia, 13. This is up on Montjuïc, part of Poble Espanyol and a great summer venue. Dance to electronic music in the open air until the early hours of the morning, with a fashionable crowd. Open from May to Oct.

Tablaos

A *tablao* is a bar/restaurant that has a flamenco show. *Tablaos* are not strictly Catalan, but this import from Andalucía has become popular among

Catalans to the point of being trendy. Check the times of the shows and whether or not dinner is obligatory.

El Patio Andaluz, Aribau, 242. Tel: 93-209 3378

El Tablao Cordobés, La Rambla, 35. Tel: 93-317 5711

El Tablao de Carmen, Arcs, 9, Poble Espanyol. Tel: 93-325 6895. A good authentic show and reasonable dinner.

Los Tarantos, Plaça Reial, 17. Tel: 93-319 1789. One of the most genuine shows.

Dance Halls

Nueva Epoca, Gran Via, 770. Old-time dancing from 6pm weekly to the sound of a live orchestra. At weekends from 11pm.

Sala Apolo, Nou de la Rambla, 113. A multi-faceted old dance hall that's mostly disco and clubbing, but one Sunday a month it has a jazz-swing night with an excellent big band *(see also Rock/Pop on page 271)*.

The Gay Scene

If you start off with these places you'll soon get to know where all the rest are. *For more details, see page 281.*

Arena, Diputació, 233. A lively, easy-going club in the heart of the Gayxample – the name given to this part of the Eixample, full of cool gay bars and clubs.

El Misterioso Secreto de Amparo, Platja de Mar Bella. Every summer this lesbian *xiringuito* opens on Mar Bella, the beach near Poble Nou. Sunday evening is party night with DJs. This hetero-friendly beach bar is just along from the gay bar **El Dulce Deseo de Lorenzo**, epicentre of the gay scene from June to September.

Metro, Sepúlveda 185. A well-known gay club. Best after 1.30am.

Salvation, Ronda Sant Pere 19–21. Very popular disco with live shows on Friday nights.

SPORT

Participant Sports

The city council has been very active in providing sports facilities for the community. Some are the legacy of the Olympic Games.

Bowling

Namco Bowling
Diagonal Mar
Tel: 93-356 2500
In the shopping centre. Sunday–Thursday noon–midnight, Friday–Saturday noon–3am.

Pedralbes Bowling
Avinguda Doctor Marañón, 11
Tel: 93-333 0352
Sunday–Thursday 10am–2am, until 4am Friday–Saturday.

Cycling

Cycling has become very popular in Barcelona. The city council issues a guide/map, available in tourist offices, which shows suggested routes and cycle lanes, and gives advice on taking bicycles on public transport.

ABOVE: join a bike tour on the waterfront.

Barcelona by Bicycle
Esparteria, 3
Tel: 93-268 2105
www.biketoursbarcelona.com
Accompanied cycling tours of the Old Town, with a meal included in the price. Also has bicycles and skates for hire.

Bici-clot
Passeig Marítim, 33
Tel: 93-221 9778

On the beach near the Olympic Village; very convenient for waterfront cycle rides.

Classic Bikes
Tallers, 45
Tel: 93-317 1970
www.barcelonarentbikes.com
Classic and folding bikes for hire in a central location. Also offers guided tours which can include tapas.

Fat Tire Bike Tours
Plaça George Orwell
Tel: 93-301 3612
City tours on US bicycles.

Filicletos
Passeig de Picasso, 40
Bicycles, tandems and child seats for hire. Open weekends and holidays 10am–dusk. Easy access to Parc de la Ciutadella, the port and the beach.

Golf

There are many courses all over Catalonia (visit www.catgolf.com to see a full list). To play, it is essential you can prove membership of a recognised club. Be aware that weekend fees are usually double the weekday fee. Three courses close to Barcelona are:

El Prat
El Prat de Llobregat
Tel: 93-728 1000
www.rcgep.com

SWIMMING POOLS

When the summer crowds get too much, a dip in a pool can be the perfect antidote to city fatigue.

Club Natació Atlètic Barceloneta
Plaça del Mar
Tel: 93-221 0010
Large indoor pool and two outdoor pools, one acclimatised and one for kids. Has loungers overlooking the sea.

Parc de la Creueta del Coll
Mare de Deu del Coll, 87
Tel: 93-211 3599
Large outdoor pool/lake in one of Barcelona's urban parks up behind Park Güell but it can be reached by metro. Boats can be hired in the winter. Swimming from June to end of August Mon–Fri 10am–4pm, Sun and

holidays 10am–7pm. Ideal for small children.

Piscinas Bernat Picornell
Avinguda de l'Estadi, 30–40
Tel: 93-423 4041
Olympic pool in a beautiful location on Montjuïc.

Piscina Municipal Can Felipa
Pallars, 277
Tel: 93-308 6047
Two indoor pools in a stylishly renovated old factory – now a community centre – in Poble Nou. Easy to reach by metro.

Piscina Municipal Montjuïc
Avinguda Miramar, 31
Tel: 93-443 0046
Two pools with a superb, panoramic view. The Olympic diving events took place here, against the dramatic backdrop of the city.

ABOVE: Barcelona Football Club merchandise.

A premier course, often host to international competitions. Hires out clubs and trolleys.

Port Aventura Golf
Tel: 902-202 220
Attraction at Salou's theme park. Two of the three courses are designed by Greg Norman.

Sant Cugat
Sant Cugat del Vallès
Tel: 93-674 3908
Includes a bar, restaurant and swimming pool. Clubs and trolleys available to hire. Closed Monday.

Terramar
Sitges
Tel: 93-894 0580
www.golfterramar.com

Horse Riding

Hípica Sant Cugat
Finca La Palleria,
Avinguda Corts Catalanes,
Sant Cugat
Tel: 93-674 8385
A bus from Sant Cugat to Cerdanyola will drop you off. Pony treks range from one hour to the whole day in the Collserola hills.

Rollerblading

Icària Sports
Avinguda Icària, 180
Tel: 93-221 1778
Specialises in rollerblades, which you can buy or hire.

Skiing

During the ski season cheap weekend excursions are available from Barcelona to the Pyrenean resorts, some of which can be reached by train (check out www.lamolina.com or www.catneu.net).

Tennis

Club Vall Parc
Carretera de l'Arrabassada, 97
Tel: 93-212 6789

FOOTBALL

Football is close to a religion in Barcelona. When the favourite local team, Barça, is playing, you will know all about it: firstly from the traffic jams to get to the match or to the television, secondly because the town goes silent during the match, and thirdly thanks to the explosion of fireworks, car horns and bugles following a victory.

The stadium, Nou Camp, is one of the largest stadiums in the world, and has a museum that can be visited.

Fútbol Club Barcelona,
Arístides Maillol, tel: 93-496 3600; www.fcbarcelona.com.

The courts, all clay, are open from 8am to midnight.

Water Sports

Agencia de Viajes Tuareg
Consell de Cent, 378
Offers organised boat trips near and far.

Base Nautica de la Mar Bella
Espigó del Ferrocarril
Platja de Bogatell
Avinguda Litoral
Tel: 93-221 0432
All types of boats available for hire by qualified sailors. Offers sailing courses for the inexperienced as well as windsurf hire.

Orsom
Tel: 93-441 0537
www.barcelona-orsom.com
Hourly and daily sails or charters in this enormous catamaran. Evening trips have live jazz.

Spectator Sports

Check the weekly entertainment guides or the sports magazines like *El Mundo Deportivo* for a calendar of events. The daily papers also have good sports coverage.

Most local fiestas have various sporting activities as part of their programme, notably the Barcelona fiesta of La Mercè around 24 September.

Basketball

Basketball is gaining almost as ardent a following as football. The Barça basketball team is part of the football club and matches are played in the Palau Blaugrana, next to Nou Camp, tel: 93-496 3600.

Motor Racing

The Catalunya Circuit home to the Grand Prix is about 20km (12 miles) from Barcelona, in Montmeló. For information, tel: 93-571 9700; www.circuitcat.com.

Tennis

The Conde de Godó trophy is an annual event at the Real Club de Tenis Barcelona, Bosch i Gimpera, 5, tel: 93-203 7562.

ABOVE: Tibidabo funfair.

CHILDREN'S ACTIVITIES

Barcelona, like everywhere else in Spain, is very child-friendly, and there will be few places where kids will be excluded. Spanish children are allowed to stay up much later than elsewhere, particularly in the summer. Eating out is quite easy with children; the variety of local food means that there will always be something to appeal to a child's palate, and restaurants are welcoming.

However, take care when out in Barcelona. Busy roads and inconsiderate drivers call for extra care. You can escape from the traffic in the Old Town, where there are many pedestrianised streets. The city's beaches are obviously wonderful options and nearly all parks now have children's play areas. When you really need to let them run wild take the 10-minute train ride to the Parc de Collserola *(see page 216).*

An invaluable website in English is www.kidsinbarcelona.com which covers what's on for kids and suitable flat rentals.

Attractions for Children
L'Aquàrium de Barcelona
Moll d'Espanya, Port Vell
Tel: 93-221 7474

A very popular venue. For full details, *see page 158.*
Zoo
Tel: 93-221 2506
Enter via the Parc de la Ciutadella or Carrer Wellington if you're coming from the seafront *(see page 138).*
Tibidabo Funfair
Parc d'Atraccions de Tibidabo
Plaça del Tibidabo
Tel: 93-211 7942
A good old-fashioned funfair. Take the FGC train, then the little blue tram and the funicular to the top of the hill *(see page 218).*
Parc de la Ciutadella
Open green spaces for riding bicycles and having picnics, a play park to keep toddlers amused, and boats for hire on the pond *(see page 135).*
Poble Espanyol
Montjuïc
This pastiche of a Spanish village built in 1929 *(see page 180)* organises activities for kids.
Skating
Roger de Flor, 168
Tel: 93-245 2800
A popular ice-skating rink.

The following museums should also appeal:
CosmoCaixa
Isaac Newton, 26

Tel: 93-212 6050
The renovated science museum is magnificent, with plenty of interactive games to keep the kids happy for hours.
Museu de la Cera
Passatge de la Banca, 7
Tel: 93-317 2649
The waxworks museum is usually a hit with older children.
Museu Marítim
Av. de les Drassanes
Tel: 93-318 3245
Contains lots of vessels from different ages, plus a chance to board a schooner.

Places further afield:
Illa de Fantasia
Finca Mas Brassó
Vilassar de Dalt
Tel: 93-751 4553
www.illafantasia.com
An aquatic park 24km (15 miles) from Barcelona in Premià de Mar, easily reached by train.
Port Aventura
near Tarragona
108km (67 miles) from Barcelona
Tel: 977 779 090
www.portaventura.es
A theme park based on five world locations: the Mediterranean, Mexico, the Wild West, China and Polynesia.

BELOW: children will love the Aquàrium.

A–Z

AN ALPHABETICAL SUMMARY OF PRACTICAL INFORMATION

A ddresses

Addresses are indicated by street name, number, storey, door. So Muntaner, 375, 6° 2ª means Muntaner Street No. 375, 6th floor, 2nd door. The first floor of a building is *Principal*, often abbreviated to *Pral*. Some buildings have an *entresol* or mezzanine. An *àtic* is a top floor or penthouse, usually with a terrace.

Admission Charges

Museums have an entry charge ranging from €4 to €8 for the main ones and as little as €2 for the smaller ones, although entry to the Gaudí buildings is more. They have the usual reductions for students and pensioners, and many are free or reduced in price one day, often the first Sunday, of each month. People eligible for discounts should carry evidence of their identity. All municipal museums are free from 3pm–closing time on Sundays.

An Articket (€25) allows entry to seven key museums: MNAC, the Picasso Museum, Fundació Miró, Fundació Tàpies, CCCB, MACBA and La Pedrera. The tickets, which last six months, are available from tourist offices, from one of the relevant museums or through Tel-Entrada Catalunya Caixa, tel: 902-101 212 (from abroad tel: +34 933 262 946), www.telentrada.com.

Some cultural centres have free entry – the CaixaForum, Arts Santa Mònica and the Casa Asia – or only charge for some exhibitions, like the Palau de la Virreina.

B udgeting for Your Trip

Gone are the days of cheap holidays in Spain. What you save on budget flights can easily be spent on meals, accommodation, shopping and clubbing. Accommodation is the main culprit, although for budget travellers there are hostels where beds are available in dormitories from €18. Self-catering is now widely available and is a good solution for families; shopping in the market is an enjoyable experience and an obvious saving.

Good restaurants are expensive but usually better value and quality than in northern Europe. Bargain-hunters should opt for a lunchtime set menu, excellent value at anything from €8–15. Even some smart restaurants offer a lunchtime menu for around €25.

On the whole, fashion items and some household goods are slightly cheaper than in northern Europe, but probably not the USA *(see Shopping, page 263).*

Cinema tickets cost from €5–8, with discounts on certain days of the week, usually Monday or Wednesday. Check listings in the daily press.

Public transport is good value with a T10 card for 10 journeys about €8 for use on the metro, bus, FGC and even RENFE trains within Zone 1 *(see pages 250–1).* Taxis are not prohibitively expensive: a short journey within the centre could be as little as €3, but the fare quickly rises on longer journeys, late at night and when stuck in the frequent traffic jams.

One option for serious travellers who intend to cover a lot of ground in a short stay is the Barcelona Card, a ticket valid for anything from two to five days which gives free public transport and entry or discounts on museums, some leisure centres, some restaurants, bars and shops. An adult card for two days is €26 and for five €42. This, the Articket and other

BELOW: information gathering.

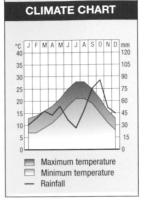

CLIMATE CHART

- Maximum temperature
- Minimum temperature
- Rainfall

offers can be purchased online at www.barcelonaturisme.cat.

Low-budget travellers can take comfort from the fact that, Barcelona being a Mediterranean city, life on the streets is free and endlessly entertaining, and no one charges for basking in the sun or swimming at the city's many beaches.

C limate and Clothing

Average temperature: 10°C (54°F) in winter, 25°C (75°F) in summer. December and January have the lowest temperatures, though the cold is often accompanied by bright sunshine.

Rain tends to fall in November and February to March. Spring and autumn are pleasant, with mild, sunny days. July and August are hot and humid. There are 2,500 hours of sunlight a year.

What to Wear

Catalan men and women dress elegantly, though casually. Ties are worn in formal situations and some offices, but not when going out to dinner. In July and August cotton and loose-fitting garments are necessary. Respect local traditions: bathing costumes and bikinis are strictly for the beach and you now risk paying fines if you are not fully clothed in the street. A light jacket is useful any

time of the year. In winter, bring a warm jacket which can accommodate various layers, especially in January and February, when the wind blows. Be sure to bring comfortable shoes – Barcelona is a very walkable city.

Consulates

Australia
Plaça Gal.la Placídia, 1
Tel: 93-490 9013
Canada
Pl. Catalunya 9, 1° 2a
Tel: 93-412 7236
Ireland
Gran Via Carles III, 94
Tel: 93 491 5021
UK
Avinguda Diagonal, 477, 13°
Tel: 93-366 6200
US
Passeig Reina Elisenda, 23
Tel: 93-280 2227

Crime and Safety

Take care, as in any large city. Loosely swinging handbags, ostentatious cameras and even rucksacks are regularly snatched in broad daylight especially from bars and terrace cafés. But do not be alarmed: Barcelona is not a den of iniquity, and with due care and attention, you can avoid dangerous situations.

The Old Town has a bad reputation for petty crime, so be alert when wandering through it or watching street artists. Wear your handbag across your chest, keep your camera hidden and do not flash your wallet around. Carry enough money for the day, leaving the rest in the safe-deposit box at your hotel.

At airports and railway and bus stations, keep your luggage together and don't leave it unattended. Never leave anything valuable in a car, even in a crowded street. Take special care when arriving in town from airports, as the professional thieves watch these spots.

Don't get caught by a few small gangs who perpetrate

various tricks to waylay you, like commenting on the dirt on your back and, while "helping" you to remove it, slip the purse from your pocket. Another is a game known as *trila*, a variation of the three-card trick, played by crooks (regulars on La Rambla), in the guise of innocent bystanders. You will *never* win. When travelling by car, be careful at traffic lights: a familiar scam is where one person causes a diversion while the other pinches your bag from the back seat, or slashes your tyres. The latest scam is performed by individuals claiming to be plain-clothed police officers and even showing their "identity". Do not show them yours.

In the case of a theft, assault or loss, call the general emergency number, 112. You will probaby be advised to go to a police station to make a statement *(denuncia)*. This is vital if you want to claim on an insurance policy or seek further help from the city police or your consulate.It may soon be possible to make a *denuncia* in hotels to ease the process.

Police

The main police station is at Nou de la Rambla, 76. There are two main types of police in the city: **Policia Municipal**. Tel: 092. The city police, known as the *Guàrdia Urbana*, are responsible for traffic, civilian care and security. They are recognisable by the blue-and-white checked band around their caps and on their vehicles. **Mossos d'Esquadra**. Tel: 088. The autonomous police of Catalonia have taken over all responsibilities from the state police, the Policia Nacional, in Catalonia. The Policia Nacional in Barcelona just handle bureaucratic paperwork like issuing IDs, passports, etc. Occasionally you see the Guardia Civil, who are responsible for customs and border controls at ports and airports.

Assistance for Tourists

The city police have a special scheme for tourists at their headquarters (La Rambla, 43; tel: 93-256 2430; daily), offering legal advice, medical assistance, provision of temporary documents in the event of loss or robbery and an international telephone line for the speedy cancellation of credit cards, etc.

The general emergency number, 112, can attend to calls in English, French and German.

Customs

Visitors from outside the EU can bring limited amounts of cigarettes, alcohol, perfume, coffee and tea. If your camera, computer, etc is new and you do not have the purchase receipt, it is wise to ask a customs official to certify that you brought it into the country with you. There is no restriction on the movement of goods between EU countries, although there are guidance levels for alcohol and tobacco for personal use: 3,200 cigarettes, 90 litres of wine, 110 litres of beer and 10 litres of spirits.

D isabled Travellers

Huge advances have been made recently for people with disabilities thanks to new local authority policies. Over 190 hotels are equipped with facilities for people with disabilities. These can be found at www.bcn.es/turisme or through the tourist office, tel: 93-285 3834. Twenty-eight city museums are wheelchair-accessible, as are many public and historic buildings; a complete listing can be found on www.bcn.es/cultura by clicking on the Directories category.

All the beaches have suitable access, and there are 14 adapted public toilets.

On public transport, nearly all bus and metro lines have disabled facilities; for details click on Transport for Everyone at www.tmb.net.

Regarding car rental, with warning Hertz can provide automatic cars.

For an accessible taxi service, tel: 93-420 8088 for information.

A very helpful organisation is Accessible Barcelona (tel: 93-428 5227; www.accessiblebarcelona.com), run by British wheelchair-user Craig Grimes, who has road-tested all his recommendations.

For general information, see www.tourspain.co.uk/disabled, or for queries specific to Barcelona, contact: Institut Municipal de Persones amb Disminució, Diagonal 233, 08013 Barcelona, tel: 93-413 2775; sap@mail.bcn.es.

E lectricity

British plugs do not fit Spanish sockets, because wall sockets for shavers, hairdryers, etc, take plugs with two round pins. British visitors should bring an adaptor, which can be bought at supermarkets, chemists and airports, or in Barcelona at El Corte Inglés. The voltage is 220v, so US visitors with 110v appliances will need a transformer.

Emergencies

In an emergency call 112 or go to the "Urgències" department (A & E) at one of the main hospitals, or visit an *ambulatorio* (medical centre). They can be found in every district – ask in any pharmacy for the nearest one.

Hospitals

Hospital Clínic
Carrer de Villaroel, 170
Tel: 93-227 5400
Hospital de Nens (children)
Carrer de Consell de Cent, 437
Tel: 93-231 0512
Hospital del Mar
Passeig Marítim, 25–29
Tel: 93-248 30 00

Emergency Numbers

Emergencies (police, fire, ambulance), tel: 112
Fire Brigade, tel: 080
Ambulance service, tel: 061

Policia Municipal, tel: 092
Mossos d'Esquadra, tel: 088
Road accidents, tel: 088

G ay & Lesbian Travellers

There is a thriving gay and lesbian scene in Barcelona, and it is considered one of the gay capitals of Europe. This is a far cry from the not too distant past when homosexuals suffered repression under Franco. Spain was the third country in Europe to legalise gay marriage in 2005, and in the first six months following the law's approval there was a gay wedding every day in Catalonia.

A whole area of the elegant Eixample district, known as the Gayxample, has fashion shops, bars, clubs, hairdressers and so on particularly focused on the gay community. In the midst of it is Europe's first gay hotel, also "heterofriendly", the Axel (Aribau 33, tel: 93-323 9393, www.axel hotels.com), a stunning *modernista* building with a designer interior.

In addition there is an annual gay film festival, the International Gay & Lesbian Film Festival of Barcelona, www.cinemalambda.com.

Nearby Sitges (just half an hour south of the city on the coast) is a real mecca for gays, particularly in summer. The drag parade during Carnival in February is renowned.

For advice and information on the latest venues, the lesbian and gay hotline is **Telèfon Rosa**, tel: 900-601 601, www.cogailes.org. A general guide is www.gay barcelona.net *(See also page 274.)*

Other useful addresses are:

Casal Lambda
Verdaguer i Callís, 10
Tel: 93-319 5550
From 5pm onwards. An information centre campaigning for gay and lesbian rights, offering help and advice.

Col·lectiu Gai de BCN
Ptge Valeri Serra, 23
Tel: 93-453 4125

Sextienda
Rauric, 11
Tel: 93-318 8676

ABOVE: taking the dog for a walk in the Barri Gòtic.

Guides and Tours

If you want to recruit a professional tourist guide or interpreter, you should contact:
Barcelona Guide Bureau
Tel: 93-268 2422
City Guides
Tel: 93-412 0674
Professional Association of Barcelona Tour Guides
Tel: 93-319 8416

H ealth and Medical Care

Barcelona is a modern European city and there are no special health risks to be aware of, and no inoculations are needed. You should take the usual travel precautions and break yourself into the climate and the food gently. Between June and September you should wear a hat and suncream when out during the day.

Food and Drink

In most areas of Barcelona tap water can be drunk without fear, but it is often dosed with purifying salts which make the taste unpleasant. Mineral water is easily available, and Vichy Catalan is soothing for queasy stomachs.

Catalan cooking is healthy and nutritious, but a change of diet can affect some digestive systems. Avoid excessively oily food.

Another danger area can be *tapas*, which in hot weather can be a source of infection if they have been left standing on a counter for too long. Most notorious is anything mayonnaise-based, such as the ubiquitous *ensaladilla rusa* (Russian salad), a potential source of salmonella; in some parts of Spain homemade mayonnaise is banned.

With common sense it is easy to spot the "tired" *tapas* which should be avoided.

TRANSPORT ACCOMMODATION SHOPPING ACTIVITIES A – Z LANGUAGE

ABOVE: much of the city was built on a grid system which aids navigation.

Treatment

Residents of EEA (European Economic Area) countries, which means EU countries plus Switzerland, Lichtenstein, Iceland and Norway, are entitled to receive state medical treatment in Spain if they have a European Health Insurance Card (EHIC), which must be obtained in their own country. In the UK this can be done online, by phone or by post (www.ehic.org.uk; tel: 0845 606 2030).

For greater peace of mind, take out private insurance, which is best organised before setting off but can be arrranged on arrival in Barcelona through any travel agency.

If you are insured privately or prepared to pay for private health care, Barcelona Centre Mèdic (Avinguda Diagonal, 612, tel: 93-414 0643), is a coordination centre for different specialists and offers an information service for consultations (www.bcm.es).

Buying Medicines

Pharmacies *(farmacias)* have a red or green flashing neon cross outside. When closed, *farmacias* post a list of other *farmacias* in the window, indicating the nearest one on duty. Pharmacies stock prescription and non-prescription medications, toiletries, baby food and supplies. Many *farmacias* also stock homeopathic remedies, or will be able to obtain them for you within a day. The following is an English-speaking chemist:
Farmacia Josep Clapés
La Rambla, 98
Tel: 93-301 2843

Alternative Medicine

The Old Town still has many charming herbalist shops, with shelves crammed with alternative health care and people queuing for advice. One of the finest, where they individually mix you a brew according to your ailments, is:
Manantial de Salud
Xuclà, 23
Tel: 93-319 1965

Dentists

Dentists in Spain are not covered by any of the reciprocal agreements between countries, so be prepared to pay for treatment. Even with insurance you may have to pay first and then make a claim on return.

The following clinics offer an emergency service:
Amesa
Gran Via, 680
Tel: 93-301 2550
Open 9am–7pm
Clínica Dental Barcelona
Passeig de Gràcia, 97 pral
Tel: 93-487 8329
Emergency service daily from 9am–midnight. English-speaking dentists.
Clínica Janos
Muntaner 375, 6° 2ª
Tel: 93-200 2333
Open Mon–Sat 9am–1pm and 4–8pm, Sun 10am–2pm.

L eft Luggage

A left-luggage service *(consigna)* is available in Sants railway station 5.30am–11pm. There are also lockers at Barcelona Nord bus station, and a left-luggage office open 8am–1am at the sea terminal on Moll Barcelona. Locker Barcelona is a great left-luggage service in the centre, near Plaça de Catalunya (Estruc, 36. tel: 93-302 8796, www.lockerbarcelona.com, 8.30am–9pm daily).

Lost Property

If you lose something on the metro or a bus, go to the TMB office (Metro Diagonal, Mon–Fri 8am–8pm); if you leave something in a taxi, tel: 902-101 564. The municipal lost-property office (Oficina de Troballes) is in Plaça Carles Pi i Sunyer, 8–10 (tel: 010, phone between 8am–10pm, visit 9am–2pm). Lost or stolen passports retrieved by the police are sent to the relevant consulate.

M aps

The tourist board issues a good general map of the city *(plano de la ciudad/plànol de la ciutat)*. A transport map is also available from metro stations. The *Guia Urbana*, the taxi drivers' bible, is the most comprehensive map of the city on sale at newsstands.

Media

Newspapers

The main daily newspapers are:
Avui
The original Catalan paper, founded in 1976, less than a year after Franco's death.
Catalonia Today
A weekly paper in English, covering international, national and local news in brief. Useful listings and features on Barcelona.
El País
Based in Madrid but with a Catalan edition, *El País* is the most internationally respected Spanish paper. An English version is published by the *International Herald Tribune*.
El Periódico
This is the more popular Barcelona newspaper, but it is limited on international news. In both Castilian and Catalan.
La Vanguardia
The traditional (and moderately Conservative) newspaper of Barcelona has good coverage of local news and publishes a very informative "What's On" magazine on Friday.

International newspapers can be found on the newsstands on La Rambla and Passeig de Gràcia, and also in several international bookshops, such as FNAC (Plaça de Catalunya).

Magazines

A wealth of magazines cover every interest and indulgence. The main fashion magazines, such as *Vogue, Marie Claire* and *Elle*, publish a Spanish edition. Most notable national magazines are:
¡Hola!
The most famous Spanish magazine, with illustrated scandal and gossip on the rich and the royal.
Guia del Ocio
A useful weekly listings magazine for Barcelona. Visit their website www.guiadelociobcn.es.

English Publications

Several freebies with information on the city and listings, such as **Barcelona Connect** (www.barcelona connect.com) and **Miniguide** (www.bcn-inside.com), are distributed to hotels, bars and bookshops. However, the most established is:
Metropolitan
Barcelona's first monthly magazine in English. Targeted at residents, it makes interesting reading and carries useful listings. Distributed free at key points in the city (and around, e.g. Sitges) – bookshops, bars and cinemas. Check out their website www.barcelona-metropolitan.com.

Television

The principal channels are TVE1 and La2 (state-owned), TV3, and Canal 33, the autonomous Catalan channels. The local channel is BTV. Commercial channels include Antena 3 (general programming), Tele 5 (directed at people at home during the day) and Canal Plus (mainly films, for subscribers only). Satellite programmes are obtainable in many of the larger hotels.

Money

The currency is the euro (€). Bank notes are issued in 5, 10, 20, 50, 100, 200 and 500; coins in denominations of 1, 2, 5, 10, 20 and 50 *centimos*, and €1 and 2.

Most banks have cashpoints (ATMs), operating 24 hours a day, where money can be withdrawn using most credit and debit cards.

Keep (separately) a record of the individual numbers of your traveller's cheques, so they can be replaced quickly if they are lost or stolen.

Tax

Tax (IVA) on services and goods is 18 percent, and for restaurants and hotels, 8 percent. Visitors from non-EU countries are entitled to tax reclaims on their return home at a Global Refund Office. Look out for "Tax Free" signs in shop windows. When you leave the EU, Barcelona Customs must confirm the purchase and stamp the tax-free cheque; you can then take it to the airport branch of Banco Exterior de España and cash the cheque into the currency required.

Banks

Bank opening hours vary, but as a general rule they are open all year Mon–Fri 8.30am–2pm, and also Sat 8am–2pm Oct–May. The

BELOW: watching the world go by on La Rambla.

cajas or, in Catalan, caixes (savings banks) offer the same service, but are open on Thursday afternoon instead of Saturday morning Oct–May.

There are numerous currency-exchange offices in the city centre, including in La Rambla and in the Plaça de Catalunya Information Centre. The larger hotels will also exchange money, although often at a less favourable rate.

Foreign banks in the city:
Barclays Bank
Passeig de Gràcia, 45
Tel: 93-214 7300
Lloyds Bank
Avinguda Diagonal, 601
Tel: 93-495 1680

Credit Cards

Major international credit cards, such as Visa, Eurocard and MasterCard can be used, although you will be required to show some form of identity or enter your PIN.
In the case of loss:
American Express
Tel: 902-375 637
Diner's
Tel: 901-101 011

Eurocard, MasterCard, Master-charge, Servired and **Visa**
Tel: 91 519 2100/900-971 231
Visa International
Tel: 900-991 124

Tipping

There are no golden rules about this. If you feel the need to leave a tip, make it a token rather than an extravagant one. Some restaurants automatically add a service charge to the total, in which case nothing extra is needed. As a yardstick, in restaurants where a charge is not added, it should be around 5–10 percent and about the same in a taxi. In a bar or café, 80 centimos–€1.50 is enough, depending on the size of the bill.

O pening Hours

In general, offices are open 9am–2pm and 4–8pm, although some open earlier, close later and have shorter lunch breaks. Most official authorities are open 8am–2pm and close to the public in the afternoon. Companies in the outer industrial zones tend to

close at 6pm. From mid-June to mid-September many businesses practise horas intensivas from 8am–3pm in order to get away early on a Friday.

P ostal Services

Stamps for letters, postcards and small packets can be bought very conveniently in the many estancs to be found in every district. These are state-owned establishments licensed to sell stamps, cigarettes and tobacco, and easily recognisable by their orange and brown logo, **Tabacs SA**. Opening hours are loosely 9am–1.30pm and 4.30–8pm. Postboxes are yellow.

The main post office is at the bottom of Via Laietana near the port, in Plaça Antoni López. It has collections every hour and is open Mon–Fri 9am–9pm, Sat 9am–1pm. Other post offices close at 2pm, apart from the one in Carrer d'Aragó, 282 (near Passeig de Gràcia) which is open until 7pm, but with limited services.

Poste Restante letters can be sent to the main post office addressed to the Lista de Correos, 08080 Barcelona. Take ID with you (preferably your passport) when claiming letters.

Public Holidays

Many bars, restaurants and museums close in the afternoon and evening on public holidays and Sundays. If a holiday falls on a Tuesday or a Thursday it is common to take a pont or puente (bridge) to link the interim day with the weekend. Roads out of the city are extremely busy on the afternoon/evening before a holiday. August is the annual holiday month and many businesses, including restaurants, close down for three or four weeks, although this is happening less in central Barcelona.

The following are the public holidays (national and Catalan):
1 January – New Year's Day
6 January – Reis Mags: Epiphany

BELOW: classical post office building near the Columbus Monument.

Late March/April – Good Friday
(variable)
Late March/April – Easter
Monday (variable)
1 May – Festa del Treball: Labour
Day
Late May – Whitsun: Pentecost
(variable)
24 June – Sant Joan: Mid-
summer's Night
15 August – Assumpció:
Assumption
11 September – Diada: Catalan
national holiday
24 September – La Mercè: the
patroness of Barcelona. This is
the city's main fiesta
12 October – Hispanitat/Pilar:
Spanish national day
1 November – Tots Sants: All
Saints' Day
6 December – Día de la
Constitució: Constitution Day
8 December – Immaculada
Concepció: Immaculate
Conception
25–6 December – Christmas

ABOVE: churches are usually open to the worshipper and the visitor.

Public Toilets

There is a notorious dearth of
public toilets in Barcelona, but
finally the municipal authorities
are remedying the situation: public urinals have been installed at
strategic points in the city. A few
coin-operated cabins exist,
although it is usually easier to
find a bar. The beaches are well
equipped with toilets, many of
which are adapted for wheelchair-
users, and others can be found in
public centres like the airport,
the railway and bus stations,
shopping centres and museums.
Bars and cafés are usually willing
to let their services be used,
especially if it is for a child.

R eligious Services

Mass is usually said between
7am and 2pm on Sunday and
feast days. Evening Mass is held
between 7 and 9pm on Saturday,
Sunday and feast days.
Catholic
Parroquia María Reina
Carretera d'Esplugues, 103

Tel: 93-203 4115
Sundays 10.30am (in English)
Anglican
St George's Church
Sant Joan de la Salle, 41
Tel: 93-417 8867
Sunday 11am (services in
English). This is off the beaten
track above Passeig de la
Bonanova (FGC Av. Tibidabo).
Jewish
The Synagogue
Avenir, 24
Tel: 93-209 3147
Muslim
Centro Islàmico Mosque
Avinguda Meridiana, 326
Tel: 93-351 4901
Toarek Ben Ziad
Hospital, 91
Tel: 93-441 9149
**Multicultural, multi-
denominational**
International Church of Barcelona
Urgell, 133
Tel: 93-894 8084

S tudent Travellers

For holders of an international
student card (ISIC), or the
Euro26 card for any people under

the age of 26, there are many
discounts on offer: reduced-price
tickets at museums and other
cultural centres, and discounts
on railways and other public
transport, hostels and shops. For
details see www.gencat.es/joventut or
www.xarxajove.net. The card is available in the UK through the
National Youth Agency (tel: 0116
285 3781; www.euro26.org).
There is a youth hostel in the
Gothic Quarter, **Gothic Point** at
Vigatans, 5, with another, also
in the Old Town, **Center-Ram-
bles**, at Hospital, 63 (just off La
Rambla). Both offer internet
access and security lockers,
and can arrange bike hire and
other activities. For other youth
hostels in the city visit www.
youth-hostels-in.com/barcelona (see
also Accommodation, pages
253–262).

T elecommunications

Telephone booths are well
distributed throughout the city,
and are easy to use and efficient, especially for international calls. Public telephones

TRANSPORT   ACCOMMODATION   SHOPPING   ACTIVITIES   A – Z   LANGUAGE take all euro coins and most accept credit cards. The minimum charge for a local call is 20 *centimos*. Telephone cards are available in *estancs* (tobacconists) and post offices. International reverse-charge (call-collect) calls cannot be made from a phone box.

There are also privately run exchanges *(locutoris)*, located mainly in the Old Town, where you talk first and pay afterwards. These are useful for making calls outside Europe and the US, or if you are planning on having a long conversation.

Principal walk-in telephone exchanges are situated in Sants railway station and Barcelona Nord bus station *(see page 249)*. US access codes are as follows:
AT&T: 900-99 0011
MCI: 900-99 0014
Sprint: 900-99 0013

Useful Numbers

Information: 1004
Directory enquiries: 11818
International directory enquiries: 11825
International operator: 11822
International code: 00
Australia: 61
Canada: 1
Ireland: 353
United Kingdom: 44
United States/Canada: 1

The Internet

There are plenty of internet cafés and lounges or cafés with Wi-fi in the city, and many of the *locutori* (telephone exchanges, see left) now offer internet service. There is even Wi-fi in some parks, indicated with a blue sign. Some of the best are:

Easy Internet Café
La Rambla, 31 and Ronda Universitat, 35
These two branches of the Easy empire are open 8am–2.30am daily for cheap internet access.
Bornet
Barra de Ferro, 3
A smaller, attractive option in the Born.

Time Zone

Spain is one hour ahead of GMT in winter, two hours in summer (when UK clocks are also advanced by an hour for summer time, so the time difference is still only one hour), and six hours ahead of Eastern Seaboard Time.

Tour Operators and Travel Agents

There are almost 400 travel agents in Barcelona, and in the centre you will find one on nearly every block. El Corte Inglés offers a good service in its Plaça

BELOW: the city is well geared up for tourists.

de Catalunya branch. Some leading companies are:
Carlson Wagonlit
Via Laietana, 16
Tel: 93-481 2704
People Express
La Rambla, 95
Tel: 93-412 2337
(for cheap flights)
Viajes Ecuador
Pau Claris, 75
Tel: 93-301 3966
To find a long list of tour agencies operating from the UK, a helpful website is www.abta.com/destinations/barcelona.

Tourist Information

For general tourist information about the city, call 010. The **"Red Jackets"** service is available in the summer. It is run by teams of young people in red-and-white uniforms, who offer help and information to visitors, usually in the Barri Gòtic, La Rambla and the Passeig de Gràcia.

Information Offices

The main tourist offices are listed below. In addition there are stands in La Rambla, Plaça Espanya, Colon and Barceloneta. Tourist cards can be bought at all of these.
Barcelona
Plaça de Catalunya
The main city tourist information centre. Well equipped and good for hotel and theatre bookings.
Tel: 93-285 3834
Open daily 9am–9pm
El Prat Airport
In both terminals
Tel: 93-478 4704
Open daily 9am–9pm
City Hall
Plaça Sant Jaume
Open Mon–Fri 9am–8pm, Sat 10am–8pm, Sun 10am–2pm
Sants Station
Open summer daily 8am–8pm, winter Mon–Fri 8am–8pm, weekends/holidays 8am–2pm
Catalonia
Tourist Information Centre for Catalonia
Palau Robert

Passeig de Gràcia, 107
Tel: 93-238 8091/92/93
www.gencat.net/probert
Mon–Sat 10am–7pm, Sun and
public holidays 10am–2.30pm
Information on the rest of Catalonia is available here, along with
reading rooms and internet connections, a garden and gift shop.
 Alternatively you can phone on
012 or 902-400 012. For information on the area around
Barcelona visit www.diba.cat/turisme.

Tourist Offices Abroad

If you would like information
about Barcelona before leaving
home, contact your nearest
Spanish Tourist Office:

Canada
2 Bloor Street West, 34th Floor,
Toronto, Ontario M4W 3E2
Tel: 416 961 3131

UK
6th floor, 64 North Row,
London W1K 7DE
Tel: 020 7486 8077 (to book a
visit) or 00 800 1010 5050
(freephone for information)
Email: info.londres@tourspain.es
www.spain.info
Note that this office is not open to
the public except by appointment.

US
666 Fifth Avenue, 35th floor,
New York, NY 10103
Tel: 212 265 8822

V isas and Passports

Passports are required for people of all nationalities entering
Spain. Carry a photocopy of the
identification page for everyday
use so that the original document
can be left for safety in a secure
place (such as a hotel safe). If
your passport is lost or stolen,
you should report the fact immediately to the police (Mossos
d'Esquadra; see page 280).
 Visas are needed by non-EU
nationals, unless their country
has a reciprocal arrangement
with Spain.
 Travelling with pets. There
are no quarantine regulations in
Spain, but you will need a pet
passport before you take your

ABOVE: there is a large student population, and lots for them to do.

own animal into the country; the
regulations vary according to its
country of origin. The require-
ments are quite complex, so
make sure you organise this
well in advance of your trip. In
the UK visit the websites
www.direct.gov.uk or www.defra.gov.uk
for detailed information.
 Once in Spain, animals are
not permitted in restaurants,
cafés and food shops. If you are
travelling with a pet, check with
your hotel before departure that
pets are allowed. On-the-spot
fines can be given for not carry-
ing an animal's papers, or not
having it on a lead.

W ebsites

A few useful sites are:
Barcelona on the web:
www.barcelonaturisme.cat
www.bcn.cat
www.barcelona-metropolitan.com
www.forfree.cat – a brilliant website
that issues information daily on
what's on that is free.
Catalonia on the web:
www.gencat.cat

www.gencat.net/turistex
Spain on the web:
www.spaintour.com
www.spain.info

Weights and Measures

Spain follows the metric system. As an approximate guide,
1 kilometre is ⅝ of a mile, 1
metre is roughly 3 feet/1 yard,
1 kilogram is just over 2lbs, 1
litre is just under 2 pints, or ⅕
of a gallon, and 1 hectare is
around 2½ acres.
 In many of the larger stores
and international chains, labels
on clothing show European, UK
and US sizes.

Women Travellers

A good source of information on
issues that are of particular
interest to women is the **Librería Pròleg**, Sant Pere Més Alt.
This is the city's specialist
bookshop for feminist subjects
and women writers. It is also an
exhibition space and occasionally holds talks.

TRANSPORT

ACCOMMODATION

SHOPPING

ACTIVITIES

A – Z

LANGUAGE

L ANGUAGE

UNDERSTANDING THE LANGUAGE

Catalan

Castilian (Spanish) and Catalan are both official languages in Catalonia. In the wake of the repression of Catalan language and culture under Franco, when its use in public was forbidden, it underwent a resurgence, encouraged by the administration, with the aim of fully implementing it in every aspect of daily life. It is often the only language used in public signs, street names, maps, leaflets and cultural information.

Catalan is a Romance language; with a knowledge of French and Spanish you should find it possible to read a little.

In the rural regions outside Barcelona you may come across people who cannot speak Castilian, but in the city even the most ardent Catalanista should respond if you communicate in Castilian, knowing you are a foreigner. Also, many people who live in the city will be from other parts of Spain and so will be primarily Castilian-speakers.

However, any attempt to speak the simplest phrases in Catalan will be rewarded with appreciation, as it shows you are recognising it as the language of their region.

English is widely spoken in most tourist areas, but even if you speak no Spanish or Catalan at all, it is worth trying to master a few simple words and phrases.

Spanish

Spanish is also a Romance language, derived from the Latin spoken by the Romans who conquered the Iberian peninsula more than 2,000 years ago. Following the discovery of America, Spaniards took their language with them to the four corners of the globe. Today, Spanish is spoken by 250 million people in North, South and Central America and parts of Africa.

Spanish is a phonetic language: words are pronounced as they are spelt, which is why it is somewhat harder for Spaniards to learn English than vice versa (although Spanish distinguishes between the two genders, masculine and feminine, and the subjunctive is an endless source of headaches).

As a general rule, the accent falls on the last syllable, unless it is otherwise marked with an accent (´) or the word ends in s, n or a vowel.

Vowels in Spanish are always pronounced the same way. The double ll is pronounced like the y in "yes", the double rr is rolled. The h is silent in Spanish, whereas j (and g when it precedes an e or i) is pronounced like a guttural h (as if you were clearing your throat).

Spanish Words and Phrases

Although it is worth trying to speak Catalan first, if you have a knowledge of Castilian it will be totally acceptable, and better than English. Here are some useful expressions:

Yes *Sí*
No *No*
Please *Por favor*
Thank you (very much) *(muchas) gracias*
You're welcome *de nada*
Excuse me *perdóneme*
OK *bién/vale*
Hello *Hola*
How are you? *¿Cómo está usted?*
How much is it? *¿Cuánto es?*
What is your name? *¿Cómo se llama usted?*
My name is ... *Me llamo ...*
Do you speak English? *¿Habla inglés?*
I am British/American *Soy británico(a)/norteamericano(a) (a – for women)*

CATALAN

Good morning *Bon dia*
Good afternoon/evening *Bona tarda*
Good night *Bona nit*
How are you? *Com està vostè?*
Very well thank you, and you? *Molt bé gràcies, i vostè?*
Goodbye, see you again *Adéu, a reveure*
See you later *Fins després*
See you tomorrow *Fins demà*
What's your name? *Com es diu?*
My name is ... *Em dic ...*
Pleased to meet you *Molt de gust*
Do you have any rooms? *Tenen habitacions lliures si us plau?*
I'd like an external/internal/double room *Voldria una habitació exterior/interior/doble*
... for one/two persons ... *per a una persona/dues persones*
I want a room with a bath *Vull una habitació amb bany*
I have a room reserved in the name of ... *Tinc reservada una habitació a nom de ...*
How much is it? *Quin és el preu?*
It's expensive *És car*
Could I see the room? *Podria veure l'habitació?*
How do you say that in Catalan? *Com es diu això en català?*
Speak a little more slowly, please *Parleu una mica més lent, si us plau*
How do I get to ...? *Per a anar a ...?*
Is it very far/close? *Es lluny/a prop?*
Where's the nearest mechanic? *On és el pròxim taller de reparació?*
Can I change this traveller's cheque? *Pot canviar-me aquest xec de viatge?*

Where can I find a dentist? *On puc trobar un dentista?*
This tooth is hurting *Em fa mal aquesta dent*
Don't take it out. If possible give me something for it until I get home *No me'l extregui. Si és possible doni'm un remei fins que torni a casa*
Please call a doctor *Truqui un metge, si us plau*
Where does it hurt? *On li fa mal?*
I have a bad cold *Estic molt refredat*
I want to make a phone call to ... *Vull trucar a ...*
It's engaged *La línea està ocupada*
I am ... I'd like to speak to Mr ... *Sóc ... voldria parlar amb el senyor ...*
What time will he be back? *A quina hora tornarà?*
Tell him to call me at this number *Digui-li que truqui al número ...*
I'll be in town until Saturday *Seré a la ciutat fins dissabte*

Eating Out

Breakfast/lunch/dinner *Esmorzar/dinar/sopar*
At what time do you serve breakfast? *A quina hora es pot esmorzar?*
Set menu *El menu*
Menu *La carta*
We'd like a table for four *Una taula per a quatre si us plau*
First course *Primer plat*
May we have some water? *Porti'ns aigua mineral*
red wine/white wine? *vi negre/vi blanc*
The bill, please *El compte, si us plau*

Some Typical Dishes

Albergínies fregides *Fried aubergines (eggplant)*
Amanida *Salad*
Amanida catalana *Salad with hard-boiled egg and cold meats*
Arròs a la marinera *Seafood paella*
Arròs negre *Rice cooked in squid ink*
Carxofes *Artichokes*
Canelons *Cannelloni*
Escalivada *Salad of roasted aubergines/peppers*
Escudella *Thick soup with meat, vegetables and noodles*
Espinacs a la catalana *Spinach with garlic, pine nuts and raisins*
Esqueixada *Salt-cod salad*
Faves a la catalana *Broad beans stewed with sausage*
Bacallà a la llauna *Salt cod baked in the oven*
Botifarra amb mongetes *Sausage with haricot beans*
Estofat de conill *Rabbit stew*
de vedella *Veal stew*
de xai *Lamb stew*
Fricandó *Braised veal*
Gambes a la planxa *Grilled prawns*
Pollastre al ajillo *Chicken fried with garlic*
Sipia amb mandonguilles *Cuttlefish with meatballs*
Suquet de peix *Rich fish stew*
Postres *Desserts*
Crema catalana *Custard with caramelised topping*
Formatge *Cheese*
Gelat *Ice cream*
Pastís de poma *Apple tart*
Postre de músics *Mixed nuts and dried fruits*

I don't understand *No entiendo*
Please speak more slowly *Hable mas despacio, por favor*
Can you help me? *¿Me puede ayudar?*
I am looking for ... *Estoy buscando ...*
Where is ...? *¿Dónde está ...?*

I'm sorry *Lo siento*
I don't know *No lo sé*
No problem *No hay problema*
Have a good day *Que tenga un buen día*
That's it *Así es*
Here it is *Aquí está*
There it is *Allí está*
Let's go *Vámonos*

See you tomorrow *Hasta mañana*
See you soon *Hasta pronto*
goodbye *adiós*
Show me the word in the book *Muéstreme la palabra en el libro*
At what time? *¿A qué hora?*
When? *¿Cuándo?*
What time is it? *¿Qué hora es?*

FURTHER READING

Good Companions

English translations of Catalan works of literature are few, and are difficult to find in Barcelona.
The Angel's Game, by Carlos Ruiz Zafón. Set in 1920s Barcelona, this thriller will please Zafón's many fans.
Barcelona, by Robert Hughes. Describes the city's development in relation to the rest of Catalonia, Spain and Europe. Good on Gaudí and modernism.
Barcelona: A Guide to Recent Architecture, by Suzanna Strum. A look at some of the city's stunning buildings.
Barcelona the Great Enchantress, by Robert Hughes. A shorter version of his earlier work *(see above)*; particularly good on architecture.
Barcelonas, by Manuel Vázquez Montalbán. Chatty book covering culture, design, history and some of the city's personalities.
Catalan Cuisine, by Colman Andrews. Describes the unique aspects of Catalan cooking; good recipes.
The Cathedral of the Sea, by Ildefonso Falcones. A novel woven around the construction of Santa Maria del Mar in medieval Barcelona.
The City of Marvels (La Ciudad de los Prodigios), by Eduardo Mendoza. Novel about an unscrupulous young man determined to succeed in Barcelona.
Forbidden Territory, by Juan Goytisolo. Autobiography by one of Spain's most important writers.
Homage to Barcelona, by Colm Toíbín. An interesting, personal view from this Irish novelist who once lived in Barcelona.
Homage to Catalonia, by George Orwell. Famous account of the author's experiences in the Spanish Civil War.
The Shadow of the Wind, by Carlos Ruiz Zafón; translation by Lucia Graves. Read the novel set in Barcelona then discover its places in a walking tour.
Teach Yourself Catalan, Hodder Arnold. Classic series of language learning books.

Other Insight Guides

The Insight Guides series includes several books on Spain and its islands, all combining the exciting pictures and incisive text associated with this series.

FEEDBACK

We do our best to ensure the information in our books is as accurate and up-to-date as possible. However, some mistakes and omissions are inevitable and we are reliant on our readers to put us in the picture. We would welcome your feedback on any details related to your experiences using the book "on the road". The more details you can give us (particularly with regard to addresses, emails and telephone numbers), the better. We will acknowledge all contributions, and we'll offer an Insight Guide to the best letters received.

Please write to us at:
Insight Guides
PO Box 7910
London SE1 1WE
United Kingdom
Or email us at:
insight@apaguide.co.uk

Insight Guides

Insight Guide: Spain contains top photography and complete background reading. The smaller format *Insight Regional Guide: Southern Spain* provides comprehensive coverage of the Costa del Sol and Andalucía, from the white towns of the sierras to vibrant Seville.

Insight Fleximaps

Insight Fleximap: Barcelona is a durable laminated map, with a list of recommended sights.

Insight Step by Step

Barcelona is one of the titles in Insight's Step by Step series. These books provide a series of timed itineraries, with recommended stops for lunch. The itineraries are plotted on an accompanying pull-out map.

Insight Smart Guides

Smart Guide: Barcelona puts the city at your fingertips. The best of Barcelona is listed by district, with detailed maps to provide orientation. Barcelona A–Z lists over 400 amazing thigs to see and do, from architecture and bars to restaurants and shopping, and much more.

BARCELONA STREET ATLAS

The key map shows the area of Barcelona covered by the
atlas section. An index of street names and places of interest
shown on the maps can be found on the following pages.
For each entry there is a page number and grid reference

Map Legend

══════	Autopista with Junction
━ ━ ━	Autopista (under construction)
═════	Dual Carriageway
────────	Main Road
════	Secondary Road
────	Minor Road
───	Track
━ ━ ··	International Boundary
─ ─ ─	Province Boundary
••••	National Park/Reserve
✈ ✈	Airport
† ✝ ✝	Church (ruins)/ Monastery
▐▌ ⌂	Castle (ruins)
∴	Archaeological Site
∩	Cave
★	Place of Interest
⌂	Mansion/Stately Home
※	Viewpoint
⌐	Beach
	Autopista
	Dual Carriageway
	Main Roads
	Minor Roads
	Footpath
━ ━ ━	Railway
	Pedestrian Area
	Important Building
	Park
Ⓜ	Metro
RENFE symbol	RENFE
	Tram
	Funicular
🚌	Bus Station
❶	Tourist Information
✉	Post Office
✝	Cathedral/Church
☾	Mosque
✡	Synagogue
🗡	Statue/Monument

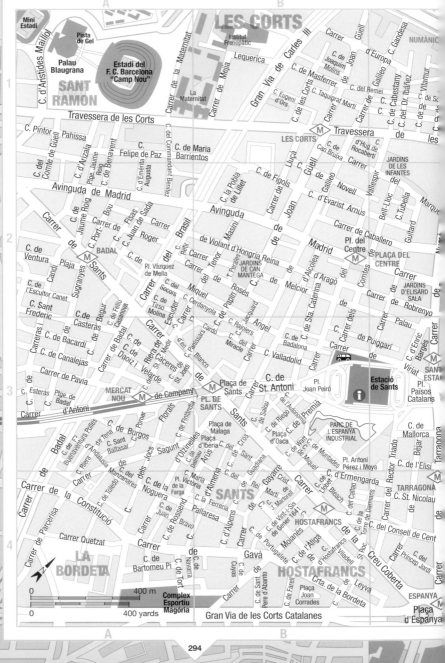

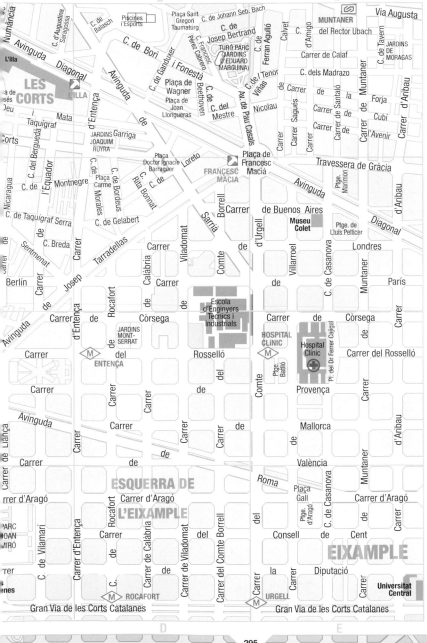

292

Gran Via de les Corts Catalanes

C. de la Química
C. de la Mineria
del
Carrer
C. de Traià
C. de Mandon
C. d'Indíbil
C. de Sant Pauli
de Nòlia
Font Florida
Carrer de la Guàtlla
C. de Santa
Dorotea
Sant
C. de
St Germà
C. de Sant Ferriot
Fructuós
C. de Mèxic
Carrer de Mèxic

SANTS-MONTJUÏC

1 C. de Crisantem
2 C. del Lotus
3 C. Begònia
4 C. del Nord
5 C. Valls

Carrer de la
Carrer
3
C. Bessora
C. Rabi Rubèn
C. d'Aiguasta
4 5
C. Miràbols
C. dels Gimbernat
C. de Montferri

Plaça d'Espanya
Cristina
Palau de la Metal·lúrgia
Fira de Barcelo

Estadi Joan Serrahima
Pl. de Llorca
Carrer
Segura
del
Plaça de Sant Jordi

Avinguda del Marques de
Passeig S. Bolívar
C. de Hortènsia
Comillas
Caixa-Forum
Avinguda de la Reina Maria
Plaça de l'Univers
Palau de Congressos
Av. de Rius i Ta

Poble Espanyol
Pavelló Mies van der Rohe

CAN CLOS

Estadi Julià Campany
Avinguda
Pl. Hidràulica
INEFC Universitat de l'Esport
Camp de Beisbol
Camp de Rugby de la Fuxarda
Av. dels Montanyans
Pista Hípica «La Fuxarda»
Plaça d'Europa

Palau de Victòria Eugènia
Plaça de Canes Burgas
Plaça Marquès de Foronda
Plaça de les Cascades
Font Màgica
Palau d'Alfons XIII
les Cascades
C. Guàrdia Urbana

Plaça Alta Can Clos
Ctra. Foment i les Banderes
C. de Pedrera del Mussol
Torre de Calatrava
Piscines Bernat Picornell
Palau Sant Jordi

Mirador del Palau Nacional
Palau Nacional
Museu Nacional d'Art de Catalunya (MNAC)
JARDINS JOAN MARAGALL
Paulet Albèniz

Mercat les Flo
Museu Etnològic
Mus d'Arqueolo
Santa
Madr

Pg. Migdia
ANELLA OLÍMPICA
Passeig Olímpic
Estadi Olímpic
Museu Olímpic i de l'Esport

Passeig
JARDINS
LARIBAL
l'Estadi
Plaça del Sol
Ne
Carrer dels Tres Pins

Muntanya de
Montjuïc
Circuito de Marcha
Zona d'Atletisme i Hoquei
PARC DE MONTJUÏC
JARDÍ BOTÀNIC
Dr Font i Quer
Carrer de la Serp
Carrer dels Tres Pins

MONTJUÏC
Pl. Gran Capità
Av. u

CEMENTIRI DEL SUD-OEST
Pg. Migdia
Camí de la Serp
Carrer de la Cartoixa
Castell de Montjuïc

0   400 m
0   400 yards
N
Ronda del Litoral

A   B

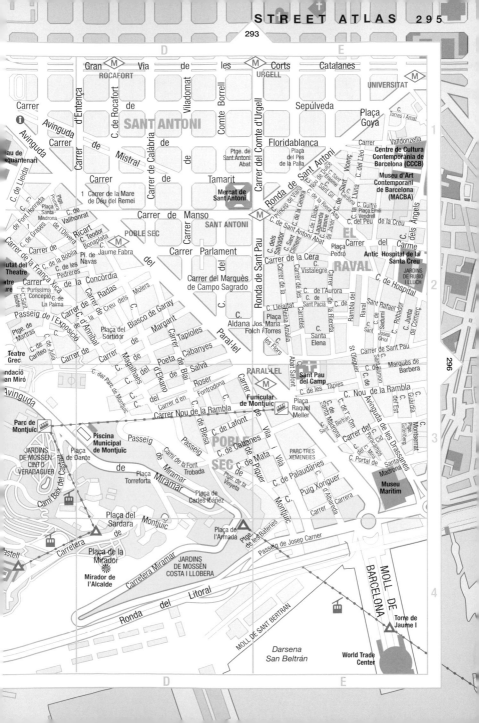

Gran Via de les Corts Catalanes
ROCAFORT
UNIVERSITAT
Carrer
Avinguda
Carrer
Avinguda
au de
quantenari
C. de Lleida
C. de Font Honrada
Plaça
Santa
Madrona
Carrer de Grases
de Font Honrada
de
Plaça
Santa
Madrona
C. de Vallhonrat
de
Carrer d'Entença
C. de Rocafort
C. de Calàbria
Carrer del Comte d'Urgell
Comte Borrell
Viladomat
SANT ANTONI
de
Mistral
Carrer
de
de
Carrer
de
de
Tamarit
Mercat de
Sant Antoni
Ptge. de
Sant Antoni
Abat
SANT ANTONI
Sepúlveda
Floridablanca
Plaça
del Pes
de la Palla
Plaça
Goya
Carrer
C. Torres i Amat
Valldonzella
Centre de Cultura
Contemporània de
Barcelona (CCCB)
Museu d'Art
Contemporani
de Barcelona
(MACBA)

Carrer de Manso
Ricart
C. Teodor
Bonaplata
POBLE SEC
Pl. de
Jaume Fabra
de Navas
del
Carrer Parlament
Carrer del Marquès
de Campo Sagrado
Ronda de Sant Pau
Carrer de la Cera
C. de Sant Antoni Abat
EL
RAVAL
Plaça
Pedró
Antic Hospital de la
Santa Creu
Carrer del Carme
de la Creu
JARDINS
DE RUBIÓ
I LLUCH
C. de Hospital

Carrer de
C. de la Bòbila
C. de les
Pedreres
de la Concòrdia
Carrer de Radas
Creu dels
Moliers
C. d'Anníbal
Blasco de Garay
Plaça del
Sortidor
Margarit
de
Carrer Tàpioles
de
Poeta Cabanyes
Paral·lel
C.
Aldana
Jos.
Folch i Torres
Plaça
Helena Amàlia
C. dels
Carretes
Santa
Elena
C. de les
C. de l'Aurora
C. de
Sant Pacià
C. de la Riereta
Rambla del Raval
Sant Rafael
St. Oleguer
Carrer de Sant Pau
Marquès de
Barbera
C. Nou de la Rambla

Passeig de l'Exposició
Ptge. de
Martras
Teatre
Grec
ndació
an Miró
Avinguda
C. de
Carteto
C. de
Júlia
Carrer de
del Parc de Montjuïc
Magalhaes
de
d'Elkano
Salvá
Roser
Fontrodona
Carrer Nou de la Rambla
C. de Blai
PARAL·LEL
Sant Pau
del Camp
Plaça
Raquel
Meller
Avinguda de les Drassanes
JARDINS
Pl. de Dante
Piscina
Municipal
de Montjuïc
Passeig
de
Passeig
Blesa
C. de Lafont
C. de Cabanes
POBLE
SEC
PARC TRES
XEMENEIES
C. de Mata
C. de Piquer
Vila i Vilà
C. de Palaudàries
Puig Xoriguer
Montjuïc
Carrer del Portal de Santa Madrona
Museu
Marítim

Parc de
Montjuïc
JARDINS
DE MOSSÈN
CINTO
VERADAGUER
Camí de la Font
Trobada
Plaça
Torreforta
Miramar
Plaça de
Carles Ibàñez
Plaça del
Sardara
Plaça de la
Mirador
Mirador de
l'Alcalde
Castell
Carretera
Montjuïc
de
Carretera Miramar
JARDINS
DE MOSSÈN
COSTA I LLOBERA
Plaça de
l'Armada
Pge. de
les Bateries
Passeig de Josep Carner
Ronda del
Litoral
Camí Baix del Castell
MOLL DE SANT BERTRAN
Torre de
Jaume I
MOLL DE BARCELONA
World Trade
Center

Darsena
San Beltrán

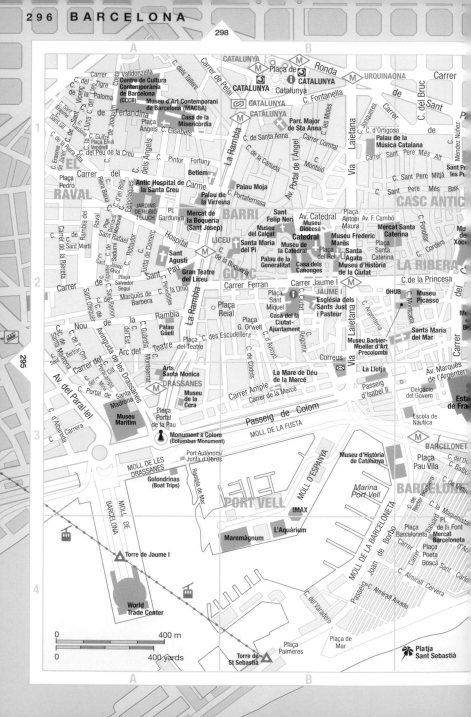

298

295

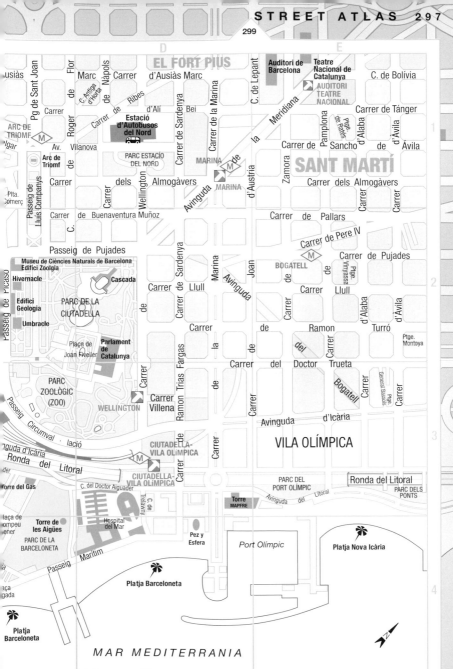

EL FORT PIUS

usiàs

Pg de Sant Joan

Flor

Marc   Carrer   d'Ausiàs Marc

de

C. Antiga d'Hora

de Nàpols

de   Ribes

Carrer   d'Alí   Bei

Roger

Carrer   de

Estació d'Autobusos del Nord

PARC ESTACIÓ DEL NORD

Carrer de Sardenya

Carrer de la Marina

C. de Lepant

Meridiana

la

de

Auditori de Barcelona

Teatre Nacional de Catalunya   C. de Bolívia

AUDITORI TEATRE NACIONAL

Pamplona

Ptge. de Ratés

Carrer de Tánger

Carrer de   Sancho   de   d'Àvila

d'Alaba

d'Àvila

SANT MARTÍ

ARC DE TRIOMF

M

lgar

Arc de Triomf

Av. Vilanova

de

MARINA

M

MARINA

d'Àustria

Zamora

Plta. Comerç

Passeig de Lluís Companys

C.

Carrer   dels   Almogàvers

Carrer

Wellington

Carrer de   Buenaventura Muñoz

Carrer   dels   Almogàvers

Carrer

Carrer

Carrer   de   Pallars

Passeig de Pujades

Museu de Ciències Naturals de Barcelona Edifici Zoolgia

Passeig de Picaso

Hivernacle

Cascada

Edifici Geologia

PARC DE LA CIUTADELLA

Umbracle

Plaça de Joan Fiveller

Parlament de Catalunya

PARC ZOOLÒGIC (ZOO)

Passeig Circumval · lació

WELLINGTON

nguda d'Icària

Ronda   del   Litoral

der

Torre del Gas

Carrer de Sardenya

de

Carrer de   Llull

Carrer

Carrer de Sardenya

Marina

Avinguda

Joan

de

BOGATELL

M

Carrer de Pere IV

Carrer   de Pujades

Ptge. Vinyassa

de

Carrer   Llull

Carrer

Ramon Trias Fargas

Carrer

la   de

Carrer

Carrer

Carrer   del   Doctor   Trueta

Carrer Villena

de   Ramon

de   del

d'Alaba

Turró

d'Àvila

Ptge. Montoya

Bogatell

General Bassols

Ptge.

Carrer

CIUTADELLA- VILA OLÍMPICA

M

CIUTADELLA- VILA OLÍMPICA

C. del Doctor Aiguader

C. de Trelawny

Carrer de

Carrer

Avinguda   d'Icària

VILA OLÍMPICA

PARC DEL PORT OLÍMPIC

Ronda del Litoral

PARC DELS PONTS

Torre MAPFRE

Avinguda   del   Litoral

Torre del Gas

laça de ompeu ener

Torre de les Aigües

PARC DE LA BARCELONETA

Hospital del Mar

Passeig   Marítim

Pez y Esfera

Port Olímpic

Platja Nova Icària

aça gada

Platja Barceloneta

Platja Barceloneta

MAR MEDITERRANIA

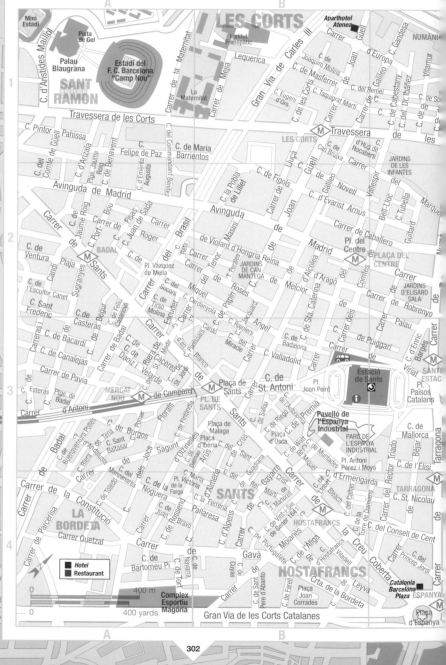

A **B**

Mini Estadi

LES CORTS

Aparthotel Atenea

NUMÀNCIA

Pista de Gel

Palau Blaugrana

Estadi del F. C. Barcelona "Camp Nou"

Institut Frenopàtic

Carrer d'Europa

Carrer Güell

C. de Candesa

Vilamur

C. de Joaquim Molins

C. de Masferrer

Gran Via de Carles III

Lequerica

C. de Carles III

C. del Remei

C. Galileo

C. del Dr. Ibàñez

de C.

SANT RAMON

1

La Maternitat

C. Eugeni d'Ors

C. Taquigraf Martí

C. del Cabestany

C. de Sò

de

C. d'Anstides Maillol

C. del Comtat d'Urgell

C. Pintor Pahissa

Travessera de les Corts

C. del Commandant Benítez

C. de Maria Barrientos

C. d'Emèrita Augusta

Travessera

LES CORTS

d'Hug de Rocaberti

de les

C. del Comte de Güell

C. d'Arizala

Ptge. Jaume Roig

C. Felipe de Paz

C. de Benavent

C. de Figols

C. de Can Bruixa

Carrer

JARDINS DE LES INFANTES

Avinguda de Madrid

C. la Pobla de Lillet

Güell

Galileo

Vallespir

Bell-Lloc

C. Tubella

Marque

Carrer

C. de Jaume Roig

Bou

Port

C. de Juan de Sada

Carrer de Brasil

de Violant d'Hongria Reina

Masini

Joan

C. d'Evarist Arnús

Novell

Carrer de Caballero

Guitard

2

C. de Ventura Plaja

Candi

Sugranyes

BADAL

PL. Vázquez de Mella

Carrer

Rentr

Llenor

J. Perdiès

Avinguda

de

Madrid

Pl. del Centre

PLAÇA DEL CENTRE

Comtes

Carrer

C. de l'Escultor Canet

Carrer de Sants

C. de

Carrer

Miquel

JARDINS DE CAN MANTEGA

de

Rosés

d'Alcolea

d'Aragó

de

Melcior

JARDINS D'ELISARD SALA

Carrer de Robrenyo

C. Sant Frederic

C. del Socors

C. Cerdanyola

C. de Papín

C. de Sta. Caterina

C. de

Palau

C. Sant Frederic

C. de Casteras

C. de Feliu Casanova

C. del Tirso Molina

Escultor

C. de Rajolers

dels

Carrer de Puiggart

C. d'Enric Barges

Carrer

3

C. de Bacardí

C. de

Begur

Carrer de Badal

Cárdo

C. del Miracle

C. de Badalona

de

SANTS ESTAC

C. de Canalejas

Riera Blanca

C. Pallars

Velarde

C. Valladolid

Carrer

Pl. Joan Peiró

Estació de Sants

Pl. Paisos Catalans

Carrer de Pavia

MERCAT NOU

Plaça de Campany

Plaça de Sants

C. de St. Antoni

i

C. Esteras

Ptge. de Badal

PL. DE SANTS

de Campany

Sants

C. de Salou

Pl. Joan Peiró

Pavelló de l'Espanya Industrial

C. de Mallorca

Carrer d'Antoni

Plaça de Malaga

de Rei

C. d'Autonomia

C. de Premia

PARC DE L'ESPANYA INDUSTRIAL

Tarragona

C. de Badal

C. de Burgos

Florals

C. de Finlandia

Plaça d'Iberia

C. de Cros

C. de Watt

C. de Muntades

Pl. Antoni Pérez i Moya

C. de l'Elisi

de

Carrer de Buenaventura Pollès

C. de Tena

Sagunt

Plaça d'Osca

C. de Sant

C. de Miquel

C. d'Ermengarda

TARRAGONA

Riera

Andalusia

Joes

Plaça Martí

Pl. Victoria

C. d'Almeria

Guadiana

Carrer

C. St. Nicolau

SANTS

Carrer de la Constitució

C. del Manzanares

Noguera

Pl. de la Farga

Martí

C. de

de

C. del Consell de Cent

LA BORDETA

C. de Juan de Rossend

Pallaresa

Ferreria

C. de Vint-i-Sis

de Gener 1641

C. Matoreni

HOSTAFRANCS

C. de Damians

Bejar

Carrer Quetzal

C. de Torelló

Bravo

C. d'Alpens

C. de Portugalate

C. de Gayarre Crist

Llobet

C. de Campo Sagrado

C. del Caño

C. del Príncep Jordi

4

Carrer de Parcerisa

Hotel

Restaurant

C. de Bartomeu Pi

C. de Navarra

de

Gavà

Molanes

C. de la Cireu Coberta

Carrer

Carrer de la Constitució

Vladell

HOSTAFRANCS

Catalonia Barcelona Plaza

ESPANYA

0   400 m

Complex Esportiu Magòria

Plaça Joan Corrades

Crta. de la Bordeta

Leyva

Plaça d'Espanya

0   400 yards

Gran Via de les Corts Catalanes

A **B**

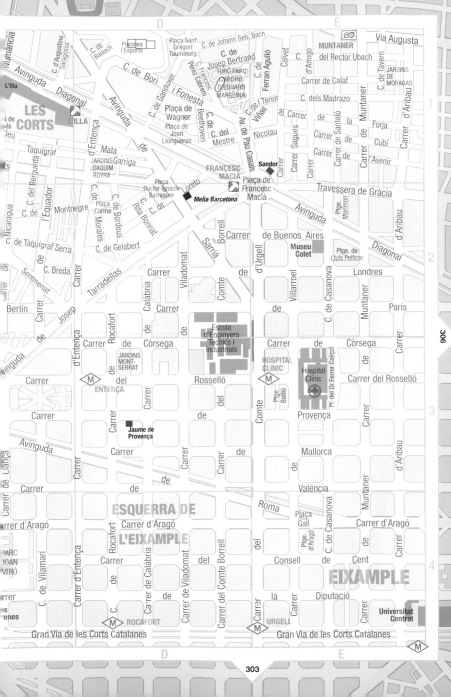

300

Gran Via de les Corts Catalanes

ESPANYA
Plaça d'Espanya

SANTS-
MONTJUÏC

CAN CLOS

ANELLA
OLÍMPICA

Muntanya de

Montjuïc

PARC DE MONTJUÏC

MONTJUÏC

CEMENTIRI DEL
SUD-OEST

Castell de
Montjuïc

C. de la Minería
C. de la Química
C. de Traja
C. de Mandon
C. d'Indíbil
C. de Sant Pau i de Nola
C. de Santa Dorotea
St. Genis
C. de Sant Ferriol
Carrer
Carrer
del
Pl. de Llorca
Segura
Carrer
Carrer de la
Carrer de la Guatlla
Font Florida
Fructuós
C. de Rabí Rubèn
C. d'Amposta
C. dels Gimbernat
C. de Morabos
de
Sant
C. de Mèxic
Palau de la
Metal·lúrgia
Cristina
Fira de
Barcelo
Plaça de la Reina Maria
Av. de Rius i Tau
Estadi
Joan
Serrahima
Plaça
de Sant
Jordi
Avinguda
Francesc
Ferrer i
Guàrdia
C. Hortensia
Caixa-
Forum
Montjuïc
Plaça de
l'Univers
Palau de
Congressos
Tablao de
Carmen
Poble
Espanyol
Av. dels Montanyans
Avinguda de la Reina Maria
Pavelló Mies
van der Rohe
Carles Buïgas
Plaça de
Guàrdia
Font Màgica
Camp de Rugby
de la Fuxarda
Palau de
Victòria
Eugènia
Palau de
Congressos
Estadi
Julià
Campany
Pista Hípica
«La Fuxarda»
Institut i
Jardí
Botànic
Plaça de
Marquès
de Foronda
Palau
d'Alfons
XIII
Pl.
Hidràulica
Passeig de
les Cascades
C. de Guàrdia Urbana
INEFC
Universitat
de l'Esport
Plaça
d'Europa
Mirador del Palau Nacional
Palau
Nacional
Museu Nacional
d'Art de Catalunya
(MNAC)
Museu
Etnològic
Mu
d'Arqueo
Camp de
Beisbol
Piscines
Bernat
Picornell
Paulet
Albèniz
Santa
Matí
Plaça Alta
Can Clos
C. de Pedrera del Mussol
Torre de
Calatrava
JARDINS
JOAN MARAGALL
JARDINS
Palau
Sant Jordi
LARIBA
Fundac
Joan M
Pg. Migdia
Passeig Olímpic
Estadi
Olímpic
l'Estadi
Plaça
del Sol
Ctra. Foment de les Banderes
Museu Olímpic
i de l'Esport
Carrer dels
Tres Pins
Circuito de
Marxa
Dr Font i Quer
Zona d'Atletisme
i Hoquei
Camí de la Serp
Carrer dels Tres Pins
Pl. Gran
Capità
JARDÍ
BOTÀNIC
Pg.
Migdia
Av.
Camí de la Serp
La Caseta
del Migdia
Carrer de la Cartoixa

Hotel
Restaurant

0   400 m
0   400 yards

Ronda del Litoral

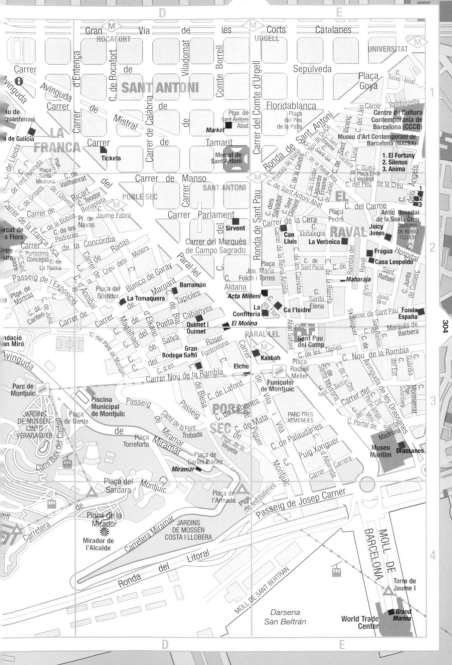

STREET INDEX

ART & PHOTO CREDITS

All Photography **Gregory Wrona/Apa** except the following:

Age Fotostock 60r
AKG-Images 28, 33tr
Alamy 8cr, 117b, 138tr, 184bl, 185
AISA 32t, 33tl, 35, 36tl, 37tr, 38, 42b, 43bl, 44tr
AR/Gau 199t
Art Archive 123, 205b
Arts Santa Mònica 105b
Axiom 23tl
The Bridgeman Art Library 30tl, 43cl, 44cl
Centre de Cultura Contemporània de Barcelona 147b
Commerc 24
Corbis 34tr, 39b, 39c, 39t, 45b, 45tl & tr, 49b, 376
CosmoCaixa 220t
Duques de Bergara 254
Annabel Elston/Apa 29 60l, 118t, 130bl, 182bl, 181cr, 189b, 195, 215tr, 253, 270
Fotolia 9CL, 87b, 122b, 133b, 237t
Fotolibra 205tl
Wolfgang Fritz 61tl
Carolina García y Eduardo Armentia/Fundació Suñol 203b
Getty Images 10t, 40tl, 40tc, 40tr, 45c, 276
Greg Gladman/Apa 3, 11b, 20, 21l, 21r, 22br, 51tl, 53b, 73, 102t, 109t, 109b, 140, 141, 144b, 145b, 171tl, 171b, 198bl, 217(all), 220bl, 222, 263t, 267, 268t, 268c, 272b, 272t, 273, 278, 288
Grand Hotel Central 256
Grand Hotel Florida 261
Hisop 74l
Hotel 1898 255
Hotel Barcelona Princess 258
Hotel Diagonal 259

Hotel Omm 206, 260
Iborra Restaurants 167t
istockphoto 8bl, 9bl, 9br, 10bl, 12tr, 12cl, 14/15, 16/17, 18, 19, 20b, 23b, 40b, 51cl, 90, 94tr, 95t, 99t, 103b, 120bl, 155b, 168, 177b, 184t, 231b, 249
Kurwenal/Prisma 42tr
Majestic Hotel & Spa 253t
Jose Martin 37l
Mary Evans Picture Library 36r, 44c, 96t & b
Serge Meiki 93tr, 95b
Meliá Hotels International 52
Mike Merchant 64
MHCat 161t
Ingrid Morato 1
Museu Blau 170t, 170b
Museu d'Art Modern 59
Don Murray 62r
Northwind Picture Archives 31t
Richard Nowitz 118r
Laura Padgett 128c
PA Photos 123t
Palau Sant Jordi 186b
Photoasia 36tl, 38
Olga Planas/Grupo Tragaluz 65, 71, 207
Poble Espanyol 175, 179t, 180(all)
Prisma Archivo Fotografico 42tr, 43t, 124, 232all
Oronoz Leefoto 30tr, 43br, 44b
Mark Read 53t
David Ruano/El Molino 190
Ronald Stallard/Museu Picasso 131t
Starwood Hotels & Resorts 160b
SuperStock 184br, 194
Tavisa 197bl, 197br
VINSEUM 234b
Bill Wassman 22tr, 31b, 147t, 239
Roger Williams 34tl, 50

PHOTO FEATURES

Pages 26–27: all images **Gregory Wrona/Apa** except **iStockphoto** 26/27t
Pages: 54–57: all images **Gregory Wrona/Apa**
Pages 66–67: all images **Gregory Wrona/Apa** except **Britta Jaschinski/Apa** 66c & **iStockphoto** 67br
Pages 68–69: all images **Gregory Wrona/Apa** except **Alamy** 69cl & **Greg Gladman/Apa** 68br
Pages 172–173: all images **Gregory Wrona/Apa** except **Fotolia** 173b & **Starwood Hotels & Resorts** 173tr
Pages 192–193: top row from left to right: **MNAC, Gregory Wrona/Apa, MNAC**; Bottom row from left to right: **Topfoto, MNAC, Museu d'Art Modern**
Pages 208–209: top row from left to right: **Corbis, iStockphoto, iStockphoto, iStockphoto**; bottom row: **Gregory Wrona/Apa**
Pages 224–225: all images **Gregory Wrona/Apa** except **iStockphoto** 224/225
Pages 244–245: all images **Gregory Wrona/Apa** except **Art Archive** 244br, **Bridgeman Art Library** 245cl, **Mary Evans Picture Library** 245tr, **Escolania de Montserrat**

Map Production: original cartography Berndtson & Berndtson. Updated by Apa Cartographic Department

Production: Linton Donaldson and Rebeka Ellam

GENERAL INDEX